Anti-Oppressive Practice

Social Care and the Law

Second edition

Jane Dalrymple and Beverley Burke

Open University Press
Maidenhead • New York

Open University Press
McGraw-Hill Education
McGraw-Hill House
Shoppenhangers Road
Maidenhead
Berkshire
England
SL6 2QL

email: enquiries@openup.co.uk
world wide web: www.openup.co.uk

and Two Penn Plaza, New York, NY 10121–2289, USA

First published 2006

Copyright © Jane Dalrymple and Beverley Burke

A catalogue record of this book is available from the British Library

ISBN-10: 0335218016 (pb) 0335 218 024 (hb)
ISBN-13: 978 0335 21801 1 (pb) 978 0 335 21802 8 (hb)

Library of Congress Cataloguing-in-Publication Data
CIP data applied for

Typeset by YHT Ltd, London
Printed in the UK by Bell & Bain Ltd, Glasgow

The **McGraw·Hill** Companies

For Peter

What you're supposed to do
when you don't like a thing
is change it. If you can't
change it, change the way
you think about it

Maya Angelou 1994

Contents

List of statutes

Access to Personal Files Act 1987
Adoption and Children Act 2002
Adoption and Children Act 2004
Care Standards Act 2000
Carers (Equal Opportunities) Act 2004
Carers (Recognition and Services) Act 1995
Carers and Disabled Children Act 2000
Children (Northern Ireland) Order 1995
Children Act 1948
Children Act 1989
Children Act 2004
Disability Discrimination Act 1995
Equal Pay Act 1970
Family Law Act 1996
Health Act 1999
Housing Act 1996
Human Rights Act 1998
Local Government Act 2000
Mental Health Act 1983
National Assistance Act 1948
National Health Service and Community Care Act 1990
National Health Social Care Act 2000
Race Relations (Amendment) Act 2000
Race Relations Act 1976
Sex Discrimination Act 1975
Special Education and Disability Act 2001
The Children (Scotland) Act 1995
The Crime and Disorder Act 1998
The Health Services and Public Health Act 1968

Preface to the second edition

It is ten years since we wrote the first edition of this book and during that time anti-oppressive practice has developed and been widely used to inform health and social care practice. *Anti-Oppressive Practice: Social Care and the Law* has become recognized as one of the first texts on anti-oppressive practice by theorists such as Healy (2005) and Payne (2005a), and has become an influential introductory text for students. However, over the last ten years the context of health and social care practice has changed and the theory base has continued to develop, influenced by critical theorists and postmodernism.

The inspiration for the book originated from a request by Guy Mitchell, then editor of *Panel News*, to write an article about implementing 'race' and culture issues using the Children Act 1989. Our initial aim was to produce an accessible textbook that linked legislation with anti-oppressive practice. The raft of legislation that has been passed over the last ten years has made this idea – of encouraging practitioners to seize the opportunities presented by legislation to improve the situation of people using health and social care services – as relevant today as it was then, if not more so.

As critical social work theorists we have taken account of the more nuanced debates which reflect the complex nature of contemporary health and social care practice. While writing the first edition we both felt very connected to practice. Beverley had only just stopped working as a social worker and Jane was working for an advocacy service for children and young people. We are now both full-time academics and we have developed our ideas over the last ten years as we have followed the critical debates regarding anti-oppressive practice. Our thinking has been informed through our work with students and colleagues. Discussions with service users have further developed our understanding of service user perspectives in relation to anti-oppressive practice. Interviews with colleagues based in practice have also been invaluable.

This edition retains the accessibility of the original text and maintains its focus on practice. Anti-oppressive practice has been described as 'innovative, evolving and contentious' rather than comprising an 'established traditional mode' (Hicks, 2002). This is reflected in the second edition, particularly in Part I, where we have made some substantial changes. The rest of the book has been revised and updated to take account of policy and legislative changes. We remain committed to the principles and values of anti-oppressive practice, however, and these guide our discussion about contemporary practice.

We are indebted to family, friends, colleagues and our respective universities, all of whom have provided us with support and space and encouraged us to complete the work. Special thanks are due to all those who have read different chapters of the book and those who have discussed ideas with us. The first edition could not have been completed without the support of Chris Hardwick, Brian Scott, Chris Kwaku Kyem, Chris Bennett and Solomon Salako. Writing the new edition we are especially grateful to practitioners who have kept us in touch with the reality of practice. Ann Farmer helped us to keep our feet on the ground. Ros Cox and Jayne Burnet helped us to unravel the details of practice, while Cliff Hoyle's comments on mental health law were invaluable. Thanks are also due to Leonie Fisher for enthusiastically sharing her experience, which contributed to one of the case studies. Pat Taylor and Karen Jones kindly read and re-read chapters, as well as being patient, tolerant and supportive throughout the process. Finally, Clive and Ian have put up with our absences and preoccupation with the work while providing endless cups of tea and good food and keeping us connected to the world outside our studies.

Acknowledgements

The authors and publisher would like to thank the following for permission to reproduce copyright material in the form of extracts, figures and tables:

art + power (2002) *Dormitory Beds*, reprinted by kind permission of the poets of art + power

Herman, J. et al (1987) *Evaluator's Handbook*, copyright 1987 by Sage Publications. Extract reprinted by Permission of Sage Publications Inc.

Holland, S. (2004) *Child and Family Assessment in Social Work Practice*. Activity 1, Chapter 10

Johns, R. (2005) *Using the Law in Social Work Second Edition*, copyright 2005 by Learning Matters. Reprinted by Permission of Learning Matters. Table, p.43

Joseph, J. (1985) *Warning*, reprinted by kind permission of Jenny Joseph

Newton, J. (2004) Learning to Reflect: A Journey' in *Reflective Practice* (5), copyright 2004 by Taylor and Francis Group. Reprinted by Permission of Taylor and Francis Group. Pages 155-166

Payne, M. (1993*) Linkages: Effective Networking in Social Care*. Activity 1, Chapter 9

Every effort has been made to obtain permission from copyright holders to reproduce material within this book and to acknowledge these sources correctly. We would be pleased to hear from copyright holders whom it has not been possible for us to contact.

Acknowledgements

Since the publication of the first edition of the book in 1995, several statutes impinging on anti-oppressive practice have come into force, and this fact alone has necessitated changes in the arrangement and content of this book.

The aim of the second edition remains that of providing a critical assessment of the theories and ideologies informing anti-oppressive practice and the legislation that impinges on the work of health and social care practitioners. Concepts such as empowerment, partnership and minimal intervention and various aspects of health and social care practice such as assessment, planning and evaluation are discussed with candour. In their assessment of law as a tool for the development of emancipatory practice, the authors note "the interconnections between pieces of legislation, which can often contradict and be confusing" and, therefore, embrace an insight in American critical legal studies that "the law" itself is "the problem" because of its contradictions and incoherence.

It must be stressed, however, that the book is not a treatise on the law relating to anti-oppressive practice but a presentation of concepts, theories, case studies, statutes and assignments that aims to amplify the lessons of practice.

Solomon E. Salako
Liverpool
November 2006

Introduction

> The law is an instrument and not an end in itself. If you learn how to use the law you can do something with it. (Margaret Simey, in an interview with the authors, November 1993)

Asked what it was that gave her the strength to continue her work, Josephine Butler replied that it was 'the awful abundance of compassion which makes me fierce'. Josephine Butler was born in 1828. Committed to fighting injustice and oppression, she spent the greater part of her life campaigning against legislation regulating prostitution. It has been said that if:

> Josephine Butler were alive today, she would still be campaigning against sexual exploitation. She would be arguing with passion against pornography. She would be out amongst the drug addicts, the AIDS-sufferers, the prostitutes of both sexes, loving them and caring for them. But at the same time she would be ruthless in her exposure of those who exploited and trapped them.
>
> (*Church Times*, 26 December 1986)

Biographers have stated that Josephine was not a born fighter. While she may not have been considered a natural candidate to lead a public cause, she did believe that women should be regarded as individuals with the same needs and rights as anyone else: 'the right to work, to be regarded as equal with men in the eyes of the law, to share with men the responsibility of making the conditions in which both must live' (Moberly Bell, 1962: 12).

Compassion is not perhaps a word that many would use to describe their motivation for working in health and social care practice. However, compassion can be described as 'sharing', and if you share the distress of people then you cannot walk away (Simey, 1993: 15). In September 1993, in a lecture to students at Josephine Butler House, Liverpool John Moores University, Margaret Simey described Josephine's 'blistering sense of outrage' not only as the quality that made her 'fierce' but also as the quality which has been lost in much social care practice. Margaret Simey, who died in August 2004, spent her life dedicated to the people of Merseyside. Her work was based in the Granby area of Merseyside, where she spoke out boldly but wisely against what she saw as injustice and oppression. This was reflected in her writing, which 'displayed a fierce commitment, written with an uncompromising

passion for not only a more just society but also a more inclusive one ...
When the issues of old age became personal to her, she said that she and her
contemporaries were excluded by a society that had no use for them. It did
not stop her seeking to remove those barriers' (Philpot, 2004: 32). Within
social care practice the sense of outrage appears to have been replaced by
indifference. For example, it has been suggested that the energy characteriz-
ing the 'heady days' of social work in the 1970s has dissipated because 'social
work now exists in a very different world' (Beresford and Croft, 2004: 55). This
world is one where social care practitioners work within managerial, bureaucratic and procedurally based organizations (Jordan and Jordan, 2000;
Adams, 2002; Ferguson, 2004). We do not need to be 'born fighters'. However,
we do need a commitment to anti-oppressive practice and a fierceness born
from both compassion and a sense of outrage.

Our practice is grounded in the law, but there is a gap between practice
and theory. The law should not be seen as something apart from what we do
but as something that is used to *inform* practice. We will consider the positive
elements of the law and try to work on those that are hidden, building on
them rather than seeing the law as totally constraining. This will be achieved
by consideration of some of the principles that underpin the legislation
bearing on health and social care practice. We are not advocating that the law
is perfect and recognize that there are paradoxes. We suggest, though, that
because work in the health and social care field is dominated by legislative
frameworks, we should try to use them to inform practice that is anti-
oppressive.

The book is written in three parts. The first part sets the terms of the
debate. In Chapter 1 we briefly examine the development of anti-oppressive
practice, going on to explore its underpinning theories in Chapter 2. Chapter
3 considers why we have chosen to use the vehicle of the law to promote
practice that challenges oppression. We suggest that health and social care
practitioners, service users and carers either work within the constraints of the
law and accept the dominant ideology underpinning legislation, or use the
law to challenge the inequalities present in society, which can be further
perpetuated through legislation. The chapter considers the contradictions
and dilemmas that are present in legislation and develops an argument for
using it as a radical tool.

By the end of Part I, you should have an understanding of the theoretical
debates informing anti-oppressive practice and legislation. This provides the
backdrop for Part II, where we go on to look at some of the elements we
consider are needed in a model for anti-oppressive practice. Chapter 4 begins
this process by discussing the value base of the law. It is important to be aware
of the values which inform legislation in order to successfully negotiate its
contradictory elements. For us, the exploration of one's personal values is a
starting point for anti-oppressive practice and we use our own experiences to

develop this. One of the aims of the book is to encourage those involved in the delivery of health and social care services to begin their own self-exploration as a part of the process of understanding anti-oppressive practice.

Having considered the need for an explicit value base, we then go on in Chapter 5 to look at empowerment, a significant element of anti-oppressive practice. It is necessary to think about what exactly this means to practitioners, service users and carers. Partnership encompasses the power relations that exist between professional workers, service users and carers, and the state. Chapter 6 therefore considers partnership, and links to the discussions about empowerment in the previous chapter. We look at how the power relationships that exist within partnerships can be used to ensure that the rights of everyone involved are upheld. Partnership includes, among other things, the joint planning of services to ensure not only that users and carers are offered choice but that intervention can be kept to a minimum. We consider minimal intervention in practice in Chapter 7, and conclude Part II by drawing these elements together to develop a framework for anti-oppressive practice.

If intervention is to be kept to a minimum, then practitioners need to develop skills in assessment and planning, in order to make decisions with service users and carers about what is in their best interests. Part III draws on the theory and principles presented in Parts I and II to reframe practice in relation to legislation. In the next three chapters we therefore consider practice in relation to preventive work, assessment and planning, addressing the importance of user and carer involvement throughout the process.

If we are committed to anti-oppressive practice, then we must continually question the work in which we are engaged. This is particularly important if service users and carers are to be provided with the best possible service. By evaluating our work we take account of the needs of service users and carers, and challenge and develop our practice wisdom. However, this book is not just a theoretical exposition. For us, an important starting point in developing anti-oppressive theory has been our experience of gender in a society that does not value the many contributions that women have made and are making. We know that women are not a homogenous group, and our experiences of 'race' and class, for example, have enabled us to appreciate the significance of differences between women, with their diverse experiences. We explore the concepts of power, difference and identity in more depth in Chapter 2.

At this point we need to note the distinction between anti-oppressive and anti-discriminatory practice. It is important to make this distinction, as all too often the terms are used interchangeably, without thought being given to their impact. For us anti-oppressive practice is about acknowledging differing power relations in society. Such practice 'works with a model of empowerment and liberation and requires a fundamental rethinking of values, institutions and relationships' (Phillipson, 1992: 15). Legislation that deals with issues of discrimination – the Race Relations Act 1976, the Race Relations (Amendment) Act 2000, the Sex Discrimination Act 1975, the Equal Pay Act 1970, the Disability Discrimination Act 1995, the Special Educational Needs and Disability Act 2001, Employment and Equality (Age) Regulations 2006 and the Human Rights Act 1998, Article 14 – is *specific* and aimed at addressing unfair treatment faced, for example, by black people or women. Anti-discriminatory practice uses particular legislation to *challenge* the discrimination faced by some groups of people. There are commentators, however, who suggest that the distinction need not be made. Thompson, for example, sees anti-discriminatory practice 'as a broad undertaking that needs to incorporate sociological, political and economic concerns above and beyond narrow legal requirements' (Thompson, 2001: x). Anti-discriminatory and anti-oppressive practice can complement each other. We acknowledge the usefulness of anti-discriminatory practice, but we feel that it is limiting in its potential to challenge oppression. We explore this further in Chapter 2.

While we are using the law as an empowering tool, we are aware of the contradictions that exist. For example, there is legislation that discriminates *against* certain groups of people, such as gay and lesbian people or travellers. Immigration legislation is used to control and regulate the lives of certain groups of people. Research evidence indicates that people working in the mental health services who have used those services are still discriminated against by employers, colleagues and educators, despite the Disability Discrimination Act 1995 (Lindow and Rooke-Matthews, 2005). Campaigns by mental health service users continue to be ignored. Richard Brook, Chief Executive of MIND, explains:

> Over the last seven years we have seen a Green Paper, a White Paper and two draft Bills, that each time we have hoped will provide the necessary legislation to deliver a workable mental health system delivering effective and compassionate mental healthcare. Yet sadly the Government has still not fully listened to the advice of the mental health stakeholders across the board.
>
> (MIND, 2005)

We acknowledge all these anomalies. However, the focus of this book is to consider how a range of legislation **can** be used to empower people and confront their oppression.

There is a wealth of legislation available to health and social care practitioners and carers. We have not attempted to cover it all and it will be seen that we have made scant reference to welfare benefits or housing legislation, for example. Both of these have an impact on health and social care practice, often in conjunction with other pieces of legislation. For instance, while looking at the Children Act 1989 in relation to the needs of homeless young people, one could discuss the necessity for young people to be given an adequate income to enable them to maintain their accommodation. This would lead to an examination of the inadequacy of the benefits legislation and the need for changes to be made. It is important to be aware of the interconnections between pieces of legislation, which can often contradict and be confusing. However, it is beyond the remit of this book to complete an analysis of all legislation that pertains to health and social care practice. The title of the book was carefully chosen with a focus on the link between anti-oppressive practice and the law. Some commentators have criticized it as misleading, thinking that it was a law text book. However, it was never our intention to write a book about the law. The focus of the second edition is the same as that of the first edition – using the law as a tool for the development of emancipatory practice.

We do not believe that it is possible to explore the concepts of oppression and anti-oppressive practice without sharing our experiences and expertise as women, as social work practitioners and as social work educators. While writing the new edition we have continued to explore the commonalities and differences that exist between us. We have been able to name and understand our oppression based on 'race', gender and class. We have also developed a fuller and richer understanding of who we are and the relationship between us. It is not easy to explore points of divergence: exploring sensitive, difficult and controversial issues between ourselves in a safe way can inevitably leave us each feeling vulnerable, although at the same time this process can be empowering. We engaged in discussions around power and oppression which require personal integrity together with an 'open and not-knowing approach' (Brechin, 2000: 32). This meant that we were able to ask difficult questions and this has helped us to think about common-sense assumptions and taken-for-granted beliefs.

This book reflects our individual experiences of *being*. For one of us, it is the experience of being black, female and heterosexual, with a working-class background but located in a middle-class occupation and enjoying a lifestyle that reflects the benefits conferred by that position. For the other, it is the experience of being white, heterosexual, female and middle class. By telling our own stories to each other, we have engaged in the process of identity formation (Dominelli, 2002a). By locating ourselves in the social context in which we live and work, we begin to understand the social construction of power and oppression. In our exploration of the issues of oppression and, therefore, our understanding of power, we draw heavily on literature written by women, particularly black women. Black women have played a specific role in documenting their experiences of oppression: 'in the struggle for racial justice this contribution has been underplayed in the past but presents rich possibilities' (Henfrey, 1988: 192). We open up these possibilities by reflecting

1 Anti-oppressive practice ten years on

Introduction

Anti-oppressive practice has developed primarily in the field of social work. It has been described as 'a dominant theory of critical social work practice' (Healy, 2005: 178) and the first edition of this book was one of the early publications[1] which led to wider recognition of this approach and its focus on social justice and challenging existing social relations (Martin, 2003). Critical social work is an encompassing term that is used to describe various perspectives that draw on critical theories. The range of perspectives and understandings within them have a number of commonalities which seem 'to be concerned with developing theory and practice in an inclusive and participatory manner that challenges social relations and structures, as well as social work itself' (Ife et al., 2005: 21). Anti-oppressive practice is a critical social work approach that draws on critical social science theories and is informed by humanistic and social justice values, taking account of the experiences and views of oppressed people. Although it is now used and recognized as an approach that informs both health and social care practice, it is useful to examine its development within social work practice, where its origins lie, in order to understand its wider applicability. This chapter will therefore look at the historical foundations of anti-oppressive practice and its development as a theory for practice. We will consider some of the debates by commentators about the strengths and difficulties of this approach and indicate how it can be used to inform current practice.

The critical tradition of social work

Anti-oppressive practice has developed as professionals have found ways of working with users of welfare services that take account of the oppression and inequality that people experience in their daily lives (Davis and Garrett, 2004: 14). Social work, in particular, has been informed by a critical tradition from its early development. For example, the settlement movement has been described by some as pioneering critical social work. The first settlement in England opened in 1884 and the idea was to provide an opportunity for university students (middle- and upper-class men and women) to 'settle' in disadvantaged (working-class) communities, living and working there to provide practical support and improve the lives of poorer people. It was described as

> simply a means by which men or women may share themselves with their neighbours; a club-house in an individual district, where the condition of membership is the performance of a citizen's duty; a house among the poor, where the residents may make friends with the poor.

> (Barnett, 1898: 11)

Samuel Barnett was the first warden of the earliest settlements in London. His work included promoting self-help, campaigning for better housing conditions for the poor, helping to establish model dwellings and setting up the Children's Country Holiday Fund. Settlements became known not only for community initiatives but also for their involvement in other movements such as women's suffrage and trade unionism.

Quoting a section from the work of Jane Addams, who established Hull House, a settlement in the USA, Fook suggests that 'awareness of social context and its importance in understanding individual experience and informing practice is therefore one of the earliest principles which holds critical potential for social work' (Fook, 2002). While, as Martin (2003) comments, not everyone would agree that the movement represented a radical approach to poverty or slum housing, within the context of the time it was challenging oppression through a structural analysis of social inequality.

The Fabian Society has also been an influential movement informing the development of critical social work (Powell, 2001). It began in 1884 as a socialist society committed to gradual social reform, with early members including George Bernard Shaw, Beatrice and Sidney Webb, Emmeline Pankhurst and H. G. Wells. Beatrice and Sidney Webb were social reformers who, together with Lloyd George and Beveridge, have been described as founders of the welfare state. The Fabians were well known for their publications, the first entitled *Why are the Many Poor?* This publication, along with other original Fabian essays, shows a commitment to social justice and a belief in the progressive improvement of society as well as indicating how the Fabians tried to encourage reform by stimulating debate. Influential Fabian authors have included Richard Titmuss, Peter Townsend, Brian Abel-Smith, Tony Benn and Ben Pimlott. Special interest groups were established that undertook research and disseminated the results. There was a separate Women's Group that was set up when women were campaigning for the vote. A Fabian Nursery was set up to support and encourage younger members. In 1900 the Fabian Society joined with the trade unions to establish the Labour Party, and has always been affiliated to it.

In their attempts to tackle poverty, the settlement movement, the Fabians and other movements such as the Society of Friends (Quakers) – many of the early reformers and members of the Fabian Society were also Quakers – believed that society had failed individuals. This critical understanding was in direct contrast to the ideology of the Charity Organisation Society (COS). The huge number of charities set up in the nineteenth century represented the 'expansion of the nineteenth century social conscience combined with social control and patronage of the poor by the wealthy classes, for whom any more radical changes in the distribution of wealth would have been unthinkable' (Brenton, 1985: 16). The COS, which coordinated the work of all the charities in England,[2] therefore operated within a perspective that believed that there were moral dangers in being too generous of help and an ideology of individualism, resulting in a belief that the 'deserving' poor, that is, those who were genuinely unemployed and of good character, could be helped to get themselves out of poverty. The undeserving poor therefore did not get any help from the COS and had to get assistance through the Poor Law.

Beatrice Webb worked as a rent collector for the COS and became disillusioned by the fact that charitable organizations had little or no impact on the causes of poverty. A necessary element of the process was an assessment to enable the decision-making process concerning whether or not a service would be provided and how much support a family would get – which in turn would also depend on what was felt to be necessary to achieve the desired goal. The volunteers involved in gathering information for the assessments did a home visit and wrote a report, which provided the basis for deciding the intervention that might or might not be offered. The origin of 'assessment' stems from this work (Payne, 2005b) and the volunteers doing this individual casework were effectively the first social workers.

The impact of these movements on social work education and practice is significant. The social justice philosophy of the settlement movement and the individualized liberal approach of the COS came together when the two organizations established the School of Sociology in 1912, and this was subsequently incorporated into the London School of Economics (founded by the Fabian Society). The two perspectives have been central in the development of social work as 'the compromise and mutual toleration that existed within an uneasy relationship between the two positions ... pervades social work up to the present day' (Lynn, 1999: 42). Lynn (1999) points out that while the two values have existed throughout the development of social work education and practice, they seem to be conflictual rather than co-existing in any creative way. Such conflict resulted in the social justice approach facing a struggle for acceptance. This, in turn, had an impact on the development of anti-oppressive practice, which, Lynn argues, can in fact include a 'social *and* an individual analysis' (1999: 48) (italics in the original).

It is generally agreed, however, that a distinct body of critical practice began to emerge during the 1960s, leading to the development of anti-oppressive practice alongside a number of other models of emancipatory social work (Pinkney, 2000).[3] Healy recognizes what she calls the 'common historical lineage' (Healy, 2005: 173) of the more recent theories of practice influencing social work, locating the theory of anti-oppressive practice between the 'strengths perspective' (which she identifies as a theory of practice focusing on the capacities and potentialities of service users) and postmodern practices. Payne (2005a) also notes that anti-oppressive approaches take in a range of social work perspectives and models that developed in the late 1980s and 1990s.

Critical social theory

Anti-oppressive practice has been informed by ideas that emanate from critical theory, which challenges taken-for-granted assumptions about social order. Critical theory has been described as 'a particular kind of theoretical orientation which owes its origin to the nineteenth century philosophers Kant, Hegel and Marx' (Ramussen, 1996: 11), although it is Marx who is primarily credited as the founder of critical theory. Later development of critical theory in the early twentieth century was through the Frankfurt School of sociologists including Horkeimer, Adorno, Marcuse and, more recently, Habermas. Critical theory has been described by Ramussen (1996) as a powerful movement not only in philosophy but also in branches of the social sciences and humanities and, as a term, embodies the optimistic view that a critical theory can change society. The changed society is one that is no longer characterized by exploitation, inequality and oppression but is emancipatory and free from domination (Mullaly, 1997). Healy (2000) points out that a significant aspect of critical theories is that they highlight that through conscious and collective action people are able to achieve such a society.

Adams et al. (2002) take three points from the ideas of these theorists to demonstrate their use for critical practice. The first is the emphasis on *social change* and the need to develop collective action to achieve it, as Healy mentions. This means, for example, that individual action is always part of wider action and, as such, is a form of political agency. Crucially, the critical professional 'is engaged in collective action, working across differences with clients and colleagues in specific local issues towards a common goal of ending injustice' (Batsleer and Humphries, 2000: 13). The second point is the focus of critical theory on *intentionality* – the conscious intention, through thinking critically, to create planned change. Thirdly, the implication of critical theories for human service practitioners is that thinking and acting critically 'needs to be placed within analyses of how the *limitations of social divisions* such as class and gender, and social assumptions about disability, sexuality and ethnic origin are created within social ideas that appear rational and that we take for granted, but are also changeable and changing' (Adams et al., 2002: 10).

Critical theories for practice have been influenced by both modernist and postmodern approaches. *Modern* society was understood as the predictable outcome of the development of science, rationality and reason. Through the development and application of science, human beings were able to create their own destiny, they were able to control nature by their superior intellect over the animal kingdom. This movement is associated with what has been described as *modernity* or *modernism*. A historical period in Western culture, modernity originated in the Enlightenment at the end of the eighteenth century and, broadly speaking, refers to the group of social, economic and political systems that emerged at that time. The modern Western world therefore brought in industrial capitalism and scientific thinking. Social work can be located within modernity, and modernist approaches challenged traditional individual 'casework' practice. This means that logic and science are used to explain and control difficult people and situations (Camilleri, 1999). Modernist approaches 'provide a lens for challenging social injustice and social inequality through transformation' (Allan, 2003: 49), the key feature being the need to recognize that macro social structures have an impact on social relations at all levels of society and provide a way of analysing the causes of oppression and transforming the structures that sustain inequality.

There is not a clearly identifiable change from modernism to postmodernism, and it has been suggested that reference to a 'postmodern turn' is more helpful (Hick, 2005). Furthermore, postmodern social theory is hard to define, as Hick notes: 'It is not an essence to be defined, but rather a constellation of discursive constructs' (2005: 40). *Postmodernism* recognizes that there is no order or certainty, nor are there any universal theories or explanations (known as 'grand narratives') as 'we now inhabit a world that has become disorientated, disturbed and subject to doubt' (Camilleri, 1999: 20). Camilleri points out that the impact of globalization and its accompanying social, economic and cultural changes is related to this paradigm. Postmodernism, then, very simply, critiques and fragments the grand narratives associated with modernism – Marxism, for example. Key elements of social transformation associated with postmodernism include:

- The increasing *pace* of change.
- The growing significance of *difference*.
- *Plurality* and the growth of various new political movements and strategies.
- The pervasive awareness of *relativities*.
- The opening up of individual *'choice'* and *'freedom'*.
- The increasing awareness of the *socially constructed nature of reality*.

(Parton and O'Byrne, 2000: 21)

Principally, reality is seen to be constructed through multiple discourses and postmodern approaches highlight multiple oppressions and difference, recognizing that power is exercised and experienced in many different ways.

There are numerous debates about postmodern theories, and it has been suggested that while discussion about modernism and postmodernism is important, 'a useful strategy is not to get too caught up with labels, but rather to use whatever analyses appear helpful in order to understand what is going on' (Fawcett and Featherstone, 2000: 9). Certainly, it has been suggested that critical practitioners should maintain the tension between the modernist and postmodern theory and practice and try to work with the inevitable contradictions and uncertainties that this might bring. The box shows the common principles between the two approaches as a helpful starting point.

Principles common to modernist and postmodern approaches to critical social work theory and practice

1. A commitment to the transformation of processes and structures that perpetuate domination and exploitation.
2. A commitment to working alongside oppressed and marginalized populations.
3. Consequently, an orientation towards emancipatory personal and social change, social justice and social equality.
4. A dialogical relationship between social workers and the people with, or on behalf of whom, they work.

(Allan, 2003: 47)

The development of postmodern and critical approaches means that a broader vision of anti-oppressive theory and practice 'which links "social exclusion", based on gender with that of "race" disability, age, sexual orientation and class, still has a foothold in the future of social work itself' (Pinkney, 2000: 128). The insights of both the 'rich tradition' (Healy, 2000) of critical social work practices and of critical theories are therefore needed for practitioners to engage with the multiplicity of current practice in what have been described as 'complex and hazardous social contexts' (Davis and Garrett, 2004: 14). In order to understand the development of anti-oppressive theory and practice, it is therefore helpful to examine its early progress before considering its applicability for progressive practice in the future.

Critical approaches to social work

1. Radical social work

Bertha Reynolds, an American Marxist social work academic and activist in the 1930s and 1940s, believed that 'to be a good social worker, one had to be radical' (Mullaly, 1997: 106). Payne points out that the word 'radical' can really mean 'anything which involves major changes' (Payne, 2005a: 229), although it is most commonly understood as expressing politically socialist (the established Left) ideals. Critiques of the traditional individual casework models of practice during the 1960s and 1970s resulted in the development of radical approaches to social work by authors such as Bailey and Brake (1975, 1980) in Britain, Galper (1980) in the USA and Throssell (1975) in Australia. These approaches recognize that problems need to be located at a structural level rather than with individuals. The emphasis is on working towards achieving social justice. Based on a Marxist analysis, the welfare state is seen as an instrument of capitalism with a social control function to meet the needs of capitalists rather than the needs of the working class. Many of these critiques see social class as the main element of oppression. By rationing services and benefits, those considered the deserving poor are appeased, as are the consciences of the wealthy classes. The role of practitioners is to challenge that oppression (Corrigan and Leonard, 1978). In community work, for example, radical approaches mean trying to move the balance of existing social relations by empowering people to question why they are living in deprivation and confront the cause of their oppression. Social workers are urged to understand how they also contribute to supporting inequality. A number of issues of concern are raised as a result of agencies being part of a capitalist welfare system:

- *Social control* and how far practitioners exercise it through the state on behalf of the ruling classes. Critical theory is cautious of controlling activities. For example, being a feminist in a statutory organization may compromise female practitioners working in child protection.
- *Professionalization* and how far it is promoted by health and social care education to the disadvantage of the interests of oppressed individuals, communities and groups.
- Is *critical practice* possible with the level of social and agency constraints on workers and the primarily individual focus of practice? Focusing on collective and political work has led to an understanding that critical practice is not possible where state agencies and charities are controlled on behalf of political elites.

(Payne, 2005a: 231)

However, while there is a range of opinion about how to challenge capitalism, the overall goal of transformation remains a common one (Mullaly and Keating, 1991). The concept of 'transformation' is particularly associated with radical social work. This means that practitioners seek to transform social institutions and the way societies create social problems by supporting service users, professional activity and political action (Payne, 2005a).

2. Structural social work

Structural social work was primarily developed by two Canadians, Moreau (1979, 1990) and Mullaly (1993, 1997). It has been described 'as part of the larger radical social work movement' (Mullaly, 1997: 104), with the same aim of critiquing traditional social work but with an emphasis on the structural aspect of individual and social problems (Fook, 2002). As a critical theory it involves connecting personal and political action (Payne, 2005a). The focus of structural social work is on power, with an emphasis on equalizing the power relations between social workers and service users. Mullaly asserts that one of the unique features of the structural approach is that it does not try to define a hierarchy of oppression, stating that 'the structural approach views various forms of oppression as intersecting with each other at numerous points, creating a total system of oppression' (Mullaly, 1997: 105). Developing the perspective and taking postmodern themes into account, he recognizes the importance of language and communication in order to develop emancipatory ways of working, stating that 'structural social work is committed to respecting the plurality of ways in which human beings find their own voices, while also being committed to solidarity with those who are struggling, against the imposition of others, to find those voices' (Mullaly, 1997: 117). However, Allan's (2003) critique of Mullaly points out that, despite his engagement with postmodernism and a recognition of the need to have knowledge and skills to work with individuals, groups, families and communities, he does not really develop ways of effectively engaging with the realities of people's lives. Nevertheless, she recognizes the value of his approach in 'addressing the root causes of oppression through social transformative practices' (2003: 36).

3. Feminist social work

The women's movement emerged alongside the development of radical approaches to practice (Langan, 1992) and, while feminists broadly agree with radical and structural analyses, the dimension of gender as a structural concern has been recognized as significant in the development of theory and practice (Pease and Fook, 1999b; Martin, 2003). Alongside other critical commentators, feminists felt that the focus of radical analysis and practice on class was too constraining (Healy, 2005). They saw the radical movement as being male-dominated and as such felt that it was not sensitive to some of the realities of practice, particularly in social work where most clients and practitioners are women (Langan, 1992). They therefore extended and widened radical definitions of oppression to take account of the specificities of oppression, placing the experiences of women's oppression alongside 'race', class, age, disability and sexuality (Langan, 1992; Dominelli, 2002c).

There are five broad approaches to feminist theory (Tong, 1989; Whelehan, 1995) which, although contradictory, can be identified with the contradictions in the lives of women (Ramazanoglu, 1989). However, feminist perspectives generally seek 'to develop an understanding of the totality of oppression and its specific manifestations as the precondition for developing an anti-discriminatory practice relevant to all spheres of social work' (Langan, 1992: 3). The feminist critique has developed and changed in emphasis from conceptualizing social work as a state institution that maintains the position of women 'in their place' within families to seeing anti-oppressive (including feminist) social work as a possible empowering element for women service users and women practitioners (Wise, 1995). The concept of 'emancipation', which is 'concerned with freeing people from the restrictions imposed by the existing social order' (Payne, 2005a: 227), is particularly associated with feminist perspectives.

4. Black perspectives and anti-racist social work

While feminists broaden radical and structural approaches on a gender basis, anti-racist practitioners focus on issues of race. Anti-racist social workers point to colonization and the impact of Eurocentricism on racial and ethnic groups (Healy, 2000). Concern that issues of racial injustice were inadequately addressed by a class-based analysis led to the emergence of distinctive ways of working, extending radical analyses to recognize racial oppression (Healy, 1996).

The development of black perspectives and anti-racist approaches in social work (Ahmad, 1990; Dominelli, 1998) emerged during the 1980s as a result of the critique of racism by black writers and urban disturbances, followed by the Scarman Report (1981) which highlighted the need to eliminate racism in the police force in London. Black perspectives emerged in response to racism and have been identified as important in enabling black people to construct their own identity based on their common experiences. Drawing on a number of commentators in this area, Keating (1997) identifies the following key elements of black perspectives:

- a reclaiming and recognition of the history and cultures (language, traditions, religions) of black people;

- valuing differences and strengths in black communities;
- a rejection of white norms;
- a political ideology from which to fight racism and promote positive images of black people;
- a political alliance between all non-white people whose commonality is their experience of racism.

Through developing black perspectives:

> Black people have been able to reclaim a space for their voices to be heard. It is the space from which to challenge and survive racism as a Black person.
>
> (Keating, 1997: 26)

Singh (2000) suggests that the development of black perspectives represents a significant step in the anti-racist struggle.

The development of anti-racism in social work has been identified as having clear, if overlapping, phases. The first phase, *assimilation*, has, as a 'dominant racialised discourse' (Pinkney, 2000: 123), informed social work theory and practice. Assimilation is about absorbing black and ethnic minority groups into the dominant culture. It is based on the belief that white society is superior and there is an expectation that black communities take on the responsibility to merge with the 'host' community – who in turn have some responsibility to understand the problems faced by them in so doing (Penketh, 2000). The presence of black service users and practitioners was not reflected in social work literature until the 1980s and the small amount of material that was available seemed to condone assimilation and blame black people for not using services properly (Denney, 1998).

The second phase is the move towards *multiculturalism*. There is no overall theory of multiculturalism but it relates to a move towards accepting and learning about other people's cultures and opposing the idea of a single dominant culture, and this, it was believed, would lead to more tolerance and acceptance of difference (Payne, 2005a). During the 1980s social work practice took account of the nature of power and the lack of power that black and minority ethnic groups had concerning their lives.

In the third phase, then, *anti-racism* developed with an agenda that brought individual and institutional racism into the forefront of people's thinking, and social work practice moved from liberal ideas about promoting change through equal opportunities to challenging dominant power relations. The approach had two elements – to increase awareness of individual racism and challenge it and to challenge institutional racism. An example of this can be seen in Rooney's inspiring account of the work of the Black Social Worker's Project in Liverpool which describes and analyses how the project 'at least exposed the nature of resistance within the social work organisation and for a time has allowed a Black working class experience to exert an influence on practice' (Rooney, 1987: 123). However, more recently, the 'failure to distinguish between the multicultural society as a fact of Britain's national make-up, arrived at through the anti-racist struggles of the 1960's and 1970's, and multiculturalism as a cure all for racial injustice, promoted by successive governments' (Sivanandan, 2005: 1) has been problematic in the fight against racism. Commenting on the reality of racism in Britain in the wake of the bombings in London on 7 July 2005, Sivanandan points out that the first is working towards a culturally diverse society whereas the second, 'not really multiculturalism, but what I term culturalism' (2005: 1), produces a society that is culturally divisive.

Anti-racism has been criticized for homogenizing the experiences of black people, ignoring the range of their oppression and the diversity of black communities. It is interesting to note, though, that, highlighting the development of good practice[4] in the provision of services for black children and their families, contributors to an edited book in the late 1980s considered both the diverse ethnic backgrounds and cultural needs of black families and the impact of poverty, poor housing and unemployment (Ahmed et al., 1986). Furthermore, Keating (1997) points out that anti-racist theory is central in the development of anti-discriminatory perspectives and suggests that the way forward is to find ways of developing a more inclusive analysis that 'will encompass the diverse and changing subjectivities of black people' (Keating, 1997: 28).

5. Critical social work

The development of critical social work, primarily by Australian writers, most notably Fook (2002, 2003) and Healy (2000, 2005), came with concerns about the limitations of radical social work, particularly its limited conception of 'power' and 'identity' and deterministic view of people, which led to 'a rather large disparity between the expressed empowering ideals of the radical tradition, and how people lived and experienced it' (Fook, 2002: 11). A search for alternatives drew on postmodern ideas to develop critical perspectives in order to further theory and practice. The key concepts of postmodern theories – discourse, subjectivity, power and deconstruction – underpin critical social work.

The aim of critical social work is to promote social justice in practice and policy. It is concerned to develop theory and practice in an inclusive, participatory way. While there are different understandings and developments within critical social work, the following components have been identified by Hick (2005):

- Critical social work examines how *structures of oppression* are reproduced in the everyday lived reality of people. By recognizing how both service providers/practitioners and service users are embedded within a complex web of power relations enables us to consider empowerment strategies and 'so guard against the tendency to see both as merely victims of social structures' (Healy, 2005: 204).
- Critical social work argues that structures of oppression are reproduced through *ideological processes*. 'Social workers transform the experienced realities of clients into the organisational relevancies of the state agency. It is in this way that ideological practices are grounded in larger social relations of power and control and operate to legitimise and sustain exploitative social relations' (Hick, 2005: 44).
- Critical social work *critiques dominant social science*, usually known as positivism. 'Social members see themselves as removed from, disengaged or alienated from the power to act on and in their situation. Therefore there is a need to develop a consciousness which is able to view "facts" as pieces of history which can be changed' (Fook, 2002: 17).
- Critical social work is political in that it believes that people can *participate in social change*.

Features of critical social work include a self-reflexive and critical analysis of the social control functions of social work practice and social policies, and recognizing that the social production of critical social work knowledge may exclude the voices of people who use services. Critical reflection within critical social work has therefore extended our understanding of reflection in professional practice (Agryis and Schön, 1976; Schön, 1983),[5] enabling practitioners to consider how they 'construct and understand their place, position, purpose, role, practice and power within and in relation to the organisation' (Fook, 2004: 73).

Other social movements

The development of anti-oppressive practice has been informed by movements other than those led by women and black people. Gays and lesbians, people with learning difficulties, survivors of the psychiatric system, survivors of abuse and domestic violence, people living with AIDS, and disabled people, for example, have all contributed to the development of anti-oppressive practice. At the same time, growing user movements emphasized the rights of service users as citizens to participate in professional decision-making and shape service provision (Payne, 2005b). The impact of service users on practice is explored more fully in Chapter 12. However, it is important to be aware that all these movements challenged social work, which led to what has been described as a 'crisis of confidence' (Lymbery, 2004b: 46) in the 1980s as the nature of social work was questioned. While this may have weakened the position of social work at the time, expressions of different ideologies and value bases did also lead to the development of models and theories by service users. For example, the social model of disability, developed by disabled people (Oliver, 1990), distinguishes between individual impairment and so-cial disablement. Beresford et al. note that similar developments have taken place within other movements, making it 'possible for people to reassess the roles and identity attached to them, the oppression they experience and ways in which their rights and needs are or, more often, are not met' (Beresford et al., 2000: 194).

Anti-oppressive practice

Most writers locate anti-oppressive practice as a response from both practitioners and academics to the social movements led by women and black people that we have outlined above. Healy (2005) points out that, like other modern forms of critical practice discussed above, anti-oppressive practice draws on the debates from other types of critical social work emphasizing:

- the structural origins of service users' problems;
- an orientation towards radical social change;
- a critical analysis of practice relations and an attempt to transform these relations in practice.

However, it also extends critical practice theory by clearly integrating the personal and cultural bases of oppression with a structural analysis and promotion of interpersonal and statutory work as justifiable sites of anti-oppressive practice.

Anti-oppressive practice develops radical approaches to include all forms of oppression and focuses on change. For Clifford, this means taking seriously 'the complex memberships of major social divisions that affect individuals' perspectives and actions, and to which they respond in different ways' (Clifford, 1998: xiii). This is achieved by practitioners, carers and service users working together towards developing a more equal society. Payne has described our perspective on anti-oppressive practice as a 'structural analysis allied with a more liberal empowerment perspective' (Payne, 1997: 254). It can be summarized as:

A radical social work approach which is informed by humanistic and social justice values and takes account of the experiences and views of oppressed people. It is based on an understanding of how the concepts of power, oppression and inequality determine personal and structural relations.

(Dalrymple and Burke, 2000: 14)

Anti-oppressive practice requires:

- An empowering approach which aims to overcome barriers for service users in taking more control of their lives (see Chapter 5).
- Working in partnership so that as far as possible service users are included in decision-making processes about their lives. This is described as a 'vexed issue' (Healy, 2005: 186) for anti-oppressive practitioners because of the constraints that derive from the unequal power relations existing between themselves and service users (see Chapter 6).
- Minimal intervention to reduce the oppressive and disempowering potential of social work intervention (see Chapter 7).
- Critical reflection and reflexivity. This involves a continual consideration of self in practice in order to understand how our values and our biographies impact on our practice relationships. (This is explored throughout the book.)

(Clifford, 1998; Beckett, 2005; Healy, 2005; Payne, 2005a)

In Chapter 2 we consider definitions of anti-oppressive practice in more depth, so here we briefly outline the strengths of the theory of anti-oppressive practice.

Commentators recognize the strengths of anti-oppressive practice by identifying how it has extended radical approaches to take account of the different bases for the oppression of various groups and inequalities and divisions in society. Payne (2005) points out that a new focus on oppression has emerged, making more directed accounts of radical social work possible, which has consequently contributed to the development of critical theory. A key strength has been identified as the reconciliation of social work values and practice methods (Healy, 2005) with the value of social justice being fundamental to all aspects of practice. By recognizing the different dimensions of oppression (which are examined in Chapter 5), practitioners are encouraged to recognize how cultural practices and social structures impact on the lives of service users rather than blame individuals for their problems. These practices and structures then become a legitimate site of intervention.

Limitations of this approach mainly focus on the structural explanations of oppression. While this is a strength – being more relevant to the daily issues faced by practitioners than economic and class-based analyses, for example (Payne, 2005a) – the structural analysis of power relations that is a central element of the theory may, argues Healy (2005), make it difficult to recognize local power relations. Such views have also been criticized for appearing to lead professionals to prescribe correct behaviour and attitudes, which in turn may be experienced as oppressive (Payne, 2005a). Healy (2005) expresses concerns about the principle of minimal intervention, particularly in situations of 'high-risk' decision-making and suggests that there needs to be more recognition of the institutional limits of the application of anti-oppressive practice theory if its development is to be critical and grounded.

Anti-oppressive practice is often linked with anti-discriminatory practice because they share a number of core assumptions. However, although there is a 'causal and interconnected relationship between discrimination and oppression' (Martin, 2003: 30) and therefore, as Thompson (2003) points out, it is necessary to tackle discrimination in order to challenge oppression, they are two distinct concepts. There are broadly two schools of thought about anti-oppressive and anti-discriminatory practice. We argued in the first edition, and put the case again in Chapter 2 of this book, that anti-discriminatory practice is different to anti-oppressive practice since it relies on legislation and policy to achieve change. However, legislation to stop discrimination invariably offers limited protection and only a minimum standard of protection in some areas.

We can see from this overview that anti-oppressive practice is informed by a rich history and, through its development, has contributed to critical theory and practice. One of the most exciting things about developing theory and practice is that the contradictions, debates and ever-changing context of practice mean that we are constantly theorizing our practice and finding ways of promoting good practice. This means that in finding ways to practice that are not oppressive:

> ...no singular or static answer is necessary or even possible. To have a fixed answer would be to close off possibilities for the future, or to perpetuate the present into the future rather than supporting many alternate futures.
>
> (Martin, 2003: 51)

Contemporary anti-oppressive practice occurs within the context of globalization, the modernizing agenda of many governments and increasing privatization of the welfare state and, in Western industrialized nations, a widening gap between the rich and poor (Martin, 2003), and it is influenced by postmodern approaches to practice. Healy points out that such approaches challenge all practitioners to reflect on how we 'contribute to the control and surveillance of people we are seeking to assist' (2005: 50). The struggle to reconcile anti-oppressive practice and the elements of social control noted by Healy is a tension that requires constant critical reflection, particularly in contexts of practice where practitioners believe that professional discretion is being managed out of their role (Baldwin, 2004). The process of critical reflection, which is an essential element of anti-oppressive practice, enables practitioners to focus on how they 'construct and understand their place, position, purpose, role, practice and power within and in relation to the organisation' (Fook, 2004: 73), which in turn should enable professional development and impact on organizational learning. The contribution by various commentators to the development of anti-oppressive practice and discussion about its limitations is incorporated into this updated text. Consideration of organizations as oppressive is the starting point and, within that, acknowledging that we have a responsibility to reflect on our own position and rethink the relationship between the state, organizations and service users.

Further reading

Payne, M. (2005) *The Origins of Social Work: Continuity and Change.* Basingstoke: Palgrave Macmillan.
This analyses changes in social work and provides a useful broad overview of its origins.

Powell, F. (2001) *The Politics of Social Work.* London: Sage Publications.
A historical overview is incorporated into this account.

Dominelli, L. (2002) *Anti-Oppressive Social Work Theory and Practice.* Basingstoke: Palgrave Macmillan.
This links theories of oppression to the realities of practice.

Thompson, N. (2006) *Anti-Discriminatory Practice*, 4th edn. Basingstoke: Palgrave Macmillan.
This is the fourth edition of Thompson's introductory text.

Allan, J., Pease, B. and Briskman, L. (eds) (2003) *Critical Social Work: An Introduction to Theories and Practices.* Crows Nest, NSW: Allen & Unwin.
This is an introductory book to critical social work that traces the historical development of critical practice in Part 1, with an exploration of the issues drawing on modernist and postmodern approaches.

Hick, S., Fook, J. and Pozzuto, R. (eds) (2002) *Social Work: A Critical Turn.* Toronto: Thompson Educational Publishing.
An introduction to critical social work and an examination of current theory and practice.

PART I
UNPACKING CONCEPTS: SETTING THE TERMS OF THE DEBATE

2 Some essential elements of anti-oppressive theory

Empowerment
Why do they speak to me this way?
What happened to my right to have my say?
Why do they speak to me this way?
What happened to my right to protection?
Why do they reject and push me away?
What happened to my opinion and viewpoints?
Why do they assess me this way?
What happened to my freedom I must say?
Why do they label me this way?
What happened to my right to the things I do?
Why do they take everything from me this way?
What happened to my possessions? feelings? emotions?
Why do they act this way?
What happened to my rights? –
They took them away.
What I need is more power.
Please let us stand together,
because I don't want to fight you.

(Chris Bennett, 1994)

We start this chapter with a poem written by a young woman in residential care. In the process of reading the poem we start to engage in critical thinking and reflection in relation to concepts of power and oppression. Through that process we become both participant and observer, bringing to our interpretation of her story our values, assumptions and practice wisdom. Telling her story provides Chris with an opportunity to articulate the situation as she sees it and offers us another perspective from which to understand both her experiences and the possibilities for resistance.

ACTIVITY

Write down your initial thoughts about this poem.

What does Chris's poem contribute to your understanding of power and oppression?

How is Chris making sense of her situation?

If work with people who are experiencing the effects of a socially unjust society, and who feel disempowered and marginalized, is to be effective, then it should locate the realities of people's lives in the context in which they exist. This context includes their family, their communities and health and social care services. Practitioners are also a part of the context. For practitioners this is shaped by the philosophies and ideas of the profession, expectations of both employers and service users and carers, and their own frameworks for practice. By understanding the concepts of power and oppression and working from a theoretically informed perspective, we are able to develop tools to enable us to work in partnership with service users and carers.

Practice and theory

If we are going to swim against the tide, we have to be strong enough to survive. This means that we have to work from an informed perspective. What gives us our direction as anti-oppressive practitioners is our view of the world. This view guides our actions. Payne has suggested that 'to take part in social work you need a view about what you are doing – an interim view perhaps, but something which guides the actions you take' (Payne, 1991). Theories, which at their simplest have been described as 'an attempt to explain' (Thompson, 2000a: 20), can provide a framework for understanding the world and so enable us to make sense of social problems. 'Theory' can range from a particular idea or concept to a set of related ideas (Fook, 2002).

Payne (2005a: 5) suggests that 'theory' covers three different possibilities:

- *Models* describe what happens during practice in a general way, applying to a wide range of situations and in a structured way, so that they extract certain principles and patterns of activity which give practice consistency. Models help us to structure and organize how we approach a complicated situation. An example of a model is task-centred work (Reid and Epstein, 1972).
- *Perspectives* express values or views of the world which allow participants to order their minds sufficiently to be able to manage themselves while participating. If you apply different perspectives then you can see situations from different points of view. Anti-oppressive and critical perspectives are good examples.
- *Explanatory theory* accounts for why an action results in particular consequences, and identifies the circumstances in which it does so. For example, attachment theory can be used to explain how children's behaviours have developed as a result of their early relationships with their care givers (Howe, 1995).

Payne (2005a) points out that all three possibilities are needed in a theory that will be useful to practice.

Many practitioners find it difficult to explicitly link theory and practice or to acknowledge the importance of any theoretical framework in relation to their practice. However, it is important to make the connections between the ideas that inform our practice and the complex processes of practice itself. The difficulty is the artificial separation between theory and practice, and often ideas from practice are not seen as having the same status as more formal theory. Sibeon (1990) provides a framework for understanding the links between formal and informal theory. Formal theory is written and debated in professional and academic arenas. Informal theory is constructed from practical experience (Payne, 2005a). Sibeon also usefully outlines three different types of (social work) theory based on theories of what social work is; theories of how to do social work; and theories of the nature of the client world. These are equally relevant for other professions (Thompson, 2000a) and are shown in Table 2.1.

We can see then that there are many different ways of 'seeing what is knowledge, how it is generated, how it is expressed and whose perspectives count' (Fook, 2002: 35). However, Fook points out that the important thing to remember is that there is a dynamic relationship between theory and

Table 2.1 Types of theory (taken from Payne, 2005: 6)

Types of theory	'Formal' theory	'Informal' theory
Theories of *what social work is*	Formal written accounts defining the nature and purpose of welfare (e.g. personal pathology, liberal reform, Marxist, feminist)	Moral, political, cultural values drawn upon by practitioners for defining 'functions' of social work
Theories of *how to do social work*	Formal written theories of practice (e.g. casework, family therapy, groupwork); applied deductively;[1] general ideas may be applied to particular situations	Theories inductively[2] derived from particular situations; can be tested to see if they apply to particular situations; also unwritten practice theories constructed from practice
Theories of *the client world*	Formal written social science theories and empirical data (e.g. on personality, marriage, the family, race, class, gender)	Practitioners' use of experience and general cultural meanings (e.g. the family as an institution, normal behaviour, good parenting)

[1] Deduction means arriving at conclusions about the particular instance from a general theory.
[2] Induction means generalizing from particular examples.

practice which is more complex than a simple split would suggest. Sibeon's framework provides an insight into some of the ways in which formal and informal theory and practice interrelate. Fook takes this further from a critical postmodern viewpoint, arguing that theory becomes both more and less than formal theories. She widens the debate by talking about 'ways of knowing' instead of 'theories', recognizing that knowledge is constructed from our practice situations and our experiences. Our understanding is informed by a multitude of factors including formal theories. These are important because they provide a starting point to engage with a new situation and make new experiences initially manageable. This is why, as indicated above, she suggests that a more useful way of thinking about theories is as intellectual tools rather than rules.

The context of contemporary practice

Anti-oppressive practice should respond to the reality of users' lives and our own lives. This is at both a personal and a structural level. Therefore, the theory needs to be interactive or reflexive (Payne, 1991: 22). As such, it will inevitably change in response to varying historical, social, political and economic factors. The context of contemporary health and social care practice is characterized by globalization, demographic change and increasing managerial-technicist approaches to practice. This leads to a number of contradictions and tensions which challenge practitioners. Globalization, a contested concept, can be described as a process whereby the world has become more integrated and interconnected economically, politically, culturally and socially. However, despite theoretical and ideological differences between commentators, most agree on the main strands of the globalization process and these are outlined in the box.

Main strands of the globalization process

- Increasing and deepening interconnectedness of societies in different parts of the world.
- Almost unimpeded flows of financial capital, news and cultural images across the world.
- Rising activity and power of multinational companies.
- Rising economic growth accompanied by rising inequalities in many countries.
- A global consumer culture in the making.
- More travel and migration by more people from more countries to more countries; faster methods of transport and electronic communication so that time and space is increasingly being compressed.

- Greater awareness by the public of what is happening in the world and of the possible implications for their own country.
- The rapid growth of governmental and non-governmental supranational organizations that supplement, supplant and support the activities of the nation-state.

(George and Wilding, 2002: 2)

The impact of globalization for practitioners is variable. It has been described as both exacerbating social problems and making them more visible – for example, environmental degradation, drug trafficking, legal and illegal immigration (George and Wilding, 2002: 208). Displacements of populations have resulted in concerns being expressed about what global responsibility should be taken in local affairs that are the result of international changes. As a consequence of this, Fook (2002) reminds us that it is of paramount importance to look at how we accommodate difference based on race and ethnic identity within increasingly fluid structures. Rossiter (2004) also warns of the need to recognize the threats to the values of professional practice that come with the changing nature of power, evidenced in global trends such as free trade, neo-conservative reorganization of society and positioning of the United States as a world hegemonic power. Other social problems include AIDS, unemployment and social dislocation. Practitioners may experience the impact of globalization through working in an environment where the purchaser/provider split has allowed multinational firms to become providers of care. Social policies that divert funds away from very dependent groups towards education and training in order to attract higher-wage investment also have an impact on social care as available resources are reduced (Holden, 2000).

Demographic changes in Europe mean that there is a growing dependent population and a smaller proportion of people in the workforce (Adams, 2002). It is projected that the proportion of people over 80 years old will rise from 10 per cent in 1960 to about 22 per cent in 2020. Most older people look after themselves, but as their age increases they may become more dependent through disability and ill-health, requiring additional support from health and social care services. Alongside this, other trends indicate that the number of informal carers is likely to decrease, because of increasing mobility, family poverty, divorce and carers growing older (Stepney and Ford, 2000).

The managerial-technicist approach has been described as dominant within the delivery of services. Harlow (2003) summarizes this approach through a comparison to other approaches to practice (Table 2.2).

There are various views about the impact of this approach on practice. For example, it has been stated that managerialism has been significant in de-politicizing practice and the professional voice can become silenced through

Table 2.2 Approaches to practice (adapted from Harlow, 2003)

Implications / Feature	Reflexive-therapeutic perspective	Socialist-collectivist perspective	Individualist-reformist perspective	Managerial-technicist perspective
Individualization	Practice aims to help individuals achieve self-fulfilment	Practice focus on individuals ignores policy implications of personal problems, and discourages collective responses	Practitioner's role treats people as individuals, while bureaucrats treat them as categories of problem	Practitioners coordinate packages of care in response to the needs of individuals
Use of knowledge	Knowledge allows practitioners to act skilfully and without risk to service users	Knowledge should be shared with service users, empowering them to act on their own behalf	Practice uses psychological and social knowledge, evidence and argument to help service users	Practitioners use knowledge of the law, policy and organizational procedures to carry out their duties
Relationship	Relationship carries communication which influences service users and also creates personal involvement which 'moves' service users to respond	Relationship with workers can offer experience of cooperative endeavour, but may also lead to manipulation through personal influence	Practice relationships personalize services and influence service users to change more readily	Impersonality increases as contact is brief, service users become consumers choosing services, and written contracts represent partnership
Organizational context	Agencies' functions give focus to therapeutic intervention	Agencies represent the interests of powerful groups in society. They reduce the pressures of an oppressive society and maintain dependence on discretionary services	The organizational context of practice sanctions social work action on society's behalf and limits and directs social work activity in accordance with socially defined objectives	In line with government directives, technologies of performance define the activity of practitioners
Need	Practice identifies and works with the needs that service users exhibit or express	Worker's role in assessing need may give or deny access to services through resource allocation or rationing	Practice defines and responds to need on society's behalf, ensuring that resources are effectively used	Indicators of need are defined centrally and practitioners work to assessment schedules

Table 2.2 *continued*

Implications / Feature	Reflexive-therapeutic perspective	Socialist-collectivist perspective	Individualist-reformist perspective	Managerial-technicist perspective
Maintenance of social institutions	Practice helps service users participate in social structures which give them support and fulfilment	Practice maintains important social institutions, such as community and family, which support the present social order and limit possibilities of change	Practice plays an important part in maintaining social institutions, which provide stability and continuity in society	Social institutions, like practice itself, are in a process of re-figuration
Advocacy	Practice helps people gain the personal power to achieve their aims in life	Practice should create structures for service users' cooperation to fight for needs	Practice advocates for service users' needs in agencies and policy changes	Coopted into budgetary responsibility, practitioners do not act as advocates and service users are expected to advocate for themselves

loss of autonomy and discretion (Stepney and Ford, 2000). It has been suggested that the use of self is also lost if practitioners merely coordinate services (Harlow, 2003). In addition, Harlow points out the 'lack of attention to the inner world of service users and the social work relationship' (2003: 29) which, in turn, may deny them voice. On the other hand, there are contradictions, as a culture does exist where practitioners are prepared to resist and meet the challenge by recording unmet need, helping service users appeal, and using what discretion they do still have to exploit opportunities to meet the needs of service users and carers within the eligibility and budgetary constraints they face (Stepney and Ford, 2000). Despite the negative consequences of managerialism, therefore, there are those who are finding more personal and holistic ways of understanding experience (Fook, 2002; Ng and Chan, 2005).

The contradictions and tensions that we have briefly visited here create the need for practitioners to develop for themselves sound theoretical frameworks which make explicit their values and commitment to what has been described as 'progressive' practice. This means 'working with service users to develop a shared understanding of a social world characterized by oppression and exclusion, so that we might be better placed to transform it' (Stepney and Ford, 2000: 25). This requires practitioners to use skills of critical engagement in relation to the range of theories and methods available to them in their work. For us, two important elements of anti-oppressive theory are the concepts of power and oppression. Both of these are subjects in their own right about which many books have been written (Freire, 1972; Lukes, 1974; Solomon, 1976; Foucault, 1980; Lukes, 1986; Clegg, 1989; Westwood, 2002). What we present here is an introduction to the theoretical concepts. In no way is this a comprehensive exposition, but it aims to provide an initial framework that can be developed. You will need to undertake further reading, personal analysis and engage in discussion with friends and colleagues in order to be able to develop a theory and practice that you can acknowledge as your own.

What do we mean by power?

> Those who profess to favour freedom yet deprecate agitation, are people who want crops without ploughing up the ground; They want rain without thunder and lightning. They want the ocean without the awful roar of its many waters.
>
> Power concedes nothing without demand. It never did and it never will. Find out just what any people will quietly submit to and you have found out the exact measure of injustice and wrong which will be imposed upon them, and these will continue till they are resisted with either words or blows or both. The limits of tyrants are precise by the endurance of those whom they oppress.
>
> (Frederick Douglas, 1857, quoted in the Gypsy Survey, 1993: 1)

As practitioners we need to recognize 'more personal, dynamic, and multiple ways in which power differences are created and maintained' (Fook, 2003: 125). Philosophers, political scientists and critical sociological theorists such as Plato and Aristotle, Hobbes and Locke, Machiavelli, Marx and Foucault have all discussed the nature of power (Westwood, 2002). Attempting to define power is an ultimately challenging task as its meaning varies, depending on context and the ideological perspective of the definer. Many interpretations of power have been put forward, which are influenced by a range of values. This means that 'the search for a single concept of power is intrinsically illusory' (Haugaard, 2002: 2). There will always be particular usages, which are suitable to certain theoretical projects. Some writers use the term in highly specific ways. For example, Parsons developed a version of power which related it to cultural consensus rather than conflict (Clifford, 1998) while Marxist theorists such as Poulantzas conceptualized power in terms of the ability of a class to realize its objective interests (Haugaard 2002: 3). This emphasis on the structural aspects of power in circumstances of conflict is taken up by critical theorists, who also stress that power is generated 'through cultural social practices which produce ideology and manufacture consent' (Clifford, 1998: 80). Lukes's (1974) influential work on power has been widely used, particularly in its application to practice and policy in community work, social work and social welfare (Rees, 1991). He developed a three-dimensional view of power – the power that you can see and can clearly challenge, the power you can see but have less clear means to challenge and the power that is less visible, because it is so ingrained in cultural norms, and social, political and legal structures.

Power has been described as a social concept which can be used to explore the public and private spheres of life (Barker and Roberts, 1992). Barbara Solomon (1987), in her discussion about power, points out that power has a number of meanings which depend on whether one looks at it from a psychological, economic, political, sociological or philosophical perspective. In her account of work with oppressed black communities in the USA she identifies power as 'a bridging concept which describes aspects of interpersonal relations at family, small group, organisational or community levels' (Solomon, 1987: 79, quoted in Rees 1991: 36). The usefulness of the concept of power as used by Solomon is that it can 'span the various dimensions of structural power and personal power and the inequalities and differences within different social relations. Thus structure, culture and biography can be analysed in a more integrated process' (McNay, 1992: 55). Loewenstein (1976) sees power as 'the overall integrating motivational concept for all human behaviour' (cited in Kolb-Morris, 1993: 104). For her, the relationships between men and women, between 'races', between different social classes and between helping professionals and their clients are all variations of unequal power relations in society (Lowenstein, 1976, quoted by McNay, 1992: 18).

Debates around the question of 'what is power?' have focused around two positions. First power is viewed as a quantitative capacity to act which implies the ability to intervene in the lives of others (Westwood, 2002). Sawicki (1991) suggests that traditional models of power involve three basic assumptions:

1. Power is possessed (for example, by a class of people).
2. Power flows from a centralized source from top to bottom (for instance, law, the economy, the state).
3. Power is primarily repressive in its exercise (a prohibition backed by sanctions).

Power understood in this way suggests that those with power who use it for themselves will have unequal relations with those who feel its dominating effects.

An alternative view of power has been influenced by the work of Michel Foucault (1980) who wrote that 'power is not something that is acquired, seized or shared, something that one holds onto or allows to slip away: power is exercised from innumerable points, in the interplay of non-egalitarian and mobile relations' (1980: 94). However, despite criticisms of Foucault, his work and understanding of power have provided what has been described as 'a new impetus' (Westwood, 2002: 19) to our analysis of power. It is useful, therefore, to briefly consider some of the elements of his approach, which provide us with an understanding of the fluid and ubiquitous nature of power – 'it is here there and everywhere, legally and militarily organized in the criminal justice system and the armed forces, but it is also in the workplace, on the streets, in our interactions and in our subjectivities' (Westwood, 2002: 139).

Sawicki (1991) summarizes Foucault's critique of the traditional conception of power and points out that his theory is different in the following ways:

1. **Power is exercised rather than possessed**
   Instead of possessing power, people use and create it. Foucault was not worried about who were the oppressors or the oppressed but about how power is exercised through social relations. No one person holds power but people are situated differently within it.

2. **Power is not primarily repressive but productive**
   Foucault argues that if power is only repressive it makes it difficult to explain why we are prepared to accept certain institutional practices. He suggests that power is at the same time creative and productive because it constitutes practices such as discourses, knowledges and 'identity'. Healy (2000) points out that Foucault asserts that people are prepared to participate in modern forms of power because not only does it subjugate but it also produces their sense of self, 'put simply, there is no "self" without power' (Healy, 2000: 44).

3. **Power is analysed as coming from the bottom up**
   Power is not located in a centralized source but is expressed in micro- and macro-level relations and structures. Foucault does not deny that there are oppressive structures (like class, capitalism or state power) but denies that understanding these is most important for organizing local resistance. His 'bottom-up' analysis of power relations helps us to understand how local relations make possible global effects of domination like class, power and patriarchy. This view of power helps us to see how power is expressed in the richness of everyday relations.

   (Sawicki, 1991; Healy, 2000; Fook, 2002)

No discussion of power can ignore powerlessness. Solomon (1976) identified three potential sources of powerlessness:

- the images that powerless people have of themselves;
- the experiences that powerless people encounter when they engage with external systems;
- systems that consistently block and deny powerless groups the opportunity to take effective action.

Powerlessness may be characterized by economic insecurity, absence of monetary support, lack of opportunity for training in critical and abstract thought, and physical and emotional stress (Sennett and Cobb, 1972; Conway, 1979). These aspects in turn generate *experiences* of powerlessness, such as exclusion, rejection or being treated as inferior, which lead to feelings of inadequacy, helplessness and dependency. If we consider that people's relations are structured by power then we are less likely to stereotype, make assumptions or misinterpret other people's actions. It is when we *do* stereotype, make assumptions and misinterpret other people's actions that we start to oppress. This is eloquently described in the following excerpt:

> When I am asked if I am a 'Real Gypsy' my answer is this: I am flesh and blood, I feel pain, I feel joy, I love, I hate, cut me I bleed, I am a real human being living in today's world who happens to be a Gypsy. Not some stereotype that fits misinformed people's ideas of what a Gypsy should be.
>
> (Gypsy Survey, 1993: 12)

Interpretations of what is meant by power therefore have a bearing on practice. In her discussion about the concepts of power and empowerment, Fook (2002: 103) suggests that we need to take into account:

- the contextual and changing nature of power;
- how power operates at different levels, often simultaneously and in contradictory ways;
- how power is experienced by different people;
- the creative, as well as controlling, possibilities power entails.

The following scenario is used to illustrate how we might use our knowledge of power to understand relations in a particular situation.

Case example: Jo and Justine

Joe (age 32) and Justine (age 30) are a white married couple who both have a learning disability. Joe also has a speech impediment, which makes it difficult for him to communicate. They have two children, Danny age 2 and Anna age 6. There is a strong bond between the two children and their parents. Joe and

Justine parent to the best of their ability and have a close supportive relationship. They have a social worker from the learning disability team who has known them for several years. Recently the school expressed concerns about Anna. She is bullied in school because her clothes are often dirty and other children say that she is smelly. She is behind other children of her age in school and seems to have little energy. Neighbours have alleged that Anna is not looked after properly. Recently a child protection case conference was held, which Joe and Justine were invited to attend. They found this very difficult, although their social worker supported them and explained what was happening. The outcome of the meeting was that the professionals involved did not feel that Anna needed to be placed on the child protection register. However a number of interventions were recommended, including parenting classes for Joe and Justine, and education social work support for Anna. A Family Group Conference was also recommended in order to address the question of how Anna could be supported in school.

In Joe and Justine's situation there are multiple layers of interacting power relationships. The fact that Joe has a speech impediment may mean that his experiences of working with professionals have been difficult and frustrating, and he will feel that he has less power in relation to Justine, whom the professionals normally address. The vulnerability of Joe as a male with a learning difficulty is magnified by his communication problem, as he is unable to express his needs or complain effectively about the way the family is being treated by professionals. This may be due to the fact that those who have power in his life fail to listen to him or help him to learn how to express himself. However, Joe has successfully lived with his disability and has managed his life to the extent that he is happily married with two children, lives in reasonable accommodation and has no rent arrears. This provides him with a sense of identity and personal strength. Justine has a powerful position within the family unit because she has the ability to articulate her needs and concerns, especially to external agencies. However, the children, because of their age, are vulnerable and under the scrutiny of professional agencies. There are differences in the level of vulnerability of the two children. Anna is older and is more exposed to the protective gaze of others. She is also able to talk about her life and what she wants, but is not necessarily listened to by the adults who have taken on the decision-making on her behalf. Danny, as a younger child, is not subject to external monitoring and could be more vulnerable.

Joe's and Justine's power as adults and parents is limited by the power that the professionals have in defining their ability to parent to an acceptable standard. Informed by a Foucauldian approach, commentators on child welfare have suggested that professionals keep families under surveillance through 'moralization, normalization and coercive intervention' (Holland et al., 2005: 73). In this case family members may find themselves caught up in the surveillance role. The Child Protection System forces the family and the social worker down such an avenue. The power of the family's social worker, who has used her professional expertise creatively to enable them to function as a family and within the community, could be challenged by the bureaucratic Child Protection processes. The Family Group Conference provides an opportunity to democratize the relationship between the family and the social worker and between individuals within the family. However, research has indicated that the radical changes in practice that are offered through Family Group Conferences are unlikely to enable true democratization without major changes within the welfare systems (Lupton and Nixon, 1999; Holland et al., 2005).

This is just a snapshot of the dynamic power relations in this situation. We can see from these initial thoughts, for example, that the divisions of age, disability and gender interact with each other and with various social structures to shape and determine the internal relations within the family as well as the external relations with professionals and the community. However, there may be other divisions that are not apparent but that shape relations. This is a fluid and changing story which needs to be constantly reviewed to understand how power is exercised and how it affects the various people involved.

Oppression

> In order for the oppressed to be able to wage the struggle for their liberation they must perceive the reality of oppression, not as a closed world from which there is no exit, but as a limited situation which they can transform.
>
> (Freire, 1972: 34)

It is from the experiences of people who have been marginalized, who have had their rights denied or violated, that we can understand what is meant by oppression. By listening to other people's experiences of oppression, we are able to extend the parameters of what is possible (Lorde, 1984). It is the *listening* that is most important, as this provides us with the information that enables us to gain a fuller understanding of the issues.

The word 'oppression' is a value-laden term that can conjure up in our minds various disturbing images. You will probably have your own definition of what oppression means to you. Think back again to your own experiences as you consider your definition. Experiences of oppression can be portrayed by literature and poetry in terms that are far more powerful and immediate than any textbook definition. The following extract from a poem very simply demonstrates the insidious nature of gender oppression:

> oppression is not a choice
> or just the misfortune of the socially deprived

> no woman has escaped
> sexism like quiet rain
> constantly, softly seeping in
> until we all become saturated
> and it gently, ever so gently
> so we hardly notice
> does us terrible violence
>
> (Aspen, 1983)

Andre Brink's novel *The Other Side of Silence* (2003) also provides an insight into the nature of human relationships that are oppressive and degrading. The novel explores individual acts of oppression and violence, showing how easy it is to behave in ways that deny the rights of another. The novel provides the reader with a particular understanding of the social divisions of disability, sexuality, racism. It raises issues in relation to lesbianism, misogyny, religious bigotry, cultural differences, questions modernist conceptions of identity and cultural representation, and looks at how identities are constructed and reconstructed. Brink poignantly describes an individual woman's experience of physical violence. The men involved could do what they did because they were supported by a patriarchal system and discourse that provided them with the means by which they could justify to themselves and others that they had the right to behave in this way. However, oppressive relations are complex and, as we noted in the section on power above, there are always elements of resistance within different power relations. The following extract from the story demonstrates 'that there are no relations of power without resistances ... like power, resistance is multiple' (Foucault, 1980: 42):

> On the face of it she has always borne whatever they chose to visit on her, but she has never yielded, she has always withheld consent. However, meek she may have seemed, this deep stern resistance has always been there.
>
> (Brink, 2003: 19)

Those who are oppressed are not passive, they resist the imposition of power in many different and significant ways.

There is no simple definition of oppression. It is a complex and emotive term. To seek to identify and explain it in a simple phrase is to deny its very complexity. Useful insights into oppression can be gained from thinking about general definitions that focus on interpersonal interaction between individuals and groups. Thompson describes oppression as:

> Inhuman or degrading treatment of individuals or groups; hardship and injustice brought about by the dominance of one group over another; the negative and demeaning exercise of power. Oppression often involves disregarding the rights of an individual or group and is thus a denial of citizenship.
>
> (Thompson, 2001: 34)

We have used Mitchell's (1989: 14) description to help us capture the essence of oppression as it impacts on social work practice:

> British society is saturated in oppression ... an empowering social work practice derived from such an understanding addresses itself to the powerlessness and loss which results from the material and ideological oppression of Black people by white people; working class people by middle class people, women by men; children and old people by 'adults'; disabled people by 'able' people; and gay people by 'straight' people. This social work practice recognises oppression not simply in the behaviours, values and attitudes of individuals and groups, but in the institutions, structures and common sense assumptions.

These descriptions are a helpful starting point as they articulate the pervasiveness of oppression, how it operates and how it is experienced. But they have their limitations. Expressing oppression in dichotomous terms does not convey a full understanding of its complex nature. Oppression is a socially constructed term, which is multidimensional and fluid (based as it is on interactions between people) and occurs at a number of levels (Dominelli, 2002b). Political and economic structures have a role to play. Together with ideology they function as a highly effective system of social control. Therefore oppression can be seen 'as a state of affairs in which life chances are constructed, and as the process by which this state of affairs is created and maintained' (Mullender and Ward, 1993: 148). The interactive nature of oppressive relations means that they are continually reproduced within daily individual activities and social systems.

A number of black women writers, in highlighting their personal experiences, demonstrate the interacting effects of gender and race (hooks, 1981, 1989; Lorde, 1984; Jordan, 1989). Their writings provide rich sources of information about the effects of multiple oppression. The oppression of the individual is grounded in the beliefs and practice of a sexist, homophobic, disabilist, ageist, racist and class-ridden society. Emma Goldman succinctly shows how the personal experiences of oppression and the structures that determine and maintain that oppression are linked when she states: 'it is organized violence at the top that permits individual violence at the bottom' (quoted in Weick and Vandiver, 1982: 9).

A black feminist perspective attempts to address the issue of difference. It argues that oppression should not be ranked, or compartmentalized, but that the interconnectedness of oppressions should be emphasized. It is only through the making of such links that a true understanding of how oppression structures an individual's life can be obtained. bell hooks makes this point clearly. In reflecting upon her experiences of, and involvement in, feminist struggle, she writes: 'at the moment of my birth, two factors determined my destiny, my having been born Black and my having been born female' (hooks, 1981: 12). Both black women and white women therefore need to take into account the following points if they are to engage effectively in the process of change:

- to end the oppression of black women, both sexism and racism have to be addressed;
- to separate racism and sexism is to deny a basic truth of black women's existence.

Marjorie Quinn (2003), telling her story as a minority white woman in Zambia (where white women constitute less than 1 per cent of the total population), over 20 years after bell hooks was writing, acknowledges the usefulness of the language of 'race', terms such as 'white' and 'Black', because it emphasizes difference, diversity and power relations. However, she warns that:

> These categories quickly and easily become reified as fixed, separate and monolithic categories of experience and identity, rather than being seen as socially constructed, blurred and changing. The reality is much more complex than these dualistic terms imply.
>
> (Quinn, 2003: 78)

Quinn describes her situation as a white woman in a country where race relations are shaped by the history of colonial exploitation and the struggle for independence. Stereotypical meanings of 'white' were of wealth, power, health, education, cleanliness, honesty and choices in life, which invoked both resentment and a kind of respect. However, there were differences between white people in terms of wealth. For example some, as she did, worked for local wages and did not have much ready money available. Others, who had been retired for a long time, had neither wealth nor power. Within the community there were some wealthy and powerful black Zambians, although the majority did live in dire poverty. Her position was made more complex because of her gender. She shared the vulnerability of black women living in a society where their roles were defined by men, with little protection (either by the law or social conventions) from abuse and exploitation. Her participation and social power were also constrained by limited knowledge and use of local languages.

Quinn's experience and analysis demonstrates that race relations are complex and particular and are connected to other oppressions. Critical postmodern theory contributes to an analysis of oppression because, Quinn suggests:

> It encourages our attempts to understand in each situation the complex and particular structures and operations of power and dominance, and subjugation and oppression, and of personal meaning. It rejects monolithic and dualistic categorization. Many threads of my social story carry with them privilege and power; others carry less privilege and power, and even some vulnerability. If we are seeking to live and work in ways which affirm difference and promote understanding and equality, we must explore, and manage ourselves through, such complexities. At the same time as engaging with these particularities and differences, we must not be blind to the fact that overall very real privileges accrue in our world from being white.
>
> (Quinn, 2003: 80)

From this discussion we can see that oppression can be specific in that it is manifested in one form or another, such as racism, sexism, heterosexism, disabilism, adultism and so on. But these forms also interconnect. The important point is that one aspect of ourselves should not be used to define the whole of us, as this is 'destructive and fragmenting' (Lorde, 1984: 120). To effectively challenge oppression, therefore, it is important to understand both the interconnectedness and the specificity of each named oppression.

Our experiences of oppression will mean that we have internalized what it means to be different and will therefore use that knowledge when we relate to others. This point is picked up by Lorde who, in sharing her experiences of oppression as a woman, said that 'as women, we must root out internalised patterns of oppression within ourselves if we are to move beyond the most superficial aspects of social change' (1984: 122). It is also necessary to examine where the power which produces and sustains specific forms of powerlessness is located. Oppression operates at different 'levels' of society, including going beyond the individual (Clifford, 1998), to include institutional structures and practices in society. 'Institutional oppression' has been used to refer to the way in which key institutions and societal structures operate to the advantage of some groups and the disadvantage of others (Singh, 2002; Quinn, 2003; Heron, 2004). Heron (2004) points out that institutional racism has been a reality and a struggle for many black people, but it was not until the Macpherson Report[1] (1999) that an understanding of its subtle, hidden, pervasive and endemic nature was brought into the public domain (Singh, 2002). Macpherson's definition of institutional racism as 'the collective failure of an organization to provide an appropriate and professional service to people because of their colour, culture and ethnic origin' (Macpherson, 1999: 28) has become the 'official' definition of institutional racism.

Identity, diversity and difference

An understanding of power and oppression is needed to enable us to consider the dynamics of power relations and their impact on individuals, groups and communities. This involves critically interrogating concepts such as identity, diversity and difference in order to make more visible the contradictions and difficulties within social relations. Williams (1996), from a background of feminism and postmodernism, has put forward some ideas about the meanings of the terms 'diversity', 'difference' and 'division', which can be seen as three aspects of 'difference'.

> *Diversity* is the difference claimed because of shared collective experience which is specific and not necessarily subordinated e.g. a shared language, nationality, regional origin, age and so on.
> *Difference* is where a shared collective experience forms the basis of resistance against subordinate status e.g. gender, ethnicity, sexuality, religion, disability.
> *Division* occurs when the difference is translated into a form of domination and forms an identity which protects a privileged position.
>
> (Williams, 1996: 70)

The term 'difference' is contested. Although Williams (1996) points out that not all discourses problematize difference, other commentators suggest that labelling and categorizing has the potential for discrimination and stigmatization. Often we label people and put them into boxes like good/bad, deserving/undeserving and so on. This focus on dichotomy leads to 'forced choices, to unnecessary competition, and to unequal relationships in which one half of the pair is viewed as inferior and the other as superior' (Kolb-Morris, 1993: 101). However, it is important to view human life from a holistic perspective. Difference can be seen as a source of strength and power.

The issue for practitioners is to find ways of recognizing and validating difference without discriminating unfairly (Fook, 2002). What such an explanation offers is a framework by which it can be argued that progressive practitioners celebrate diversity, acknowledge difference and are committed to challenging division (Davis and Garrett, 2004). The potential of what has been called 'identity politics' arises from this. The concept of 'identity' has enabled people to resist domination through recognizing difference and consequently creating affirming identity categories. Disabled people, black and ethnic minority groups, older people and people who use mental health services, for example, have mobilized around particular divisions to protect their rights and become empowered in articulating their needs and defining themselves. Self-definition has been actively sought by black women. Parmar (1990) explains that the creation of black British women's identities is not '"in relation to", "in opposition to", "as reversal of", or "as a corrective to" ... but *in and for ourselves*' (Parmar, 1990: 101). This undermines the universalist and essentialist ideas of black women by dominant groups. Marginalized groups also use their structural position and experience of marginality to make links between other social divisions and contribute to the experiences of others (Dominelli, 2002a). The main point for practitioners from this type of analysis is that the politics of identity construction become central in resisting and confronting oppression.

The concept of identity, then, is one of the elements of anti-oppressive practice. As practitioners we need to be aware of our social location, of the social divisions membership of the people with whom they work, and of the nature of the interaction between the social divisions. For Weeks (1990: 98):

> Identity is about belonging, about what you have in common with some people and what differentiates you from others. At its most basic it gives you a sense of personal location, the stable core to your individuality.

He further explores the concept, explaining that we all live with many potentially contradictory identities and that it is the dynamic interplay between the differences that exist between people which defines and identifies. It is important, therefore, to appreciate the various complex and competing factors that shape and inform our identities.

Identity is a social construction – 'everyone is implicated in creating "the gaze" whether it is to produce dominant versions of it, challenge it from the marginalized position, or seek to create alternatives to it' (Dominelli, 2002c: 63). Some identities are constructed as privileged in relation to others, for example white, European, heterosexual males without a disability at the expense of those identities that are deemed as inferior – not part of the mythical norm. For example '"women" are (re)cast as inferior to "men"' (Dominelli, 2002c: 63). The implication for practitioners of understanding that identity is not fixed is that they must provide a holistic needs-led service. By sensitively assessing the individual's situation we are less likely to engage in a stereotyped response to an individual's difference. One's identity is a prism through which the individual views social interactions and in which social relations are mediated. Anti-oppressive practitioners therefore need to be self-aware, have an understanding of power relations, acknowledge and work with the individual's sense of self.

What is anti-oppressive practice?

Theorizing the elements of anti-oppressive practice is a precursor to thinking about how it has been defined. As we have already pointed out, definitions are never fixed and static – rather, they reflect the debates, emerging discourses and changing contexts of practice. 'The choice of words used to define reveals not only the value and ideological base of the definer, but also the nature of the practice that would emanate from that definition' (Burke and Harrison, 1998: 230). We conclude this chapter by providing a number of definitions that reflect the development and understanding of anti-oppressive practice and its underpinning principles. We start with the work of Phillipson (1992), who developed a framework for thinking about the universal elements of power and oppression as well as the specific manifestations of power in the form of sexism and racism. Within the framework she distinguishes the differences between anti-oppressive practice as challenging injustice and suggesting alternative ways of working and anti-discriminatory practice as specified by law. Her diagram, which we have adapted in Figure 2.1, helps us to explain the differences between anti-oppressive practice and anti-discriminatory practice.

In this diagram Phillipson has used black and feminist perspectives as an example to demonstrate how holding a particular perspective can lead to transformatory practice. In the diagram we see that black and feminist perspectives are potentially more anti-oppressive than anti-discriminatory practice. Anti-oppressive practice is the overarching framework for linking the universal features of oppression. She then shows how black perspectives and black feminism can combine together to inform a view (black feminist) that can lead to radical practice. She sees anti-discriminatory practice as a way of working that is only possible within the legal framework, using the examples of anti-sexist and anti-racist practice as a specific form of anti- discriminatory practice. In her exploration of anti-oppressive practice Phillipson was trying to build a framework to show the interrelationship between anti-discriminatory and anti-oppressive practice while at the same time demonstrating the potential for anti-oppressive practice to promote change without being constrained by legal frameworks.

In 1993 Dominelli brought together ideas about anti-oppressive practice in a statement that reflects the development of anti-oppressive practice and

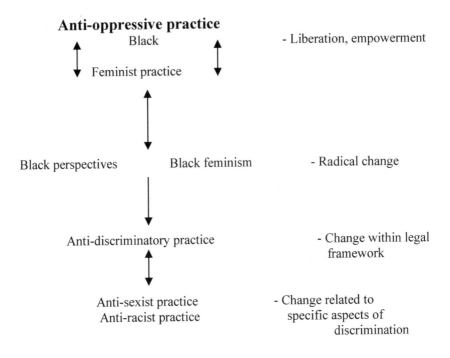

(adapted from Phillipson 1992: 20)

Figure 2.1   A framework for anti-oppressive practice concentrating on black and feminist perspectives

its underpinning principles. For Dominelli, anti-oppressive practice is informed by:

> ... a person-centred practice, an egalitarian value system concerned with reducing the deleterious effects of structural inequalities upon people's lives; a methodology focusing on both process and outcome; and a way of structuring relationships between individuals that aims to empower users by reducing the negative effect on hierarchy in their immediate interaction and the work they do together.
>
> (Dominelli, 1993, cited in Adams et al., 1998: 7)

Drawing on our previous writing we attempt in the following definition to provide an understanding of anti-oppressive practice in order to help practitioners recognize and challenge oppression within their work. Working with people has both a personal and a political dimension. This means that we have to be aware of the political nature of our work and also to find ways of making private issues public concerns in order to have an impact on policy and legislation. Alongside this is the need to be reflective and reflexive. Reflective practice in this respect goes beyond just being reflective (which does not contribute to transforming practice) to a critical approach that uses understanding gained from the reflective process to question the taken for granted in order to achieve change. Reflexivity is about being aware of who we are as practitioners and the impact that we have on others and that they have on us. It has been described as a way of responding to the uniqueness of each individual (Parton, 2000). This means that anti-oppressive practice is a dynamic and ongoing process based on the changing complex patterns of social relations:

> Anti-oppressive practice is a radical social work approach which is informed by humanistic and social justice values and takes account of the experiences and views of oppressed people. It is based on an understanding of how the concepts of power, oppression and inequality determine personal and structural relations.
>
> Practitioners are required to analyse how the socially constructed divisions of race, age, gender, class, sexuality and disability and the impact of differential access to resources, interconnect and interact to define the life experiences of individuals and communities. From this position, practitioners are provided with the means to recognize and challenge situations of oppression within their work.
>
> Anti-oppressive practice is based on a belief that social work should make a difference, so that those who have been oppressed may regain control of their lives and re-establish their right to be full and active members of society. To achieve this aim, practitioners have to be political, reflective, reflexive and committed to promoting change.
>
> (Dalrymple and Burke, 2000)

The influence of postmodernist thinking can be seen in the next account. Here Jan Fook's discussion of postmodern and critical social work practice highlights how an understanding of social relations and structures can be used to develop inclusive practice. The critical dimension of anti-oppressive practice, which includes recognition that there are many explanations of apparently similar situations that can be used to challenge dominant ideas, is clearly stated in this definition.

> A postmodern and critical social work practice is primarily concerned with practicing in ways which further a society without domination, exploitation and oppression. It will focus both on how structures

> dominate, but also on how people construct and are constructed by changing social structures and relations, recognizing that there may be multiple and diverse constructions of ostensibly similar situations. Such an understanding of social relations and structures can be used to disrupt dominant understandings and structures, and as a basis for changing these so that they are more inclusive of different interest groups.
>
> (Fook, 2002: 18)

Latterly, the term 'transformational practice' has been used to describe practice which attempts to tackle inequality and oppression and ensure that the work we do now has an impact on our individual and collective futures.

> Transformational practice ... meets the objective of promoting well being by changing current configurations of inequality and diswelfare that prevent people from realising their full potential as self-determining agents. Additionally, securing these improved relationships in practice requires us ... to connect our interpersonal interactions with our political objectives and thereby model and demonstrate our increased sociality to remove barriers that cause inequalities and promote social change.
>
> (Adams et al., 2005b: 2)

Healy (2005) locates anti-oppressive practice theory as being on the cusp of modernism and postmodernist thinking. In the definitions discussed here we can see the interrelationship between modernist and postmodernist concepts, how language reflects specific ideas of the time. Some words, for example 'transformational', with roots in radical structured approaches,[2] have been reclaimed to reflect current understanding of practice which is aimed at tackling inequalities. Although the term 'anti-oppressive practice' was not widely used until the 1990s, the above definitions reflect a more sophisticated understanding of anti-oppressive practice as it has emerged as a dominant theory of critical practice (Healy, 2005). All acknowledge that society is unequal and that the problems faced by service users have a personal, cultural and structural dimension. Therefore, in order to challenge inequalities, practitioners need to engage in meaningful dialogue with service users and carers and link the personal stories of individuals, groups and communities to the wider political processes.

Reflective thoughts

With an understanding of the concepts outlined above we have the building blocks to develop the tools we need to work with service users and carers. However, learning is a continual process, which, to be effective, requires us to be reflective, and this reflection needs a 'critical edge' (Baldwin, 2004: 43). Put simply, critical reflection means linking a reflective approach with a critical analysis. This involves using the process of reflection to reveal assumptions relating to power relations and structures. By examining the role of these assumptions in constructing dominant power relations and structures, a theory of power can be reconstructed in order to disturb such domination. This then enables us to deconstruct and reconstruct the knowledge informing our practice so that we can evaluate its effectiveness and develop ways of working that are not oppressive (Baldwin, 2004; Fook, 2004).[3] The changing context of practice for health and social care means that practitioners are working with complexity and uncertainty which managers try to control through rational organizational procedures. While this can make it hard to question accepted and powerful ways of working, especially in environments that are less supportive, critical reflection can help workers to 'transform the ways they act within and in relation to their organisations' (Fook, 2004: 72).

We began this chapter with a personal account of Chris's experiences as a young person in residential care. Being looked after in local authority care contributed to creating her identity, her sense of herself. She had been marginalized, discriminated against and felt invisible. Chris wants to assert her individual identity and she is aware of the need to organize with others, rather than work against them. In this way she is using her social location and experience of marginality to make links between others to renegotiate and re-create her identity. Chris understands power relations – her questioning shows how she has reflected on her position and her awareness of how power is used and how she can engage in a more meaningful dialogue with those who appear to have power. A Foucauldian analysis of power and resistance can help understand her situation. Foucault talks about the interplay of power and resistance: 'power relations open up a space in the middle of which the struggles develop' (Foucault, 1989: 187). Her questions, the tools of her resistance, are the questions that she asks of us.

Chapter summary

In this chapter, through an analysis of what is meant by *power* and *oppression*, we lay the foundations of a *theory* of anti-oppressive practice. Critical postmodern and poststructural writers suggest that theories can be seen as intellectual tools

(Healy, 2000; Fook, 2002). This does not mean rejecting formal theories, which are necessary to enable dialogue with other people, but to use our practice and experiences to develop our theorizing in order to help us to engage with the complexity and diversity of practice. It is therefore necessary to connect with 'theory in a way that does not ignore the context within which professional practice takes place and looks for alternatives to the technicist and in-strumentalist role imposed upon professionals' (Batsleer and Humphries, 2000: 12). We concluded therefore with a number of definitions that encapsulate the dynamic relationship between the lives of service users and practitioners. Over time, these definitions have changed, reflecting our increasing understanding of the nature and the impact of power and oppression on people's lives.

Further reading

Theory

Payne, M. (2005) *Modern Social Work Theory*. Basingstoke: Palgrave Macmillan.
This offers a complete introduction to the theories of social work practice. The first two chapters in particular help practitioners think about links between theory and practice. Chapter 13 includes an analysis of anti-oppressive practice. Although aimed at social workers, it is relevant for a range of practitioners.

Thompson, N. (2000) *Theory and Practice in the Human Services*. Buckingham: Open
University Press.
This book takes as its starting point the principle that theory is an important element of informed practice and provides a comprehensive approach to the subject for practitioners across all human services.

Power

Foucault, M. (1980) *Power/Knowledge: Selected Interviews and Other Writings 1972–*
1977, edited by C. Gordon. New York: Pantheon Books.
A useful introduction to some of Foucault's ideas.

Rees, S. (1991) *Achieving Power*. Sydney: Allen & Unwin.
An interesting and useful book about power. Chapter 4 in particular explores 'Power, Politics and Language'.

Oppression

Dominelli, L. (2002a) *Anti-Oppressive Social Work Theory and Practice*. Basingstoke:
Palgrave Macmillan.
This text looks at the theories underpinning anti-oppressive practice, linking identity and empowering practice using case studies to explore the issues.

Reading novels is a good way to further our understanding of the reality of oppression. There are many to choose from – here are a few:

Angelou, M. (1984) *I Know Why the Caged Bird Sings*. London: Virago Press
Brink, A. (2003) *The Other Side of Silence*. London: Vintage
Gilman, C.P. (1981) *The Yellow Wallpaper*. London: Virago Press
Morrison, T. (1987) *Beloved*. London: Picador
Primo Levi (1979) *If This is a Man*. London: Abacus
Shields, C. (1994) *The Stone Diaries*. London: Fourth Estate
Winterson, J. (1985) *Oranges are Not the Only Fruit*. London: Pandora Press

Poetry has also been used to powerfully express individual experiences of oppression:

Kay, J. (1991) *The Adoption Papers*. Newcastle Upon Tyne: Bloodaxe Books
Angelou, M. (1986) *And Still I Rise*. London: Virago Press
Poetry by Disabled Writers (1992) *Rainbow in the Ice*. Manchester: Crocus Books
Schiff, H. (ed.) (1995) *Holocaust Poetry*. London: Harper Collins
Voice for the Child in Care (2000) *Shout to be Heard*. London: Voice for the Child in Care

Anti-oppressive practice

In addition to the text by Dominelli, above, the following books are helpful:

Brechin, A., Brown, H. and Eby, M. (eds) (2000) *Critical Practice in Health and Social Care*. London: Sage Publications.
A useful book to help practitioners to think about working within changing situations.

Healy, K. (2005) *Social Work Theories in Context: Creating Frameworks for Practice*. Basingstoke: Palgrave Macmillan.
Chapter 9 of this book focuses on anti-oppressive practice and considers the strengths and weaknesses of this approach.

Mullaly, B. (2002) *Challenging Oppression: A Critical Social Work Approach*. Ontario: Oxford University Press.
A good introduction to the theories of anti-oppressive practice.

Tomlinson, D.R. and Trew, W. (2002) *Equalising Opportunities, Minimising Oppression: A Critical Review of Anti-Discriminatory Policies in Health and Social Welfare*. London: Routledge.
This book critically analyses anti-racist, anti-discriminatory and anti-oppressive practice. The distinctions and the links between the three approaches to practice are looked at, as well as the contribution that these perspectives have made to our understanding of issues of oppression and inequality within the area of health and social care.

3 Use of the law: contradictions and dilemmas

The crisis in the law concerns an institution which is incapable or unwilling to adapt to a different order: a system unable to recognise its own failings. I hope I have demonstrated that while the law is in a lamentable state it can be changed; it can be challenged and is being reformed to some degree.

(Kennedy, 1993: 264)

A decade of legislation

In the UK over the last ten years we have seen the demise of eighteen years of Conservative government and the rise of New Labour. Tony Blair's election in 1997 was welcomed by many, including health and social care practitioners. The following comment by a social worker interviewed in research undertaken by Jones (2001) demonstrates both the optimism and the reality of New Labour's modernization agenda (Department of Health, 1998):

I voted for Labour in 1997 and like all my friends was really excited to see the Tories defeated. But my life as a social worker has been no better as a consequence. They don't seem to like social workers any more than Thatcher's lot. They don't have any real feel or concern for poverty and how people have suffered in these sorts of areas for 20 years.

(Jones, 2001: 555)

Since 1997 the UK government has initiated a range of policy reforms such as prevention, reintegration of those who are defined as 'socially excluded', minimum standards and partnership working between agencies. New Labour policies are committed to ideas of equality, autonomy, community and democracy which many health and social care practitioners identify with. The New Labour leadership has named its political philosophy and strategy *The Third Way*,[1] which emphasizes 'a more active achievement-orientated style of welfare state, stressing responsibility and work as well as support' (Jordan and Jordan, 2000: 218). Jordan points out that the ideas behind the Third Way's policy programme set out a new relationship between those who provide social services and those who receive them, which represents a more effective communication of key values, especially 'reciprocity' (meaning something for something) and 'responsible community' (meaning respect for order and the needs of others).

One of the problems of the New Labour Agenda is that in taking on the legacy of the Conservatives they have perpetuated policies and reforms of the Right while incorporating socialist ideologies in a way that has led to the pragmatic organization of welfare which lacks any ideological commitment or consistency and is organized on a 'what works' basis (Lymbery, 2004b). Jones (2001) points out that as far as state social work and its clients are concerned there has not been any decisive break in the neo-liberal project. The needs of service users still have to compete with economic and political priorities. Services are beset by target setting and means testing. Practitioners' professional autonomy is constrained by the impact of 'managerialism', which makes innovative, service user focused practice difficult, and has not resulted in the additional resources necessary to meet the identified needs of individuals, families, groups or communities While on the positive side the accountability by managerialist principles has raised practice standards and led to the effective use of scarce resources, from an anti-oppressive perspective there are concerns about the benefits of managerialism and the effectiveness of neo-liberal welfare policies to address issues of social exclusion (Ferguson, 2004).

For practitioners the reality of the last ten years is that increasing legalism has become a feature of contemporary practice. This can be seen in the emergence of national standards in many areas of work, court involvement in decisions that used to be made by professionals on their own, and increasing guidance and regulations prescribing practice. It has been argued that this statutory mandate can promote and encourage good practice (Brayne and Broadbent, 2002). This is because it stresses the importance of prevention and rehabilitation as well as providing legal safeguards when compulsory intervention is needed. On the other hand, Humphries (2004), drawing on Jordan (2001), points out that there is evidence that the controlling and restrictive elements of legislation can draw practitioners into the moralistic aspects of New Labour policy rather than those concerned with attempts to 'empower'. In relation to immigration legislation, she suggests that 'social workers have increasingly become a part of the surveillance process' (Humphries, 2004) of legislation that she describes as repressive and punitive.

This chapter, then, looks at how the law can be used to promote anti-oppressive practice. We will consider the contradictions and dilemmas that are present in the law, which means that it can be seen as constraining and oppressive but can also be used as a radical tool.

The debate

Andy and Charlie are two practitioners who have views concerning their use of the legal authority invested in them. Charlie is trying to convince her colleague that the law can be used positively to promote change. The debate reflects their principles, their knowledge and their application of the law in relation to health and social care practice.

Andy: I find it difficult to think about how the law can be used anti-oppressively as sometimes it does seem to have a lot of potential for denying people their rights, especially in situations like child protection or mental health.

Charlie: I know what you mean. It is quite worrying now in child protection that the threshold for triggering action to investigate is only 'reasonable cause to suspect', which is quite low. But the law doesn't have to be about state control of children and their families – we can see it as something that can be used to promote change and used as a positive resource to promote good practice. For example, all four countries of the UK now have a Children's Commissioner and the importance of involving service users in decision-making is also written into guidance and legislation.

Andy: Yes that's right. But then if we look at the immigration legislation it just seems to be really racist – it's difficult to see how legislation like that can be used to promote good practice.

Charlie: It's a dilemma isn't it? But I guess when you can't use it to promote good practice then you have to work to change it – which is easier said than done I know!
            But what I am thinking about is the wider debate. Sometimes I know that I don't think enough about issues like citizenship and rights.

Andy: No, nor do I – and I know it's really important.

Charlie: But, if you think about it we do have control over how we use legislation to promote the rights of people we work with and care for.

Andy: It's difficult though – even campaigning groups like Family Rights Group, MIND or disability rights groups find it hard.

Charlie: But the law is very powerful. So I think that what we need to try and do is use that power and make it work for service users.

Andy: The trouble is that all I feel that I'm doing some days is monitoring parents and their children, especially mothers: discriminating against them and labelling them as 'inadequate'. It just feels so oppressive and controlling.

Charlie: Yes, the law is complex and can be contradictory. But as practitioners we have to question the moral dilemmas that we face and
understand how the law can help us get through them and not see
the law as an obstruction. Maybe we need to try and find more
time to discuss these issues in a team meeting.

Andy: Even if we only did that once every couple of months it would keep
the issues alive and help to think about different ways of working. I
always learn from sharing practice issues in a group discussion.

Charlie: I would have liked an opportunity to talk about Neil with the team
a few weeks ago – he has moderate learning difficulties and also
takes Ritalin for attention deficit hyperactive disorder. He got a
place at college and I was really pleased about how he was getting
on. Then he had a new tutor who refused to hold his medication
for him. So then Neil was excluded from college. I was really annoyed about this and felt that there must be something I could do.
So I got in touch with the Disability Rights Commission (DRC) to
find out. They advised us of Neil's rights and when I got in touch
with the college about the situation they agreed to hold his
medication and let him go back to college.

Andy: That sounds like a good piece of work – but what gave you the idea
to phone the DRC?

Charlie: Well I was so frustrated as well as annoyed and after trawling the
Internet I realized that this could be a possible source of information and advice. It was not that easy for his parents and it wasn't
just about Neil as an individual – I felt that I needed to make the
institution see that it should be part and parcel of their responsibility in providing an inclusive service. Anyway, a couple of months
later there were more problems when, for medical reasons, Neil
needed to use the toilet on a frequent basis, and he was actually
threatened with exclusion from college for leaving lectures without
permission. Imagine that! We asked the DRC to help us again and
they wrote to the college pointing out its obligations under the
Disability Discrimination Act 1995, and then the college agreed to
further reasonable adjustments. Neil is back there now but we have
all had to work on re-establishing good relationships with his
tutors.[2]

Andy: Doesn't that make you feel like a law enforcement officer rather
than a social worker? I see my job as using my skills and values and
professional judgement to work with individuals to help them solve
problems in their lives.

Charlie: Yes, but in many ways a statutory social worker **is** a law enforcement officer – the clue is in the title! But seriously, I'm not just
taking a legalistic approach to practice, Andy. I see that the law can

be a resource which we can use to support practice – in Neil's case it made his life richer being able to attend college and not feel constantly discriminated against. In the college there was eventually a change of culture both with regard to access and by the tutors who began to understand disability equality issues. Personally I feel angry by the way that Neil was treated and it undermines my values and my view of my role as a social worker.

The above dialogue demonstrates some of the contradictions, dilemmas and tensions that characterize the uneasy relationship which appears to exist between practitioners, service users and the legislative framework. Andy's perspective reflects practitioners who may view the law with some ambivalence. He struggles with the contradictory nature of the legislation and finds it more difficult than Charlie to find a way through – and this contributes to his own role ambiguity (Braye and Preston-Shoot, 1992). Charlie recognizes the complex relationship that exists between the legal framework and the objectives of social work intervention. Her competence is demonstrated by her ability to integrate relevant legislation, policy and procedures into her practice, and she has been able to critically evaluate them in relation to the anti-oppressive values she holds. She has used the law creatively to challenge oppression and powerlessness (Preston-Shoot, 2001). However:

There will always be debate between those who are sceptical about the power of the law to change society and those whose legal training makes them reluctant to acknowledge the law's limitations or to dismiss the law entirely.

(Morris and Nott, 1991: 193)

Using the law

The law is not usually the first resort in our interactions with others. For it to be available we have to know what it states and be able to apply it to the different situations that we encounter. In addition, we have to be able to critically analyse the ideological base of the legislation. We are now in an age when human rights are at the forefront of our work (Laing, 2003) and when there is a movement towards legislating values or rights (Preston-Shoot, 2001; Williams, 2004). This can be seen in the Care Standards Act 2000, which requires practitioners to legally recognize privacy, dignity and lifestyle; the Carers and Disabled Children Act 2000, which gives carers rights to have their needs assessed; and the Human Rights Act 1998, which focuses on upholding and promoting rights and provides a chance for practitioners to 'promote best practice' (Brammer, 2003).

However, particular discourses dominate various pieces of legislation, which is why it is necessary to critically analyse the law. For example, when thinking about immigration legislation, we need to be aware of its inherent racism. In relation to the Mental Health Act 1983, proposed reforms have been driven by an imperative to protect certain sections of society from people who have been diagnosed as having a dangerous severe personality disorder, rather than concern about providing services for those in need of them. Criticisms of proposed reforms have highlighted the failure to address civil rights and the disproportionate response to risk posed by such individuals to the community (Williams, 2004). The Crime and Disorder Act 1998 similarly responds to community concerns about the behaviour of young people rather than any commitment to social welfare principles and the needs of many young people for support. Anti-social behaviour orders established under section 1 of this Act are intended to enforce supervision with a view to preventing further offending and 'epitomises the government's approach to community safety' (Brayne and Carr, 2003: 579). However, Asboconcern, a campaigning organization, believes that anti-social behaviour orders are not only a punitive measure that can criminalize people for behaviour that is not criminal (because people receive a custodial sentence for breaching an ASBO even though the 'offence' that attracted the ASBO would never have attracted a custodial offence) but also, importantly, they fail to deal with the causes of anti-social behaviour. What is needed to support young people and their families are properly funded community and youth resources. As Goldson has pointed out, the young people on orders:

> ...come from the poorest families and the most distressed communities. They are already the victims of poverty, injustice and inequality. It is taking a group of kids who have been failed and punishing them again – that's a very strange sort of justice.
>
> (Goldson, 2003: 2)

The challenge for anti-oppressive practitioners, particularly those based in youth offending teams, is to balance need, risk and criminal justice objectives by engaging in creative practice in order to resist a policing role (Grier and Thomas, 2005).

Some commentators have argued that the law is not an instrument that can be used to promote anti-oppressive practice. 'The legal powers and remedies available do not always empower [practitioners] to protect vulnerable people' (Braye and Preston-Shoot, 1992: 3). It has been described as a 'blunt instrument' in relation to domestic violence (Brayne and Carr, 2003: 562) designed not to enhance people's positions but to maintain them. To take the law on is often seen as an arduous, thankless task (Braye and Preston-Shoot, 1992: 3). However, along with others, we believe that, despite the complexity of the relationship between the law and health and social care practice, using the law alongside professional codes and guidance can contribute to the development of good practice which is beneficial, supportive, and promotes anti-oppressive values (Brayne and Broadbent, 2002; Johns, 2003; Williams, 2004).

Promoting good practice: the law in action

The functions of the law can therefore be seen to have contradictory elements, but at the same time provide the opportunity to promote good practice. Pinkney (2000) points out that practitioners who are committed to anti-oppressive practice will always find ways to use legislation to support practice that challenges inequality. The legislative mandate defines the roles and responsibilities of practitioners and directs practice in the areas of protection, prevention and rehabilitation. However, this does not mean that practitioners 'merely implement the law' (Adams, 2002: 4), as the legal mandate:

> ...cannot accurately reflect the complexity of many people's lives, locating problems and solutions, as it predominantly does, within individuals and families, without acknowledging structural inequality, disadvantage and exclusion.
>
> (Brayne and Broadbent, 2002: 62)

In the following section we will outline two pieces of legislation, identify their positive elements, consider any barriers and problems, and engage in critical discussion. Through this we will illustrate how practitioners might take into account the complexity of people's lives and the impact of the legal mandate for service users and carers.

Community Care (Direct Payments) Act 1996

Community Care (Direct Payments) Act 1996

In England the Community Care (Direct Payments) Act 1996, which came into force in 1997, gave local authorities the power to make cash payments to disabled people who had been assessed as needing community care services (under section 47 of the NHS and Community Care Act 1990) so that they can arrange their own support in lieu of services. Older people were included in the legislation in 2000, and under the Carers and Disabled Children Act 2001 eligibility was extended to 16–17 year olds, carers (including young carers aged 16–17) and people with parental responsibility for disabled children and disabled young people. This means that the following groups of people may be eligible to receive direct payments:

- Older people and disabled people aged 16 and over
  This includes in particular older people who, despite being the largest single group of people using community care services, have been the least likely to be offered and to get a direct payment. This may also include disabled adults and disabled young people aged 16 or 17.
- A person with parental responsibility for a child
  This may include a parent or others, such a grandparent, with parental responsibility for a disabled child. It may also include a disabled person with parental responsibility for a child.
- Carers aged 16 and over
  People whom the council decides need services because they provide or intend to provide a substantial amount of care on a regular basis for someone aged 18 or over. Carers (but not employees, persons working under contract or for a voluntary organization) may obtain direct payments in respect of their own needs for services but not for services in respect of the needs of the person they care for.

(Department of Health, 2003, s20)

Research by Stainton and Boyce (2004) indicates that people in receipt of direct payments experience having increased control over their own lives, improved self-esteem, deeper and more lasting relationships, and new, interpersonal, vocational and lifestyle opportunities. Direct payments facilitate more continuity of care as personal assistants often provide support to just one person. The relationships between personal assistants and their employers have been described as 'warm and friendly ... and personal assistants talk about feelings of affection, loyalty and friendship towards their employer' (Leece, 2004: 216). Service users enjoy this relationship, as one respondent in Stainton and Boyce's research indicates: 'We go out, we are good friends, nothing is too much trouble for them' (2004: 451).

Leece (2004) suggests that direct payments may be the start of a new way of providing support for disabled people that not only means social care is nearer to a 'true' market economy but also that disabled people will be better able to take their rightful place as full participants in society. Research in Norfolk has shown that for most people direct payments can be a positive alternative to direct services. For disabled people the positives included:

- employing whom they choose;
- determining the hours of employment;

- determining the tasks they require the personal assistant to undertake;
- the flexibility of the employment relationship, which allows them to vary their routines and activities with greater ease;
- the level of support offered in their role as employers;
- reduced involvement with professional agencies.

(Dawson, 2000: 47)

The examples below, taken from the Department of Health Guidance on Direct Payments (Department of Health, 2003), illustrate how they work.

Case examples: Martin and Jennifer

Martin, who has profound and complex disabilities with high-level support needs, began to use direct payments when he became 17 years old. Although at first some professionals involved expressed lots of concerns, Martin and his family persevered, encouraged by his Circle of Support. There have been plenty of ups and downs with recruiting and retaining personal assistants, but receiving direct payments has made a big difference to Martin's daily life. He is no longer totally dependent on his parents to organize interesting things to do each day, or support him to do them. He has help to do ordinary everyday activities such as shopping, visits to interactive museums, swimming, eating out and going out with his friends. Most exciting for Martin, he has support during the family holiday, giving him freedom to choose when to go out, and not having to rely on the rest of the family. For the first time ever, Martin now spends weekends in his own home without his parents, supported by two friends who act as personal assistants, giving him all the support and attention he needs.

Jennifer is a 17-year-old with a physical disability who wishes to move away from home to go to college. To help her do this she wants to engage her own personal assistant to help her get ready for college in the mornings, rather than rely on the local council domiciliary service. Her parents were unhappy at the decision as they felt that she would be unable to manage her needs independently. In addition they are reluctant to have her leave home. The local council has worked closely with the local support and advocacy services. Jennifer's parents have accessed separate advice and information and now fully support her decision.

Barriers and problems

A number of commentators have identified problems about how cash payments are made and attitudes that discourage independent living (see, for example, Leece, 2004; Morris, 2004; Stainton and Boyce, 2004; Ungerson,

2004). Social workers have been identified as 'gate-keepers' to direct payments (Dawson, 2000) since the mechanism by which disabled people can obtain direct payments is through assessment by social workers rather than self-assessment. Morris (2004) argues that these assessments are driven by dependency levels and eligibility criteria (reflecting a medical model of disability) rather than by needs and disabling barriers. This means that rather than reflect what the individual needs and wants, they reflect professional views, knowledge and convenience (Leece, 2004).

Morris (2004) points out that there are problems with the framework of legislation under which people can get support for independent living:

- It places duties on local authorities to provide services rather than give rights to individuals to receive support.
- There is no entitlement to live at home instead of institutional care.
- It does not adequately cover assistance for leisure, work, having relationships or looking after children or other family members.
- There is no entitlement to advocacy.
- Enforcement of existing entitlements involves negotiating an inaccessible legal system with inadequate support.

In addition, the way the legislation is implemented creates barriers. For example, Morris argues that there are a number of financial incentives to provide residential care, instead of supporting independent living. Assumptions about 'capacity', and concerns about 'risk', also contribute to people being discouraged to use direct payments. Morris (2004) indicates that even where there are entitlements under the legislation, 'custom and practice' may take precedence. For example, while people living in residential care cannot pay for it using direct payments, they can use it to have more choice and control in their lives – such as supporting activities outside the home.

Problems have also been identified concerning care being treated as a commodity. This 'commodification of care' means that the relationship between money and care is complex. One example is that the boundaries between paid and unpaid care have become blurred, and, as the quote from Stainton and Boyce's (2004) research above shows, the relationship between employers and employed is often defined in terms that are more applicable to the informal care provided by friends and family. Other arguments about the employment of family members focus on fears that relatives who are not paid may be unwilling to provide support. Leece (2004) expresses concern about the potential of the cash payment system to reproduce inequalities. She suggests, for example, that employers have to open a bank account with cheque facilities – not an easy option for those who have poor credit records or no driving licence or passport for identification. Similarly, working-class people may have less experience of employing and managing people and so choose not to use the direct payment option. There are indications that it may be the middle classes who are disproportionately benefiting from the direct payments system, as many have backgrounds of supervising or management.

There is a potential, then, for disabled people to be denied the opportunity for choice and control over their lives that the direct payments system offers. Morris (2004) points out that this is exacerbated by the fact that recruiting and employing personal assistants is no easy task. The time needed and pressures in doing it right can be experienced as 'weighty' (Dawson, 2000). Furthermore, some personal assistant support services are being set up by organizations that do not appear to have much understanding of the principles of independent living, and problems in recruiting personal assistants at poor rates of pay mean that service users cannot provide good working conditions for them.

Critical discussion

The provision of direct payments came about following campaigns by disabled people and their allies, supported by commissioned research evidence (Ungerson, 2004). In order to work with the complexity of the legislation and challenge the barriers to its implementation, the critical practitioner needs to understand the competing discourses that underpin the Act. The development of health and social care from the 1970s was informed by market principles, creating a 'mixed economy of welfare'. Rather than care being provided solely by the state, the voluntary and private sectors were opened up to allow users of services a range of provision to meet the various needs and choices of individuals. Arguments that social services departments in particular were 'costly, ineffective, distant and oppressive, leaving the user powerless and without a voice' (Parton, 1996: 10) influenced the development of the market economy, which is reflected in the NHS and Community Care Act 1990. This gave local authorities a duty to assess the needs of individuals and devise care plans, but they are then expected to purchase the majority of the services through the competitive 'quasi-market' (LeGrand, 1990). It was argued that these initiatives would promote less costly use of resources and expand consumer choice.

At the same time, the social justice and rights discourse was also having an impact on service development. The social model of disability (Oliver, 1990) regards society as disabling people from full participation. So the social justice and rights discourse states that environments, structures and legislation need to be changed if disabled people are to have equal rights of citizenship. The legislation is therefore influenced first by market principles and consumerism, which see cash payments as giving disabled people power, choice and control through being able to buy their care from various providers in a competitive market place. Secondly, it is influenced by the social justice and rights perspective which welcomes the legislation as empowering because it improves the lives of disabled people through enabling them to have choice and control over the management and delivery of their services.

For direct payments to work, it has been argued, local authorities need to make what Leece describes as a 'cultural shift' (2004: 214) in the way risk and control is approached. Morris (2004) points out that negative assumptions about 'capacity' and concerns about risk mean that even when service providers indicate a commitment to empowerment principles, concerns about safety and liability dominate. In the case of direct payments, where an assessment is made by a social worker, the discourse of social work, defining not only who and what the client and the practitioner is but how they interact (Pease and Fook, 1999a), competes with and may potentially silence other discourses. Social workers have an ethical obligation to value and respect service users' self-determination and so their right to take risks in the process of establishing their independence. At the same time, there is a legal obligation to their employing authority who will expect them to act responsibly in rationing services. The dilemma is that most practitioners do not necessarily want to rock the boat and risk losing their job and career prospects (Leece, 2004). Nevertheless, good practice can be developed if perspectives change and public services start from an assumption of disabled people's competence, rather than their incompetence, in the assessment process (Dawson, 2000).

The Children (Scotland) Act 1995

The Children (Scotland) Act 1995

The Children (Scotland) Act 1995 is founded on the following key principles:

- Each child has a right to be treated as an individual.
- Each child can form his or her views on matters affecting him or her and has the right to express those views if he or she wishes.
- Parents should normally be responsible for the upbringing of their children and should share that responsibility.
- Each child has the right to protection from all forms of abuse, neglect or exploitation.
- In decisions related to the protection of a child, every effort should be made to keep the child in the family home.
- Any intervention by a public authority in the life of a child should be properly justified and should be supported by services from all relevant agencies working in collaboration.

In support of these principles, three main themes run through the Act:

- The welfare of the child is the paramount consideration when his or her needs are considered by the courts and children's hearings.
- No court should make an order relating to a child and no children's hearing should make a supervision requirement unless the court or hearing has considered that to do so would be better for the child than making no order or supervision requirement at all.
- The child's views should be taken into account when major decisions are to be made about his or her future.

The Children (Scotland) Act 1995 provides a legal and procedural framework in which practitioners can ensure that the voices of children and young people are not only heard within adult decision-making processes but that they are acted upon. The United Nations Convention on the Rights of the Child (UNCRC) has had an impact on both policy-makers and wider society. Article 12 of the Convention commits signatories to take account of the views of young people on matters or procedures that directly affect their lives. This principle was incorporated into legislation introduced in the 1980s and 1990s across the UK, such as the Children Act 1989 and the Family Law Act 1996 for England and Wales, the Children (Northern Ireland) Order 1995, and the Children (Scotland) Act 1995. Enabling children to actively take part in decision-making processes 'is now seen as a moral, legal, and practical obligation' (Barford and Wattam, 1991).

Positives

Tisdall et al. (2002) undertook a detailed analysis of the Children (Scotland) Act 1995 and its accompanying regulation and guidance as part of a feasibility study commissioned by the Scottish Executive. The study sought to 'examine how best to conceptualise and evaluate the ways in which decision-making in children's lives takes due account of their views within the context of, and as a result of, the Children (Scotland) Act 1995' (Tisdall et al., 2002: 386). The Act strengthens the rights of children to have their views heard in court decisions in three main ways:

1. Children can initiate proceedings or become party to private proceedings.
2. There are mechanisms in place for children to state their views.
3. Children's views have to be considered by their parents when making 'major decisions'.

Barriers and problems

Despite the proliferation of guidance, development of procedures, and policies to facilitate effective inclusive practice, evidence suggests that participation of children and young people is at times more rhetoric than reality (see, for example, Schofield and Thoburn, 1996; Thomas and O'Kane, 1999; Shemmings, 2000). While there is a stated commitment to involve and enable children and young people to participate in decisions that will affect them, research based on interviews with children who experience divorce and separation suggest that children 'feel significantly ill informed' not only of the legal process but in relation to what was happening in their own homes (Tisdall et al., 2004: 23). There is also 'considerable reluctance towards children's more direct involvement through appearing in court, becoming party to the proceedings or initiating proceedings' (Tisdall et al., 2004: 24).

Success in involving young people in decision-making 'seems to be highly dependent on professional practice and attitudes' (Tisdall et al., 2004). A number of suggestions have been put forward to improve practice in this area:

- Practitioners within social work and the legal profession need to be provided with training in relation to direct work with children.
- Practitioners should have the appropriate knowledge base.
- Funding should be made available so that the spaces that children have to wait in are child-friendly and promote an ethos of participation.
- One of the prerequisites for children and young people to engage and fully participate is that they should be informed, for example about their legal rights.

(Tisdall et al., 2004)

However, to make a difference, changes in practice need to be matched by fundamental changes within the legislative system. It has been suggested that there are two conceptual flaws in the current system. Firstly, court proceedings regard separation as an event rather than a process that children and their parents are going through. Secondly, the formal and informal processes of parental separation and divorce are primarily linked to the needs of parents rather than the needs of children (Tisdall et al., 2004).

Critical discussion

Discourses of participation are central to the involvement of young people in decision-making and in turn are influenced by the discourses of childhood and rights. Participation has been described as 'the keystone of the arch that is the United Nations Convention on the Rights of the Child' (Badham, 2002: xi). Although the term 'participation' is difficult to define (Murray and Hallett, 2000), it is often associated with values such as user control and leadership, trust and respect, equality between professionals and service users, and mutuality (Healy, 1998). Murray and Hallett (2000) remind us, though, that participation rights usually exist because the right to self-determination is absent, that is if children and young people had the right to self-determination then the right to participate would not be necessary, as is the case for many adults.

Participation means 'taking part in' and has been defined as 'the process of sharing in the decisions which affect your life and the life of the community in which you live' (Lansdown, 1995: 17). Practices based on this ideal assume that children and young people have the status of citizens. Participation can then be described as a process that provides a structure for children and young people's decision-making. However, the level and nature of participation may vary from 'taking part in' or 'being present at' to knowing that your actions and views are being taken into account and might be acted on (Department of Health, 2001c). Participatory practice does not mean denying the power of adults but is about assessing the varying power relations that will exist within different practice contexts. Rather than viewing children and young people as powerless and needing to have power transferred to them, participatory practice acknowledges the complex power relations present in a given situation. Within that process adults need to listen to and respect the views of children and young people, be prepared to enter into dialogue with them, and be open and honest in all their communications. The relationship then is neither a hierarchical 'adults know best' position nor an approach whereby the adults renounce their power completely. Instead, it is one in which adults are reflective and reflexive in their relations with children and young people.

Implementation of the United Nations Convention on the Rights of the Child (UNCRC) and of the Children Act within the four nations of the UK depends on adults. Franklin (1995) points out that in fact 'children have been excluded from participation in formal decision making for so long, that it seems unlikely they could enter this arena without the initial support and advocacy of adults' (Franklin, 1995: 14). The link between rights and responsibilities is not that children have to learn to take the responsibilities that go with rights but rather that adults have a responsibility to ensure that children have opportunities to exercise those rights, or they will be meaningless. Children's rights of participation are dependent on responsible adults providing the necessary information to enable children to make choices, give consent and learn to develop the skills necessary to move from sharing decision-making to taking it over (Flekkoy and Kaufman, 1997).

Implementation of the Children Act (Scotland) 1995 demonstrates the complexity of participatory practice. Unlike other UK children's legislation such as the Children Act 1989 (England) and the Children (Northern Ireland) Order 1995, the Children (Scotland) Act 1995 has a distinctly different approach because it consciously promotes key legal principles of the UNCRC. The starting point for the other two Acts are 'overarching' principles for courts rather than the rights of children. However, in Scotland the government decided not to do this. The end result was that the requirement to listen to children, along with other key legal principles such as the paramountcy of children's welfare and due regard to a child's religious persuasion, was included in particular sections with particular applications. Unfortunately, the subsequent legislation has resulted in inconsistent application of the principle of listening to children's views within decisions and the processes set out in the Act. A review of the legislation (Marshall et al., 2002) suggests:

a. that there has been a dedicated attempt to include and think through how children's views should be heard; but
b. that the final result is a complicated collage that is not easily grasped, particularly in its details.

The review suggests that such complexity raises questions about what legal professionals, service providers, parents, and children and young people themselves actually know about its requirements and procedures, especially if they become involved in parts of the Act with which they are unfamiliar. This discussion therefore identifies the importance of being confident in our knowledge of the law and ability to apply it. We also need to actively work with everyone involved to provide a seamless child-centred service. The law only becomes effective when it is implemented sensitively and purposefully by informed practitioners.

Rights, duties and obligations

In order to be able to use the law effectively, it is helpful to understand the concepts of rights, duties and obligations. Although the legislation primarily defines the duties and powers of local authorities, we also need to consider our actions in relation to the rights of service users and our own obligations.

Rights

Rights have been described as 'valuable commodities' (Wasserstrom, 1964: 628, quoted in Freeman 1983: 33), 'important moral coinage' (Freeman, 1983: 33) or, concerning legal rights, 'indispensably valuable possessions' (Feinberg 1966: 1, quoted in Freeman, 1983: 33). Brayne and Broadbent (2002) point out that while human rights are often expressed as if they had always existed, waiting to be discovered, they may more accurately be seen in the political, economic and social context developed over the last three centuries. For example, the United Nations Convention on Human Rights passed in 1948 was a response to prevent the horrors of the Second World War.

There are, however, a number of distinctions which it is useful to briefly explore. First, it is important to recognize that there are basic universal rights, like those enshrined in documents such as the European Convention on Human Rights. Declarations of Rights and Conventions do not have legal status – they may bind governments at a rhetorical level, but it has been argued that unless there is a mechanism for enforcing them they are worthless (Brayne and Broadbent, 2002) and no more than a statement of ideals (Jenkins, 1995). Nevertheless, by signing up to Conventions and Declarations, nation states are making a statement about their commitment to changing legislation, policy and practice. Furthermore, it is possible to use some Conventions, under the auspices of the United Nations, as a way of measuring complicity with basic human rights. For example, every five years the United Nations receives reports on progress from each country on implementation of the Convention on the Rights of the Child. While this does not provide a means of redress for individuals, it does publicly highlight particular unacceptable policies and practices. Declarations covering the rights of disabled people (1974) and eliminating discrimination against women (1981) operate in a comparable way (Johns, 2003).

Helena Kennedy highlights the impact of such documents when she describes how the Universal Declaration of Human Rights 'spawned a new generation of rights' (Kennedy, 2004: 310). She indicates that the values of liberty and justice, dignity and equality, community and responsibility are now central to the UK Human Rights Act 1998. This means that human rights are now embedded into the very fabric of UK society, resulting in a framework underpinned by human rights and anti-discrimination legislation within which health and social care practitioners are 'attempting to create a world where each individual has equal value and equal rights' (Brayne and Carr, 2003: 74). Human rights represent a 'powerful discourse' (Ife, 2001) that seeks to unite people by overcoming difference. However, there is tension in some situations where existing legislation does not fit with the Human Rights Act. The government may then make a *Statement of Incompatibility* and undertake to address the situation through future legislative changes*.

Despite criticism of rights discourses and competing rights, there is general agreement by both lawyers and critical commentators that human rights can be dynamic and inclusive. It has been suggested that using the language of rights, service users and service user organizations have been able to articulate their perspectives (Roche, 1996). This language redefines the relationship between individuals; users and providers of services; and in relation to the state (Brayne and Carr, 2003; Kennedy, 2004). The Human Rights Act 1998 then demonstrates how, through its impact on the nature of our society, it can be a 'vehicle for social change and the realisation of ideals' (Brayne and Carr, 2003: 16). Kennedy eloquently describes the importance of the law in this respect when she says that: 'rights have to be given the force of law for that is how we link our dreams to the acts of daily life' (Kennedy, 2004: 301).

It is also possible to identify different kinds of rights, that is legal, social and civil rights. The concept of legal rights can also be considered in two ways: substantive and procedural rights. Substantive rights can be understood as rights that give individuals power, enforceable by law, to take action to protect their own interests. Procedural rights ensure fairness in the decision-making process.

An element of anti-oppressive practice is to ensure that people's rights are not violated. In terms of anti-oppressive practice and the law, we need to understand how rights are enshrined within the legislation as well as to recognize how it can be said to deny people their rights. We need to be aware of our role in ensuring that minimizing the oppressive aspects of such legislation serves to maximize the rights to which they are entitled. How do we do this? It is not always easy. In the following examples we will consider some of the dilemmas practitioners may face when using the legislation.

Practice dilemma 1

Amy (24) is a white mother with two children, 7-month-old Brent and 6-year-old Leanne. She has type 1 diabetes and so needs to test her blood sugar levels and take her insulin daily. She finds it hard to cope with a baby who does not sleep well and demands a lot of attention. She has had several mild hypoglycaemic episodes since Brent's birth as a result of failing to take her insulin. On one occasion she had a serious episode when Leanne phoned for help and Amy received paramedic attention. Amy has limited family support.

Amy's situation poses a number of practice dilemmas. It could be argued that Amy is irresponsible as a parent in not testing her blood sugar levels on a regular basis or taking her insulin. The worker has to make a professional judgement about the risk that might be present in this situation. The legislation could be used to protect and balance the rights of all those involved. The philosophy of the Children Act 1989 is that Brent and Leanne should be brought up in their family and that the local authority should work in partnership with Amy to provide a range of services appropriate to their needs (Volume 2, Guidance and Regulations on the 1989 Children Act). Brent and Leanne also have a right to family life, enshrined in Article 8 of the Human Rights Act 1998, which states that a public authority should not interfere with this right unless it is to protect health, morals and rights. The children also have a right to be safeguarded from harm. This means:

- all agencies working with children, young people and their families take all reasonable measures to ensure that the risks of harm to children's welfare are minimized; and
- where there are concerns about children and young people's welfare, all agencies take all appropriate actions to address those concerns, working to agreed local policies and procedures in full partnership with other local agencies.

(Department of Health, 2002b: para 1.5)

Amy has a right to parental autonomy but not the right to endanger the life of her children should she go into a coma and leave them without adequate care. The paramountcy principle is key to the Children Act 1989 in England and Wales and in the balancing exercise required by Article 8 of the Human Rights Act the needs of the children may override those of their mother. In Amy's case the decision is made easier by the fact that Leanne has safely reached the age of 6 years old – and therefore we know that Amy has the capacity to care for her children. It would be less easy if Brent was an only child as there is then less predictability about the situation. Our understanding of the possible risk posed to Brent is mediated by the fact that Leanne has grown up in this situation and now is an additional protective factor as a young carer. In this instance, the situation could be seen as assessment and management of uncertainty rather than of risk. Parton (2001) points out that we need to distinguish between what is predictable and what is unpredictable, identifying the first as 'risk' and the second as 'uncertainty'. There is also an issue about Leanne's rights as a young carer. Some young people see themselves as carers, others do not acknowledge this role. We therefore need to listen to Leanne and assess how she views her situation. We may need to be pro-active in identifying her as a young person with caring responsibilities (see box).

Legislation and young carers

Statutory services have a duty to assess and support young carers under:

- Children Act 1989
- Carers (Recognition and Services) Act 1995
- Carers and Disabled Children Act 2000
- Carers (Equal Opportunities) Act 2004
- National Service Framework for Mental Health (Standard 6)
- Human Rights Act 1998
- UN Convention on the Rights of the Child
- Framework for the Assessment of Children in Need and their Families (Department of Health, Department for Education and Employment, Home Office, 1999)

and to recognize young carers and their needs under:

- Quality Protects Initiative (DoH, 1998)
- Caring About Carers: A National Strategy for Carers (DoH, 1999c)
- Young Carers – Making a Start (DoH, 1996b)
- National Health Service Priorities Guidance (DoH, 1999d)
- National CAMHS Strategic and Implementation Plan
- Social Inclusion: Pupil Support (Circular 10/99) (DfEE, 1999b)
- National Healthy Schools Standard: Guidance (DfEE, 1999a)
- Jigsaw of Services (DoH, 2000)
- Fair Access to Care Services (DoH, 2002)

In the second practice dilemma a number of legal interventions could be considered. Since the psychogeriatrician did not make any recommendation for action under the Mental Health Act 1983, this is not really an option. While Lil may be in need of medical attention she does not appear to have a mental illness.

Practice dilemma 2

Lil Scholes is a 72-year-old woman who lives alone. Her next-door neighbour called the local GP after seeing Lil in the garden seemingly in some pain and unable to move freely. A visiting district nurse contacted social services. A community care worker called and found Lil living in a corner of one room in the house; the other rooms were stockpiled with bags of rubbish and things that Lil had accumulated over years. She had just a chair which she sat on and slept in.

Lil, who is sharp-minded, was looking undernourished – her mobility problems had prevented her from doing her shopping. A friend who regularly collects her shopping with her on Thursdays was on holiday for two weeks. The community care worker offered a home care package until her friend returned home, but Lil wanted nothing to do with social services, saying they weren't going to put her in a home. The worker was worried about Lil's health due to the state of the house as well as through lack of food. But Lil refused to go to hospital and refused to leave the house. He arranged for a psychogeriatrician to visit and he concluded that Lil would die if she wasn't treated, yet she continues to refuse to leave her house despite hours of attempting to persuade her.

(Adapted from *Community Care*, 22 July 2004, 'She won't let us help her')

A radical option would be to remove Lil against her wishes under the National Assistance Act 1948. Her situation seems to meet the criteria laid out in section 47 which provides the authority to compulsorily remove an adult from their home:

... for the purposes of securing the necessary care and attention for persons who –

(a) are suffering from grave chronic disease or, being aged, infirm or physically incapacitated, are living in insanitary conditions, and

(b) are unable to devote themselves, and are not receiving from other persons, proper care and attention

... in the interests of any such person ..., or for preventing injury to the health of, or serious nuisance to, other persons, it is necessary to remove any such person...

In Lil's situation any decision to use compulsory powers to protect her demonstrates the 'messiness' of ethical problems concerning older people (Stevenson, 1989) and judgements about the degree of risk to the person concerned. Professional intervention could be seen as a response to the needs of the professionals to protect her rather than to her needs for a service. In this way the use of legislation would be oppressive. Lil has the right to make decisions about her life and she is clear that she does not wish to be treated. Her human rights may be breached if she is taken away from home. On the other hand, if her condition and home environment are so bad then there is a possibility that she will die in pain or discomfort, which could also influence any decision taken. In relation to this case *Knowsley Older People's Voice*, an advocacy service, commented that Lil seemed desperate to keep her independence and did not want support from social services. They point out that hours of trying to persuade Lil to accept help may have done more harm than good, by cementing Lil's view that she does not want support. They suggest that practitioners would need to help Lil understand that care services exist to enable her to remain in her home rather than insist she is cared for elsewhere. Alternative ways of working are also suggested, for example voluntary sector resources could be used to help with shopping and providing meals. This could lead to helpers developing a relationship with Lil, with a view to persuading her to accept further services in the future (*Community Care*, 22 July 2004).

Duties

A duty, imposed by statute, has to be carried out. There is no choice in this and, however difficult it might be, there is no acceptable reason for not doing so. The key word in the legislation is *shall*. So, for example, under the National Health Service and Community Care Act 1990 there is a duty for local authorities to carry out an assessment of needs for community care services:

... where it appears to a local authority that any person for whom they may provide or arrange for the provision of community care services may be in need of any such services, the authority

(a) shall carry out an assessment of his needs for those services; and

(b) having regard to the results of that assessment, shall then decide whether his needs call for the provision by them of any such services.

Sometimes people confuse duties and powers. A power is something that statute gives to individuals or bodies but they can choose whether or not to exercise that power – there is no obligation to do so. Power gives authority to act in a particular way, but authorities have the discretion to decide how to act. It is the imposition of duties that people in health and social care practice may feel contributes to the oppressive elements of legislation. However, a duty can also be a powerful force in promoting rights and ensuring adequate provision of services.

Obligations

Case example: Veronica

Fifteen-year-old Veronica is pregnant to John, who is 32 and known to be involved in a prostitution ring. Veronica has recently moved in to live with him. Although she is aware of his activities, she believes that within the relationship her needs are being met. Her social worker is concerned that the relationship is abusive and that she is being exploited. She feels that she has a legal obligation to protect Veronica and is considering using the child care legislation to prevent her continuing in this relationship. This course of action causes the social worker a number of dilemmas. The social worker is aware of how much the relationship with John means to Veronica, who considers that John meets her emotional needs. Veronica can be considered to be 'Gillick competent',[3] and is therefore able to make her own choices and has a right to do so. The worker has a good relationship with Veronica and has tried to give her as much information as possible about her concerns should Veronica remain in the house. After some discussion about the options available the social worker told Veronica that, having considered the situation and Veronica's views, she was going to call a strategy meeting. The purpose of strategy meetings is to bring together in a formal setting representatives from agencies who hold key information relating to children, their families or have details regarding an allegation or incident which has taken place. The most important thing to consider at this strategy meeting was keeping Veronica, her unborn child and possibly other young people safe from harm. The social worker, a police officer and a senior from the Children and Families Service discussed their information and decided that prosecution of John was not in the public interest, but the police had been made aware that he is involved with Veronica. It was agreed that the social worker would continue to work with Veronica and eventually she persuaded Veronica to move out to live with professional foster carers who had experience of supporting young single mothers. She eventually ceased further contact with John of her own volition.

An obligation can be understood as a morally binding relationship between individuals based on reciprocal biographies. We all feel obligations at various times to various people. At times, such obligations can be competing and we have to make choices (Jordan, 1990; Finch and Mason, 1993). What choices did Veronica have? She had a relationship with John which she felt was satisfactory. But through her social worker she had access to information which made her question that relationship. The social worker, through her work with Veronica, had access to information about John. She also had an understanding of the risks that Veronica and the unborn child faced. In providing her with information the social worker tried to assist Veronica to make informed choices. The social worker had a legal obligation to ensure that Veronica's wishes and feelings were taken into account, to consider her physical and emotional needs and any harm she was likely to suffer.

The worker felt that she had an obligation to protect Veronica and the baby and used her knowledge of policy and procedures about safeguarding young people to facilitate this, having also fulfilled her obligations to involve Veronica completely in the decision-making process and keep her informed throughout that process. Having instigated a strategy meeting, recommendations for further enquiries or actions to be undertaken could then be made. For example, if there were different concerns about John, the strategy meeting should consider the appropriateness of instigating Section 47 Enquiries under the Children Act 1989 or decide that a Child Protection Conference was necessary. This decision would be a professional judgement based on whether Veronica or her unborn child would be likely to suffer significant harm.

The law and anti-oppressive practice

Case example: Zenab

The mother of 11-year-old Zenab, Hasina suffers from bipolar affective disorder. Zenab was placed in a foster home after her mother had gone into hospital for treatment and was then unable to seek medical treatment for Zenab's asthma. The foster carer, after talking to her and observing her play and drawings, became aware that while Zenab said that she wanted to go home she also indicated that she felt unsure about this. Zenab clearly had a good relationship with her mother but at times, when her mother was ill, she became unhappy and this made her anxious about a possible return home. The social worker also recognized the confusion felt by Zenab. In the foster home her physical health and school performance improved considerably. Hasina continued to require regular hospital admissions.

Andy and Charlie continue their debate by discussing Zenab's situation:

Andy: Working in this situation is hard when you have to think about competing needs. For me good practice must involve listening to Zenab. But if you do that you would have let her go home to Hasina even though you are aware of the possible impact of her illness on Zenab.

Charlie: Yes, anti-oppressive practice is about listening to the child, but it is also about knowing your own value base which informs how you work with people. I am committed to an anti-oppressive practice perspective and empowering people with whom I work. So that means taking account of the context, listening and respecting Zenab's confusion and working with her to help her through that. It's about making a full assessment without making assumptions – for instance, just because she's doing well with the foster carers doesn't mean she wants to stay there for ever. It just means that they have the resources that her mother doesn't currently have to look after her. We have to take account of Hasina's resources in view of her mental health.

Andy: Well, as far as I'm concerned my primary consideration would be Zenab and her welfare would be paramount. So if she's doing well with the carers, then I would have to start thinking about permanency planning.

Charlie: My assessment would be that if Zenab is confused it could well be that it is because she does really want to live with her mother but that she wants it to be OK. And equally important is the welfare of Hasina and her wishes and feelings.

Andy: If she is regularly admitted to hospital this could have an impact on her ability to care.

Charlie: Hasina has looked after Zenab for a long time. They have a good relationship. We need to consider the times when she's well and look at supporting her – which you could do under Part III of the Children Act 1989. She has parental responsibility and has a right to be involved in any decisions about Zenab's life. It is up to us to work with her. Hasina still has the capacity to make decisions despite her illness and we need to provide the right support to help her to do so.

Andy: Of course, it is easy to assume that Hasina is unable to make decisions – the principles of the Mental Capacity Act 2005 are a useful reminder here aren't they? But don't you find it difficult to take into account the wishes of Hasina as well as Zenab? How do you make a professional assessment?

Charlie: Just because I'm a professional doesn't mean my views should override everyone else's. I have to take responsibility for the views I express and the judgements that I make, and I'd rather do this in partnership with everyone involved – the foster carer, Hasina and Zenab.

Andy: Well, maybe the foster carer thinks that Zenab shouldn't go home.

Charlie: If that's the case then her views also have to be listened to – it's about making a decision which takes everyone's views into account and it may be that my view is not the accepted view. What is important is that everyone has been involved in that process and a plan is made which everyone understands and accepts as the right way forward. I agree with you that we need to develop a solution which isn't oppressive to Hasina but the solution also needs to protect Zenab's welfare. There are several pieces of legislation we could use to help us do this and the National Service Framework for mental health is helpful for promoting inter-agency working and multi-disciplinary assessments.

Andy finds it more difficult to be creative in his use of the law – he uses it more as a means to an end. He genuinely believes that he is working in the best interests of Zenab, that is, from a liberal traditional perspective. Charlie, on the other hand, is incorporating the best interests of Zenab in her practice but is aware of the rights of all the individuals involved and so from her perspective uses the law to enable a more radical approach to her practice.

Michael Freeman (1992: 4) reminds us that 'legislation is a political act with political consequences, using political language and political symbols'. Our knowledge, values, theories and skills provide the framework which informs our practice. To use it in a transformative way we have to acknowledge its weaknesses and harness its strengths.

Chapter summary

As practitioners we have to continually address the impact of structural inequalities and discriminatory legislation on people's lives. We have seen through the dialogue between Charlie and Andy that a legalistic model of working is not enough to address the complexity of people's lives. On the other hand,

sometimes we can find ourselves in the strange place of working within restrictive legislation and at the same time advocating for people's rights. In this
chapter we have examined the contradictions and dilemmas that can occur in
such situations and the need to find ways of using the law in a creative way.
While acknowledging the limitations and restrictive elements of the law we have,
through discussion of case examples and specific pieces of legislation, shown
ways of using the law positively in practice situations.

Further reading

The following books have been chosen because they consider the application of
law to practice. Other texts exist which are more specific about the law in particular situations.

Cull, L.A. and Roche, J. (eds) (2001) *The Law and Social Work: Contemporary Issues
for Practice*. Basingstoke: Palgrave.
An accessible edited book that provides information about how the law can guide
decision-making. Although specifically concerning social work, it covers three
broad themes, including a range of practice issues and user perspectives that can
be used by all professions.

Braye, S. and Preston-Shoot (1997) *Practising Social Work Law*, 2nd edn. Basingstoke: Macmillan.
The second edition of this book provides an overview of skills and dilemmas for
practitioners and a critical appreciation of the law.

Johns, R. (2005) *Understanding the Law in Social Work*, 2nd edn. Exeter: Learning
Matters.
An introductory reader aimed specifically at social work degree students.

Dimond, B. (2005) *Legal Aspects of Nursing*, 4th edn. London: Longman.
This introduces nurses and other health care professionals to the law via everyday
nursing situations. The book takes a practical approach through fictional 'situation' boxes that highlight the relevance of the law to health care professionals.

Brammer, A. (2006) *Social Work Law*, 2nd edn. Harlow: Pearson Education.
A social work text that is practical and accessible and considers issues of anti-
oppressive practice.

Brayne, H. and Carr, H. (2005) *Law for Social Workers*, 9th edn. Oxford: Oxford
University Press.
Comprehensive legal text providing clear information with an introductory case
study for each chapter and questions for discussion. A companion website is also
helpful: *www.oup.co.uk/best.textbooks/law/braynecarr8e*.

Clements, L. (2004) *Community Care and the Law*. London: Legal Action Group.
An excellent, comprehensive and accessible book covering all aspects of community care law.

PART II
A MODEL OF ANTI-OPPRESSIVE PRACTICE: PRINCIPLES FOR ACTION

4 Values

THE LAW is the bedrock of a nation; it tells us who we are, what we value, who has power and who hasn't.

Almost nothing has more impact on our lives. The law is entangled with our everyday existence, regulating our social relations and business dealings, controlling conduct which could threaten our safety and security, establishing the rule by which we live. It is the baseline.

(Kennedy, 2004: 3)

What do we mean by values?

'Values are in essence a set of beliefs, ideas and assumptions that both individuals and groups hold about themselves and the society they live in. Values are a part of the culture and societal norms that guide people's daily lives' (Eby, 2000: 118) and are used in everyday language to refer 'to one or all of religious, moral, political or ideological principles, beliefs or attitudes' (Banks, 2001: 6). Reamer, looking at the area of social work values, suggests that values are:

> generalized, emotionally charged conceptions of what is desirable; historically created and derived from experience; shared by a population or group within it; and they provide the means for organizing and structuring patterns of behavior.
>
> (Reamer, 1995: 11, cited in Bisman, 2004)

However, values are often viewed as unproblematic, universal and agreed and, as such, do not need to be critically analysed (Timms, 1983; Powell, 2005). But this is far from the truth of the matter, as becomes evident when we begin to explore exactly what is understood by the term. Values 'resist satisfactory definition' (Clark, 2000: 26) as they are, 'inescapably, relative to the actor's view; plural and inherently contradictory; contingent on time, community and situation' (Clark, 2000: 30). Engagement in a critical debate about personal, professional and organizational values is essential for professions that deal on a daily basis with ethical dilemmas. By making the ambiguities, complexities and the moral dimension of social situations explicit – by talking about ethical issues or dilemmas that challenge our personal beliefs, assumptions and our professional integrity – we begin to attain clarity about the nature and purpose of the work we are engaged in as well as consider how individual, professional, organizational and societal values interconnect and interrelate.

However, if values are socially constructed, historically specific and open to individual interpretation, is it possible for health and social care professions to reach some consensus regarding the values that are appropriate for working with people? Is it possible to identify a set of values which promote 'egalitarian discourses' (Dominelli, 2004: 62) and action aimed at eliminating oppression and inequality? We do not underestimate the difficulty of attempting to agree a set of values that are pertinent to professions that work with people who are relatively vulnerable, who have limited access to physical and emotional resources, who are socially disadvantaged, and who experience a range of oppressions because of their social division membership. We would, however, propose that it is possible to identify those values and principles which underlie practice that shows care and concern about the position of others and which demonstrates an unwillingness to accept inequality and oppression in any form. For us, anti-oppressive practice encompasses a number of 'identifiable values', principles or value statements, such as social justice and personal caring (Lynn, 1999); compassion (Simey, 1996); respect for the individual, valuing uniqueness and diversity, promotion of user self-determination (Banks, 1995: 92); and challenging discrimination and oppression (Burke and Harrison, 1998). It could be argued, therefore, that practice that is informed by anti-oppressive values and principles is practice that is not 'economically, politically, aesthetically, or morally neutral' (Payne, 1999: 256).

Practitioners working in the area of health and social care are often faced with a number of competing and at times contradictory values. The practitioner's personal values may well conflict with the values of the profession, and these may be in tension with the values of the organization in which the individual is located, and the perspectives held by service users and carers. Practitioners will in this situation be required to critically reflect on the different value positions, which will enable them to understand how different discourses impact on their decision-making. Where values do not match humanitarian ideals, this process of critical reflection enables us to 'seek to change social structures which perpetuate inequalities and injustices' (BASW, 2002, Section 3.2.2.d, cited in Bisman, 2004).

Personal values

Ursula's story contains a number of competing discourses about the nature of the social work task and the role and function of social work within contemporary society. While reading her story, try to identify the different values, beliefs and ideals Ursula holds and which inform her practice.

Ursula

Ursula is a black 24-year-old social worker who has been employed as a care manager for the last two years. Reflecting back on her reasons for entering the profession and her training she was quite concerned that the work that she was currently engaged in did not reflect her initial idealism of entering a profession which, amongst other things, was about working with people. Ursula feels that she is caught up in numerous administrative activities – completing endless forms, working out budgets and attending meetings. The parts of her work that she most enjoys – professional autonomy and the relational and caring aspects of practice – are becoming increasingly marginalized. Ursula's motivation to become a social worker was informed by a range of experiences and factors: her Christian upbringing, her experiences of living in a socially deprived but culturally rich community, growing up with a brother who had converted to Islam and who was bullied at the school which they both attended. Ursula's experiences of working in a local youth club helped her to develop her skills, knowledge and values for working with socially excluded young people. During the course of this work, Ursula met a number of social workers. Ursula found their experiences of working with people interesting; she considered that she too had what it required to be a social worker. However, resource constraints, increasing bureaucratization, staff shortages and the shift from preventive work to more reactive protective interventions have limited Ursula's opportunities to utilize her experiences of advocating, advising, supporting and engaging in social action. Making decisions with which she personally feels uncomfortable is the norm rather than the exception these days for Ursula.

- What impact does Ursula's story have on you?
- Is it possible to manage, or reconcile, the different value positions that are evident within the story?
- How can Ursula maintain her commitment to working with people in a way that is meaningful for her?

Ursula's values and experiences affect her understanding of social situations, and textures the relationships she has with a range of people. Ursula's narrative illustrates how professional practice is shaped by a number of factors, which ultimately place limitations and restrictions on the professional autonomy of the practitioner. Ursula's biographical details, the range of ethical and political issues raised by practice situations, and the organizational context provide a rich and complex backdrop against which her personal and professional values, the values of the organization, and societal values compete, conflict and interrelate.

The ability to be aware of one's values and to understand how they inform practice is essential in beginning to work anti-oppressively. Quoting the work of Downie and Telfer (1980), however, Bisman notes that this requires practitioners to spend 'more time analysing the moral ambiguities of their authority, rights and function' (2004: 118). Critical practitioners are not only aware of their values and the ideological perspective that they hold in relation to social issues, but are conscious of the fact that they are active participants as well as observers within social situations. Consequently, they have the ability to act in ways that demonstrate that they are cognizant of the different values held by others, but more importantly are able to consider how different value perspectives will define the nature of practice engaged in. An important aspect of being able to locate where our values originate, and how they inform our practice and understanding of social situations, is that we are able to use this knowledge to discern the appropriate use of the law when faced with making decisions in morally complex situations.

Ursula's personal values, assumptions, cultural and religious background, and her view of the world direct and inform her understanding of social issues and her practice. By engaging in a process of 'ethical reflexivity' (Banks, 1995; Banks and Williams, 2005), Ursula is able to critically examine the ideals and values that prompted her decision to enter the profession. She is aware of the difficulties of attempting to construct her moral and professional identity within an organization which is increasingly subject to political and managerial control and where professional autonomy and discretion is diminished. Ursula's commitment to work with service users openly, honestly and transparently (Clark, 2000) and, where possible, to challenge 'dominant assumptions that serve to humiliate and oppress service users (Banks and Williams, 2005: 1020), inform her approach to anti-oppressive practice.

The managerialist perspective that is currently directing the actions of many workers within health and social care agencies cuts across and ultimately undermines some of the fundamental values and principles that have been associated with the social professions. Values expressed in terms such as effectiveness, efficiency and quality standards,[1] coupled with the belief that social problems can be solved by the implementation of robust managerial systems, we would suggest, are not values that assist in a critical analysis of the causes of social problems and inequalities. Humanistic values and principles which inform care practice appear to have little currency within a world where human need and the causes of social inequality are dealt with as though they are mere commodities. We would agree that effective management of people and resources is necessary, but we would concur with the view that management 'is a means not an end. To elevate management to the level of an "-ism" is to give it a comprehensive power that is beyond its appropriate function – to assist and facilitate the delivery of human services' (Tsui and Cheung, 2004: 441). It is therefore essential that practitioners have the ability to negotiate a path between the managerialist contexts in which practice takes place and their commitment to anti-oppressive principles and values of justice and equality.

Values and codes of ethics

Professional codes of ethics generally aim to promote ethical awareness and behaviour. They usually incorporate a range of values which have been found to be 'useful in structuring moral life. These may include seeking justice, equality and liberty for all, and respect for persons and their autonomy' (Pattinson, 2001: 7). Professional codes vary in length and detail but on the whole they can be seen to embody the theoretical, practical and ethical basis of a range of professional groups. The United Kingdom Central Council for Nursing, Midwifery and Health Visiting (UKCC) Code of Professional Conduct and the British Association of Social Workers Code of Ethics are examples of such documents and in essence provide practitioners with the relevant professional framework which guides and regulates the conduct of its members. Codes make tangible the nebulous qualities of values. They are the bridge between values and putting those values into practice. They can be used to assist the practitioner to negotiate the contradictory terrain of practice.

The values associated with social work are incorporated within the British Association of Social Workers (BASW) Code of Ethics and the Codes of Practice for Social Care Workers and their Employers published for the first time by the General Social Care Council (GSCC) in 2002. The codes reflect a commitment to both traditional liberal individualistic values and values that emphasize justice and equality principles. Banks (2004), who has made a study of various codes of ethics in relation to different professions, including social work and health-related professions, found that contemporary codes generally contain all or some of the following points:

- Statements about the **core purpose** or service ideal of the profession. For example: the purpose of social work can be seen to include a commitment to social justice and equality principles, the promotion of social change, engagement in work which maximizes the development of human potential and the fulfilment of human needs. Both the Australian Association of Social Workers (AASW) Code of Ethics, the National Association of Social Workers (NASW) and the British Association of Social Workers Codes of Ethics reveal a number of similarities regarding what is considered to be the primary purpose of social work.

- Statements about the **character/attributes or virtues** of the professional. For example: professional practitioners should be open, honest, trustworthy, reliable and impartial. The ability to 'work co-operatively within teams and to respect the skills, expertise and contribution of colleagues and other professionals' (The Nursing and Midwifery Council, 2002: 6) is also considered necessary and appropriate for practitioners working with people. Patience, tolerance, courage, imagination and perseverance are also thought to be important 'professional virtues' (Begley, 2005: 626).

- While codes may vary greatly in their wording and the types of rules that they may include, statements that convey **ethical principles** can be found within them. For example, the Kantian ethical principle of respect for the individual and self-determination is encapsulated in the BASW statement 'respect service users' rights to make informed decisions, and ensure that service users and carers participate in decision making processes' (BASW, 2002: para 3.1.2e). The Nursing and Midwifery Council Code of professional conduct alerts the health practitioner to the importance of 'respecting the role of patients and clients as partners in their care and the contribution they can make to it' (The Nursing and Midwifery Council, 2002: para 2.1:3) and the need to respect 'patients' and clients autonomy – their right to decide whether or not to undergo any health care intervention – even where a refusal may result in harm or death ...' (The Nursing and Midwifery Council, 2002: para 3.2:4).

- **Ethical rules**: It is expected that health and social care workers do not: abuse their 'own and their organisation's informal or coercive power on involuntary and potentially involuntary service users' (BASW, 2002: para 4.41d), or by exploiting the trust of service users and carers or misuse personal information that they may have about the people they are working with (GSCC, 2002; The Nursing and Midwifery Council, 2002).

- **Principles of professional practice** are contained within professional codes; they reflect existing good practice as well as identify what workers should aspire to in relation to their own practices – statements such as helping service users and carers to make complaints, taking complaints seriously and responding to them, or passing them to the appropriate person and 'working openly and co-operatively with colleagues and treating them with respect' (GSCC, 2002: para 6.5) convey to practitioners what is expected of them.

- **Rules of professional practice** provide very specific guidance relating to professional practice. So, for example, practitioners are reminded that policies and procedures exist in relation to accepting gifts and money from service users and carers. Within the health professions staff are reminded that their registration status should not be used in the promotion of commercial products or services (The Nursing and Midwifery Council, 2002).

The form and content of the codes are linked to the multiple purposes that they are intended to fulfil. The codes identify the importance that the profession attaches to what it believes are fundamental values and practice principles. By clearly stating what can be expected of the professional practitioner, codes can be used to protect service users, establish, enhance and maintain professional identity, provide guidance to practitioners about how to act ethically and make ethical decisions, and identify the qualities expected of the people who belong to the profession. Codes also serve as surveillance and disciplinary tools to ensure that practitioners do not behave in ways that are 'unethical' (Ife, 2001: 103) and would bring the profession into disrepute. Codes then serve a number of purposes. They are aspirational, educational and political documents (Banks, 2004).

How far codes can assist practitioners who are engaged in very complex moral situations to make the right decisions is, however, a question which needs to be addressed. Should codes of ethics be seen as tools to promote ethical practice or do they merely act as a conduit through which the power that professionals have over relatively powerless service users is legitimated? Some commentators have suggested that codes do not of themselves produce 'ethically competent, responsive, responsible professionals who exercise autonomous, rational, and critical judgement and choice in the light of universally important moral principles and concerns' (Pattinson, 2001: 17). Therefore they should not be used as a substitute for practitioners engaging in ethical reflection and discussion of moral dilemmas and issues. They should be viewed as a useful framework, which can assist practitioners to think about particular issues – they are a helpful guide for practice and need to be used in conjunction with legislation and associated guidance, agency policy and procedures.

Codes of ethics have been criticized on a philosophical and sociological basis. Some professional codes over-simplify moral requirements (Beauchamp and Childress, 2001), and by presenting moral principles as unproblematic, fail to recognize that they are in fact underpinned by complex philosophical ideas. Little guidance, if any, for example, is provided to help the practitioner manage decisions in relation to *competing* moral principles. The right to self-determination at times conflicts with the authority of professionals to intrude into private life, particularly if a person's actions are seen to endanger their life. How does the practitioner decide what is the right decision to make when the needs of the individual conflict with the interests of other family members, the community and society? There can be conflicts between the legal mandate and one's ethical obligations. What would be the right action to take in these situations of moral complexity? Codes of ethics may suggest that there is only one way of practising, when in reality there may well be alternative ways of working with people.

However, trying to 'encompass the varied and complex roles of social workers into a single ideal way of practising' (Ife, 2001: 106) is not only unhelpful and impractical but unachievable, as practitioners would have to develop a comprehensive code of ethics to cover every eventuality. Assiduously following the rules of the codes will not guarantee practice that is morally acceptable. They are helpful guides but they are not a substitute for practitioners critically engaging in complex moral decision-making. It is evident that values can contradict and be in tension with each other. By emphasizing personal morality, responsibility and accountability, codes fail to address the relationship between individual situations and group, organizational and managerial ethics, imperatives and responsibilities (Pattinson, 2001). Codes, it could be argued, can lead to practitioners engaging in individualistic responses to moral situations which may require an organizational or policy response.

Ife argues that codes of ethics are 'essentially modernist' in their formulation and function (Ife, 2001: 106) and are a tool of the powerful rather than an instrument that attempts to reflect the diverse perspectives of those who are often subject to those who have power and control. However, if their content is critically analysed and it is appreciated by practitioners that the principles and language of ethics and values that are found within them, 'is often partial, narrow or essentially misleading' (Pattinson, 2001: 17), then the codes can provide the starting point for practitioners to think about the ethical dimension of their practice, engage in practice informed by personal care, concern and interest, and encourage practitioners to work with others in relation to making real social change.

Values and the law

When we initially put forward our idea that the law could be used to develop practice that was anti-oppressive, we became engaged in many debates with friends and colleagues who challenged our assumption. The discussions highlighted some of the difficulties practitioners faced when using the law to assert the rights of service users. The law was often viewed as a powerful, monolithic structure, which was seen in negative terms as representing a particular form of power. It was regarded as an insensitive tool, which had limited use in assisting practitioners to engage in less oppressive interventions in people's lives. The following statements encapsulate some of the points of view that we encountered:

- The law is inflexible and insensitive. It over-simplifies the difficult moral issues we have to try and deal with.
- The law adds to the dilemmas we face – it doesn't help us at all.
- How can the law support anti-oppressive practice when some areas of discrimination are still lawful?

Ten years on, the contradictory relationship that exists between practitioners and the law is still evident. Research has indicated that practitioners continue to be ambivalent about the use of the law, which is often seen as 'offering protection to vulnerable people and as a tool to be used creatively, but [is] also likely to compound inequality and elevate control over justice' (Preston-Shoot, 2003: 468). We acknowledge that the law does not always reflect or is informed by anti-oppressive values, that it can often be reactionary, regulatory and procedural. We are aware that the 'extent to which the law can change assumptions about older people, people with disabilities, children or people with learning disabilities is debatable' (Williams, 2004: 46). That the law can be used to deny the basic rights of those who seek asylum, as well as to restrict the liberty of those who are deemed to be 'dangerous', is not disputed by us. However, despite these very valid concerns and limitations of the law, we would argue (along with other commentators such as Braye and Preston-Shoot, 1997; Roche, 2001; Williams, 2004) that the law can be used to promote practice that is beneficial, supportive and promotes anti-oppressive values within the helping professions. The law can be used to directly support values that promote self-determination, equality and rights. For example, the Mental Capacity Act 2005 provides a statutory framework to empower and protect vulnerable people who are not able to make their own decisions (Department of Health, 2006). Three of the five principles underpinning the Act support principles of anti-oppressive practice:

- Every adult should be assumed to be capable of making their own decisions unless proved otherwise.
- Everyone should be given all the support they need to make their own decisions, before they are judged incapable of doing this.
- People should be able to make 'eccentric' or 'unwise' decisions – it is their capacity to make decisions, not the decisions themselves, that is the issue.

(Mental Health Foundation, 2005: 1)

Another example can be found in the Criminal Justice Act 1991, of which section 95 makes it a duty to avoid discrimination on the 'ground of "race" or sex or any other improper ground'. Finally, in relation to rights, the use of the Family Law Act 1996 to enable an individual to gain an injunction to exclude an abuser from the home may well contribute to them gaining control over their lives (Brammer, 2003). But equally, the use of the Act promotes the right not to be subjected to inhuman or degrading treatment under Article 3 of the Human Rights Act 1998. The Children Act 2004 and the Disability Discrimination Act 2005 incorporate themes of empowerment and partnership and facilitate user involvement in the processes of assessment and care planning. However, for the anti-oppressive potential of the law to be realized practitioners should use the law critically; an unreflective use of the law can lead to practice that is defensive, conservative and disempowering. Practitioners need to critically reflect on their use of the law and ensure that they do not use it as a prescriptive framework which directs rather than guides and supports practice. Complex practice situations require practitioners to actively engage in situations of moral uncertainty and to use the opportunities that the law provides to engage in positive practice. In short, the law 'provides authority and a structure for decision-making rather than solutions: it provides a framework in which individual social workers have to act' (Cull and Roche, 2001: xiii).

The law defines the roles and responsibilities of practitioners and directs practice in the areas of prevention, protection and rehabilitation. However, practitioners do not use the law in isolation, they draw on a range of academic disciplines, such as psychology, sociology, politics, social policy. Evidence from research informed by service user experiences and grounded in practice realities is also used to explore and understand the context in which the problems people face are located. Consequently, the relationship between social work and the law is not unproblematic. There is inevitably, in reality, a dynamic relationship between the law and practice. The law itself reflects certain values and norms in society – some of which we may regard as antithetical to principles of liberty, justice and equality. Use of the law is not an impartial activity as the relationship that exists between the legislative and policy framework and the provision of services reflects political and ideological agendas. Using the law is an ethical and value-based action. The law is underpinned by 'values and assumptions about people, relationships and their place in society' (Braye and Preston-Shoot, 1997: 31).

The law can be seen to function as a tool in which particular ideologies are sustained and the status and interests of certain groups are maintained. For example, the differences in power that exist between adults and children are reflected in child care legislation, where two contrasting ideologies 'care and protection' and 'control and correction' can be seen to underpin legislation and policy development. These distinct ideologies do not co-exist in a creative way but conflict. Children are viewed as out of control and in need of correction (Goldson, 2002) by the Crime and Disorder Act 1998. The Children Act 1989, hailed as a Children's Charter, challenges the idea that children are the property of their parents. Yet the Education Act 1985 assumes that children have no voice and are the property of their parents, so that all decisions concerning their education are made with parents. Children's behaviour is also seen to be the responsibility of their parents, as failure to ensure that their children attend school leaves parents liable to be fined £2500 and/or a three-month prison sentence. The introduction of Parenting Orders under the Crime and Disorder Act 1998 and on-the-spot fines for parents of truants under section 23 of the Anti-Social Behaviour Act 2003 (Grier and Thomas, 2005) firmly places the responsibility onto parents for their children's actions. Practice that promotes the rights of children and young people therefore has to be mindful of the competing discourses that contribute to a particular social construction of children and young people. Critical anti-oppressive practitioners should use available legislation and social policy that focuses on the rights of children and young people to participate and be involved in decision-making. The Children Act 1989, which incorporates various rights that are enshrined in the United Nations Convention on the Rights of the Child (see Table 4.1), can be used to promote practice that is anti-oppressive.

Table 4.1 United Convention on the Rights of the Child and links to the Children Act 1989

Article	Focus
2.2	No discrimination on account of what parents do or say
3	'Best interest' of the child to be a primary consideration for courts and administration, for child protection, safety and health
12	Right to participate in decision-making
32.9	Protection from exploitation, drugs, sexual abuse, abduction, inhuman treatment or punishment, deprivation of liberty without advocacy, participation in armed conflicts

(taken from John, 2005: 43)

The majority of decisions in social work involve a complex interaction of ethical, political, technical and legal issues. Practitioners, if they are not to contribute to exclusion, injustice and a denial of citizenship, have to be critically aware of the 'moral basis of social relations and social work practice' (Jordan, 1990: 78) and use this understanding to inform their practice so as to engage in social action which challenges the social structures sustaining and supporting inequality. The ethical principles, values and critical perspectives we hold will influence how we interpret, use and critique the law and social policy (Jordan, 1990; Banks, 2001). If used without reference to the 'moral and human framework of compassion, care and empathy' (Banks, 2001: 104;

and see Jordan, 1990), the law can be an inadequate, insensitive and an imprecise tool with which to understand and resolve the delicate and complex nature of peoples' lives.

Taking a purely legalistic approach to human problems or social issues fails to address directly questions of inequality, and the social conditions which generate and sustain social divisions. In fact, such an approach can compound the oppression felt by individuals, families and communities who have, for example, sought asylum within Britain. The treatment of children and families seeking asylum provides clear evidence of the unequal and oppressive relationship that exists between the state and those who are deemed not to be its citizens. It has been argued that practice in this area is that of systematically denying and violating their rights under the United Nations Convention on the Rights of the Child (Cemlyn, 2003). The detention of unaccompanied asylum-seeking children continues and is rising (Children's Rights Alliance for England, 2004). Consequently, practitioners will be increasingly faced with the challenges of working with these children within a particular legal and policy context which is not particularly supportive. For example, government dispersal policies break and fragment family ties and inhibit the ability of refugee and asylum-seeking families to integrate within local communities and further contribute to the isolation and vulnerability of these families. Located as they are in areas that are not well served with good-quality housing stock or education and health services, their quality of life is compromised. They not only have to recover from the traumatic experiences of war, rape, torture, murder and state-organized oppression (Humphries, 2004), but they have to cope with the stress of surviving in communities which are not always welcoming.

The use of section 9 of the Asylum and Immigration Act 2004, which provides officials with the right to stop all benefits to those who do not voluntarily return to their home countries once refused asylum, has further compounded the experiences of many asylum seekers who face the prospect of being made homeless. Without financial support, families struggle to provide for themselves and their children and often have to contend with the very real possibility that their children will be removed from them and placed into care (Batty, 2005a, 2005b; Ward, 2005). The experiences of people at the receiving end of New Labour's policies, whose aim is to deter those who wish to seek asylum and protect resources for those deemed to be citizens, reminds practitioners of the need to be aware of the ideological basis of the law.

However, the engagement in anti-oppressive practice requires more than an awareness of the ideological basis of the law – this is an important starting point, but 'law that is inherently anti-liberty requires social workers to engage in anti-liberty practice' (Williams, 2004: 50). Practitioners wishing to oppose rather than work with racist, nationalistic and chauvinistic legislation (Humphries, 2004) have to acknowledge the political dimension of their practice. This involves 'campaigning, contributing to the debate on social rights, and submitting evidence to influence social policy' (Cemlyn, 2003: 176) and at the same time engaging in practice that is informed by the very real experiences of those who are subject to legislation that is unjust. Working in this way is not easy, as practitioners will be faced with numerous personal and organizational challenges when they attempt to work from an anti-oppressive perspective in environments which are antithetical to principles of social justice and equality. A critical understanding of the nature of power will assist practitioners to construct or reconstruct themselves as active con-tributors to the processes of change. On an individual basis, we have a certain amount of power arising from our social division membership and our pro-fessional status, which can be used in the interactions we have with others. For example, as practitioners we have specialist knowledge and skills which can be used to support people in need. We also potentially have access to a range of resources and support systems within the organizations in which we work that can be accessed when necessary. By fashioning new ways of thinking about power, practitioners begin to discover new possibilities for developing individual, collective and community-based responses to legisla-tion which is oppressive. Transformative practice that challenges aspects of the law seen as unjust is emotionally demanding and intellectually challen-ging. Immigration and asylum law and policy can be a particularly difficult area for social workers to engage in practice which is anti-oppressive but there are spaces where good practice can be developed.

The following general points provide possibilities for engaging in work that is consistent with the core values of anti-oppressive practice:

- Focus on the experiences of people on the receiving end of draconian and punitive legislation. The incorporation of this perspective should enable practitioners to work from a standpoint that truly acknowledges the realities of people's lives.
- Work from an informed perspective – what are the implications of working with a particular piece of legislation for yourself and the service user(s)?
- Use opportunities provided by supervision, team discussions, train-ing and conference attendance to engage in critical reflection and discussions (Baldwin, 2004).
- Critically analyse research evidence, policy and practices from an anti-oppressive perspective. For example, 'ask critical questions about the motives behind the ideologies which inform social po-licies' (Humphries, 2004: 105).
- Engage in research that provides alternative ways of working within a framework of rights, justice and cross-cultural principles (Cemlyn, 2003).

- Work collectively with others who are committed to operating from an anti-oppressive perspective. By working collectively the individual experiences of oppression and ways of challenging oppression can be pooled together. Collective working also provides the opportunity for support networks to be developed.
- Use existing legislation such as the Human Rights Act 1998 as a tool to combat oppression. Section 20 assessments under the Children Act 1989, rather than section 17, can be used to 'ensure a full package of *appropriate* accommodation and support' (Hayes, 2005: 193).
- Actively engage in campaigns against legislation and policy that is oppressive.
- Engage in dialogue across disciplinary boundaries so that issues can be fully understood from different perspectives.
- Actively engage with service user forums, which can influence the development or the reform of legislation.
- Become involved in groups within the organization that you are working for which may be able to influence policy and practice. The production of alternative discourses not only challenges dominant ideas and ways of practising within the organization, but can provide the impetus for change within organizations that are open to working with rather than coopting new perspectives.

By way of conclusion, the passing of the Human Rights Act 1998 has resulted in a more explicit discussion of the value base of the law. Despite its imperfections, the Act is underpinned by values such as 'tolerance; respect for the dignity and lifestyle choices of others; allowing others to speak their mind or to protest without obstruction; and treating others fairly without discrimination or degradation' (Klug, 2000: 197): values and principles consistent with our view of anti-oppressive practice. The Human Rights Act 1998 therefore provides a framework in which debates regarding tolerance, diversity, inequality, individual and collective rights and responsibilities can take place. Human rights provides a structure in which we can begin to discuss issues of power which shape the relationships we have with each other locally, nationally and internationally (Ife, 2001; Kennedy, 2004). Health and social care practitioners can use the Human Rights Act 1998 as an important 'benchmark' (Williams, 2001: 843) for reviewing policies, practices and procedures so that they comply with the Act, but are also consistent with anti-oppressive principles.

Chapter summary

'Practitioners have statutory duties, underpinned by professional codes and personal values to support the most vulnerable members of society' (Brayne and Carr, 2005: 724). The law can be used to challenge decisions that deny people's access to resources, and on behalf of people who have been discriminated against on the basis of their gender, disability or 'race', or who have been discriminated against within the workplace. For the law, social policies, and guidance documents to be of assistance in relation to the development of good practice, the underpinning value base needs to be looked at – questions need to be asked about how far they address the difficult questions of equality, justice and rights. The statutory framework in which social work and the health care professions is embedded also has to be critiqued in relation to questions of values and ethics.

The law is a product of social, cultural, political, economic and historical factors. In essence, it reflects the dominant values of the society that constructs it. Our ethical principles or values will influence how we interpret the law. The culture of the organizations in which we practice also influences how we use the law (Braye and Preston-Shoot, 1997). A critical understanding of the ideological basis of the legislation may help practitioners to identify inherent oppressive elements within and between various pieces of legislation. In turn, this knowledge can assist practitioners to negotiate the difficult path that exists between 'oppressive legalism' (Jordan, 1990: 106) and the creative possibilities of engaging in anti-oppressive practice. The law can be used as a creative, effective and 'forceful tool' (Spelman, 2006: 22) and can be used to '... distribute and negotiate resources, rules and power itself, making it at once a powerful medium and a medium for power ...' (MacKinnon, 2005, cited in Spelman, 2006: 23). Used positively, the law can protect, enable and support people who are marginalized, vulnerable and in need. The law can be used to make demands and used as a mechanism for accountability, but ultimately to use the law justly requires that we challenge it when it fails to promote equality and translate 'standards of human rights into reality' (Kennedy, 2004: 318).

Further reading

Banks, S. (2001) *Ethics and Values in Social Work*, 2nd edn. Basingstoke: Palgrave. This book will assist students to further develop their understanding and encourage critical thinking of ethical dilemmas encountered in practice situations. The inclusion of case studies assists students to discuss and debate ethical dilemmas and issues regarding values.

Banks, S. (2004) *Ethics, Accountability and the Social Professions*. Basingstoke: Palgrave.
This book usefully looks at professional ethics and values within social work, community and youth work.

Dominelli, L. (2004) *Social Work: Theory and Practice for a Changing Profession*. Cambridge: Polity Press. See Chapter 3: 'Values, Ethics and Empowerment'.
This chapter critically analyses traditional values of social work and looks at the links between values, ethics and empowering practice.

Brechin, A., Brown, H. and Eby, M.A. (2000) *Critical Practice in Health and Social Care*. London: Sage Publications. See Chapter 6: 'The Challenge of Values and Ethics in Practice'.
This accessible chapter focuses on some common approaches to the understanding of ethics.

Activity 1: Locating yourself – What is my story?

Reflect back on Ursula's story. Can you identify your reasons for your choice of profession? Can you trace how your personal values and beliefs about the social world contribute to the way in which you practice?

The following questions may assist you in your personal exploration of experiences which have had an influence on your life.

- When and where were you born – what local, national, international events coincided with your birth?
- Family composition – for example, were you an only child, did you live in an all-female household?
- What type of community did you live in?
- Where did you go to school – locally, mixed, private or public? Were you educated at home?
- What significant relationships did you have within the family, in the community, within the school system or any other social systems?
- Have you, or anyone close to you, ever used services?
- Can you identify any experiences that enabled you to critically reflect on the values you hold?

When you have completed your reflections, you may want to record significant events or feelings/emotions that have contributed to the person you are and have shaped and informed your current practice.

Commentary

Having completed this personal exploration, did you consider how issues of power and oppression shaped and determined you as a person and the relationships that you have with others? What value did you identify as important to you, and how has this value informed your practice?

Did you include answers to, or consider, the following questions?

- Did your family experiences influence any decisions in your life?
- What difference, if any, does it make to your practice that you belong to a different or similar class background as the people you are working with?
- What significance does your gender have?
- What impact does your sexual, racial, cultural identity have on your practice?
- Did you consider what impact your experience of disability/ablebodiedness has had on your life experiences?
- What impact did your experience of receiving a service(s) or knowledge of someone close to you receiving a service(s) have on you?
- What impact has your experience of the law had on your current practice?
- What significance have national and international debates (such as poverty, world debt, environmental issues) had on how you conduct your life?

Activity 2: Language and values

Within language are embedded the values, beliefs and ideas which reflect the social, economic and political context in which social work is practised (Rojek et al., 1988). Language can be used to illustrate the power inequalities that exist between individuals and the value judgements that can be made about situations in which people find themselves. With this in mind, please read the following poem.

Tomorrow I am going to re-write the English language

Tomorrow I am going to re-write the English language.
I will discard all those striving ambullist metaphors
Of power and success
And construct images to describe my strength.
My new, different strength.
Then I won't have to feel dependent
Because I can't Stand On My Own Two Feet
And I will refuse to feel a failure
Because I didn't Stay One Step Ahead.
I won't feel inadequate
When I don't Stand Up For Myself
Or illogical because I cannot
Just Take It One Step At a Time.
I will make them understand that it is a very male way

To describe the world
All this Walking Tall
And Making Great Strides.

Yes, tomorrow I am going to re-write the English language,
Creating the world in my own image.
Mine will be a gentler, more womanly way
To describe my progress.
I will wheel, cover and encircle

Somehow I will learn to say it all.

(Morris, 1989)

This poem challenges our assumptions of gender and able-bodiedness and illustrates the way in which our everyday language takes so much for granted. Think about the value judgements that are portrayed in other poems that you have read.

Activity 3: Value statements

An example of how the language of values can be used by those whose mission could be said to be in opposition to that of health and social care practitioners is provided below:

'Blueprint for Behaviour'

Trust. We believe everyone embracing the values of the division will do what is best for the customer, each other and the enterprise.

- Expects people to perform their mission and be accountable.
- Demonstrates openness and honesty in business relationships.
- Eliminates the fear of breaking away from familiar ways of thinking and acting.
- Shares information freely in all directions, both good news and bad news.
- Respects and honours matters of confidentiality.

Mutual Respect. We treat everyone with dignity and courtesy. Makes everyone feel important and able to make a contribution.

- Listens without interruption when someone is speaking.
- Makes no distinction based on position.
- Recognises the uniqueness of individuals.

Empowerment. We believe people must work in an environment where they feel enabled to make decisions that contribute to customer satisfaction and performance of the division.

- Balances decision-making authority and responsibility.
- Seeks and shares information with others on decisions that affect them.

Commitment. We deliver what we promise to each other and our customers.

- Recognises action rather than rhetoric as the true measure of commitment.
- Promises only what can be delivered.
- Demonstrates personal commitment to continued learning and up-grading of skills.

(Extract taken from *Nine Common Values – Blueprint for Behaviour*,
Despain et al., 2003)

The box above contains an extract from *Nine Common Values – Blueprint for Behaviour*, a vision and values statement which was put together by the Track-Type Tractors Division Management Team who are part of Caterpillar Incorporated, an American company (Despain et al., 2003). It reflects the relative nature of the term 'values', and the fact that values gain specific meaning from the context in which they are located.

Task

You may wish to compare and contrast this 'blueprint' with the mission statements or value statements found within the organizations where you work or have worked, where you have undertaken voluntary work or where you are currently on placement.

What impact do you think the mission or value statements you have looked at has had on professional relationships or the delivery of services within the organization?

Commentary

The 'Blueprint for Behaviour' was developed after a comprehensive investigation to find out why the Division, despite producing a quality product with a highly experienced workforce and state-of-the-art equipment, was operating at a considerable loss. It was identified that if the business was going to succeed then there needed to be a significant culture change within the organization. The implementation of the 'Blueprint', to which both staff and management had to be committed, led to a cultural shift within the work environment from that of 'conflict and adversarialism to one of support and caring' (Despain et al., 2003: 409) and ultimately to an increase in profit margins.

Activity 4: Media reporting

An understanding of popular language and the values it implies can be obtained by scrutinizing media reporting. Read the following newspaper story.

Home alone at Christmas

In the early hours of Christmas Eve 1993 three small girls were taken into care. They were sisters aged between 10 months and 10 years. Their mother was 25. The family lived together in a council house. The house was in a poor state of repair, it was dirty, carpets were covered with cat and dog faeces, half-eaten food littered the front room. The cooker in the kitchen was encased in grease; the fetid air made it difficult for police and social workers to breathe without feeling as though they were going to be physically sick. The children were found alone when police and social workers called.

The social worker's story

This is not a 'home alone' case. The mother was with her children. Concern was about neglect – neglect linked to poverty. The poverty was not caused by any extravagant lifestyle but by an insensitive benefits system. This case is one of many that this office deals with. What should be of concern is that this is a case we are aware of. There are many others that are not brought to our attention.

But what we are sure of is that this case highlights the nature of deprivation, poverty and inequality that some families experience.

The mother's story

It hurts to see your story splashed all over the newspaper, particularly when all the facts are wrong. I have had social workers calling round all the time, checking on my children and helping me with the housing and the social. Things were going all right for a time until my fella, Ronnie, walked out on me and the kids. That was in August. I was upset by this but you have to get on with your life, so I carried on best I could.

I met Peter in November and that's when things really got difficult. Ronnie saw me and Peter together and started getting funny with me. He didn't want to know before, but because I was with someone else he felt he owned me. Anyway, Ronnie called round saying he wanted to see the children, but he called at eight, nine or ten o'clock at night sometimes and I would say no, he couldn't, because they were in bed. There would be an argument. Peter would say something, Ronnie would tell him to 'shut it', 'cos he wasn't the girls' father. The baby would wake up and that would be the end of my night with Peter.

Just before Christmas, Ronnie wanted the children to spend Christmas with him. I said no and a row started. Ronnie left, saying he was going to get the social workers and the police on to me. He said that I was too busy with Peter to mind the children properly. Social workers and police have called a few times now – he tells them a pack of lies, but it's their job, they have to check the children are OK. Ronnie has applied for an order to see them. I didn't mind him seeing the children – it's the time. You can't come round at night to see a baby can you?

Anyway, on Christmas Eve morning, Ronnie called round, said he had presents for the children out in the car. So I let them go out to get their presents. I was standing by the door. Next thing, Ronnie drives off with the children. So I called the police, told them what had happened. I went out to look for them. When I got back, the police were at the house. Ronnie had just gone round the block. He had come back and got in the house, left the children and then called the police on me. When I got in, the police asked why I had left the children on their own. They said that they were taking them into care and that social workers had found somewhere for them. I saw red then, and grabbed my kids. I was crying and screaming and so were they. When the social workers came I just ran out of the house. I couldn't take any more. Now my girls are in care.

The resource manager's story

I cannot comment on a specific case but this case has to be seen in a wider context of poverty and deprivation. The benefits system has failed this family. People like this mother find it difficult to manage on the limited income they get from the state. Christmas is a financially difficult time, particularly when you have children. But these cases don't just come to light at Christmas. We see cases like this every day of every week. People find it hard to cope, they are not parents who do not care. They care very much. But they do not have the financial resources to care properly for their children. They know this, and the stress of knowing, of being unable to do something, is very great and sometimes people break and that is when we have to step in and take control of the situation.

1. What basic values are being expressed through the media and the stories of the people involved?
2. What impact does the mother's story have on you?
3. What impact do you think the media has had on the mother?
4. What are the arguments put forward by the media to the public by their presentation of her story?
5. How would your own value base affect your response at a practical, policy and legislative level?
6. You are one of the people involved in the mother's life (you could, for example, be the babysitter, personal friend, health visitor, or school nurse). What is your story? Once you have written it, write an imaginary letter to the paper that printed the article.

(This exercise is based on an article printed in *The Guardian*, 19 January 1994.)

5 Empowerment

Warning

When I am an old woman I shall wear purple
With a red hat which doesn't go, and doesn't suit me,
And I shall spend my pension on brandy and summer gloves
And satin sandals, and say we've no money for butter.
I shall sit down on the pavement when I'm tired
And gobble up samples in shops and press alarm bells
And run my stick along public railings
And make up for the sobriety of my youth.
I shall go out in my slippers in the rain
And pick the flowers in other people's gardens
And learn to spit.

You can wear terrible shirts and grow more fat
And eat three pounds of sausages at a go
Or only eat bread and pickle for a week
And hoard pens and pencils and beer mats and things in boxes.
But now we must have clothes that keep us dry
And pay our rent and not swear in the street
And set a good example for the children.
We will have friends to dinner and read the papers.
But maybe I ought to practise a little now?
So people who know me are not too shocked and surprised
When suddenly I am old and start to wear purple.
(Jenny Joseph, 1985)

Introduction

To move empowerment from rhetoric to reality requires leaping
some well established hurdles, among the most significant of which
are: the credibility and legitimacy of the power exercised by health
care professionals, the needs and career aspirations of many professionals, and the bureaucracy of the health service.
(Lamont, 1999, cited in Descombes, 2004: 94)

The term 'empowerment' is a relatively new concept that has had a considerable impact upon the nature of health and social care practice. It was the 'buzz word' of the late 1980s (Adams, 1990) and it became popular in the 1990s as a term used to reflect the nature of health and social care (Stevenson and Parsloe, 1993). In Chapter 2 we introduced the concepts of oppression and power and the idea that all interactions are characterized by power relations. In this chapter we will continue to explore these concepts in our discussion of empowerment practice. Practitioners, working from an empowerment perspective with individuals, need to be aware of the wider context in which people's personal issues are located. This link between the personal and wider structures of society is encapsulated in the international definition of social work, which states that:

> The social work profession promotes social change, problem solving in human relationships and the empowerment and liberation of people to enhance well-being. Utilising theories of human behaviour and social systems, social work intervenes at the points where people interact with their environments. Principles of human rights and social justice are fundamental to social work.
>
> (International Association of Schools of Social Work (IASSW) and
> International Federation of Social Workers, 2001: 29)

Similarly, modern definitions of nursing also link to the wider structures impacting on health:

> Nursing is not only concerned about health and functioning but with quality of living and dying, lived experience, and universal lived experiences of health.
>
> *en.wikipedia.org/wiki/Nursing*

The Royal College of Nursing (RCN) is committed to a view of patients as equal partners in their own health care. It states that health professionals need to 'modify their position to ensure that power re-balance is effectively achieved' (Royal College of Nursing, 2000: 25).

Rappaport also identifies and links the personal and political aspects of empowerment, describing it as a way in which 'people, organisations and communities gain mastery over their own lives' (1984: 3). For Rappaport, it 'conveys both a psychological sense of personal control or influence and a concern with actual social influence, political power, and legal rights' (1987: 121). Jordan with Jordan (2000) suggest that the ideas of inclusion and empowerment have characterized a practice with users of services in the 1980s and 1990s that is sensitive to their needs and perspectives. However, it has been recognized that 'the very term empowerment does not do justice to the changes it attempts to describe' (Braye and Preston-Shoot, 1995: 110). With the establishment of the notion of empowerment has also come a critique of its meaning. So what does the term really mean? Is it just a word that has become fashionable for use by professionals and politicians? Has it, as Thompson suggests, become a term 'used by some right wing commentators to promote a notion of self-reliance as part of a process of discouraging re-liance on collective or state measures' (Thompson, 2003: 76)? Is it used as a synonym for enabling? Does it, as Ward and Mullender (1991) state, lack specificity and gloss over significant difference? Or, as Croft and Beresford (1989) argue, is it a much abused and devalued word? A number of writers note that empowerment has the potential to be both regulatory and libera-tory (Croft and Beresford, 2000). For example, Fawcett and Featherstone (1996), drawing on work by Baistow (1995), question the unproblematic nature of empowerment and empowering strategies in relation to 'carers' and 'caring'. Thompson (2003) also notes the need for clarity in how the notion of empowerment is used. Humphries (1996), exploring why such care needs to be taken, highlights contradictions in the development of a discourse of empowerment, concluding that the culture of empowerment embodies containment and collusion. She is therefore sceptical of any radical change being brought about as a result of empowerment strategies.

In this chapter we will briefly consider the history of the term and some contemporary reformulations of the concept. We will then present a model of empowerment practice. Finally, we consider how legislation and policy in-itiatives have incorporated empowerment principles.

Development of the concept of empowerment

In tracing the historical development of the term 'empowerment', we start with Solomon's influential work *Black Empowerment*. Solomon (1976: 12) re-fers to empowerment:

> as a process whereby persons who belong to a stigmatized social category throughout their lives can be assisted to develop and in-crease skills in the exercise of interpersonal influence and the per-formance of valued social roles.

The major thesis of her book is that individuals and groups in black com-munities have been subjected to negative valuations from the wider society to such an extent that powerlessness in the group is pervasive and crippling. Although Solomon is specifically thinking about black communities in the United States of America, her work has major relevance to other negatively valued groups in society. She argues that empowerment is about engaging service users in the problem-solving process. Discussing social work with black people, she states that:

> empowerment is the process whereby the social worker engages in a set of activities with the client or client system that aim to reduce the powerlessness that has been created by negative valuations based on membership in a stigmatized group.
>
> (Solomon, 1976: 19)

Similarly, Gutierrez (1990: 149) identifies empowering practice as 'a process of increasing personal, interpersonal, or political power so that individuals can take action to improve their life situations'. This process serves to counteract the oppressions that shape and inform the lives of those who do not have access, or have limited access, to the power structures of society.

How can we engage people in the problem-solving process? One of the ways of doing this is by enabling people to talk about their experiences of oppression. By documenting the experiences of black women, black female writers (hooks, 1989; Hill-Collins, 1990) have shown that if women are to take control of their lives they need to articulate and share their experiences of oppression. By making visible their personal experiences, they begin to value themselves – which of itself is empowering. They are then able to start the process of rejecting the system which perpetuates their oppression. Taking this point into consideration, we must therefore look at the structure and process of service delivery systems that have the greatest potential for facilitating empowerment of service users. Our services must be sensitive – a sensitivity that can only be brought about by practitioners listening to and taking account of people's experiences. As Solomon (1976: 29) points out, 'the success or failure of empowerment is directly related to the degree to which [the] service delivery system itself is an obstacle course or an opportunity system'. In order to engage in this process, we therefore need to understand the power that agencies have to determine access to services (service power); the power they have to define and specify service (strategic power); and the power they have to decide which issues are important and who has access to decision-making. All three levels of power need to be addressed so that service users and carers have the chance to access services (Skelcher, 1993).

A study of the literature about empowerment practice indicates that most writers view it as a dynamic process (Rappaport, 1985; Rees, 1991; Phillipson, 1992; Stevenson and Parsloe, 1993). However, it is also a goal, product or outcome (Swift and Levin, 1987; Holdsworth, 1991; Sohng, 1998) – the 'end state'. Contemporary concepts of empowerment take account of changing understandings of power from postmodern and critical perspectives. Recognizing that 'the very term empowerment does not do justice to the changes it attempts to describe' (Braye and Preston-Shoot, 1995: 110) re-formulated concepts of empowerment take into account:

- the contextual and changing nature of power;
- how power operates at different levels, often simultaneously and in contradictory ways;
- how power is experienced by different people;
- the creative, as well as controlling, possibilities power entails.

(Fook, 2002: 103)

Fook is influenced by the work of Foucault, who highlights 'the slippery and ambiguous nature of empowerment' (Ward, 2000: 50). As mentioned in Chapter 2, Foucault argues that power is not a fixed entity and that in order to engage with the essence of power, people 'have to participate in, influence and begin to engage with defining the facts, priorities and responsibilities which we take as given – in fact to challenge the discourses in which we are all enmeshed' (Rees, 1991). Lukes' (1974, 1986) analysis of power also focuses on both the behaviour of decision-makers and the way that the interests of people may be defined by systems that work against their interests. Ward (2000) points out that thinking about the analyses of Foucault and Lukes helps us to appreciate that empowerment is not a commodity to be passed from one person to another, resulting in the empowerment of one person and disempowering another. A Foucauldian analysis sees power as exercised rather than possessed and productive. This helps us to see that 'empowerment is a process of change through achieving power and transforming it. Just as oppression is experienced through personal, everyday events, so empowering practice offers people the chance to experience new ways of being involved in those events' (Ward, 2000: 51). Empowerment seeks to help clients to gain power of decision and action over their own lives (Payne, 2005a).

Ferns (1998) views empowerment as: 'fundamental to equality ... Enabling access to legitimate forms of power and removing discriminatory barriers' (cited in Brechin, 2000: 41). These ideas are reflected in definitions of empowerment from the perspective of service users, for whom it 'means challenging their disempowerment, having more control over their lives, being able to influence others and bring about change' (Croft and Beresford, 2000: 116). Features of an empowerment approach have been described as recognizing and building the capacity of service users to help themselves and their communities and to 'promote a mutual learning partnership between workers and service users' (Healy, 2000: 157). However, this is not always easy. In her research with service users in a hospital environment, Platzer (2005) notes that while it is invariably hard to obtain the views of disempowered service users, 'to do so in a psychiatric hospital environment, with its climate of fear is particularly problematic' (2005: 87). The development of participatory ways of working with service users from consumerism to empowerment and partnership has been identified by Barnes et al. (2000) in a case study about the involvement of service users in a postgraduate programme. They state that partnership is a more realistic way of thinking about working with service users as it recognizes differences in power without expecting equality. This is reflected by a social worker we spoke to while writing this edition, who described her commitment to empowerment practice as 'attempting to work from an equality perspective in unequal circumstances' (Ann Farmer, personal communication). She identified the dilemmas of empowerment practice when working with the complexity of the reality of people's lives. Added to this is the fact that however motivated and committed front-line managers may be, they can also be 'compromised by organizational structures and audit cultures' (Carr, 2004: 19).

For professionals there is a continual tension between autonomy, protection and empowerment (Braye and Preston-Shoot, 1995). Practitioners who work with vulnerable adults have to balance 'the provision of protective strategies and the type of services contributing to the prevention of abuse, while enabling vulnerable adults to make their own informed decisions wherever possible' (Cooke and Ellis, 2004: 133). Similarly, in child protection work practitioners face a number of dilemmas. For example, take the situation of Jenni, who is drug-dependent and lives in inadequate housing in an unsafe neighbourhood. She is a young single mother struggling with parenting her 2-year-old. The dilemma for practitioners wishing to engage in empowerment practice is how to work in partnership with Jenni to help her feel safe and in control of her life (autonomy) and at the same time make the right decisions together about keeping her child safe (child protection). This means that the worker needs to engage in practice that is negotiated rather than imposed. This is made more complex by the context in which practice takes place. The worker has to balance needs, rights and resources, which can pull in different directions (Braye and Preston-Shoot, 1995).

In addition, there is a big issue for workers concerned about their own safety when visiting a neighbourhood where there is a high level of violence and aggression. In areas where gun crimes and robberies associated with drug use are routine, all authority representatives are feared. The question then is how to work in a fair and honest way with people who are ultimately in a position to hurt you. For the social worker we talked to about Jenni, the challenging part of statutory child care work is reconciling health and safety issues with empowerment practice. Anti-oppressive practice can help us to understand fear in a situation like this. It has been suggested that fear is about the struggle between power and powerlessness. So service users who violently threaten practitioners 'may themselves be fearful, feeling trapped, marginalized and resentful' (Smith et al., 2004: 558). Social workers, whose conditions of work are acknowledged and who feel they have been taken seriously in relation to their fears and concerns, are more likely to maintain a dialogue with people like Jenni and enable them to take part in difficult, oppressive systems such as child protection (Ferguson, 2005).

We can see then that empowerment is not a straightforward process. It cannot provide a sufficient foundation for practice on its own. To be meaningful it needs to be related to challenging injustice, inequality and oppression (Ward, 2000):

> ...empowerment, if connected with a notion of oppression ... can become a distinctive underpinning for practice, and one which does not become colonised or domesticated in the service of the status quo.
>
> (Mullender and Ward, 1991: 19)

Just as oppression is experienced through personal everyday events, so it is important to offer people the opportunity to experience new ways of being through empowering practice (Ward, 2000).

Principles and assumptions of empowerment

DuBois and Krogsrund Miley (1992) list a number of guiding principles and assumptions underlying the process of empowerment which have been described by various authors (Solomon, 1976; Rappaport, 1981; Pinderhughes, 1983; Swift, 1984; Swift and Levin, 1987; Weick et al., 1989).

- Empowerment is a collaborative process, with service users and practitioners working together as partners.
- The empowering process views service user systems as competent and capable, given access to resources and opportunities.
- Service users must first perceive themselves as causal agents, able to effect change.
- Competence is acquired or refined through life experiences, particularly experience affirming efficacy, rather than from circumstances where one is told what to do.
- Solutions, evolving from the particular situation, are necessarily diverse and emphasize 'complexities of multiple contributory factors in any problem situation' (Solomon, 1976: 27).
- Informal social networks are a significant source of support for mediating stress and increasing one's competence and sense of control.

- People must participate in their own empowerment; goals, means and outcomes must be self-defined.
- Level of awareness is a key issue in empowerment; 'knowledge mobilises action for change' (Swift and Levin, 1987: 81).
- Empowerment involves access to resources and the capacity to use those resources in an effective way.
- The empowering process is dynamic, synergistic, ever-changing and evolutionary; problems always have multiple solutions.
- Empowerment is achieved through the parallel structures of personal and socio-economic development.[1]

These are helpful as principles to underpin our practice if it is to be truly empowering.

The legislative mandate

In the current legislative context the statutory powers available to workers in health and social care practice are being continually enhanced. There is the potential, therefore, for service users to feel further disempowered by such legislation. However, the notion of empowerment in social care is an expected element of practice in both official and professional arenas (Royal College of Nursing, 2000; Cree, 2003). Labour's modernization agenda in relation to the planning and delivery of public services is underpinned by Third Way[2] values (see box). The philosophy of empowerment included in these values is manifest within legislation, guidance and professional codes of practice through the discourses of rights, choice, participation, involvement and consultation. For example, carers' rights have been recognized through the Carers (Recognition and Services) Act 1995, which extended the duty of assessment for carers to have their needs evaluated alongside the person they were caring for. The Carers and Disabled Children Act 2000 provides for carers to have an independent assessment of their needs. The Human Rights Act 1998 focuses on promoting and upholding rights.

The Green Paper *Independence, Well-Being and Choice* (Department of Health, 2005b) addresses the challenges for social care of a changing and ageing population. This paper identifies independence, empowerment and choice as the key themes, which are embedded in proposed outcomes for adult social care. National Service Frameworks stress the need to consult with service users on all aspects of decision-making. Children and young people have to have their wishes and feelings taken into account in any decisions concerning their lives (Children Act 1989) and more recently legislation places a duty on local authorities to arrange advocacy services for looked-after children and young people leaving care in the context of complaints

(Adoption and Children Act 2002). The five aims at the heart of the Children Act 2004 for children to be healthy, stay safe, enjoy and achieve, make a positive contribution, and achieve economic well-being were identified by children and young people consulted by the government in 2003. In addition, the requirement to involve service users and carers in all aspects of planning and delivering the social work degree, which was introduced in 2003, has been described as the 'fullest expression so far' (Beresford and Croft, 2004: 61) of the commitment to the involvement of service users and carers. These are just a few examples of the wealth of legislation that now recognizes the importance of empowerment practice.

Third Way values

The values of Labour's modernization agenda are:

- Equality – equal moral worth of all human beings; equality of opportunity, not outcome; protection of the vulnerable;
- Autonomy – personal freedom; choice; political liberty;
- Community – individual responsibility; reciprocity; obligations corresponding to social rights; social inclusion as the basis for social justice;
- Democracy – empowerment; devolution of power.

(Jordan with Jordan, 2000)

Empowerment as a process

> During the depression years of the 1930s, cookery classes were organized for women in poor communities in an attempt to help them to provide nutritious meals for their families despite their low incomes. One particular evening a group of women were being taught how to make cod's head soup – a cheap and nourishing dish. At the end of the lesson the women were asked if they had any questions. 'Just one', said a member of the group, 'whilst we're eating the cod's head soup, who's eating the cod?'
>
> (Popay and Dhooge 1989: 140).

The first stage of empowerment is about making the links between our personal position and structural inequalities. For the woman in the cookery class the question indicated the start of a process of awareness about her position. This position was not about knowing that she was poor, that is her personal position, but was about making the links between the personal and the structural, that is access to power and resources. We have outlined how empowerment can be seen in terms of process and goal (Swift and Levin, 1987; Stevenson and Parsloe, 1993). It is about replacing powerlessness with 'some sense of power' so that 'confusion can give way to a feeling of co-herence' (Rees, 1991: 21). Health and social care practitioners do not instantly *give* people power; rather, as indicated by Barbara Solomon, they aim to help reduce the powerlessness that individuals and groups experience.

An empowerment perspective which assumes that issues of power and powerlessness are integral to the experience of the service user enables us to move away from pathologizing individuals to increasing personal, inter-personal or political power so that individuals can take action to improve their life situations. Within the existing models of social care practice there is a focus on the individual – problems are individualized (blame the victim syndrome). Interventions often focus on assisting individuals to cope with or accept a difficult situation rather than changing the situation on a structural level.

At a micro level, empowerment is described as the development of a personal feeling of increased power or control without any change in struc-tural arrangements. Empowerment on a macro level is seen as a process of increasing collective political power. A third level of empowerment relates to the interface of these two approaches: individual empowerment can con-tribute to group empowerment and, in turn, the increase in group power can enhance the functioning of its individual members.

Effective empowerment practice involves understanding the process of change that enables us to feel less powerless. This multifaceted and multi-dimensional process will go through a number of stages and occur at a number of levels (Rappaport, 1984). Rees (1991) develops a model for practice based on the work of Friere (1972), Rose and Black (1985) and Rosenfeld (1989) that involves a mutuality of interaction between the stages, which he describes as an 'educational device' rather than something to be rigidly fol-lowed. Individuals who make the connections between their personal con-dition and the society in which they live begin to make changes within themselves, within their families and community and wider social structures. People who become aware of the connection between their personal condition and the society in which they live have the means to evaluate their position critically. Through this process of self-discovery we are able to name our op-pression, but equally we can begin to address the causes of our oppression.

Many marginalized and oppressed groups, through personal and collec-tive struggle, have challenged oppressive practices and structures. For ex-ample, at a conference in Birmingham in 2001 called *Ask Us!* a group of disabled children and young people launched a series of six PowerPoint presentations on CDs sharing their experiences of exclusion. *Survivors Speak Out* is a national group of survivors of mental health services who campaign for better treatment for people with mental health problems and provide advice and information. *Stonewall* is a lobbying organization which challenges the discrimination of gay men, lesbians and bisexuals. An example of their work involves mobilizing thousands of individuals around the country to campaign, especially in the run-up to the votes on discriminatory legislation in Parliament. More recently, their work has involved partnerships with organizations outside Parliament to ensure that the rights and needs of lesbians, gay men and bisexuals are addressed in the wider community. *Art and Power* is an organization based in the southwest of England whose aims include the following:

- to impact on the treatment of disabled people in the wider population by the dissemination of art and learning resources through performance, exhibitions, publications and the society's website; and
- to develop and enact an access and inclusion strategy so as to develop a fully inclusive membership group in which disabled artists are involved in the running of the society and to ensure full and equal access to the work of the society.

An example of their work is Dormitory Beds (see box), an exploration of oppression through sculpture, sound and light which was first shown at Bristol New Vic Basement in 2002, and at the Brewhouse Theatre, Taunton, in January 2003.

Dormitory Beds

In the past they have turned us into dormitories
Rows and rows of the same beds, made in the same way,
The same colour mugs hung-up on the same row of hooks.
They made the world into a cold room, with us lined up in neat rows
So they knew we were alive, so they could see if we went missing
Because they didn't want us anywhere else
And then they could make us the way they wanted us
Like row after row of dormitory beds
Stripped back and made the way they wanted us
All sealed up with hospital corners
With the sheets tight and tucked like an envelope
And us pinned in their beds, each like a letter from a different world.

(art + power poets)

Norton (1978) provides a framework from which we can make sense of the complex relationships that exist between the individual and social structures. She calls this framework the dual perspective and defines it as:

> the conscious and systematic process of perceiving, understanding and comparing simultaneously the values and attitudes and

behaviour of larger societal systems with those of the client's immediate family and community system.

(Norton, 1978: 3)

This idea holds that every individual is part of two systems:

1. The societal system that functions within the norms and values of the dominant groups within society.
2. The smaller system that functions in a person's immediate environment. This latter system could be the cultural system.

When the two systems do not agree concerning norms, values, expectations and ways of functioning, then difficulties arise for individuals, families and cultural groups (Johnson, 1989). The process of understanding and comparison identified by Norton enables individuals to acknowledge differences as well as points of contact between the larger dominant system and the world of oppressed people. The dual perspective is a particular way of viewing the world – it is informed by a critical evaluation of the similarities and differences between the powerful and those who feel powerless. The perspective can inform practice with groups who have limited power and presents a way of working that is empowering. Norton uses the work of Chestang (1972) to emphasize 'the importance of an affirming attitude within the family to balance the negative effects of racial prejudice' (Kolb-Morris, 1993: 102). Chestang (1972) described the black experience in terms of two interacting systems. The society at large was described as the *sustaining* system, providing an individual with status and power, this being determined by an individual's access to resources. Embedded in this is what can be called the *nurturing* system. This system provides an individual with positive images, role models and support. The nurturing within this environment of family and community provides the space for individuals to develop coping strategies. The individual is then able to develop a sense of self and so have the resources to counteract the *'negative valuations'* (Solomon, 1976; Small, 1986; Ahmad, 1990) placed on her or him by the dominant culture.

Other writers also discuss empowerment practice taking place on different levels. Hasenfield (1987: 479) identifies three levels: the *worker–client* level, which is involved with 'improving the client's power resources'; the *organizational* level, which is aimed 'generally at harnessing the agency's power advantages to increasingly serve the needs of the client'; and the *policy* level, which ensures that 'the formulation and enactment of policy decisions are influenced by those directly affected by them'. Troyna and Hatcher (1992), in their model for analysing racist incidents in schools, move through eight levels from the interactional to the structural. However, these can be broadly grouped into three levels which, like the others, can equate with the perspective put forward by Rappaport (1985) that a person can take control of her or his own life at the level of feelings, the level of ideas and the level of being able to make a difference to the world around him or her, or the level of activity.

Thompson (1993) develops a model of anti-discriminatory theory that identifies empowerment taking place at three levels, personal/psychological, cultural and social/structural, which, Payne (2005) points out, is similar to Norton's position. At the personal (P) level practitioners can help individuals gain more control over their lives. This takes place within the cultural context (C) in which practitioners challenge assumptions and stereotypes which are rooted in the culture and values of the dominant group. These levels are in turn embedded in a structural level (S). Empowerment at this level seeks to remove structured inequalities through a collective political response or social action. Practitioners' influence is primarily at the personal level, but has less impact at the cultural and structural levels. Dominelli (2002a) is mindful of the multi-layered context of people's lives. The different levels of context that impact on individuals and practitioners working together are:

- the personal level
- the institutional domain that encompasses the family, school, welfare state, social policies and legislation
- religious or faith affiliation
- the spiritual realm
- the cultural sphere
- the local community
- the national domain
- the economy – local, national and global
- the physical environment

(Dominelli, 2002a: 22)

Locating the individual and the practitioner within his or her social context politicizes practice. Dominelli argues that understanding the interaction between the different levels which shape people's lives helps practitioners engage in empowering practice.

A model to analyse the process of empowerment

In order to understand the process of empowerment we have developed a model (Figure 5.1) that is informed by the work of a number of the writers discussed above and by 'a belief that power is not a scarce commodity but rather one that can be generated in the process of empowerment' (Gutierrez, 1990: 150). The model operates on three levels but it is difficult to express a dynamic process in a static diagram. Therefore, while the levels have been described in an order, the empowerment process does not occur in a systematic way. It is an ongoing process with shifting goals. The changes can often occur at the same time at various levels and so enhance one another. As Gutierrez (1990) notes, empowerment is a continual process of growth and change which can occur throughout one's lifetime (Freire, 1972; Kieffer, 1984).

The level of feeling or personal biography

The level of feeling is located in the centre of the model. This is the core of the empowerment process. This level is concerned with the personal experiences of the individual who is feeling powerless – which may be the service user or practitioner (Thompson, 2001; Dominelli, 2002a).

It is difficult to begin change without first being able to locate oneself. Rees (1991: 86) points out that 'the processes of empowerment may cover the story of a lifetime'. He talks about the 'promise of biography', which he explains as 'the telling of a story with a view to participating in a different way in future events' (Rees, 1991: 21). From the telling of the story, Rees explains, the one who is being listened to will become more confident in the knowledge that she or he is being taken seriously. This confidence is empowering. Certain *themes* will also emerge, so that links can be made between personal and social issues. This notion is based on the work of Friere (1972), who, by involving people oppressed by poverty in critical *dialogue*, enabled them to engage in praxis – analysing social situations and acting on that analysis. Hill-Collins (1990) points out that the process of self-conscious thought is an essential element of the empowerment process, with personal experience being a key component. In their model for analysing racist incidents, Troyna and Hatcher (1992) begin with three stages, which all concentrate on the 'feelings' level. The first is *interactional*, concentrating on the actual incident: what was done, what was said. The next is *contextual*: the immediate history of the racist incident. The third is *biographical*: the factors and characteristics specific to the individuals involved in the incident. It is this level that Hill-Collins would call the process of self-conscious struggle.

The level of ideas or changed consciousness

The second level is a continuing process of self-conscious struggle, which in turn leads to a changed consciousness – self-knowledge, self-actualization, self-definition. This will lead to increased self-respect as people learn to evaluate their self-image and gain knowledge about themselves (Rees, 1991). This equates with Thompson's 'C' level (2001) and Dominelli's cultural sphere (2002a).

At this level, then, people are able to reduce self-blame – Gutierrez (1990) explains that powerlessness leads to depression and immobilization. Raised consciousness and an understanding that we are not responsible for the negative situation enables us to 'shift focus'. We then move from feeling powerless to feeling more capable of changing the situation. We can manage this by locating problems within existing power relations. Much of the process at this level has connections with humanist and existential models and 'emphasises values of self knowledge and self control which also accept that clients have rational cognitive control of their lives' (Payne, 1991). Troyna and Hatcher (1992) identify three stages within the level of ideas in relation to young people in school: the *subcultural*, the *institutional* and the *cultural*. At the institutional stage are what they call the 'ideologies, procedural norms and practices which are promoted, sanctioned and diffused by the school', while at the cultural level they also refer to experiences of young people in terms of their 'lived experience and common-sense understanding', both locally, particularly through family networks, and within the community generally.

Developing self-knowledge and, at the level of ideas, a sense of personal power, enables people to develop new language. Rees (1991) sees language not merely as a device for communicating but also as 'a means of creating social relationships and realising the self involved in those relationships' (Rees, 1991: 95). The insight gained as connections are made between one's own story or personal biography and the biographies of other people will be indicated by new words which form a language that expresses power, for example 'I want to make my own choices', 'I know my rights', 'I'm in control'.

The level of ideas is represented in the second band of Figure 5.1.

The level of activity or political action

This level is concerned with making changes in the systems which adversely affect service users. Here practitioners are trying to promote change in social, economic and political structures in order to establish more equitable distribution of material resources and social power (Healy, 2005). One of the five skills identified by Solomon (1976) as necessary for empowerment practice is the need to facilitate organizational change, which she sees as an agency-related form of intervention in both policy and practice. This is made possible through the development of raised consciousness and the subsequent awareness of the possibility of political and social action. Hill-Collins (1990) states that the process of political action is not an end in itself for any one particular group. It is about an ability to work with others to change social institutions. For example, progressive practitioners can 'transform reactionary agencies' (Beresford, 2004: 65) in which they are located in order to provide positive experiences and services for users. However, it is assisted through the development of group consciousness, which involves the development of an

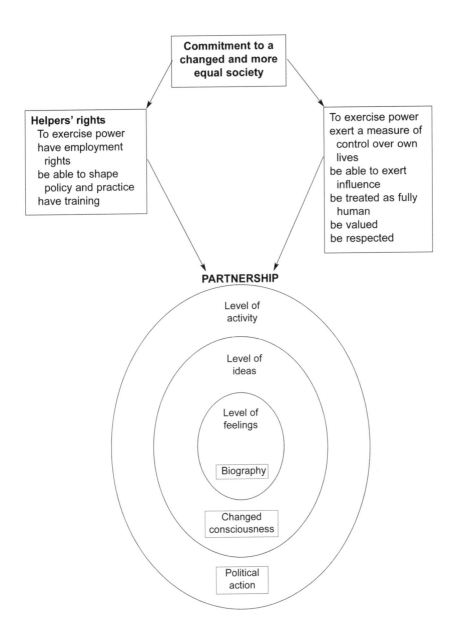

Figure 5.1   The process of empowerment: a process of personal growth that may occur at any time. Change at any one level will affect change at other levels.

awareness of how political structures affect both individual and group experiences (Gutierrez, 1990). At this level there is a very real danger that people feel doubt about the action they have been taking. This is an inevitable part of the process of growing stronger and may be evidenced in a desire for the familiar. It is often far easier to return to a difficult but familiar situation than it is to carry on. It is at this point, therefore, that the person will need the appropriate support if she or he is to resist returning to the former state of powerlessness (Rees, 1991). The objectives of empowerment at this level may be about changing legislation or policies, but can equally be about the small changes that may affect the life of one individual, which in Rappaport's (1985) terms is about making a difference in the world around us.

A continual process

The model we have developed provides a framework to cover both the micro and the macro, that is the personal and the political (Phillipson, 1992). In the diagrammatic representation of the model (Figure 5.1) the circles represent the process of empowerment at the different levels. This can only successfully operate when all those involved in the process are working in partnership with a joint commitment to a changed and more equal society.

The level of activity is an all-encompassing element of the process, taking in both the personal and the structural and involving change through political action. The diagram identifies how the process is one that is interlinked but also occurs at any or all of the levels at any one time. The process is ongoing. Change at the level of feelings will affect the level of ideas as self-awareness develops. This enables mobilization of resources at the level of action, which in turn affects one's biography at the level of feelings, as inevitably change has occurred. This is a continual process.

It may well be, however, that the process begins at the level of action, which will lead to a changed consciousness and again affect one's personal biography. Essentially change occurring at one level will affect change at other levels. The relationship between health and welfare practitioners or carers and the person they are working with is crucial, however, to enable the process to take place.

Making the connections

In trying to understand what empowerment really means, we need to bear in mind our discussions about oppression in Part I of the book. Oppression is a complex term – it is not one-dimensional but multifaceted and it is easy to be overwhelmed by the sheer scale of the problem. As with 'empowerment', the word 'oppression' can often be used without an understanding of what it means, as discussed in Chapter 2. Oppression itself is a powerful force. On a personal level it can lead to demoralization and lack of self-esteem, while at a structural level it can lead to denial of rights.

To illustrate, let us briefly analyse the case of *R v Devon County Council ex parte L* [1991] 2 FLR 541. We have used this case, which can be seen to be controversial, because:

- it is a documented case, which actually happened;
- it presents a number of ethical and moral dilemmas;
- it enables us to consider issues about men who abuse children;
- it enables us to consider issues about adult/child power relations;
- it provides the opportunity to consider the principles of empowerment in a difficult situation;
- in working with offenders, practitioners will often find themselves working in oppressive situations, and it is important not to intensify this position for the offender or alleged offender.

The answers we provide are hypothetical, based on the facts made available to us.

The facts

The case concerns an alleged child sexual abuser, Mr L. In 1986 he moved into the home of a Mrs B and shortly afterwards they began to live together as man and wife. However, he moved out in August 1987. Mrs B had two children. In December 1987 the headteacher of the school of the elder child (born 1982) contacted social services because of concern about her disturbing behaviour. Mrs B's daughter was examined by a consultant paediatrician and stated in the presence of the doctor and a social worker that Mr L had been touching her in an inappropriate manner. Some inflammation of the vagina was found but no bruising or contusions. The paediatrician took the view that although there was no physical evidence of abuse the examination findings were consistent with manipulation of her genital area.

Following a visit by representatives of the NSPCC and a female police constable, a report was written which indicated that Mr L had sexually assaulted Mrs B's daughter. He was arrested and interviewed on the same day and he denied the allegations. No criminal proceedings were ever instituted against Mr L.

In June 1988, the applicant started to live with Mrs G. She became pregnant by Mr L and later gave birth to his child. Three incidents occurred between June 1988 and September 1990. On each occasion Mr L started to live with women who were subsequently advised by social workers that if he remained in the household a case conference would have to be held to discuss possible registration of the children who lived there. In the first two cases Mr L moved out following a request to leave by the women concerned. In the third case he did not leave immediately and there were several visits by social workers as well as some correspondence. On one occasion a letter to one of the women suggested that the local authority might have to consider care proceedings in the case of her granddaughter.

The issues

1. At no time was Mr L's name on a list of abusers or child abuse register.
2. Social work intervention was not as a result of any case conference decision.
3. Four social workers believed that they were carrying out their duties.
4. None of the social workers had interviewed Mr L, but they knew that he had been interviewed by police – although no police action had been taken.
5. Each believed the allegations made by the child.
6. Mr L was illiterate and so had a different understanding of the allegations.

It was stated by Hayes (1992) that 'The social work practice in the Devon case is open to criticism on three main counts. It was high handed, it was partly ineffectual and it was unfair.' Let us consider these questions from an anti-oppressive perspective. It could be argued that if the practitioners had been informed by an empowerment perspective this case might never have been brought before the court.

Q: What was the evidence that this action was high handed?

A: The social workers made no real attempt to work in partnership with the various women that Mr L had been involved with: they could have involved the women in plans about protecting their children; they could have explained clearly the options available rather than taking a coercive approach.

Q: Why was it partly ineffectual?

A: Two of the women managed to conceal the fact that Mr L had at some stage returned to the household. Therefore contact with the children thought to be at risk was not prevented.

Q: Why was it unfair?

A: First, Mr L was not given an opportunity to be heard. Secondly, he was not given the opportunity to be a part of the assessment of risk. This meant that he could not discuss whether he still posed a threat to the children concerned.

Therefore, a just and comprehensive assessment for preventing Mr L from living in households with children did not take place.

Analysis

It is important to take account of the various power relations that exist. In this case there were a number of competing interests:

- between different professionals;
- between professionals and Mr L;
- between professionals and the women;
- between professionals and the children;
- between Mr L and each of the three women;
- between Mr L and the various children involved (that is, from the child who had originally made the allegations, his child by Mrs G and the children of the other families).

It is important also to take account of gender, race, age, class, disability, sexuality and other social divisions which play a part in determining the power relations in this situation. This also adds to the miscommunication. From the evidence, the starting point for practitioners was that the child was at risk, which started the investigation. Mr L experienced a number of feelings, one of which was a sense of powerlessness, and therefore sought the assistance of a solicitor, which brings a new element into the equation.

If we view the situation from Mr L's perspective for a moment, he was insufficiently involved in the local authority's decision-making process. That process led to a number of his personal family relationships being broken up and to him losing contact with his own child. If work had been in partnership with Mr L, he would have been given the opportunity to understand what risk was presented and to work jointly towards change in order to minimize that risk. In that assessment there would be some recognition of whether it was possible for him to live within a household with children. An effective way of working, which would also be good practice, would be to have two workers involved in the case in order to minimize the conflict of roles. By entering into dialogue with Mr L, the social workers would be engaging in the process of empowerment. Mr L may then feel able to use the law (actively seeking the help of a solicitor to take his case to court). It also enables the social workers to open up creative ways of working which means that they are less likely to violate anyone's rights.

Mr L could continue in the same pattern for a number of reasons, including feeling disempowered by the process and his treatment by the professionals involved. He also could seek further recourse to the law. Failure to afford Mr L proper procedural safeguards when intervening to this degree in his family life could be challenged under Articles 6 and 8 of the Human Rights Act 1998.

Anti-oppressive practice is about ensuring that people are not oppressed because of the protective nature of our role. It is difficult to think about anti-oppressive practice when working with someone whom we believe may well have abused his own power (as a male adult). So the practice is about helping that person to understand why his action has been seen as an abuse of power. The purpose of anti-oppressive practice in situations like this is summed up in the following comment: 'We should stop the perpetrator of sexual or domestic violence from damaging others. At the same time we should aim to free them from the social and personal bonds which lead to their behaviour' (Payne, 1994: 6).

When working with risk and protection issues, then, we need to reflect upon and evaluate our practice when using legislation. This means:

- being informed about and understanding the policy and legislative mandates underpinning health and social care practice; and
- using legislation positively to facilitate change.

A helpful checklist of questions that incorporates these points and can be used to ensure good practice in risk and protection work has been put forward by Cree and Wallace (2005):

- What is the risk? Is it positive or negative, and for whom?
- What is the relevant legislation?
- What procedures and policy frameworks apply to the situation?
- Whose rights and whose responsibilities need to be safeguarded?
- What values issues need to be considered?
- What methods of assessment should be used and why?
- How can decision-making and tasks be shared between agencies?
- What support systems are in place for you as a worker?
- What are the lines of accountability? How can these be shared?
- How will the work be monitored and reviewed?

Chapter summary

In this chapter we have briefly introduced the concept of empowerment. Our understanding of empowerment recognizes that it is not a value-free idea, and is in fact a politicized concept. Our analysis, informed by the work of a number of writers, develops a practice model involving the practitioner and service user in a partnership committed to change. The model operates at three levels: the level of feelings, reflecting the biographies of both service users and the practitioners; the level of ideas, working to achieve a changed consciousness; and the level of political action in wider society. The model therefore recognizes that the process of empowerment occurs on individual, interpersonal and institutional levels. The levels interconnect, recognizing that empowerment is not a straightforward process.

Further reading

Adams, R. (2003) *Social Work and Empowerment*. Basingstoke: Palgrave.
A general account of empowerment, particularly relevant to community and groupwork approaches to promoting self-help.

Braye, S. and Preston-Shoot, M. (1995) *Empowering Practice in Social Care*. Buckingham: Open University Press.
This provides an overview of issues of power and partnership in professional practice, focusing on the area of community care. It examines the concepts underpinning empowerment practice.

Gutierrez, L. M., Parsons, R. J. and Cox, E. O. (1998) *Empowerment in Social Work Practice: A Sourcebook*. Pacific Grove, CA: Brooks/Cole Publishing Company.
A useful book which provides specific examples of empowerment practice in various settings which will interest readers from a range of disciplines.

Activity 1

What does the term 'empowerment' mean to you?

You may find it helpful to jot down a few ideas that come to mind. Think of a time when you have felt empowered.

Describe the situation. Who was involved? How did you feel? How did you respond?

When reflecting back on that experience, what did you find helpful and unhelpful?

How might you use learning gained from this exercise to inform your practice?

How might you need to change your practice to manage the dilemmas of empowerment practice?

We all have different experiences of being empowered which lead us to an understanding of what empowerment means. Having completed the exercise, you will have come up with at least some of the following ideas about empowerment, which involves:

- gaining more control over your own life;
- becoming aware of and using your personal resources;
- overcoming obstacles to meeting your needs and aspirations;
- having your voice heard in decision-making;
- being able to challenge inequality and oppression in your life.

(adapted from Kirton and Virdee, 1992)

This is not an exhaustive list. You may wish to add to it.

Activity 2

Read the following case scenario.

> *B v B* (*Grandparents: Residence Order*) *Re*
> An application made for a residence order in respect of a girl aged 11 by her maternal grandmother and supported by her mother was refused by the justices on the grounds that the court should not make an order unless doing so would be better than making no order at all (Children Act 1989 Section 1(5)). Since the girl had lived with the grandmother for all but the first six weeks of her life and it had been agreed by the mother and

- Bearing in mind the principles of empowerment that have previously been discussed, and referring to the checklist identified by Cree and Wallace on p.xx, do you feel that this was the right decision by the court in terms of empowering the grandmother and her granddaughter?
- The grandmother went to appeal. What grounds do you think she might have for an appeal?
- Think about what might have motivated the grandmother to use the law in this way in the first place, as it is not an easy thing to do. Bear in mind how the granddaughter might feel when she cannot immediately get a response to a request to go on a school trip. Think about the grandmother's situation in a medical emergency.
- What conclusions do you come to about anti-oppressive practice and the making of an order?

Commentary

This is what actually happened. On appeal an order was made because:

1. The grandmother had found that the education authorities were reluctant to accept her authority in matters where consent was required (such as school trips) and had insisted on having the written authority of the mother.
2. There were likely to be situations in the child's life when emergency medical attention was required and the grandmother's consent was deemed inadequate.
3. There were reasons to believe that the mother's behaviour was sometimes impulsive and that pressures upon her might lead to her removing the child from the grandmother.
4. There was evidence that the child was disturbed by the seeming lack of stability in the arrangements made for her.

In this instance it would be better for the child if the order were made, particularly as Section 12(2) also provides that the person in whose favour the residence order is made shall have parental responsibility (Hargrove, 1992).

6   Partnership

His social worker came to visit,
And went through the work she had begun.
Everything he had asked
Was almost done.
Together they discussed possibilities
of the future – which was to come.
Many options she gave him
Which made it hard to decide which one.
She asked for his permission,
To do the things she wanted to do.
Happily he agreed.
The fact is she asked!

(Chrissie Elms Bennett, 1994)

The notion of including service users as participants in decisions about the
organization of social care services is not new. The Seebohm Report (1968)
mentioned citizen participation in its outline of a community-based, family-
orientated service. The Barclay Report (1982: 198) suggested 'that personal
social services must develop a close working partnership with citizens, focusing more clearly on the community and its strength'. Citizens here are
partners who directly participate in agency decision-making, while workers
are accountable to all those with whom they have a partnership relationship.
More recently core legal mandates – the National Health Service and Community Care Act 1990 and the Children Act 1989 – make the concepts of
partnership working and user involvement central to the provision of services. Joint working between health and social services is emphasized in
services for adults and service users should be involved in the assessment and
care management process. The need to share information is emphasized in
various pieces of legislation and guidance with recognition that service users
and carers will find it easier to be involved if they have information and
explanations from professionals about decision-making. Work with children
and families is underpinned by a partnership approach and the need for the
view of children and young people and their parents to be given consideration in decision-making processes. The cornerstones of partnership outlined
in the Children Act 1989 and its accompanying guidance have been identified
as:

- information
- consultation
- written agreements
- reviews
- access to complaints procedures
- access to advocacy

(Braye, 2000: 14)

The document *Working Together under the Children Act 1989: A Guide to Inter-Agency Co-operation for the Protection of Children from Abuse* (Department of Health, 1991c) was first produced to facilitate interprofessional and inter-agency cooperation and enable local authorities to work in partnership with parents and children in protecting children from abuse (although Parton (2006) reminds us that the importance of partnership working has been a key recommendation of inquiries concerning child abuse since 1973). This document stressed the need for social services departments, police, medical practitioners, community health workers, schools, voluntary organizations and any other concerned parties to develop close working relationships. In 1995 the Department of Health and Social Services Inspectorate identified 15 principles for partnership working in child protection (Department of Health Social Services Inspectorate, 1995). In relation to the care and protection of severely mentally ill people, guidance (Department of Health, 1995) looks at the roles of health service purchasers, local authorities, health service providers and other agencies and their relationships in developing a care programme approach. A further document, *Developing Partnerships in Mental Health*, was published in 1997.

Following the election of the Labour government in the UK in 1997, partnership working became central to the development of public services with the notion of 'joined-up' government through partnerships and cross-cutting approaches to solving what have been termed 'wicked problems' (Parton, 2006). Indeed, it is hard to find a policy document or good practice guidelines that does not have partnership as 'a central strategy for the delivery of welfare' (Miller, 2004: 145). The range of partnership working includes:

- partnerships between public, private and voluntary sectors;
- broad partnerships to address complex issues such as substance misuse, teenage pregnancy, regeneration, crime and disorder and social exclusion; and
- partnerships between public services and the people who use these services.

(Glasby and Peck, 2004)

We can see here that there are different kinds of partnerships:

1. partnerships between different stakeholders – agencies, community groups and so on – which involves bringing different sectors together; and
2. partnerships between practitioners and service users.

For practitioners, therefore, a range of skills are needed in order to engage in all forms of partnership working. Partnerships between individuals require different skills to working together in some of the broader partnerships, and service users need to experience positive working relations with practitioners before they are able to engage in any wider partnership arrangements. Furthermore, while the concept is now embedded within health and social care provision, informal connections remain essential to the life of communities since they 'create a web of links and relationships which support communication and cooperation between organisations and agencies and enable better coordination of community activity' (Gilchrest, 2003: 147).

In the fields of health and social care in particular, policies to improve inter-agency working include statutory obligations and financial incentives to promote and sustain partnerships (Hudson, 2002). As Holton observes, 'The message is clear: partnership is no longer simply an option; it is a requirement' (2001: 430). For example, the Health Act 1999 introduced a number of partnership-focused approaches followed by the institution of new Care Trusts through the NHS and Social Care Act 2000. While partnership working has always been an element of the delivery of these services, the imperative now is to make sustainable progress and new alliances to contribute to wider aspects of community and individual well-being (Poxton, 2004). The Act expects health and social service departments to have planning agreements that say which services will be provided, by whom, and how people will be assessed. The Local Government Act (2000) brought Local Strategic Partnerships into being so that local authorities, residents, private, voluntary and community organizations in areas eligible for support under the Neighbourhood Renewal Fund are brought together under one umbrella (Miller, 2004). In the box partnership initiatives under New Labour are identified. These primarily refer to broader partnership arrangements, although partnership working between practitioners and service users is implied.

Partnership working under New Labour

Partnership initiatives include:

- a duty of partnership between health and social care;
- joint planning frameworks;
- powers to enable health and social care agencies to work together more flexibly;

- intermediate care services to prevent unnecessary hospital admissions, facilitate swift hospital discharges and prevent premature admission to long-term residential or nursing care;
- single assessment of older people so that they do not have to give the same personal information to a large number of different health and social care professionals during assessments;
- integrated community equipment stores;
- Health Action Zones to improve health of local communities in areas of high social exclusion;
- national service frameworks applicable to both health and social services to ensure consistent access to services and quality of care across the country;
- overarching strategic frameworks to bring together key players locally from the public, private and voluntary sectors;
- Children's Trusts to integrate health, education and social care.

(Poxton, 2004)

Within this context we will now explore the concept of partnership, bearing in mind our discussions about empowerment in the previous chapter. We will then consider various partnership approaches and look at the skills needed for effective partnership working.

What do we mean by partnership?

Many different kinds of relationship are described by the word 'partnership'. Between individuals it can be as personal as an emotional relationship between two people or it can be a business relationship. People can enter into temporary or permanent partnerships with either informal agreements or legal contracts with obligations for both parties. Some partnerships include recognition of power relations by identifying senior and junior partners and most partnerships have a common goal or interest, even if it is defined rather vaguely. In most partnerships there is an element of choice, so that if one partner wants to change the arrangement it is seen as possible by the other, even if it is not welcomed (Murray, 2000; Miller, 2004).

Generally, then, partnerships can be described as formal structures of relationships which should bring together a combination of interests between more than one agency and/or individual and where the activity is characterized by:

- commitment to a common cause – often purposive change (Peckham, 2003);

- a shared responsibility for developing common aims and a strategy for achieving them;
- negotiation between people committed to working together over more than the short term and sharing risks, resources and skills;
- an intention to seek mutual benefit and synergy which could not have been provided by a single agency working alone.

(adapted from Hutchinson and Campbell, 1998;
Glasby and Peck, 2004)

This implies that partners are equal; that they 'have a right and an obligation to participate and will be affected equally by the benefits and disadvantages arising from the partnership' (Carnwell and Carson, 2005: 6). In reality this does not often happen. Commitment may vary from one context to another, and partners will have different values, levels of power and resources (Peckham, 2003; Carnwell and Carson, 2005). As Murray points out in relation to partnerships between parents and educational professionals:

> Neither the parent nor the teacher necessarily chooses the partnership – we certainly do not choose it on an individual basis as both parents and teachers are 'given' to each other. We cannot end the relationship when and if we might want to, neither can we extend it if we think it is working well; within the relationship it is assumed our common goal is one of in 'the best interest of the child' – as this is an entirely subjective matter it is a goal that cannot be assumed.
>
> (Murray, 2000: 694)

While the focus of formal partnerships is on agencies, and the needs of service users have been promoted as one of the main justifications of new partnership arrangements, it has been argued that a significant user perspective is lacking (Parrott, 2005). Experiences of service users indicate that partnership working has a long way to go to challenge the oppression felt by those representing user perspectives in organizations and those in receipt of services who want to be involved in decision-making processes concerning their lives (Brodie, 2004; Minhas, 2005). For practitioners partnership has also been described as 'not only a value but also a highly skilful form of practice' (Thompson, 2002: 2). As well as working with other professionals and communities in the situations outlined above, it also crucially means working in partnership with service users and carers. In this respect partnership can mean anything from the most cautious interpretations (as in the Barclay Report, 1982) to the most radical (Beresford and Croft, 2004), including non-participation, varying degrees of tokenism and user power (Arnstein, 1969). What links both ends of the spectrum is the notion that service users must be included as far as possible as citizens in the decision-making processes which affect their lives. Partnership working in this respect involves 'working to-wards a consensus about *what* is to be achieved and *how* it is to be achieved' (Thompson, 2002: 59). Partnership working is then about creating a climate of inclusion and collaboration which acknowledges everyone's contribution to the process (Trevithick, 2000). In particular, this involves taking the time to explore cultural differences. The social construction of partnerships as 'equal' *can* help to break down barriers – for example, actual hierarchical differences can be challenged if the philosophy is equality. But, as Miller notes, the skills of patience, commitment and perseverance are also needed, as the parties involved are likely to come to the partnership with 'a history of mistrust and antagonism, seeking to maximise their own interests' (Miller, 2004: 157).

Most commentators agree that there is no easy way to define partnership (see, for example, Peckham, 2003; Carnwell and Carson, 2005; Lloyd et al., 2005). Context is significant in thinking about the term not only because the concept of partnership has changed in use over time (Carnwell and Carson, 2005), but also because no one definition can be used across all sectors (Hutchinson and Campbell, 1998). Use of the term 'collaboration' perhaps illustrates the importance of thinking about the context of the concept. This is described as 'rather a strange term' (Golightley, 2004: 126) to use in view of the fact that one meaning of the word is to cooperate with the enemy. Nevertheless, there has been a level of suspicion between health and social care professionals in the past, which has made partnership working difficult. Policy reforms around partnership aim to encourage different groups to break down barriers and Carnwell and Carson (2005) suggest that terms like 'working together' are beginning to be used as an alternative to partnership, which, together with language like 'breaking down barriers', brings together the two concepts of 'partnership' (who we are) and 'collaboration' (what we do). For Miller (2004), however, the notion of collaboration is central to all the views that try to describe relationships between stakeholders involved in delivering services. Formal partnerships, as they are developing, are currently moving towards integration at a number of levels. For example, national policy underpins the development of Primary Care Trusts and Children's Trusts; locally there are strategic partnerships; and at an international level there are integrated responses to issues such as poverty or diseases like HIV/AIDS.

We can see from this brief overview that while the terms 'partnership' and 'collaboration' figure most prominently, alternative terms are used in a range of situations so that what could be described as a 'terminological quagmire' now exists (see box).

Terms associated with partnership working

Inter-agency working: when more than one agency work together in a *planned and formal way.*

Joined-up: deliberate and coordinated planning and working which take account of different policies and varying agency practices and values. This can refer to thinking or to practice or policy development.

Joint working: professionals from more than one agency working directly together on a project, for example teachers and social work staff offering joint group work. School-based inter-agency meetings may involve *joint planning* or it may be *sequential.*

Multi-agency working: more than one agency working with a service user, a family or on a project (but *not necessarily jointly*). It may be *concurrent,* sometimes as a result of *joint planning* or it may be *sequential.*

Single agency working: where only one agency is involved; this may still be the consequence of inter-agency decision-making and therefore may be part of a joined-up plan.

Multi-professional working: the working together of staff with different professional backgrounds and training.

Inter-agency communication: information sharing between agencies – formal and informal, written or oral.

(adapted from Lloyd et al., 2005)

Working in partnership with service users

Traditionally, in both statutory and voluntary agencies, service providers have seen themselves as official protectors of vulnerable people and so, despite legislation recognizing the need for empowerment and participation and the genuine commitment of many service providers to involve people who use their services, partnership working is not easy.

We noted earlier that the Department of Health (1995) has described 15 principles for working in partnership in child protection.[1] In summary, these indicate that working in partnership means enhancing the capacity of service users to consolidate and extend their ability to know themselves, make decisions and problem solve (Trevithick, 2000). Since partnership working involves embracing diversity and understanding the power relations between ourselves and service users, we need to appreciate how we work alongside others, which involves:

- trust
- respect

- honesty
- shared risk-taking.
  (Allison, 2005)

This, Allison suggests, means that we will be encouraged towards an eman-cipatory practice that involves service users in a process. It enables us to reach a mutual understanding of the problem and, through the process of nego-tiation, find a possible resolution: 'who might do what to help, or who might best influence behaviour seen as undesirable or self-damaging' (Smale et al., 2000: 132). How far service users feel able to contribute – perhaps because they have limited communication or they lack confidence to take on the responsibilities implied in the notion of partnership working – will have an impact on the power relations experienced by both ourselves and the people we are working with, and this is one of the challenges of partnership working: ensuring that service users remain engaged with the process and feel that their contribution is valued (Trevithick, 2000).

Thompson (2002) identifies a number of pointers for working in partnership:

- *Establish shared goals and shared plans of action* – we cannot realisti-cally expect service users to work with us if we cannot agree what outcomes they would like or what needs to happen to achieve them.
- *Recognize and build on strengths* – partnership emphasizes the ex-pertise, strengths and personal resources of service users and the contribution they can make to resolving their own personal difficulties.
- *Being self-aware* – by developing an awareness of how we come across to people, we place ourselves in a stronger position in terms of de-veloping the necessary working relationships for effective partner-ship work.
- *Mediation and conflict resolution skills* – helping to resolve conflicts through principled negotiation is a creative approach that involves looking for the common ground between parties and looking for a way forward that both can be happy with. It can be helpful in working in situations where there are unresolved conflicts, because, unlike positional negotiation, which is likely to produce a win-lose situation at best and a lose-lose situation at worst, it is less likely to generate ill-feeling.
- *Addressing the emotional dimension* – the complexity of people's lives and the situations they are in when using health and social care services means that they can and do generate 'emotional heat'. We therefore have to be *willing* to tackle complex and sensitive matters and *equipped* to do so in terms of knowledge and skills.

- *Promoting change: recognizing and dealing with obstacles* – in our work with service users we are effectively trying to promote positive change. This is unlikely to be straightforward and so we have to recognize the obstacles and deal with them as well as we can – removing them, side-stepping them and/or minimizing their impact (for example, resistance brought about by fear of change).

We should not underestimate the skills we need to develop in situations where there are clearly unequal power relations. As professionals, especially when we have a statutory role, we need to be clear about our power and authority and to be open about our power and duties (Trevithick, 2000; Ward, 2000). For example, Di Bailey (2002) describes a situation with Sally, a 25-year-old woman who had been experiencing difficulties with anorexia nervosa since her late teens. Her experience of mental health professionals following a compulsory admission to hospital and a difficult relationship with her consultant psychiatrist meant that, when she first met with Sally, Di felt that it was important to be honest about her status as an approved social worker in relation to the Mental Health Act 1983. She wanted to look at the power relationship together:

> being clear that just as easily as I could take a decision to pursue a formal mental health act assessment I could equally decide that I actually preferred to work with Sally without recourse to legislative measures, but that this required some joint effort to establish a collaborative relationship on which we might start to build some trust.
> (Bailey, 2002: 178)

From that point, Sally offered her own position in negotiating the relationship and they were then able to move on through establishing some 'ground rules' for working together to explore Sally's hopes and fears for the future rather than focusing on her eating disorder and attempts to self-harm. This suggests that working in partnership then means moving away from 'the historical tradition whereby coercion has often been wrapped up as part of the "service"' (Bates, 2005: 56) and recognizing the range of different perspectives that need to be taken into account within a partnership.

For some groups of people there may be a number of perspectives that could impact on the relationship. For example, black and anti-racist perspectives support the strengths of black communities and are designed to meet need in ways considered appropriate by black people (Ely and Denney, 1987; Graham, 2002). For Graham:

> Partnerships in the context of black communities require focus upon community strengths and capacities, and the recognition and

validation of knowledge and skills as an integral constituent of how best to ensure community involvement in the regeneration of communities.

(2002: 143)

The impact of ideology on working in partnership with service users

Although partnership is a key principle of recent legislation, it is also underpinned by familial ideology. In Chapter 4 we considered how values concerning such ideology affect legislation. This makes it all the more important to emphasize the notion of partnership and shared care as a way of facilitating families, children and young people and developing anti-oppressive practice. Consider parenting. Jordan (1990) points out that parenting is not the exclusive activity of two people carried out in their own territory. Often it is shared between a number of kin or a group of friends or an employee and employer (nurse, nanny), and involves others, such as health visitors, playgroup leaders, child minders, nursery staff or teachers, who are not usurpers of parental rights but have a complementary task in bringing up children. Graham (2002), in her critique of the Eurocentric nature of Western social work, provides a similar argument to Jordan. She suggests that an African-centred worldview regards children as the collective responsibility of communities – that is, they are valued and cared for by the whole community.

Ideally, social care services should be a part of this network. If we start from the premise of services being voluntarily received and supportive, parents would be encouraged to see services as assisting in their children's upbringing rather than compensating for their own perceived inadequacies – and this could include reception into care. Just as periods of living with friends are normal features of any family's supportive network, parents should be able to request periods of respite care, or even total care, be closely consulted about placement and be involved in the decision-making.

Case example: Danny

Five-year-old Danny is severely brain-damaged and requires round the clock medical care. His parents refused to take him home from hospital following a particularly severe epileptic fit which caused further brain damage. They felt unable to give him the care that he needed and requested that he be accommodated by the local authority. He was placed in a residential establishment managed by a voluntary agency. The residential home was only a couple of miles from where the family lived and they developed an excellent working relationship with Danny's key worker. However, the local authority considered that

Danny's needs would more adequately be met within a family environment and proposed to find a foster placement for him. The parents were unhappy about this. They wanted to work in partnership with the local authority in providing for their son, whom they loved and cared about. However, they were denied access to meetings, did not understand the decision-making processes and were not given information about reasons for decisions being made. They were told that they would be taken to court if they opposed the plans of the local authority. The clash of ideology between familial perspectives and community/shared care perspectives and the problems that can occur is evident in this story.

Since the 1948 Children Act, the principle that the family is the best place to bring up a child and that a substitute family is preferable to residential care has been written into child care legislation and underpins the United Nations Convention on the Rights of the Child (Crimmens and Milligan, 2005). Based on research evidence that residential care was not a positive option (Barclay Report, 1982; Berridge, 1985; Bamford and Wolkind, 1988; Rowe et al., 1989), it has been seen as a temporary, last resort option rather than as a positive choice for many years. Some of the reasons for this are theoretically based, particularly with reference to familial ideologies. There is therefore an expectation that families should care for their children, and it is only if the family is perceived to have failed that the state intervenes in the form of care. This then compounds the negative views of care rather than considering it as part of a process of 'shared care'. Frost and Stein (1989) argued that only by developing more flexible state support and preventive programmes would the drift towards policies which – in a divided and unequal society – act as a market transferring children to dominant class and racial groups, be stopped. Subsequently, reports by Utting (1991), Skinner (1992) and the Welsh Office (2003) have been described as setting a new national agenda for the recovery of residential child care in the UK (Crimmens and Milligan, 2005), with the situation for children looked after in state care being a commitment of the New Labour agenda. The legal obligation of professionals to take the views of young people into account when planning placements and more recent research indicating a preference by children and young people to be looked after in residential accommodation rather than foster care, is leading to changes in attitudes (Crimmens and Milligan, 2005). This points to a more prominent role for residential staff as key partners with children and young people, their parents and other professionals in care planning.

The rhetoric of partnership embraces the belief that the most neglected resources in the current systems are the ideas and experiences of service users, members of the community, basic grade workers, home helps, and so on (Rojek et al., 1988). However, health and social care agencies have been described as 'junior partners' in terms of provision (Coulshed, 1988) – relatives, friends and neighbours do most of the work. This raises a number of questions:

- Is real partnership a myth?
- Does it really support networks without taking them over?
- By engaging in partnership with users and carers, are professionals in effect exploiting those who feel a moral obligation to care?

While partnership may not be the answer to everything (Rojek et al., 1988), the skills and talents of health and social care practitioners working in partnership with carers and service users can be used to build systems of care which are more relevant to felt needs. Confusion or disagreement about what might be the shared goal of a worker and a family, for example, will make partnership working difficult. Furthermore, research examining unequal power relations within child protection indicates that the key requirements for establishing a working relationship may often be missing (Pinkerton, 2002). For example, service users (and other colleagues) need written information, manageable practical arrangements, advice and emotional support. In addition, Pinkerton notes the following advice from his work with a group of parents whose children were identified as being at risk:

- Use everyday language we can understand.
- Be realistic about how well you really know us and only write reports on us when you do.
- Don't put us under a microscope.
- Don't come across as threatening and sticking too rigidly to rules and regulations.
- Deliver on what you say you'll do and don't expect of us more than you would of anyone else in our situation.

(Pinkerton, 2002: 103)

This provides a useful set of principles for effective partnership working with service users.

Partnership working with agencies and other professionals

The editor of a volume containing the personal accounts of social workers notes that there appears to be 'a certain degree of ambivalence to "joined up working"' (Cree, 2003: 163). Cree comments that while it is mainly a positive experience which involves both learning from and contributing to multi-disciplinary ways of working, 'joint work can also be frustrating, isolating and difficult' (Cree, 2003: 163). Examples from these accounts include confronting a dominant medical model within adult mental health services (Chima, 2003) and being the only social worker in a school inclusion project (Howell,

2003). The policy imperatives for partnership working mean that agencies, professional workers and carers are encouraged to develop partnership-based approaches, enabling service users to be full citizens rather than excluding them from decision-making processes. However, some of the problematic issues around the notion of partnership can often be ignored, such as the relationship between professionalism and participation, social control and democracy, consumerism and elected representation. Cautious interpretations especially emphasize the need to identify and contain those who are defined as 'dangerous' or labelled as 'disturbed'. Dilemmas are then raised around notions of 'risk' and partnership working.

Working within the effects of existing stereotyping and labelling may also cause difficulties as other professionals may have different priorities, values, worries and concerns, pressures and constraints, objectives, legal obligations and expectations (of the service user, themselves and other professionals) (Thompson, 2000b: 137). Such differences can make multidisciplinary partnership work difficult, as well as leading to discriminatory and oppressive practice as a result of tension, mistrust and poor communication. Despite the barriers, though, a report about partnership working in mental health (the Sainsbury Centre for Mental Health, 2000) identified some common themes for successful working based on five sites in England and Wales (see box). This means that partners have to be prepared to change their culture and ways of working to accommodate all the participants in the partnership (Taylor, 1997).

Prerequisites and obstacles for effective joint working

Prerequisites:

- the attitude of senior management in seeing joint working as a priority, and a commitment to removing obstacles;
- a willingness to pioneer new approaches, if necessary going beyond central guidance;
- a history of good communication coupled with coterminosity, especially at team/local level;
- joint posts or some other form of clear management accountability for joint working;
- integrated training and supervision of staff;
- monitoring of progress.

Obstacles:

- a lack of role clarity between different professions;
- different terms and conditions of service across health and social care;

- the creation of new boundaries when joint working arrangements are introduced;
- particular professions acting as a block on change;
- the desire for all professions to defend their separate identities.

(the Sainsbury Centre for Mental Health, 2000)

Practically, Thomson (2000b: 136) identifies a number of ways individual practitioners can make sure that partnership principles are incorporated into their work, which is a positive step towards promoting anti-oppressive practice:

- Keep the channels of communication open, with service users, carers and others involved.
- Make sure that you consult with the relevant people when forming your view of the situation – work together on assessing the situation as far as possible.
- Work *with* people when carrying out your intervention – do not do things *to* them or *for* them, unless this is required by the specific circumstances of the case.
- Do not rely on stereotyped or untested assumptions in relation to either service users or colleagues.
- Remember that responsibility for resolving the situation is shared – you should not act independently of the others involved in order to deal with your own anxiety about being responsible for the outcome of the situation.

Chapter summary

The legislative mandate for partnership has developed as a mechanism for change and formal partnership arrangements now exist in all public sector work. The language of partnership is complex, however, and there are both positive and negative elements of partnership working. We have examined the terminology and identified different kinds of partnership arrangements that now exist within public sector services. The skills required for successful partnership working require practitioners to be mindful of the power relations that have an impact on the provision and delivery of services. While the legislative mandate can be seen as a positive force for change, effective partnerships require us to be mindful of the obstacles that may prevent good practice, to continue to use our skills to maintain informal partnerships and to use principles of anti-oppressive practice to develop good working relations.

Further reading

Barratt, G., Sellman, D. and Thomas, J. (eds) (2005) *Interprofessional Working in Health and Social Care: Professional Perspectives*. Basingstoke: Palgrave Macmillan.
A practical book for pre-qualifying health and social care professionals.

Burley, D. (2005) *Working in Partnership to Support Families*. London: Contin You.
A useful pack for helping practitioners to work in partnership with families.

Carnwell, R. and Buchanan, J. (eds) (2005) *Effective Practice in Health and Social Care: A Partnership Approach*. Maidenhead: Open University Press.
A helpful reader.

Glasby, J. and Peck, E. (eds) (2004) *Care Trusts: Partnership Working in Action*. Abingdon: Radcliffe Medical Press Ltd.
Illustrated with case studies throughout, this accessible book examines the rationale, skills and conditions required for interprofessional working, and provides insights into the roles and perspectives of professionals involved in health and social care.

Leathard, A. (ed.) (2003) *Interprofessional Collaboration: From Policy to Practice*. London: Brunner-Routledge.

Activity 1

Partnerships, as we have said, need to be worked at. Think of a situation in which:

- a partnership would be difficult;
- a partnership would be impossible; and
- a partnership is ideal.

This could be either in your work situation or within your personal experience. Write down your feelings about each of these situations.

- Now identify from these situations:
    - What makes you feel positive about partnership?
    - What makes you feel uncomfortable and why?
    - What makes you feel undermined or threatened by a partnership?

Activity 2

Case study

> Debra (age 22) is a white young woman with a long-standing drug habit. Her 3-year-old son Ricky, who is white, lives with his grandparents, Mary and Peter. Debra is expecting a baby and her partner, Assim (age 22), who is black, is the father. Assim is aggressive and hostile towards professionals and has been convicted of several violent offences. In the last three months of the pregnancy Debra has managed to reduce her drug use and make a home for the forthcoming baby. However, she still sees Assim regularly and they are both saying that they are committed to each other.
>
> The week before the baby is due there is a big domestic incident with Assim and the police are called. Debra is injured. As a result of the police enquiries it comes to light that Debra has been regularly assaulted by Assim throughout her pregnancy. Mary says that she feels the baby will not be safe with Debra and has offered to care for the baby after it is born. The social worker has tried to discuss with Debra and Assim the concerns raised by Mary and by the professionals involved with the family. Assim, during that interview, becomes hostile and threatening and has now refused to engage with the social worker in any further assessment. Debra is saying that she will do anything to keep the baby, including agreeing to seek further help with her drug dependency and separate from Assim.

There are a number of issues to think about here. First of all, the primary concern must be to safeguard the baby when it is born. This involves the assessment of Debra and Assim's parenting capacity, which the social worker has already started to do. Mary's offer to care for the baby would be an easy option and resolve many of the problems identified by the professionals. A potential problem here, though, for the baby, growing up in a predominantly white household, could be the development of a positive black identity. The social worker is aware that under Section 47 of the Children Act 1989 and her statutory responsibilities in relation to *Working Together to Safeguard Children: A Guide to Inter-Agency Working to Safeguard and Promote the Welfare of Children* (Department of Health et al., 1999) and the *Framework for the Assessment of Children in Need and their Families* (Department of Health et al., 2000), there are a number of concerns to be addressed. However, Debra has the right to an opportunity to see if she can care for the baby and Assim also has a right to be a parent. The social worker is working with Debra to identify her strengths. However, assessing the situation in the context of drug use and violence is complex. There needs to be re-engagement with Assim, but working in a climate of hostility to social services involvement is likely to be difficult. Debra's drug use structures her life in a particular way. She is a parent alongside trying to find money to feed her habit

– this is difficult if she has to spend all day looking for a dealer while avoiding people she owes money to. Furthermore, for the social worker, if Debra is out and about, it is difficult to make a thorough assessment and/or to observe her interactions with her baby when it is born.

Focus on those aspects of the case study which relate to partnership working with Debra, Assim, Mary, Peter, Ricky and the other professionals involved.

Consider some of these questions in relation to the case study:

*   Make a note of your immediate personal reactions to this situation.
*   What professional issues are raised for you?

Bearing in mind your answers to these questions:

*   How would the family know that you were genuine in your concern to keep them together as a family?

You need to work in partnership with Debra and Assim, and at the moment Assim is not engaged with the process. So:

*   How would you begin to establish a dialogue with Assim?
*   How would you work with Mary so that she is supportive of Debra's desire to look after her baby?
*   How would you maintain and further develop your relationship with Debra in view of the issues raised?

7 Minimal intervention

It's nice to know somebody cares
Who is interested in my welfare
A person who is always there.
Sometimes I want my freedom:
Do things for myself,
A chance to learn.
Why don't they encourage me
Instead of doing everything for me?
They don't think I am capable.
Maybe they are too scared.
Give me some responsibility
and let me make decisions.
I know I'm in a wheelchair –
but I can do things from there.
                    (Chrissie Elms Bennett, 1994)

Thelma Lewis had suffered mental disturbance for 15 years before she was found wandering the streets naked. The body of her handicapped daughter Beverley lay emaciated in a strange house which had become their fortress, stuffed with debris like a concrete representation of the chaos of Ms Lewis's mind (Jervis, 1989: 22).

Beverley Lewis was born unable to see, unable to hear and with learning difficulties as a result of rubella. Although it was considered that Thelma Lewis did not welcome intervention, it was apparent that the bond between mother and daughter and Thelma's devotion to her daughter were never in question. Beverley died starved, naked and in conditions of squalor following inadequate care by her mother, who was subsequently diagnosed as suffering from schizophrenia and admitted to a psychiatric hospital. One of Ms Lewis's daughters had been told that her mother's disturbed behaviour 'was normal for someone from Jamaica' (Jervis, 1989: 22). Thelma was an informal carer who herself needed care as her own condition deteriorated. In essence, 'Beverley was strangled in a web of ideology which has been woven to get the "nanny state" out of our lives' (Morgan, 1989).

The case of Beverley Lewis graphically brings to our attention the issues we face in discussions about intervention into people's lives: care in the community, compulsory treatment, the strain upon carers, the problems faced by health and welfare agencies in providing appropriate coordinated services, and the application of relevant legislation in directing effective intervention strategies. Commentators at the time of the death of Beverley Lewis focused on the issue of civil liberties and the fact that while the rights of Thelma Lewis were preserved, her daughter's were sacrificed – to the extent of her losing her life.

> Victoria spent much of her last days, in the winter of 1999–2000, living and sleeping in a bath in an unheated bathroom, bound hand and foot inside a bin bag, lying in her own urine and faeces. It is not surprising then that towards the end of her short life, Victoria was stooped like an old lady and could walk only with great difficulty.
> (Department of Health and Home Office, 2003: para 1.4)

When 8-year-old Victoria Climbié died in February 2000 she had 128 separate injuries and scars on her body. Victoria originally lived on the Ivory Coast with her parents, who then entrusted the care of their daughter to her aunt, Marie Therese Kouao, when she was 7 years old. She eventually moved with her aunt to London, where they lived with her aunt's partner, Carl Manning. The situation had been looked at from varying perspectives and different conclusions had been made by people from a range of professions and cultures, and this contributed to a failure to appropriately intervene and tragically ended in Victoria's death. The social worker interpreted Victoria 'standing to attention' in front of her aunt and Carl Manning as a relationship 'that can be seen in many Afro-Caribbean families because respect and obedience are very important features of the Afro-Caribbean family script' (Department of Health and Home Office, 2003: para 16.4). Medical practitioners who noticed marks on Victoria's body considered that 'children who have grown up in Africa may be expected to have more marks on their bodies than those who have been raised in Europe' (Department of Health and Home Office, 2003: para 16.4). At least two pastors at her local church told Victoria's aunt that she was possessed by an evil spirit.

As in the case of Beverley Lewis, the story of Victoria Climbié makes us face the complexity of practice when discussing intervention into people's lives. Health and welfare agencies find it difficult to provide appropriate coordinated services. Application of the relevant legislation continues to be an issue for the implementation of effective intervention strategies. Within the Children Act 1989 there are duties to both provide support services for children in need (section 17) and duties to investigate allegations of abuse (section 47). Both agendas need to be born in mind as assessment under section 17 of the Act led to a failure to appreciate the riskiness of Victoria's situation.

The case of Victoria Climbié also vividly shows the need to address the issues of 'race', culture and religion in child protection situations. Other dilemmas in working with children and families are about the paradoxes around issues of the management of risk, preserving families and acknowledging their strengths while at the same time safeguarding children (McAteer, 2002; Ferguson, 2003b; Mistry and Chauhan, 2003; Munro, 2005).

It is therefore impossible to talk about minimal intervention in any meaningful way without first discussing:

- the role of the state;
- our relationship as workers to the state;
- our relationship to those we are involved with – are they clients, patients, service users, consumers, welfare citizens, deserving poor, undeserving poor or people we work with?[1]

We will briefly explore each of these three areas in turn, which should help us to understand how and when, as either professionals or carers, we intervene in the lives of others.

The role of the state

Within health and social care practice, clients, patients or users are viewed as citizens who have paid for services either directly or indirectly, and to whom the provider of services should be accountable. This emphasis is part of a consumerist trend within public services. Supported by central and local government policies, services have attempted to be more accountable to those who use them. Citizens' charters were put forward by John Major when he was prime minister as an embodiment of this striving to be accountable. Citizenship emerged as a key concept at the time of the creation of the welfare state. William Beveridge acknowledged the central significance of citizenship in his report 60 years ago, and it appears once again as we seem to be moving into a post-welfare state age. Citizenship is not a politically neutral term. Both the left and the right have made concentrated attempts to own and control the concept. In the UK the current Labour government's view of citizenship sees the achievement of a relationship between the state and the citizen through:

> Creating opportunities for engagement in political life, ensuring that the citizen is sufficiently informed, and emphasising the social obligations and responsibilities attached to the concept of citizenship.
>
> (Miller, 2004: 40)

Citizenship 'is concerned with how the individual and the state relate to each other across public concerns and how public institutions, such as the judiciary and the polity, mediate that relationship' (Ungerson, 1993: 143).

The idea of citizenship has a long and distinguished history. It is a contested and disputed concept – different groups, all with different interests, have claimed the term (Soydan and Williams, 1998). Within health and social care practice today service users are constructed as active participants 'rather than simply being the passive bearers of rights or the recipients of services' (Lister, 1998a: 15). Citizenship implies empowerment, membership and rights. However, historically citizenship has carried with it another powerful set of values and ideas: exclusion, obligation and duty. For example, as a result of their immigration status asylum seekers are excluded from access to full citizenship rights. Therefore, only when excluded people have a say in the democratic process are they able to achieve full citizenship and inclusion (Rimmer, 2005).

It has been argued that the modernization agenda is mainly concerned with regulating the behaviour of professionals through a range of measures that prescribe practice – such as national targets, quality standards, performance indicators and national service frameworks (Jordan and Jordan, 2000). The relationship between state and local government has changed as legislation has increased state powers, duties and responsibilities, with local authorities responsible for ensuring the delivery of increasing and complex services (Adams, 2002). Local government is no longer the sole provider of services but has become more involved in commissioning and purchasing services with a mix of provision by public, private, voluntary and informal sectors. This means that practice has become caught between a number of conflicting imperatives:

- economically, within the public sector there is constant pressure to reduce costs and do more for less;
- the political climate is increasingly unsympathetic to public services;
- groups of service users have become more assertive in their demands.
  (Lymbery, 2004b)

While services aim to provide consumer choice, there is fragmentation of service provision. For example, care management has been described as 'going to a supermarket' to buy goods up to a certain price limit; or resembling street or stock markets where people are 'wheedling', 'persuading', 'doing deals', and 'juggling' (Leat and Perkins, 2000). This means that services become commodities and 'the creative work which goes on in the "space" between assessment of need and purchase of services' (Leat and Perkins, 2000: 273) has become neglected. The opportunities for creative work are grasped by practitioners but it is within the context of managing resources and the processes of the contract culture. While managers control the formal aspects of the work of practitioners, it is important to remember that there are many chances in our daily face-to-face work with service users to reinterpret agency policies and counteract managerial dominance (Lymbery, 2004b). Lymbery notes that we need to identify ways of developing empowering reflective practice which involves challenging the imposition of managerialist structures and processes.

Our relationship as workers to the state

How we interpret government legislation in the form of the policies and procedures which guide our practice will depend on how we view our relationship as workers to the state. Spending cuts and privatization policies have added to the complexity of the relationship between health and social care practitioners and the state. For example, social workers have been subject to political and media pressure to respond to the behaviour of young offenders, who in the eyes of society are being treated too leniently for their misdemeanours. There has been a consistent 'drive to press social workers into assuming a more coercive and interventionist role in policing deviant families' (Langan and Lee, 1989: 3), and in particular *irresponsible* single parents. The view that 'parenting' is 'very much a public concern and therefore a legitimate site for state intervention' leads to a triangular relationship between the state, parents and children (Parton, 2006: 99). The increasing orientation of health and welfare agencies to the needs of a market economy has meant that success is based on measurable outcomes, which places additional burdens on the worker. Public inquiries and investigations into social tragedies have blamed health and welfare practitioners either for failing to intervene or for being overzealous in their interventions into the private sphere of family life. Debates following the deaths of both Beverley Lewis and Victoria Climbié noted the need for better interprofessional working relations.

The growth of active, campaigning user groups representing those who have not traditionally benefited from health and social care services has also affected the work of social care agencies. Such groups have developed as a result of the impact of policies, procedures and practices which have not taken account of the needs of all individuals who make up the diverse society in which we live. All these factors mean that professionals are rethinking their relationship to the state and, in turn, how they should intervene in people's lives.

Our relationship to others

Personal reflection and an understanding of the theoretical frameworks that have been offered to explain what is meant by the purpose of health and social care are the precursors to any action that we take. The quality and type of intervention should be based on our understanding of the relationship that exists between practitioners, service users and carers. If our interventions are informed by a belief in partnership and empowerment, then we maximize the effectiveness of intervention with minimum intrusion into people's lives.

The language that we use to describe the people with whom we are working characterizes the nature of the relationship and, in turn, how we will intervene in their lives. Language is not neutral (Croft and Beresford, 1993; Fook, 2002). Language conveys personal, structural and ideological messages (Phillipson, 1992). It reflects the different power relations within society. Through language we make sense of our world and communicate our ideas. This is referred to as discourse, although discourse goes beyond just words (Parton, 1999) because it 'places emphasis on the context in which individual people live, in particular linguistic context, and how this not only frames our understandings of our social world but also how we construct our own identities within and through social relations' (Fook, 2002). Dale Spender (Spender, 1980), for example, has argued from a feminist perspective that in fact language is *man-made*. The term 'client' has been criticized because of its implied inequality and separateness, and other terms such as 'service user' and 'consumer' have entered our language. 'Clients' may also be 'patients' to practitioners based in the health professions; to others they will be 'consumers' of purchased services (Payne, 1994).

Different terms can also convey certain ideologies and reinforce divisions. For instance, use of the terms 'carers', 'caring' and 'dependent people' can have a massive impact on how people are perceived. People who need help with their daily living activities cannot receive the respect and autonomy they should have if they are regarded as *dependent* people. Equally, their personal relationships cannot be respected if their partner, parent or relative is treated only in relation to their role as *carer*. Therefore, it has been suggested that we need to reclaim the word 'caring' to mean caring *about* someone rather than caring *for*, with 'its custodial overtones' (Morris, 1993a: 174). Use of the term 'citizen' has been preferred by some writers, because of its link to civil rights rather than refer to people in relation to service provision (Croft and Beresford, 1993). However, the term 'citizen' has also been linked with racist immigration policies and so will always have negative connotations for black communities, who already experience discrimination.

In our intervention, therefore, we have to be aware of the way in which language can reflect power relations and have an impact on people with whom we are working. This means using the words that people themselves understand and the words by which they wish to define themselves. The language of health and welfare has been said to be a form of power (Rojek et al., 1988; Fook, 2002). It enables workers to label others and define what is acceptable and unacceptable behaviour. Terms such as 'disturbed', 'at risk' and 'in need', for example, describe behaviour from a particular value perspective and also the relationship we have with the people concerned.

Minimal intervention in practice

Having considered the context of practice we can now go on to look at the impact of minimal intervention on service users, carers and practitioners. Minimal intervention means that practitioners should try to intervene in people's lives with as little intrusion as possible and can be seen as a key principle of anti-oppressive practice (Healy, 2005). However, it also requires an understanding of the need to protect people who are vulnerable. This means that we have to be aware of the contradictory nature of our role and the impact of our intervention on service users. The concept of minimal intervention is an overarching principle but cannot be successful without a commitment to preventive strategies:

> Providing effective interventions in response to relatively low levels of need not only is a legitimate intervention but could alleviate the need for more 'heavy-ended' interventions later.
>
> (Leigh and Miller, 2005: 262)

Leigh and Miller's research confirms that minimal intervention might lead to quite major changes. Their interviews graphically show that all service users wanted was for social workers to listen and give them time and space so that they felt that they were valued and their problems were worth addressing. When they did get this, not only were they 'enormously appreciative', but 'it also appeared to work' (Leigh and Miller, 2005)! For example, a father, clearly considered to be only a 'low-risk' case, had managed to get some advice and support by telephone for concerns that he and his wife had about their 13-year-old daughter. Both the parents and their daughter felt that this small contact made a big difference. The daughter explained that things were better because they had subsequently talked together as a family about the problems. Another young woman who was regularly truanting from school had met a social worker several times. Here the social work contact was valued because the worker took time to speak to everyone in the family as well as teachers. She spoke to the young woman on her own but also respected all the family members, which was evidenced through:

- asking the parents' permission to talk to the young woman;
- not acting as an expert; and
- acknowledging that she 'could not work miracles' (that is, the limitations of her role).

The relational aspects of the intervention are clearly important and a key skill for critical practitioners is to be able to communicate across difference and put into action the values that underpin anti-oppressive practice. Holland and Scourfield (2004) use the work of Sennett (2003) to suggest that the concept of respect, which is highlighted in the research outlined above, is also essential to working in high-risk situations such as child protection. Partnership with service users goes beyond a rights-based approach to one that recognizes the importance of human relationships, which we discuss further below.

Links to practice: Beverley Lewis

Let us look back at the case of Beverley Lewis and consider some of these issues. The state provided the legislative framework within which intervention could have been facilitated. Despite criticisms of the lack of available legislative powers at the time, the intervention appeared to focus on the need for compulsory powers rather than a consideration of the preventive measures available. The lack of appropriate intervention could be attributed to racism within society, attitudes about the privacy of the family, and the protection and control of vulnerable people. What were the dilemmas posed to professionals by this case? We can begin to answer this by posing the following questions:

- Should the practitioners have acted as guardians to Beverley?
- Should the practitioners have respected Thelma's wishes in refusing intervention?
- Did Beverley have the right to intervention against the wishes of her mother?
- Was the role of practitioners to maintain this family and support Thelma as a carer – bearing in mind the close bond between them (as the coroner commented, to have separated Beverley from her mother would not have been in her best interests)?
- Should the focus have been merely on these two people or on assistance given to the wider family and community networks to support the mother in the face of her hostility to statutory intervention?
- Should people deemed to be schizophrenic have the right to look after their own children?
- Should support services be based on the carer's needs rather than the person cared for or vice versa?

The story of Beverley Lewis sadly indicates the problems of intervening appropriately in the lives of vulnerable people. Workers were given the power to intervene, which could have enabled Beverley Lewis to live a fuller life. The practitioners in this case appeared to see the law as a stumbling block rather than a vehicle for change. Because they considered that they had no *powers* to intervene, they were able to claim that they had no *duty* to intervene. But ethically they had obligations. At the end of the day, *no action at all* can be as oppressive as intrusion into people's lives. If there are high-quality and reliable support services then private care, in the context of a strong bond between two people, can be supported within state provision of care (Ungerson, 1993).

When to intervene?

The concept of minimal intervention is enshrined in legislation; for example, in the Children Act (Section 1(5)):

> Where a court is considering whether or not to make one or more orders under this Act with respect to a child, it shall not make the order or any of the orders unless it considers that doing so would be better for the child than making no order at all.

However, as Braye and Preston-Shoot (1997) point out, the law does not provide the answers as to when or how to intervene, and so a practice as well as a legal rationale is needed for intervention. Furthermore, intervention occurs at individual, family, group, organizational, community and societal levels and requires the ability to use effectively a range of skills and methods at varying times (DuBois and Krogsrund Miley, 1992).

Perhaps the most severe form of intervention is the use of compulsory powers. The justification of compulsorily removing someone from their home is that the person concerned is at risk, which may be because:

- of other people, usually their own relatives;
- of their own actions;
- they are placing others (known or unknown) at risk.

(Stevenson, 1989)

Stevenson suggests that these risks fall into five basic categories.

1. *Physical injury or neglect.* The focus has primarily been on children in the past, but local authorities are also required to have adult protection procedures and a service plan as a result of guidance issued under 'No Secrets' (Department of Health, 2000b).

2. *Those considered to be at risk either socially or emotionally (rather than physically)*. It is difficult to define such abuse. It is, however, possible to intervene in the lives of children and young people in such situations using child care law, but there are no legislative powers for adults.

3. *Those who are a physical risk to others in the immediate environment which the behaviour of the individual may occasion*. While it is more usual in the case of mentally ill adults, this can include children and young people alleged to be uncontrollable by their carers, or older people who may perhaps be aggressive towards a partner.

4. *Social risk*. Young offenders can be identified in this category and can be seen as a risk to the community in terms of the breakdown of law and order rather than any physical risk (unless the offences are violent or endanger life). Stevenson suggests that this category is more open to exploitation by those with power, particularly in the case of young people.

5. *Environmental risk*. This is where the lifestyle of an individual causes problems for others; for example, where squalid living conditions lead to infestation, causing health hazards to others in the community.

Braye and Preston-Shoot point to the need for a framework for decision-making, which they say is both a 'safety device and a moral imperative' (1997: 76). Such a framework, they say, provides for consistency of practice and consists of three parts.

1. *Structure*. This is a series of questions which can be used to assist judgement. They may be asked of service users, colleagues, managers or themselves and come under the headings of what, when, who and how?

2. *Substance*. This is essentially a combination of theory, knowledge and practice wisdom which informs the decision-making process. In particular, Braye and Preston-Shoot cite examples of checklists which can be used to appraise a situation and are increasingly suggested in policy and guidance.

3. *Principles*. These are the values which underpin the decision-making processes.

A framework for decision-making has to take into account a number of factors. In particular, it has to provide for legal knowledge and practice wisdom to work together. Of course, it is not easy to do this and to use the law positively. As Braye and Preston-Shoot point out, the lack of precision over definitions and the power it gives to professionals means that there are many different interpretations that can be made. In using the law positively, however, to promote anti-oppressive practice and to minimize intervention in people's lives, it is important to make informed decisions.

Discussing investigation in child protection, Brayne and Martin (1990: 166) consider the vital words in the legislation to be 'safeguarding and promoting the welfare of the child'. Safeguarding and promoting, they say, are 'positive words', whereas inaction is 'rarely positive' (p.170). The dilemmas for those investigating arise because of the tensions between outcomes. Corby notes that while intervention is justified when children are considered to be at risk of serious harm, 'the issues are rarely clear cut and in Britain there has traditionally been much circumspection about intervening into families' (Corby, 2002). But those involved in an investigation will be involved in trying to balance societal demands and the needs of the young person. In the light of this, Brayne and Martin (1990: 167) suggest that practitioners will always be involved in the following issues.

- *Therapeutic intervention.* This means trying to help the young person (which can be achieved through using various powers, duties and services).
- *Statutory control.* Using the courts and statutory powers to produce evidence that the grounds for an order are satisfied.
- *Prosecuting the perpetrator.* In the murder of a child, prosecution is acceptable. In the case of abuse, the situation is more difficult and so 'investigating the facts with the child and the child's family for this particular end, whilst still trying to give therapeutic support becomes even harder'.

It is important to remember that there are other ways of protecting children than recourse to legislative action. This is emphasised in policy documents which indicate that 'providing access to a wide range of support services to help children in need is likely to be equally important' (Brayne & Carr 2003: 292)

The fear of infringing civil liberties was at the heart of the controversy about levels of intervention concerning the care of people with a mental illness or mental disorder living in the community. There has always been media stigma attached to the 'dangerous paranoid schizophrenic' which has been fuelled by some high-profile cases.

The most significant case of recent times is that of Christopher Clunis, a paranoid schizophrenic who stopped taking his medication while living in the community. Lack of powers to enforce community treatment led to him stabbing Jonathan Zito to death in 1992. Borne out of this came the Zito Trust (available online *www.zitotrust.co.uk*) who set out a charter to:

- work towards the reform of mental health policy and law;

- provide advice and support to victims of community care breakdown;
- carry out relevant research into services for the severely mentally ill and disordered.

Following on from Clunis came the case of Ben Silcock. He was also diagnosed with a schizophrenic illness and by choice lived alone in a council flat, supported by his family. Limited support was provided by the day hospital but he had been banned from a local centre run by the charity MIND after he had been violent towards a member of staff. However, he stopped taking his medication and, after he entered a lion enclosure in a zoo to share his New Year's Eve lunch with the animals, he was mauled to death. At the time, the legal director of MIND, Ian Bynoe, commented that discharged patients should be allowed to take risks if they are capable of living in the community with the proviso of intervention if it is needed. In Ben's case, when he stopped taking medication, he felt part of a colourful world and powerful, which as his mother commented, was more exciting to him than the real world. One could argue that we all have a right to choose a life that we find exciting – and if the real world was deadened by drugs, then perhaps we too would choose not to take them.

Debates following situations like that of Christopher Clunis and Ben Silcock have led to calls for community treatment orders and proposals for the radical overhaul of the provisions of the Mental Health Act 1983. Discussions focus on protection of the public and management of risk, on the one hand, and patient autonomy[2] and rights on the other (Bartlett and McHale, 2003; Laing, 2003). In the box, we look at how these debates have informed changes in policy and practice where human rights issues are raised as a result of the compatibility of the Human Rights Act 1998 with mental health legislation;[3] the concept of mental capacity; and the way that the law can be used (in the absence of community treatment orders) to enable detained patients to live in the community.

Some challenges and changes in mental health legislation

Significant developments have come in the form of challenges from the implementation of the **Human Rights Act 1998**. When legislation appears to breach the Convention rights, a court can declare it 'incompatible'. The government then has the power to correct the problem by quickly introducing new legislation. For example, breach of the Article 8 right to a private and family life for detained patients is especially apparent in the case of who their nearest relative is for the purpose of the Mental Health Act 1983. A declaration of incompatibility allowed the government to continue with existing legislation with the promise that the legislation would be reviewed. The effects of the National Health Service and Community Care Act 1990 and the National Health Service Plan; recognition of fragmented mental health services leading to policy implementation of the National Service Framework for Mental Health; and other significant case law, directed policy-makers to the need for new legislation. The review promised by the government was an overhaul of the Mental Health Act 1983 in the form of the highly publicized Mental Health Bill.

One further and extremely significant challenge to existing legislation concerned a 49-year-old man with autism who was an in-patient at Bournewood Hospital. The case was heard at the European Court of Human Rights and addressed issues of capacity (see Chapter 12, 'Tony's walks'). This important case contributed to the rapid introduction of the **Mental Capacity Act 2005**. At the time of writing the new Mental Health Bill is in its third draft and still does not look likely to be presented to Parliament in its current form. However, parts (some say the best bits) of the original draft of the Bill found their way into the Mental Capacity Act 2005.

The impact of the legislative review since Christopher Clunis (1992) resulted in extensive review and radical overhaul of the mental health legislation. This followed the outcry from various sectors on the issues of persons using medication in the community. The proposed new Mental Health Bill sought to address this issue in the form of **Community Treatment Orders** (CTOs). However, existing legislation and subsequent case law have effectively given us 'community treatment orders'. This is because a detained patient can now be granted indefinite leave by the responsible medical officer under section 17 leave (Mental Health Act 1983) with a recall to hospital if the patient fails to engage in treatment. The responsible medical officer can renew the original detention if he/she 'considers that hospital treatment constitutes part of the patient's care plan' (Jones, 2004b: 108). Extended hospital leave of over one year is not uncommon and, although threat of hospital recall if the patient does not engage in the treatment programme is coercive, it is also an option for *minimal* restriction in the care of a person with a serious mental illness. Understandably, there have been challenges to the use of extended section 17 leave such as *L v Sweden*, app. no. 10801/84 (cited in Jones, 2004b: 109) but the European Commission held that granting leave of absence with a condition that a patient accepts medication did not contravene their human rights. This welfarist approach to continued use of legislation in effect (paradoxically) empowers the service user to live in the community as independently as possible with a functional care plan and community support, where the alternative would likely be continued admission. This is a welcome step forward in finding ways of working anti-oppressively with service users in this position.

Jones, R. (2004b) *Mental Health Act Manual*. London: Sweet and Maxwell.

Cliff Hoyle, ASW Bristol, 2006

Commentators, including campaigning organizations such as MIND and Rethink, argue that such differences are symptomatic of confusion in the government's thinking and approach to the reform of mental health services (Bartlett and McHale, 2003; Laing, 2003). Debates in cases such as these are necessary so that legislation does not become more oppressive, and indicate how important it is for practitioners, carers and service users to understand the scope of powers under the law.

Finally, within these debates we must remember the people concerned. So many professionals and interested parties have an opinion. But often those who are the subject of such intense scrutiny have no one to represent them. In all these cases their silence is concerning. For example, we do not know about Victoria Climbié's probable experiences of being frightened, confused and in pain during the time that she was living in England (Cooper, 2005). One of the reasons why we may not hear their voices is that Victoria and others like her may well bring out in us mixed emotions – including fear and even disgust at 'the smells, dirt and the notions of disorder' (Ferguson, 2005: 790) which surround them – and we may be resistant to engaging with the pain of individuals. This is a tension for anti-oppressive practitioners, who are committed to understanding the situation of marginalized people yet experience the 'feelings of disgust which appear to judge and oppress people who are invariably already subordinated' (Ferguson, 2005: 790), and this can be taboo to acknowledge. Such feelings can stop us from intervening appropriately – either doing too much or too little.

The response of welfare states to deaths of children has been the creation of more bureaucratic solutions through legislation, procedures and guidelines (Ferguson, 2004), resulting in a reconfiguration of the relationships between the state, professionals, children and their families as the role of the state has become 'broader, more interventionist and regulatory all at the same time' (Parton, 2006: 139). Ferguson points out that reorganization of child protection services following the Laming Report (2003) has not paid attention to 'the complexities of the relationships involved in the work' (2004: 215). Countering the increasing interventionism of legislation and guidance requires us to develop 'emotionally alive' relationships with families in order to gain a real understanding of the nature of relations within them, which in turn alerts us to any 'potential risks, dangers and disturbances' (Cooper, 2005: 7). This does not give us grounds to act, but it should inform our practice and understanding of the lives of children and families. While practitioners are expected to raise and share concerns at an early stage to safeguard children, we have to be aware of the danger of intrusive practice within a framework of what is now effectively a mandatory reporting system. Minimal intervention involves hearing, listening and taking account of their voices. Hearing the voices of service users is the starting point to enable people to gain control of their lives. In relation to children, Parton points out that:

This is a major challenge. In a period of increased anxiety about childhood, it is understandable that there is an emphasis on adults wanting to regulate the lives of children more and more. It takes considerable maturity to give the primary control to children and young people themselves so that they can report what they want, where and when, and how 'their concerns' should be addressed, so that they feel that they have a large degree of control about what happens to them.

(Parton, 2006: 186)

We would argue that this applies to any situation in our work with service users.

Judgements are made according to our value position, our experiences and available facts. Our decision to act is based on how we interpret a given situation, which in turn guides our level of intervention. In considering risk, the issues of *needs, rights* and *harm* have to be balanced. This balance is about recognizing the power we have rather than being patronizing and over-protective. It is also about ensuring that everyone involved has access to necessary information. For those who are unable to articulate their needs, it is about ensuring that they have someone who can act as an *advocate*. The *assessment* of risk, therefore, is no easy task and needs to be made in *partnership* with all concerned.

The word 'intervention' conveys a notion of intrusion into people's lives and so, it could be argued, it is oppressive and by its very nature indicates where the dominant power relations are situated. Given such an observation, perhaps a more useful term could be that of 'interaction' rather than intervention. This reminds us that we should be working in partnership and so we may be less likely to be accused of either violating rights or, at the other end of the spectrum, neglect. This is not to legitimize a vague and unfocused approach to the work that we do, but reminds us to think about such work and how we can promote anti-oppressive practice. Of course, it can equally be argued that to call the process 'interaction' is dishonest in situations of compulsion, and that the word 'intervention' more accurately reflects what is happening. To describe the process as interaction would only be relevant, therefore, in cases of *minimal* intervention. The language used conveys the type of relationship that the worker has with the service user – it relates to the practice that is carried out.

Chapter summary

In this chapter we have looked at the context of our practice in relation to the state. The principle of minimal intervention means that we aim to intervene in the least intrusive ways possible in order to ensure the oppressive elements of health and social care practice are challenged. Minimal intervention is an over-arching principle which requires a commitment to preventive working and creative ways of responding to need. Through reference to a number of well-known situations, we consider the concept of minimal intervention in more detail and the dilemmas that practitioners face when intervening in the lives of service users.

Further reading

Burke, B. and Dalrymple, J. (2002) Intervention and empowerment, in R. Adams, L. Dominelli and M. Payne (eds) *Critical Practice in Social Work*. Basingstoke: Palgrave.
Using a case study of Dawn, this account examines the dilemmas of intervention and empowerment.

Healy, K. (2005) *Social Work Theories in Context: Creating Frameworks for Practice*. Basingstoke: Palgrave Macmillan.
Chapter 9 of this book provides a useful analysis of anti-oppressive practice, locating minimal intervention as one of the key principles.

Parton, N. (1999) Reconfiguring child welfare practices: risk, advanced liberalism, and the government of freedom, in A.S. Chambon, A. Irving and L. Epstein (eds) *Reading Foucault for Social Work*. New York: Colombia University Press.
This chapter analyses changing discourses of social work, focusing on risk and risk management.

Sayce, L. (2005) Risk, rights and anti-discrimination work in mental health: avoiding the risks in considering risk, in R. Adams, L. Dominelli and M. Payne (eds) *Social Work Futures: Crossing Boundaries, Transforming Practice*. Basingstoke: Palgrave Macmillan.
An exploration of discriminatory risk practice in relation to disabled people and mental health service users and how to avoid limitations imposed by risk thinking.

Activity 1

Debra and Assim – case study revisited

Debra (age 22) is a white young woman with a long-standing drug habit. Her 3-year-old son, Ricky, who is white, lives with his grandparents, Mary and Peter. She is expecting a baby and her partner, Assim (22), who is black, is the father. Assim is aggressive and hostile towards professionals and has been convicted of several violent offences. In the last three months of the pregnancy Debra has managed to reduce her drug use and make a home for the forthcoming baby. However, she still sees Assim regularly and they are both saying that they are committed to each other.

The week before the baby is due there is a serious domestic incident with Assim and the police are called. Debra is injured. As a result of the police enquiries it comes to light that Debra has been regularly assaulted throughout her pregnancy by Assim. Mary says that she feels the baby will not be safe with Debra and has offered to care for the baby after it is born. The social worker has attempted to discuss with Debra and Assim the concerns raised by both the professionals involved with the family and Mary. Assim, during that interview, becomes hostile and threatening and has now refused to engage with the social worker in any further assessment. Debra is saying that she will do anything to keep the baby, including agreeing to seek further help with her drug dependency and to separate from Assim.

The next morning Mary phones the social worker and tells her that Assim had been to see her the previous evening and had told her that he would never allow her to look after his baby. He apparently threatened Mary and Peter, telling them that if they interfered he and Debra would move away and make sure that they did not know where they were living. Mary was frightened that they would take Ricky as well. Ricky was really upset after Assim's visit.

The situation introduced in the previous chapter has now developed. There are a number of decisions you could make in working with this family in the light of the current situation. These need to recognize the needs within the family but also acknowledge the level of risk that may exist. Any strategy developed has to appreciate the strengths of the various members.

- What do you think are the strengths of this family?
- How might you ensure that your intervention with the family is not experienced as intrusive?
- How do you ensure that the rights of this family are respected – that they are neither overlooked nor drive the family apart? Consider all the people involved: the baby, Debra, Assim, Ricky, Mary and Peter.

Activity 2

How would you define risk?

Think of three situations where you have consciously taken a risk:

1. What were the advantages of doing so?
2. What were the disadvantages?
3. Do you feel that vulnerable people should be allowed to live in conditions that are hazardous to their health and place them in danger if they refuse help?
4. Should residential care be used to protect people from risk at the cost of depriving them of their liberty?
5. How can vulnerable people prevent medical treatment from being forced upon them?

8 Implications for practice

Be Sure

If you want something real badly
And you're feeling insecure
There is only one thing I've got to tell you
And that is to be sure

Be positive It's your prerogative
You're the only one who can open up the doors
Life is full of decisions
Make sure yours are not poor
        (Christopher Richard Kwaku Kyem, 1994)

Framework for anti-oppressive practice

We hope that from Part I you gained an understanding of the theories and ideologies informing anti-oppressive practice and the legislation that impinges on the work of health and social care practitioners and carers. We do not for one minute suggest that this is easy, nor should you assume there is a straightforward flow from theory to practice. However, our intention was to provide a theoretical basis for Part II, where we went on to look at some elements of anti-oppressive practice.

In this chapter we present a conceptual framework for practice. This is informed by the preceding chapters and based on Phillipson's (1992) model of anti-oppressive practice. We have arrived at this modified version through our own experiences of working with people in various situations. You may wish to use this model, adapt it or develop your own – but we offer it as a first step.

The framework, shown in Figure 8.1, acknowledges the reality of oppression and inequality that exists in society. Our experiences of oppression (our biography) determine our responses and shape our *value* base. Our understanding of that reality then assists us to research and select information which increases our *knowledge* base. This then helps us to develop the *skills* necessary to help us practice in ways that do not further oppression and inequality. In practice, our knowledge, values and skills are brought together

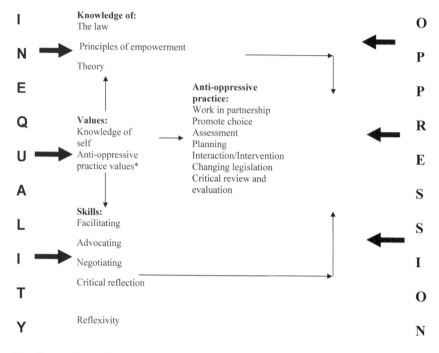

* See Chapter 4 for anti-oppressive practice values.

Figure 8.1   A framework for anti-oppressive practice

in such a way that our work with others is empowering at both personal and structural levels.

The framework is not static, and through constant evaluation we refine our responses as we continue to seek out knowledge, interrogate our values and develop our skills. To do this we need a system of self-evaluation to enable us to develop an anti-oppressive perspective. Since anti-oppressive practice is about transformation, we can only develop such a perspective if we are able to critically analyse situations as well as have a system for critical self-analysis (Adams et al., 2005a). The self-assessment questions in Chapter 13 (Activity 1) can be used to assist our personal critical evaluation of practice.

Working with Sieta

Case example: Sieta

Sieta is an 84-year-old black woman whose husband died a year ago, leaving her on her own. She was born in Jamaica and moved to Manchester to work as a nurse in the 1950s. She is becoming forgetful and has been diagnosed as 'depressed' since her husband died. Sieta uses a walking stick to move around the house due to a long-standing back problem. She finds it hard to socialize with others as she did most things with her husband after he retired. Sieta has a care line, which she does not always remember to put on and once or twice recently has left the front door open. She finds it difficult to carry out personal care tasks and her daughter-in-law, Ruby, helps her with daily tasks such as dressing, showering and preparing food. Sieta enjoys cooking but does not always remember to turn the cooker off and has had a couple of accidents recently when she has left a saucepan on. Sieta's son, Delroy, takes her to appointments and a neighbour, Mark, calls in most days and helps with bits of shopping. Occasionally her granddaughter, Emma, calls in and helps out. Everyone is becoming concerned about Sieta, and after seeing her GP a referral is made to a psychogeriatrician and social services.

Sieta

I really like living here and want to try and manage on my own but I miss Edwin – he did so much to help me. Ruby and Delroy are good, but it's not the same as having someone here all the time. Mark keeps telling me I shouldn't be here on my own but Dr Burns seems to understand that I want my independence. The trouble is that Delroy has said another doctor is coming to see me. I don't know why because I always go to the surgery to see Dr Burns.

Delroy

Poor Mum seems to have gone downhill since Dad died. I hope the specialist can help – I've tried to explain to Mum why he is coming but she doesn't seem to take it in. I love seeing Mum but it is hard trying to manage her life as well. But she has done so much for me and the family over the years and always been a good grandmother to Emma, that I feel now that this is my opportunity to show her how much she means to me.

Ruby

I can see Sieta getting worse each day. It is getting more and more difficult trying to get things done for her in the morning. It's a good job I only work part-time, but it's very tiring. I hardly see my own mum these days, which I miss. If I could just pop in and have a cuppa with her like I used to – it would be so much nicer. Mark's good but he is worried that she will burn the house down one day. She is so independent, it is difficult to know what to do. I don't know how she'll take the specialist visiting – it wouldn't surprise me if she just ignored him. I can't talk to Delroy about it . . . he doesn't see her every day like I do and thinks I'm moaning, when really I am just concerned. She is very kind and thoughtful – Emma just loves to call in to chat with her, but she is a teenager and has her own life to lead. I can't ask her to help out.

Mark

Sieta is a part of my life – I know she's not family, but I've lived next door to her for over 20 years and watched Delroy, and now Emma, growing up. She's always been there for others – I don't know what everyone in our street would have done without her over the years. I just worry now that one day she will have a serious accident and no one will be there when she needs them.

What next?

It is clear from the individual stories that each person in the family has her or his own feelings and experiences of the situation. It is our role to respectfully listen to all those viewpoints as part of engaging in a process of dialogue (Powell, 2005). Milner and O'Byrne suggest that 'storying the separate lives of the person and the problem, encourages a sense of authorship of one's life, a sense that service user and worker can co-author a future story . . .' (Milner and O'Byrne, 1998: 155). You may think that it is unlikely that everyone in the family will tell you their story. You are right. They will not, and if they do, it will take time. We therefore need to be aware of what might be happening for each individual and be aware of their stories as part of the wider structures. If we are committed to providing the means by which people can realize their potential and access their rights, we must be aware of how we can use legislation to mobilize resources, however hard that might be, and use our skills to increase available choices.

We can see that the stories of the various people involved present a number of dilemmas, both for the family members themselves and for any professionals who might be involved with them. The stories can therefore be seen as issues about personal responsibility, structural disadvantage or legal duty (Jordan, 1990; Fook, 2000; Parton and O'Byrne, 2000).

If we consider these stories, first, in terms of the *moral obligations* of the people involved, then we have to think about individual rights and responsibilities people have to each other within personal relationships and communities. Jordan points out that 'moral duties arise out of lives which are interdependent, commitments which are mutual, and communities with common interests' (Jordan, 1990: 21). Here are some questions to think about:

- Should Sieta be helped to keep her independence?
- What responsibilities do Ruby and Delroy have in relation to Sieta?
- What role does Mark have?
- What are the responsibilities of the professionals involved?

These pose ethical dilemmas for everyone involved and the perceptions of these different people will depend on various personal and social factors (Littlechild and Blakeney, 1996). We therefore need to acknowledge the moral and political dimensions of our practice.

Secondly, the same stories could be considered in terms of the *structural disadvantages* faced by those involved. The context of care is that the family is often the provider of 'community care' (Thompson, 1995; Watson et al., 2004). There is a continuing assumption that 'if you care about someone you should be willing to care for them' (Means and Smith, 1998: 40). The care and nature of support in families is complex (Finch and Mason, 1993), and women often take on caring responsibilities (Orme, 2002), which feminist perspectives suggest relate to the unequal power relations between men and women (Finch and Groves, 1980; Dalley, 1983; Ungerson, 1993). However, the gendered nature of care could be changing in the UK, as statistics increasingly indicate the diversity of carers. For example, the 2001 Census suggests that approximately 175,000 young people are carers, while the General Household Survey 1995 (published in 1998) showed that 42 per cent of carers are men. Carers' organizations argue the need for more support services to be available for carers, whose work is often unrecognized. This compounds the failure of services to meet the needs of frail older people despite the development of National Service Frameworks and legislation such as the Carers (Recognition and Services) Act 1995. As a black service user, Sieta is likely to find that because racism also structures the delivery of health and social care services (Penketh and Ali, 1997; Adams, 2002) mainstream services may not be able to meet her needs (Chahal and Ullah, 2004).

Older people from black and minority ethnic communities

(Extract from National Service Framework for Older People)

10. The proportion of older people from black and minority ethnic communities is small but growing. It was estimated that between 1981 and 1991, the percentage growth of people of pensionable age from black and minority ethnic groups increased by 168 per cent (from 61,200 in 1981 to 164,306 in 1991). Figures from the 1991 Census estimated that the total black and minority ethnic population was just over 3 million (5.5 per cent of the total population of Great Britain).

11. Local health and social care services should recognize the greater prevalence of some illnesses among specific groups of people, for example increased rates of hypertension and stroke among African-Caribbeans and of diabetes among South Asians. This will become increasingly significant as these populations continue to age.

12. At the same time, all services should be culturally appropriate, reflecting the diversity of the population that they serve, and ensuring that services are accessible for those who do not have English as their first language. The needs and wishes of each individual should be recognized and taken into account as far as possible in planning their health and social care.

(Department of Health, 2001)

Ageism[1] and stereotyping have a pervasive influence on our behaviour. Ageism compounds the discrimination that marginalized groups experience throughout their lives (Gorman, 2005). Under-use and restricted choice of services in relation to community care for black and minority ethnic people is significant (Butt, 1996). Despite the growing proportion of older people from black and minority ethnic communities (see box), few attend local authority day centres or care homes. The lack of other black service users and Eurocentric approaches to activities and food mean that black service users prefer to use local voluntary organizations that will meet their specific needs (Webb and Tossell, 1999). The ontology of old age (Thompson, 1995) helps us to understand Sieta's particular situation as a Jamaican woman living in an English city. 'Ontology' is the *study of being* and in relation to old age it raises questions about what it is to be old in society, which in turn means taking into account issues of life, death, grief and loss. Sieta has experienced multiple losses, including:

- her family and country of origin;
- her dignity and respect as a result of racism and ageism;

- her role as an independent person;
- the death of her husband; and
- her declining mental and physical ability.

Thirdly, the stories could be considered from a managerialist perspective, focusing on *legal duty*. The dominance of managerial values of 'efficiency, economy and effectiveness' undermine anti-oppressive values such as 'fairness, justice, participation and rights to representation' (Payne, 2000: 31). This is evidenced in the operation of care management systems which dominate work with older people and have resulted in a mechanistic approach to working with complex situations. Debates about prioritizing recipients of care packages and the resulting complex assessment forms (Means and Smith, 1998) mean that care management is characterized by:

- Routinized working – swift assessment, unimaginative planning and cursory review.
- Large caseloads, with the emphasis on processing a high volume of work rather than client outcomes.
- Proliferation of forms for various aspects of practice.
- Tasks are split, and provided by different workers, leading to a general deskilling of the workforce.
- Emphasis on formal services rather than the linking of formal and informal services.
- Discouragement of the counselling and interpersonal aspects of social work.

(Sturges 1996: 49, cited in Lymbery, 2004a)

These points are echoed in comments made to us by care managers we spoke to in the course of writing this book. Their experience of working as care managers was that they felt bogged down by procedures. The time that they spent with service users was limited because of the workload, amount of time spent filling in forms, and agency time allocated to each visit for assessment. Resentment and guilt is felt about the situation they find themselves in:

> I sometimes want to spend more time with service users but I feel very guilty, when I do, because I am aware of the competing demands on my time. Obviously spending time with one service user restricts my availability for other work, but I consider that face to face contact with service users is one of the most important aspects of my work.
>
> (Jayne Burnett, personal communication)

Such experiences indicate the frustration practitioners feel when trying to develop creative user-centred care management systems (Means and Smith,

1998). The use of panels as a form of budgetary management (Lymbery, 2004a) is also experienced as managerial control. These panels make the final decision about allocation of resources and so limit the professional discretion of care managers. From this perspective, Sieta and her family could experience a routinized response to her needs. A procedural model of assessment is management-led and based on the eligibility criteria of the authority for access to services. The goal of this model is to provide a cost-effective way of finding out who is eligible for available services and ensure scarce resources are allocated fairly (Smale et al., 2000).

Using the framework that introduces this chapter, we therefore need to take into account the personal obligations of everyone involved, including our own, the structural context of the lives of Sieta, Delroy, Ruby and Mark and the demands of working within managerialist cultures of practice. We need to use the legislation as a resource to ensure that the rights and choices of all those involved are respected. We focus on their needs and try to ensure that resources are available to meet them. This may seem idealistic, but anti-oppressive practice is about moving towards the ideal. While the law cannot make us into good practitioners, it can and should assist and encourage good practice (Johns, 2003).

The process of assessment[2]

The starting point therefore is to have a sound knowledge and understanding of the law, the assessment process and our own power in this situation both in terms of organizing our time and using our personal power to work creatively with Sieta, her family and the community. The initial assessment can be viewed in two ways – as a tick box exercise or a 'purposeful, in-depth activity requiring use of social work skills' (Charles and Butler, 2004: 67). As practitioners we are in control of the process of developing a relationship with Sieta. This means understanding her experience as an individual with her own identity as a black woman, who in her youth started a new life in a new country and who has a story to tell. The NHS and Community Care Act 1990 requires local authorities to make assessment of individual need for community care services with good case management being the 'cornerstone of high quality care' (Means et al., 2003). A creative care manager will ensure that Delroy, Ruby and Mark are involved in the assessment process, but without making assumptions based on their concerns. Clearly, Delroy, Ruby and Mark are significant people in Sieta's life. The document *Caring about Carers* (Department of Health, 1999a) recognizes the importance of supporting carers in their caring role and in terms of looking after their own health and well-being.[3] Support for informal carers (usually family, neighbours and friends) is contained within the Carers (Recognition and Services) Act 1995 and the Carers and Disabled Children Act 2000.[4]

A second area of legislation and policy that is relevant in this situation relates to services for minority ethnic communities. One of the problems of the National Health Service and Community Care Act 1990 is that, unlike the Children Act 1989, there is no specific reference for the need to take into account race, religion, language and culture in the process of the assessment and provision of services. However, the Race Relations (Amendment) Act 2000 is significant in that it strengthens and extends the provisions of the Race Relations Act 1976. Local authorities have a statutory duty under section 71 of the Act to ensure that their functions are carried out with due regard to the need to:

a. eliminate unlawful racial discrimination;
b. promote equality of opportunity; and
c. promote good relations between people of different racial groups.

(Commission for Racial Equality, 2002)

In community care this duty applies to the assessment process, and the planning and provision of the service, which should ensure that adequate, appropriate and accessible services that meet the needs of all members of the community are provided. To ensure that providers of services are actively engaged in eliminating racial discrimination and promoting racial equality, policies should be subject to an assessment that identifies the impact they will have on race issues. Race equality impact assessments involve critically evaluating proposed or existing policies in relation to the duty to effectively promote racial equality (Commission for Racial Equality, 2002). We have already noted the underuse of services by black and minority ethnic people. This may be compounded by assumptions about extended family support networks (Brammer, 2003). Chahal and Ullah (2004) note that the experiences of people from black and minority ethnic groups indicate that they can feel ignored by service providers because of myths about family support. Guidance issued in 2002 about Fair Access to Care Services (see box) does aim to ensure equality of access to services but its long-term impact on the experiences of older people remains to be seen (Means et al., 2003). One social worker told us, however, that:

> I think the fair access to care criteria has had a great impact on the way we work ... if a service user got a 'moderate' or 'low' need,[5] then they are often signposted to other agencies or other options. I think it is difficult to distinguish between these needs which are substantial to those which are moderate.
>
> (Ros Cox, personal communication)

Fair Access to Care

The framework is based on individuals' needs and associated risks to in-dependence, and includes four eligibility bands – critical, substantial, moderate and low. When placing individuals in these bands, the guidance stresses that councils should not only identify immediate needs but also needs that would worsen for the lack of timely help.

At the heart of the guidance is the principle that councils should operate just one eligibility decision for all adults seeking social care support; that is, should people be helped or not? Councils should not operate eligibility criteria for the type and depth of assessments that they carry out; likewise, they should not operate eligibility criteria for specific services. The guidance explains how as-sessments and subsequent care planning should be carried out, in proportion to needs and in good time.

The guidance emphasizes that reviews of individual service users' circum-stances should be carried out by appropriate council professionals on a regular and routine basis. These reviews should incorporate reassessments of individuals' need, and will help councils to reach decisions on continuing eligibility. Councils are advised of the action they should take when significantly reducing and withdrawing services following a review, and of the particular sensitivity they should exercise in situations where reviews have not been carried out for some time prior to the implementation of the guidance.

(Department of Health, 2002)

Sieta's personal experiences of being black, female and old must be analysed in relation to understandings gained from an exploration of her experiences of oppression. Sieta is an older woman who will become in-creasingly frail and more dependent on the support of her family, friends and significant others. She may also need to access relevant public services. This position of 'dependency' is not one that Sieta wishes to gracefully slip into, but it is a position that some might see as inevitable. However, Sieta's wishes need to be at the forefront of any action that is taken. Self-respect and au-tonomy are part of human rights (Gorman, 2005) and the Human Rights Act 1998 supports these principles. The concepts of 'caring', 'dependency' and 'need' therefore have to be critically understood in relation to our work with Sieta and her family. These terms are 'inextricably bound' together (Watson et al., 2004: 342), although their meanings are contested and context-specific.

The fact that Sieta's powers of decision-making may be impaired by her physical and mental capacities has to be considered as well. We need to be aware of the web of power relations in which Sieta is located as well as those external to her social and family networks. A detailed social history from Sieta and her family and the agencies that she has been involved in is required in order to gain a holistic picture before decisions are made. Our social division membership, knowledge of resources that are available, and experience of working with older people from a particular background, will all contribute to the quality of the dialogue we have with Sieta.

One of the first problems that a worker will face when meeting Sieta is that she has already expressed feelings of disempowerment about the visit by a psychogeriatrician: 'another doctor'. The potential for her to experience intervention as oppressive is very real – she is already worried about losing her independence and her vulnerability is being exposed as a result of the referral. Respecting her wishes and understanding her need for independence is crucial for Sieta's overall health and well-being. We therefore have to start by thinking about how we listen to Sieta's story, but also how we work with other professionals to ensure that she develops a trusting relationship with everyone involved. In this situation, having visited Sieta, the psychogeriatrician made a clinical judgement that Sieta is suffering from dementia which could feed into apparent concerns about her ability to continue living alone. Dementia is defined as:

> The impairment of higher mental functioning including the loss of memory, problem-solving ability, the use of learned skills, social skills and emotional control. The consciousness of the sufferer is not impaired. The condition is both progressive and irreversible.
>
> (Victor, 1991, cited in Gorman, 2005: 158)

We also have to be aware that Sieta has already been diagnosed as depressed, and links can be made between depression and dementia (Crawford and Walker, 2005). Depression has been described as:

> . . . a more persistent condition in which a number of feelings, such as sadness, hopelessness or lack of energy, dominate a person's life and make it difficult for them to cope.
>
> (source: *www.alzheimers.org.uk*)

However, the causes of Sieta's depression may also be linked to other aspects of her life. For the social worker, understanding Sieta's story means taking time to think about the loss of Edwin, which still has a huge impact on her life. His death may also have awakened other losses. A point that may well need to be considered is that many Jamaican people moving to England in the 1950s left behind young families with their own parents, thinking that their children would join them once they were settled into their new life. For a variety of reasons, the families remained separated. Sieta and Edwin subsequently brought up another family in their new country and effectively 'lost' the experience of parenting their first family. As practitioners, then, we need to think about issues of grief and loss and their impact on older people. Thompson points out that in old age the loss of meaning that accompanies loss generally is amplified by the ideology of ageism that marginalizes older people and dismisses their feelings (Thompson, 1998).

We can see from this discussion that Sieta's feelings of anxiety, finding it difficult to remember, problems in looking after herself, finding it hard to socialize with others and low self-esteem are symptoms of both dementia and depression.

The *single assessment process* is helpful here. This process, which is promoted by the National Service Framework for Older People (Department of Health, 2001c), integrates social work assessments into a single assessment that includes health care input and aims to:

> ...ensure that older people are treated as individuals and they receive appropriate and timely packages of care which meet their needs as individuals, regardless of health and social services boundaries.
> (Department of Health, 2001c, Standard 2)

This means that active coordination of the different professional groups is a crucial element of effective practice (Lymbery, 2004a).

Informed by values such as 'the centrality of user need, the importance of good assessment and the benefits of preventive work' (Lymbery, 2004a: 169), we therefore need to facilitate the telling of her story in order to complete the assessment and work with everyone involved to put together a care plan. In addition, our work with Sieta needs to hold at the forefront her right to independence. Gaining knowledge about her experiences will help us to understand Sieta's fierce desire to maintain her independence – she learned and developed this as a black woman establishing a new life in Birmingham, a large industrial city in England, with Edwin as her main source of support. Recognizing and acknowledging changes in her abilities will be difficult and frightening for Sieta. Therefore, together with other professionals and her family, we need to be able to help her to cope with her illness. This requires the use of effective communication skills which confirm her sense of self, informed by a strengths perspective that focuses on her capacities and potentialities (Gorman, 2005; Healy, 2005).

In addition, the stories of Ruby, Delroy and Mark need to be understood. As care managers we would need to build a realistic plan around whether they feel able to continue to provide a level of informal care. The Health Services and Public Health Act 1968 sets out (in section 45) a general responsibility to promote the welfare of older people. A local authority might offer:

- social work support and advice;
- information;

- meals;
- recreation;
- help with travel;
- foster care schemes ('boarding' in the Circular);
- aids and adaptations and similar practical assistance;
- residential care;
- home care and laundry facilities.

Intervention at this point could prevent breakdown of the situation at home in the future. Clearly, the family and Mark are thinking about her inability to manage and the impact of her illness on their lives. A support package of domicilary care that acknowledges their concerns and also respects her wishes to stay at home can be agreed. Caring has different dimensions, combining feelings and the practical tasks of everyday life. This has been conceptualized as 'caring about' – the feeling part; and 'caring for' – the practical side (Watson et al., 2004). If the physical task of caring is reduced, Ruby is more likely to enjoy seeing Sieta and engage in her emotional care. Frozen meals and a microwave may reduce the danger of accidents with the cooker and perhaps alleviate some of the concerns of Mark.

Working with Sieta and her family will take time – a problem for managers who need assessments to be completed speedily because of the volume of work. Lymbery suggests that there are three factors that can help creative practitioners:

- Although the loyalties of first-line managers are divided between service users and organizational priorities, many of them have a commitment to the importance of meeting user need and will respond positively to a well-constructed plan.
- Therefore, it is essential that the quality of the care manager's work be of the highest order, as this represents the best defence against managerialist intrusion.
- The core argument is that investment of time in the relatively early stages of a problem may help to improve the situation such that future financial expenditure can be minimized.

(2004a: 69)

Judgements are likely to be made about the riskiness of Sieta's situation. At the moment, Sieta is happy at home and has a right to private life. Practitioners need to remember that breaches of the Human Rights Act 1998 can be pursued. Gorman points out that human rights are about 'acting in an anti-oppressive way, being mindful of the potential for discrimination against older, mentally frail people and making sound judgements that can be evidenced and supported by good recording practices ...' (2005: 164). We need to be mindful that Sieta's situation may change and, if in the future Sieta does need to move from her home, then we would need to allow space for this life transition to take place. This means taking care not to minimize any risk in the future while at the same time working in ways that respect her dignity rather than being driven by managerialist approaches. The skills of the practitioner are about ensuring that Sieta remains central to any decision-making and is involved in subsequent planning. This requires, in particular, skills of partnership working and negotiation – with Sieta, the other key people in her life and other professionals – as well as being able to manage uncertainty, conflict and complexity.

Chapter summary

Having introduced a conceptual framework for practice, we have demonstrated in this chapter how it can be applied to a practice situation. In thinking about Sieta's story one response, in a busy day with limited resources, could be to react to pressures from other professionals, the family and the community by taking a bureaucratic managerialist approach to the situation. This could lead us to using the law oppressively rather than creatively. However, it is possible to use our knowledge of the law, our values and skills (the basis of our framework) in applying the law to work from an anti-oppressive perspective – to use legislation as a resource whereby we can provide services which allow service users and user groups an element of choice.

Further reading

Parton, N. and O'Byrne, P. (2000) *Constructive Social Work: Towards a New Practice.* Basingstoke: Macmillan.
This book outlines an approach to practice that focuses on dialogue, listening to and talking with people. It provides an in-depth exploration of narrative work.

Means, R., Richards, S. and Smith, R. (2003) *Community Care Policy and Practice.* Basingstoke: Palgrave Macmillan.
A useful handbook about community care.

Kitwood, T. (1997) *Dementia Reconsidered: The Person Comes First.* Basingstoke: Open University Press.
A radical and seminal work that focuses on the personhood of men and women who have dementia and demonstrates the possibility of a better life for them.

For information about carers, we recommend the following websites:
Carers UK: *www.carersuk.org*
The Princess Royal Trust for Carers: *www.carers.org*
The Department of Health site: *www.carers.gov.uk*

PART III
REFRAMING PRACTICE IN RELATION TO LEGISLATION

9 Prevention

> One person's prevention is another person's intervention.
> (Dartington Social Research Unit, 2004: 18)

In considering the concept of prevention we are instantly faced with the question of what is to be prevented. Skidmore et al. (1991: 328) suggest that prevention is about 'keeping the vase intact, rather than trying to repair the broken pieces'; that is, instead of 'gluing together human parts that have been cracked, broken apart or splintered', prevention is about keeping human personalities and interrelationships operational. But it could be argued that legislation which is aimed at encouraging the market economy and competitive tendering is unlikely to promote an increase in preventive service provision. Keeping the vase intact is about preventive work at the personal level, but what about the structural level? The chapter will first consider what we mean by prevention. We then go on to look at what attention it has received from policy-makers and practitioners. Finally, we will consider some preventive strategies with various user groups.

What is prevention?

The notion of prevention has been an acknowledged element of health and social care provision since the 1960s. There have been varying understandings of the concept based on traditional reactive models of prevention and more proactive models that build on strengths (Colton et al., 2001; Mason et al., 2005). Differences have also been noted between statutory and voluntary agency definitions, between understandings in urban and rural settings (National Evaluation of the Children's Fund, 2004). The Seebohm Report (1968) referred to general prevention which emphasized well-being and universal services, whereas specific prevention focused on minimizing risk for individuals or families.

More recently, various stakeholders within Children's Fund[1] partnerships identified a number of definitional responses to the term, such as:

- Services provided to assist children and their families where there is a risk or a danger that those children would not fully develop educationally, emotionally or socially without the provision of some type of assistance.

- Preventive services are not seen as universal but are those services targeted at certain children in need within the definition of the Children Act 1989.
- Intervention, rather than waiting for a whole range of issues to escalate to a point where there must be intervention. Prevention is a universal, non-stigmatizing service developed in partnership with service users.
- Service provision away from heavy-end interventions towards earlier intervention and prevention.

(National Evaluation of the Children's Fund, 2004)

Looking at children's services, the thread of prevention that informed child care practice became identified as the criteria for eligibility of services under the Children Act 1989: the two categories being 'in need' and 'at risk'. Different services have been provided within these categories: preventive services to keep children and their families out of the health and social care systems and services provided for children assessed as being at risk of significant harm. More recently, a drive to strengthen preventive services was outlined in the green paper *Every Child Matters*[2] (Department for Education and Skills, 2004) which focused on four themes:

- increasing the focus on supporting families and carers;
- ensuring necessary intervention takes place before children reach crisis point and protecting children from falling through the net;
- addressing underlying problems identified in the report into the death of Victoria Climbié – weak accountability and poor integration;
- ensuring that the people working with children are valued, rewarded and trained.

These themes are incorporated into the Children Act 2004.

Despite the preventive mandate since the Children Act 1989, the requirement to provide a supportive preventive service to children and their families has often been overtaken by surveillance of families through the assessment and management of risk (Parton, 1999; Behan, 2003). Effectively this means that 'prevention', 'in need' and 'at risk' have become technical terms with an administrative purpose (Smith, 1999: 268).

What are we preventing?

Health and social welfare practice has drawn on medical models in developing preventive strategies. Five levels of prevention are, for example:

- health promotion;
- specific protection;
- early diagnosis and treatment;
- disability limitation;
- rehabilitation.

(Skidmore et al., 1991)

Levels of prevention in public health have also been described as primary, secondary and tertiary. In social care practice, the primary level is the 'health promotion' level: working positively with people to protect them for future 'good health'. The secondary level is about early diagnosis and treatment: relieving distress and reducing symptoms. At the tertiary level prevention tends to be more therapeutic and to enhance quality of life. Similar levels have been used in the Children's Fund Guidance, which uses a framework adapted from Hardiker et al. (1991) identifying four levels of prevention:

Level 1: Diversionary

Here the focus is on thinking about problems before they occur. So prevention strategies are likely to focus on whole populations such as community networks where practice is likely to be community action or community development. For example, the NSPCC,[3] in an attempt to increase public awareness about child abuse, launched FULL STOP Week as part of *Talk 'til it stops* – one of the organization's campaigns to help stop child cruelty. FULL STOP Week was launched as a new report revealed that abused children helped by the NSPCC waited an average of two years and four months before telling someone about their abuse. The report found that the children spoke to an average of three people before anyone helped them. During FULL STOP Week, the NSPCC sent out packs to nine million adults with advice on how people can act on concerns about a child.

Level 2: Early prevention

This implies that problems are already beginning to manifest themselves and action is needed to prevent them becoming more serious. Preventive strategies are likely to be based on multi-agency supportive work with family systems. Other examples at this level are services that allow people to identify their needs. *Parentline Plus*, for example, works to offer help and support through a range of free, flexible, responsive services – shaped by parents for parents. *ChildLine* is the free 24-hour helpline for children and young people in the UK. Since it was launched in 1986, ChildLine has saved children's lives, found refuges for children in danger on the streets, and helped children feel that someone cares and will listen to them. ChildLine also campaigns on behalf of children by working with policy-makers.

Level 3: Heavy-end prevention

This focuses on multiple, complex and long-standing difficulties that require a customization of services to meet the needs of the individual concerned. For example, NEWPIN[4] is a voluntary organization working with families to help break the cycle of destructive family behaviour by:

- placing emphasis on emotional abuse as a precursor to physical and/ or sexual abuse;
- developing the self-esteem and emotional maturity of parents;
- bringing about lasting change in the quality of life for both parents and children;
- empowering parents and children to take care of their lives.

NEWPIN works through a network of centres where parents and their children develop in an atmosphere of equality, empathy and respect. This demonstrates the commitment of the organization to principles of anti-oppressive practice. The agency works with parents and other primary carers of children who are in need of support in their role as parents. Individuals may refer themselves or be referred by social workers, health visitors, GPs, courts, the probation service or others. This project works with very vulnerable families, in which, for example, a mother may be suffering from post-natal or other forms of depression. Parents may feel unable to cope with raising children or to give their children the nurturing and care they need. They may be hurting their children or taking their anger out on them, they may feel isolated from their family and society, and feel valueless as individuals and parents.

Level 4: Restorative prevention

This focuses on reducing the impact of an intrusive intervention. The objectives at this level could be to secure the welfare of a child or young person or reduce risk. This is the level of prevention that would apply to young people who are in local authority care, permanently excluded from school, in young offender institutions or supervision, and/or those receiving assistance within the child protection framework. For example, **fsu**[5] works with vulnerable and excluded families and aims to engage with the most marginalized. Working with families who do not have the personal support and resources to manage situations of adversity, **fsu** helps them to achieve positive changes in their lives. The case study, Hana's story, is a good example of their work.

Hana's story

Hana was 15 years old when she arrived in the UK, unaccompanied, from Rwanda. More personally she had witnessed the murder of her father and other close relatives. When she arrived in the UK she was supported by social services and placed in semi-independent accommodation. She was diagnosed with suffering from post-traumatic stress disorder and was seeing a psychiatrist. Hana was referred to **fsu** when she was 17 years old and had been granted Indefinite Leave to Remain (refugee status). This meant that her support and accommodation provided by social services was cut and she was passed on to mainstream services. At this stage she was living in Foyer accommodation and in receipt of benefits but she was becoming increasingly isolated. Initially Hana was coping well but after a few months her mental health declined and she began suffering from severe depression, chronic insomnia and nightmares, anxiety attacks and suicidal feelings. **fsu** provided emotional support and counselling, sometimes four times a week. During this difficult period Hana was not coping with paying her rent, however this didn't come to light until it was too late, and she was asked to leave her accommodation. **fsu** fought for Hana to access council housing, although they initially refused to see this young woman as vulnerable. It took a number of months and many letters and reports written on Hana's behalf before she was provided with a council flat. **fsu** continued to provide emotional support and helped Hana get basic furniture and appliances for her flat. They also began to teach Hana basic budgeting skills. With this continued support from **fsu** and also her psychiatrist, Hana's mental health and abilities to cope alone began to improve. At the final meeting with her worker Hana thanked **fsu** staff for their support, saying that there were times when she really thought 'it would be easier to be dead but **fsu** were always there, never too busy to listen either at the end of the phone or in person'. She said she felt that **fsu** had helped her find the strength to cope.

www.fsu.org.uk, 13 October 2005

In considering why preventive work is such a difficult issue, we have to think about the impact of complex social policies, inadequate resources and changing attitudes. For example, much child care practice focuses on child protection rather than on looking at the needs of children. This may remove some oppressed and vulnerable families from the arena for preventive and supporting services.

There is also the problem of prioritizing not only within various user groups but also between them. Policies of prevention and health care mean that people are living longer and enjoy better health. However, the likelihood is that in the end they will become more dependent and therefore increase the calls on resources. The question could then be asked, who should the housing department consider a priority when a transfer to a ground floor flat becomes available: the lone parent with small children or the older person who finds difficulty with stairs or lift?

Preventive work with older people raises a lot of other questions. Again, we have to ask what the object is of prevention for older people (Tinker, 1981). It cannot be avoidance of death because that is inevitable. It may be possible to prevent expensive forms of care if preventive measures are introduced early enough. Or it may be that preventing an accident or entry into institutional care can save money and human suffering. Government guidelines have stated that prevention is the key to healthier living and a higher quality of life for everyone. So, for example, chiropody services and greater attention to feet can prevent older people being unnecessarily housebound. Equally, adequate dental care, eye care and attention to hearing can only assist in maintaining older people within the community. The role of health visitors and occupational therapists is vital in this respect, to provide support in the community and arrange aids and adaptations. Again, this indicates how the principles of partnership between agencies are never more important than in preventive work.

Generally speaking, it can be argued that preventive work is necessary to avoid the need for more intrusive alternatives in the long term. In many ways it could be said that preventive work is the most empowering form of health and social care practice. So what are we required to do by law? And how can we use the legislation to maximize the development of preventive strategies?

Networking

One of the practitioner's roles in prevention is that of networking (Gilchrest, 2004). Networking has been identified as a useful way of working preventively with children and families, for example (Colton et al., 2001). Five strategies can be used within practice situations to build up social networks:

- Building on the personal links of service users, such as with relatives and neighbours.
- Where there is not a lot of personal support for individual users of services, practitioners may link them with volunteers who have experience and are skilled to work with them to tackle their problems.
- Bringing together those with similar experiences or problems – this can lead to informal grouping for mutual support.
- Identifying and building on existing local networks, such as neighbours or communities.
- Forming groups to address local needs. This is a more political way of

working and may include engaging with organizations such as local voluntary agencies, trade unions and churches.

(Reigate, 1997: 217)

An element of all anti-oppressive practice is about 'making and maintaining links between organisations and between individuals involved in caring and the organisations that might help (or hinder) them is a vital part of social care' (Payne, 1993: 1). By sharing resources and making links, organizations can work together to develop preventive strategies see box. Networking enables health and social care service providers to identify gaps and barriers. This then enables inter-agency collaboration in planning services to address unmet needs. Recent legislation envisages such collaboration as an essential aspect of health and social care practice, which in itself brings together many aspects of anti-oppressive practice.[6]

Rose Hill – Littlemore Sure Start

The Sure Start project started in 1999 in an area of Oxford with the second largest 0–16-year-old population. The area also had the highest number of people reporting a limited long-term illness and high levels of unemployment. Rose Hill had a high proportion (25 per cent) on the school roll of children from Asian families and a high number of children on the special education needs register. There were no locally based health services in the area and few resources for under-4s and their families.

The project has worked with local parents to establish a centre based at the First School for 0–13-year-olds providing a community café, health clinics, crèche, playroom and so on. The project has also worked with the local early education project.

The project is a partnership between statutory and voluntary services and local families. There are parent representatives on the project group, and a research group is conducting a local evaluation of the project.

The focus of work is on preventive rather than crisis intervention and thus should be seen as playing an important role in addressing local health and welfare issues from a public health perspective.

(Taken from Peckham 2003: 76)

Strategies for action

Here we present some strategies for action and examples of preventive work with different user groups.

Young runaways

If a young person is considering the choices and options available to resolve a particular problem, it could well be that the preferred option is to run away. Indeed, this could, on occasions, be the least detrimental alternative.

Janice

Janice was terrified of her father. When he was drunk he would hit her and when he was sober he would ridicule her. She was frightened to tell anyone in case they didn't believe her. She was convinced that life would get worse if he found out that she had told anyone. So she ran away.

Running away is often the only way young people can be heard. A report by the Social Exclusion Unit,[7] for example, stated that young people are more likely to run away when:

- They have no one to talk to.
- They don't know what else to do.
- They don't know where to go for help.
- The help they need is not available.

(Social Exclusion Unit, 2002: 2)

Research from the Central London Teenage Project (CLTP) indicates the importance of providing somewhere for young runaways (Newman, 1989). While it may be hard immediately to see how this fits into the category of preventive work, one of the social workers interviewed in the research believed that safe houses not only empowered young people in care but also gave them the opportunity to talk to professionals who would work with them to negotiate possible alternatives.

Perhaps one of the most important aspects of the research was that the safe house gave the young people the opportunity to take stock. It identified the importance of addressing the reasons why young people run away if their situation is to be resolved. It demonstrated the need for resources to give young people ongoing support on their return to their homes or care placements. So safe houses can prevent further incidents of running away. They also provide shelter, care and a place of safety – this last being vital since in order to support themselves some young people 'who had found themselves hungry, penniless and with no place to go had turned to prostitution', which of course means that they 'risked both their health and their lives' (Newman, 1989: 142). Other positive comments from social workers indicated that safe houses can give workers a 'lever to push for action' or empower young people by giving them a bargaining position.

Section 51 of the Children Act 1989 recognizes the need for refuges for young people at risk and gives the secretary of state power to issue certificates with respect to voluntary or registered homes or foster carers approved by local authorities or voluntary organizations. Children and young people can be taken into and remain in a refuge if they appear to be at risk of harm (Reg. 3(2) The Refuges (Children's Homes and Foster Placements) Regulations 1991). There are limitations placed on the length of time a young person may stay in a refuge (Reg. 3(9)), but if the people running the refuge feel that leaving would cause significant harm there are options available to safeguard that young person (Section 46, Police Protection; Section 44(1), Emergency Protection Order). The guidance acknowledges the need for safe houses when it states that:

> Refuge workers can work with the youngsters to help them to return to parents or local authority care, or to sort out some other solution if a return home is not appropriate (e.g. where a child has been, or may have been, sexually or physically or emotionally abused at home).
>
> (DoH 1991c: 4, para. 9.4)

Centrepoint[8] (2001) acknowledge the role of refuges within the range of services needed to meet the needs of young runaways. However, they also note that a flexible range of services is needed for a preventive strategy to work. A strategy, which takes account of the experiences of young people, needs to address problems which cause young people to run away, support them while they are away from home and reduce running away (see box). Services could include family services, school-based services, personal advisors (through services such as Connexions).[9]

Groundswell

The work of Groundswell involves helping people to make informed choices about their lives and find solutions to their own problems. The organization works from the premise that homelessness can only be tackled by involving homeless people and by helping people to take control of their own lives.

The values underpinning the work of Groundswell are that homeless, poor and excluded people:

- are not 'the problem' – they must be part of the solution;
- hold the key to solutions in their experiences and knowledge;

- have a right to the information they need to make informed choices about their lives;
- can build communities and create positive change by acting together.

Groundswell encourages and supports people who have first-hand experience of being disempowered and excluded from decision-making, working with a wide range of groups and individuals, including:

- homeless people, including rough sleepers, asylum seekers, users of homeless services, ex-homeless people and those recently resettled;
- 'hidden homeless' people, particularly people from ethnic minorities, women, young people, elderly people;
- community groups, including tenants' associations, residents' groups, local action groups and co-ops;
- people with health problems, particularly those with mental health problems, people with drug or alcohol dependencies, people with physical disabilities.

Working together in partnership with homeless people, the organization aims to:

- enable homeless people to set up and run their own projects;
- increase homeless people's influence in policy and decision-making;
- increase homeless people's meaningful involvement in the services they use.

Protecting women and children in violent situations

One could argue that for women trying to escape from situations of domestic violence we must be talking about gluing the vase back together rather than keeping it intact. In the case of domestic violence more intrusive intervention could occur in relation to child protection. Links between domestic violence and child abuse have been apparent for over a decade (Kelly and Lovett, 2005). Social services departments have no statutory responsibility to protect women, and 'the law is a blunt instrument in protecting a person from domestic violence' (Brayne and Carr, 2003: 562). However, social services departments do have a statutory responsibility to protect children and to help women to protect their children, and social workers and other professionals can take on a liaison and support role (Brammer, 2003).

It has been suggested that the basic principle for good practice must be that the protection and empowerment of women and girls is the most effective form of child protection (Marchant, 1993; Kelly and Lovett, 2005). If a woman is worried about leaving her home because of very real fears about money and a roof over her head, then practitioners need to know how to apply to a court for maintenance for the woman (if she is married) and to the

Child Support Agency for the children. Equally, workers need to be aware that a woman cannot be treated as intentionally homeless under the Housing Act 1996 if she leaves a violent situation. However, the Family Law Act 1996 provides a number of remedies for violence within families – although the violence cannot be prevented, there are measures to help families to be safe. For example, the Act provides for occupation orders which can protect the survivor and any children from further abuse by excluding the perpetrator of the violence and preventing any return. These orders can also help the applicant to regain access to accommodation if they have left to escape the violence. While domestic violence is not mentioned in the Children Act 1989, the Women's Aid Federation England has pointed out that children who are in refuges as a result of domestic violence are children 'in need' and as such qualify for all the support and preventive services of any child defined as 'in need'.

Thinking about violence against women from a human rights perspective means that the obligations of the government in relation to preventing and addressing violence are clarified. The human rights legislation also makes us aware that failure to acknowledge unequal power relations between men and women and the gender violence that can be perpetrated as a result can deny women and girls the right to life, liberty, bodily integrity, freedom of movement and dignity of the person (Article 5 Human Rights Act 1998). Finally, the human rights perspective is important because it ensures that violence against women and children is not a private matter but a public concern. This makes governments accountable if they do not take steps to address the issues, including prevention (Kelly and Lovett, 2005).

The Womens National Commission (WNC) has campaigned for changes in legislation and government policy in relation to violence against women. A government consultation with 100 women who experienced domestic violence concluded that what was required was a comprehensive government national strategy on violence against women which effectively amounted to a well-resourced preventive strategy (Womens National Commission, 2003). A later report has called for an integrated approach to ending violence against women:

> The basic contours of an integrated approach must, in the short term, support and empower women and girls and ensure sanctions for abusive men, whilst over the longer term seeking to reduce and ultimately end violence.
>
> (Kelly and Lovett, 2005: 26)

Their proposal for an integrated approach which requires a single co-ordinated and consistent government policy is a radical step and, significantly, recognizes that:

- Achieving women's equality requires addressing violence.
- All forms of violence against women are connected, and have the same underlying causes.
- These are not only individual experiences of victimization they also have a gendered pattern.
- Victims need support, advocacy and redress; perpetrators must be held to account.
- National and local government can and should take a leading role in seeking to prevent violence against women and children.

Preventing violence against women: practice examples

Glasgow City Council

- Glasgow City Council is well known for its Violence Against Women (VAW) approach.
- It is one of the earliest and most sustained supporter of the Zero Tolerance awareness-raising strategies of VAW.
- It has developed innovative work around prostitution and the sex industry, including a Routes Out of Prostitution Partnership established in 1999.
- Inter-agency work addressing indoor prostitution, the proliferation of lap dancing establishments and trafficking, within the context of gender equality and addressing VAW more broadly.
- See *http://www.glasgow.gov.uk/en/YourCouncil/PolicyPlanning_Strategy/ Corporate/Equalities/Women/*

(Kelly and Lovett, 2005)

Southall Black Sisters

- Combines service provision for black (Asian, African and Caribbean) women and acts strategically at regional and national levels.
- Assists women suffering violence in both public and private spheres.
- Aims to mainstream the experiences of black and minority women of domestic and sexual violence into practice and intervention strategies.
- See *http://www.southallblacksisters.org.uk/*

(Kelly and Lovett, 2005)

Improving the quality of life for older people

With the population of older people increasing across Europe, strategies for improving their quality of life are becoming part of policy and practice. In

England, for example, the number of people over the age of 65 has more than doubled since the 1930s. It is expected that between 1995 and 2025 the number of people over 80 years old will increase by nearly a half and the number of people over 90 will double (Department of Health, 2001c). Thompson (1995) points out that it is a 'natural' process to grow old, that is, we move from birth through the life course to death. There is, then, a bio-logical dimension, but he points out that other writers argue that old age can also be seen to have been constructed by demographic, economic and work processes. This social construction of old age, Thompson suggests, challenges traditional views of old age that do not really take account of the wider social context of ageing.

We have indicated throughout the book that across the life course we need to be constantly aware of difference and diversity. However, when working with older people it is also important to take into account different dimensions of age. As practitioners working with older people, the following broad categorizations of older people offered by the government (Department of Health, 2001c) inform our understanding of age:

Entering old age

These are people who have completed their career in paid employment and/ or child rearing. This category can include people as young as 50, or from the official retirement age. These people are active and independent and many remain so into late old age.

Transitional phase

This group of older people are in transition between a healthy active life and frailty. This transition often occurs between the ages of 70 and 90, but can occur at any stage of older age.

Frail older people

These people are vulnerable as a result of health problems such as stroke or dementia, social care needs or a combination of both. Frailty is often ex-perienced only in late old age.

In addition, we have to be aware that older people are more likely to have a complex range of needs within these categories and therefore need to be able to use the range of primary, community, acute hospital and social ser-vices. For example, older people are more likely to have a disability in addi-tion to chronic health needs: 80 per cent of people over 60 have a visual impairment; 75 per cent of people over 60 have a hearing impairment; and 22 per cent have both a visual and hearing impairment. There is also a greater prevalence of some illnesses among specific groups of people. For example, among African-Caribbean people there are higher rates of hypertension and stroke, and there are increased rates of diabetes among South Asian people (Department of Health, 2001c).

Some older people also experience poverty, which may be the result of an extended period on low income or a continuation of previous circumstances. Other problems may include:

- isolation, as friends and family die or move away, and there are fewer opportunities to make new friends or link into new networks;
- bereavement, when partners die;
- housing: old people often live in older housing, which may be deteriorating;
- the problems of carers; many old people are looked after by women who are themselves ageing;
- lack of leisure facilities.

(Thompson, 1995; Department of Health, 2001c)

Against this background there is recognition of the need to develop preventive strategies to support independence, promote good health and develop specialist services and to promote a culture in which older people and their carers are treated with respect, dignity and fairness. The government has developed a National Service Framework (NSF) for Older People (Department of Health, 2001c) which is a ten-year programme to ensure fair, high-quality, integrated health and social care services for older people. The NSF is a policy driver for a prevention agenda that has been launched by the government called Partnerships for Older People Projects (Kaur, 2005). This is a three-year programme of work that aims to improve the health, well-being and in-dependence of older people through better coordination of care and en-couraging investment in preventive approaches to care.

An example of preventive approaches in work with older people is to take action to prevent falling (see box). Standard 6 of the National Service Fra-mework recognizes that falls can cause serious problems for older people. They are the major reason for accident and emergency hospital admissions – a third of the people who are aged over 65 fall in the UK each year. Falls are also the leading cause of mortality due to injury in people over the age of 75 years in the UK.

Preventing older people from falling: practice examples

Handypersons scheme

Letchworth Primary Care Trust in Hertfordshire has a handypersons scheme.
    The aim is to help people to keep their independence in the community and reduce hospital admissions.

Vulnerable people living at home can call on someone to do everyday jobs such as mending taps, fitting smoke alarms and changing bulbs. Not being able to do these things can lead to a loss of confidence and ability to live independently. Also, those who might 'have a go' could risk falling.

London Older People's Service Development Programme

Projects in Wandsworth and Greenwich have piloted different ways of identifying older people who have fallen or who are at risk of falling.

Wandsworth project

- Aimed to improve outcomes for older people who had fallen, or were at risk of falling, through timely intervention.
- Focused on the relationships between practitioners to produce speedier and more appropriate outcomes.
- Identified where services overlapped, were duplicated or fragmented.
- Used a validated screening tool.
- Developed a screening tool that doubled as a resource for contact information.
- Developed a multi-agency falls care pathway that was capable of risk identification, screening, referral, treatment, rehabilitation and monitoring.

Greenwich project

A screening tool was used either face to face or over the phone to identify older people who fall by:

- social service initial contact team;
- district care managers;
- in-house home care service;
- community alarm service;
- a multi-disciplinary team in hospital accident and emergency department.

If the person scored 3 or more on the screening tool, they were asked if they would agree to be referred to a new community falls team.

The outcome from this project was that it identified risk, found cases that may not have been referred to mainstream services, enabled workers to access multidisciplinary services and advice, helped older people who may not have been able to stay at home otherwise, demonstrated that falls are preventable and not a natural consequence of ageing and raised the profile of falls and fracture prevention, leading to ongoing funding.

Keeping children out of prison

'In recent years juvenile crime has attracted sustained high-profile attention from politicians, child welfare services, criminal justice agencies, the media and the public' (Goldson, 2002: 120). NACRO[10] has suggested that there needs to be a cultural change in the way we deal with children who offend if we are to stop children ending up in prison. Statistics for children locked up in the UK show that:

- The number of children in penal custody has risen from 3130 in October 2004 to 3423 in September 2005, an increase of 10 per cent in a year.
- The majority of children are detained in prisons, with 2933 in prison service custody, 245 in local authority secure children's homes, and 245 held in secure training centres.
- The number of children remanded into prison service custody has increased by 26 per cent, from 403 in October 2004 to 507 in September 2005.
- The number of girls in penal custody has increased by 35 per cent from 198 in October 2004 to 267 in September 2005. The number of girls held in prisons has increased by 31 per cent from 85 to 111.
- The number of boys held in prisons has increased from 2589 to 2822 in a year.
- Two boys died in prison in 2005: a 16-year-old hanged himself in Lancaster Farms prison and a 17-year-old was found in his cell in Hindley prison with a ligature round his neck. This latter boy was known to be at risk of suicide but had not been designated as vulnerable.

(Howard League for Penal Reform, 2005)

These statistics are horrifying for a number of reasons – not least because they indicate the punitive relationship that exists in the UK between children and the state. A preventive strategy is clearly necessary at both individual practice levels and at the structural level if the situation for young offenders is to improve. Campaigning organizations such as NACRO and the Howard League for Penal Reform have highlighted a number of ways to prevent the incarceration of children.

Government responsibility
There needs to be a shift in the youth crime debate from a punitive agenda to promoting public confidence in alternatives that work. This could be achieved by educating the public about a framework for youth justice that is expert-led rather than led by exaggerated public anxiety.

Currently there are financial incentives that operate locally in favour of custodial sentences. This is because the cost of detention is a central concern, whereas community-based alternatives are a local responsibility.

There are not enough low-level alternative interventions. The use of intensive supervision and surveillance programmes appears to be replacing other less punitive options and escalating young people up the sentencing 'ladder'.

Practitioners' responsibility

Principles of anti-oppressive practice would inform an anti-custodial outlook. This involves understanding the context of the lives of the young people concerned and a personal and professional commitment informed by a genuine concern for them as people. This means being prepared to use alternatives to custody and argue for them in court.

Magistrates need to be informed about local provision that provides alternatives to custody.

Chapter summary

> The logic of prevention suggests that resources should be focused on potentially successful situations where by putting in resources at an earlier stage, the point of collapse is not reached.
>
> (Twigg and Atkin, 1994: 149)

The impact of complex social policies, inadequate resources and attitudes changing from a reactive response to problems to looking at the origins of problems makes preventive work difficult. Prevention requires creative thinking and imaginative use of resources. The prevention argument assumes that collapse can be avoided, or that it is possible to keep 'the vase' intact. Realistically, one of the challenges for health and social care practitioners is how personal, family and community problems can be prevented. The connection of preventive policy initiatives to systems of surveillance (Parton, 2006) is problematic for practitioners committed to principles of anti-oppressive practice. This means being aware of inequalities, and particularly of how to use what legislative frameworks are available, to prevent further discrimination against vulnerable groups of people. In this chapter we have looked at definitions of prevention and examined the question about what we are trying to prevent. We have illustrated the issues through consideration of strategies for action with particular service user groups.

Further reading

Parton, N. (2006) *Safeguarding Childhood: Early Intervention and Surveillance in a Late Modern Society*. Basingstoke: Palgrave Macmillan.
Through an analysis of responses to child abuse, Parton examines policies and argues that we are moving towards a 'preventive state' which is characterized by regulation and surveillance. A thought-provoking and interesting text.

Activity 1

The following exercise will enable you to assess the aims of the links that you currently make with other organizations. From this, you should be able to identify – in terms of your networking – whether you are constantly working in a reactive way, or are developing proactive strategies which will promote preventive ways of working.

The aims that may be fulfilled by making links can be divided into service, maintenance and policy aims. *Service aims* are concerned with providing effective services to the public. An essential aspect of linking which meets the aims of your service might be good practical relationships with agencies that refer potential users of the service, accept referrals from you or assist users. *Maintenance aims* are about keeping the agency in existence so that the service aims can be met, for example regular contact with funding bodies and the support of other departments or councillors, if the service is a local authority one. *Policy aims* are concerned with changing policies which affect the service users in your area – these can be policies in other organizations and departments, or in government.

1. List all the links with other organizations that you have, and should have.
2. In each case decide whether the link meets service aims, maintenance aims or policy aims, or a combination of these, and the reason why it meets those aims.
3. For each list (service, maintenance, policy) rank the organization in order of priority for meeting that aim (that is, top priority = 1, next priority = 2, and so on).
4. For each organization, add up the number given under each list to give the priority for linkages for that organization overall (the lower the number, the higher the priority).
5. If you are working alone, look at each priority ranking, and consider whether it fits with your judgement of the priority. Are there factors that give it a higher or lower priority in the exercise which you are not thinking of in your work? If you are working with others, try sharing your judgements and testing with colleagues the reasons for them. If you are working on a team's links, how do your judgements agree? Are there significant differences in

priority? How could you handle this (for example by each member taking on links that he or she personally gives high priority to)? Should you be trying to agree priorities? (taken from Payne, 1993: 16).

Activity 2

Debra and Assim – case study revisited

Debra (age 22) is a white young woman with a long-standing drug habit. Her 3-year-old son, Ricky, who is white, lives with his grandparents, Mary and Peter. She has given birth to a little girl, Jasmine, and her boyfriend, Assim (age 22), who is black, is the father. Assim is aggressive and hostile towards professionals and has been convicted of several violent offences. In the last three months of the pregnancy Debra managed to reduce her drug use and has made a home for Jasmine, who is now 2 months old. Debra continues to see Assim regularly and they are both saying that they are committed to each other. However, Mary has told the social worker that she suspects that the relationship is still volatile. Debra has had some bruising when visiting, but is vague about how she got it. Ricky loves his little sister and would like her to stay with him at his grandparents' house. He can't understand why his mum does not see him as much as she used to. Mary and Peter tell him that she is busy looking after Jasmine.

Bearing in mind the government's emphasis on prevention while strengthening protection, consider the following questions:

- What preventive strategies could be put in place to assist Debra to care adequately for Jasmine?
- Debra is committed to the relationship with Assim, so how can she be supported and empowered in this situation?
- How would you work with Assim to reduce/stop his violence?
- What resources are you aware of that could assist Debra and Assim's parenting?
- What role could Mary and Peter have in contributing to a preventive strategy?

10 Assessment

Why do they write things about me?
Details of everything I do.
Why do they always watch me?
Wherever I may go.
Why do they make me stay in?
And if I go out, it's with them.
Why do they send me a counsellor
To find out things about me?
Why do they watch how I react
To problems we face each day?
Why do they assess me
When I have the right to be free?
Why do they label me –
When I am only being me!

(Chris Elms Bennett, 1994)

What is assessment?

The poem by Chris draws our attention to the fact that assessment is not a neutral and objective activity. It has particular meaning for all involved in the process. For Chris, the process is driven by the needs of the professionals; her concerns, desires and needs are peripheral to the process. Assessment is not experienced as a sensitive, helpful or even therapeutic process, but as an intrusive act that she is subject to. Chris's needs are defined for her (Pitts, 1990).

The attitudes and values of the assessor as well as the situation of the person(s) being assessed will have an impact on the assessment process. Practitioners face moral and ethical dilemmas when they are engaged in the processes of assessing people's needs – assessment therefore can be considered to be a value-laden activity (Clifford and Burke, 2004). 'Ideally, the assessment should be a forum in which hypotheses are devised and theories tested; a place where conflicting ideas are encouraged. The totally "objective" assessment remains an elusive ideal' (Pitts, 1990: 54). Assessment should allow for multiple, changing and contradictory understandings of social situations (Fook, 2002).

Returning to Chris's poem, the failure to ensure that the assessment process incorporated her views and understandings of her situation has meant that 'professional assumptions of what need is and how it should be met' (Morris, 1989: 175) prevail and remain unchallenged. The view of assessments as political and value-laden processes which are used to distribute limited resources has some support within the literature (Morris, 2004). Indeed, a focus on resources, rather than needs, often underpins local authority decisions where they have interpreted the concept of need as taking into account 'not only the unmet need of the individual but also the wider resource implications of meeting that need' (Hitchings, 2005: 333). In this chapter we will consider some of the dilemmas faced by practitioners when engaged in the process of assessment, discuss the link between assessment and the legislation and the need to think anti-oppressively when assessing social situations.

Assessment is a central task of social work. However, a systematic review of the textbooks and frameworks on assessment did not reveal a clear definition or conceptualization of assessment (Crisp, 2005). This lack of a universal definition may well reflect the tension that exists between the different approaches to assessment as 'the ways in which we assess problems, and the way in which we describe and define them are of course integrally connected with the ways in which we construct knowledge of our world and more generally our place within it' (Fook, 2002: 115). Holland notes that there is 'tension between searching for assessments of measurable scientific validity and those that reflect the individually situated nature' (Holland, 2004: 2) of people's experiences. She suggests that the first approach produces assessments that are 'scientific', while the second approach is based on practitioners using their expertise and knowledge to inform their professional judgements. By problematizing social situations and the information provided by service users, practitioners begin to construct a variety of perspectives to enable them to make sense of those situations. This latter approach to assessment challenges conventional empirical approaches. But equally, it does not mean that assessment is a subjective and relativistic process – which relies on the values, skills and knowledge of the individual worker. Assessment should be viewed as a theoretically informed practical activity that includes 'elements of personal skill, judgement and art' (Clifford, 1998: 233) and 'involves wisdom, skills, appreciation of diversity and systematically applied knowledge in practice' (Parker and Bradley, 2003: 4).

Approaches to assessment

Holland's discussion of assessment practice is informed by social constructionism, a critical perspective concerned with how 'knowledge and understanding is historically and culturally determined' (Holland, 2004: 2). A social constructionist approach to assessment emphasizes the processes through which people define themselves and their environments: '*construct-ing* is seen as an ongoing aspect of people's lives and relationships' (Parton and O'Byrne, 2000: 16). The ideas inherent in social constructionism challenge the view that assessments can be objective, accurate and consistent and that the person making the assessment is a 'relatively objective and passive party, who simply gathers empirical facts, puts them together and makes a judgement based on what the "facts" say' (Fook, 2002: 115). A postmodern and constructionist critique 'alerts us to the ways in which assessment tools carry an overarching and inherent emphasis on client "problems", thus prioritising a deficit-based discourse as opposed to a language of "potentials"' (Iversen et al., 2005: 695). Assessment viewed as a 'collaborative inquiry' (Iversen et al., 2005: 699), allows for the creative exploration of multiple and diverse meanings of social situations between the practitioner and the service user(s).

This informed, reflexive approach to making assessments enables prac-titioners to 'balance the regulatory aspects of their work with more empow-ering possibilities' (Iversen et al., 2005: 701) as well as resist the dominance of problem-centred professional discourse within the assessment process. As-sessment then becomes more than a fact-finding task but a dynamic process through which practitioners make sense of a mass of information relating to issues and problems of service users and carers. Practitioners need to be re-flective and reflexive in their approach to assessments. Values, the context of practice, knowledge and experience will all influence the way in which practitioners resolve ethical dilemmas. For example, in the area of child protection, values will influence 'the importance given to competing de-mands to keep the child within the biological family, to refrain from inter-vening in the lives of families, and to protect the child' (Benbenishty Rami et al., 2003: 150). Equally, the nature of caring relationships across the 'spec-trum of illnesses and disabilities' (Keywood, 2003: 356) has to be clearly un-derstood, as it is essential that assessment and service responses are sensitive to 'the nature of care-giving and the relationship between unpaid carers and those who provide services to support them' (Nicholas, 2003: 34). Such an understanding will have implications for the assessment process (Nicholas, 2003). The incorporation of service users and carer perspectives 'challenges the established power relations in the production and application of knowl-edge, thus acting as a key mechanism for anti-oppressive practice' (Braye and Preston-Shoot, 2005: 13). In conclusion, assessment is a highly skilled, multi-dimensional activity which has 'intrinsic', 'therapeutic' benefits beyond the goal of gathering information *en route* to the allocation of resources or to judgements of 'risk' (Millar and Corby, 2005: 3). The practitioner, service user(s) and carers are all active participants in the assessment process and will each bring to that situation their own meanings and constructions. Assessment, therefore, does not just consist of applying technical skills, but is a process whereby, informed by research evidence, we make professional and personal judgements about complex social situations (Clifford and Burke, 2004).

Assessment, needs, rights and services

The socially constructed concept of 'need' has been criticized from various 'sociological perspectives including Foucauldian, critical and feminist theories' (Clifford, 1998: 121). The term 'need' has been used as though it is an objective phenomenon that can be unproblematically identified and measured (Ife, 2001).

What are basic human needs? Are some needs more important than others? Is it possible to establish an agreed definition of need? Understanding need and practising in ways which ensure that people's identified needs are met is seen as the domain of health and social care practitioners. But the very concept of need is problematic and open to numerous interpretations.

If we take, for example, the well-known psychological-based concept of need by Maslow, who outlined five levels of human needs (Maslow, 1970). His hierarchy starts with what he considered the most fundamental of human needs – physiological needs, such as for food and drink. Next are safety and security needs. Once these are satisfied, needs that can be 'fulfilled in satisfying relationships emerge, such as those for love, attention, and belongingness' (Mayhew 1997: 49). Needs for esteem and self-actualization are at the top of the hierarchy. The important feature of Maslow's hierarchy of needs is that needs at one level have to be met before an individual can reach the idealized state of being self-actualized, that is an individual who has 'desire for such things as truth, beauty, wholeness and meaningfulness' (Maslow, 1973, cited in Mayhew, 1997: 49).

However, it could be argued that viewing needs in this objective and fairly mechanistic way fails to appreciate that needs do not come in discrete packages, that they in fact at times cannot be separated out, as they interact and overlap with each other and are influenced by factors external to the individual. It could also be argued that this 'positivistic conception of need fails to take into account power or differences between ways of understanding social concepts' (Clifford, 1998: 121).

Ife suggests that rather than considering needs as factual statements we should understand them as statements of values and ideologies (Ife, 2001). Need, it could be argued, is defined and controlled by agencies and professionals – therefore assessments of need are not neutral or objective but reflect the 'tendency of professionals to appropriate the right of individuals, families or communities to define their own needs' (Ife, 2001: 79). This particular perspective is one that is often supported by official guidance. The Care Management and Assessment: Practitioners' Guide published by the Department of Health Social Services Inspectorate in 1991 acknowledges, on the one hand, that 'need is unlikely to be perceived and defined in the same way by users, their carers and any other care agencies involved' (Department of Health, 1991: para 3.34, p.53). Ultimately it is the professional definition that takes precedence because, as the guidance states, 'having weighed the views of all parties, including his/her own observation, the assessing practitioner is responsible for defining the user's needs' (Department of Health, 1991; Social Services Inspectorate, 1991: para 3.35, p.53).

A purely objective concept of need is of limited value according to Doyal and Gough (1991), because we come to understand what our needs and capabilities are through our interactions with others. Doyal and Gough suggest that personal autonomy is an important basic human need. According to Doyal and Gough, without autonomy or the freedom to be able to decide and choose, human beings are unable to participate fully in life or achieve other valued goals (Blakemore, 1998). Realizing our aspirations, being able to actively participate in the process of defining one's needs, is what makes us human. This useful conceptualization of one universal need – autonomy – is an important one in relation to understanding need within an anti-oppressive framework. Judgements about the needs of an individual, family, group or community and, crucially, how they can be met, relate therefore not only to the knowledge, values and skills of the practitioner, and the wider political, economic, legal and organizational contexts, but more importantly morally and ethically, should include the views of the service user(s), who should be provided with opportunities to define and clearly state their needs. Anti-oppressive practitioners committed to values of human rights and equality should bring to their understanding of the concept of need an awareness of the relative nature of any definition, and the role played by dominant social discourses at particular times and places in its definition. The definition of need, we would argue, must be arrived at through dialogue with and working in partnership with those whose needs are being assessed.

The legislation embodies within it a vision of the needs of individuals, which will enable them to achieve their full potential. It contains 'expressions, if not definitions, of the concept of "need"' (Braye and Preston-Shoot, 1997: 35). For example, section 1 of the Chronically Sick and Disabled Persons Act 1970 requires local authorities to identify the needs of certain groups (Braye and Preston-Shoot, 1997: 35). The Special Educational Needs and Disability Act 2001 addresses the provision of education for children and students with special needs (Johns, 2005: 44). The Children Act 1989 also introduces the concept of need, and Part III of that Act is devoted to outlining the provision of services for children defined as 'in need', for example section

17 of the Children Act 1989 places on the local authority a duty to 'safeguard and promote the welfare of children within their area who are in need' (Brayne and Carr, 2003: 253).

The Care Management and Assessment: Practitioners' Guide (Department of Health, 1991a) recognizes that needs are unique to the individual concerned and these needs have to be identified and addressed; however, they have to be met within the available resources. The guide clearly links the assessment of need to resource availability. The concept of need therefore presupposes that:

- we have a common understanding of what human need is;
- some needs are more deserving of resources than others;
- need is based on everyone being able to compete equally within society and to reach their full potential;
- need is based on maintaining a quality of life that enables us to participate in society; and
- we can accurately assess need and provide the resources to meet it.

Assessment of need, strengths and risks has to take into account the social context of people's lives. For example, social division membership of the individual will give rise to a range of different and specific needs.

The guidance accepts that need is a complex concept. It defines need in terms of 'the requirements of individuals to enable them to achieve, maintain or restore an acceptable level of social independence or quality of life, as defined by the particular care agency or authority' (Department of Health, 1991a: 12). Clearly, the notions of user involvement, partnership and choice are severely limited by this definition. This point can be illustrated by consideration of the legislation for people with disabilities. Guidance on developing assessment procedures placed emphasis on enabling people to 'live a full life in the community' and to 'be in charge of their own lives and make their own decisions, including decisions to take risks' (Department of Health, 1991a). Disabled people do have the right under the Disabled Persons (Services, Consultation and Representation) Act 1986 to ask for a comprehensive assessment of their needs. Local authorities also have a duty to provide services under section 2 of the 1970 Chronically Sick and Disabled Persons Act. A genuine needs-led assessment incorporates the self-defined needs of disabled people. An anti-oppressive perspective would ensure that self-assessment and advocacy services are an essential element of community care policies, which then promote the rights of users (Morris, 1993b).

In July 1993, Mark Hazell won a court battle to live in the home he had chosen. Avon[1] Social Services, working from a service-led philosophy within certain financial constraints, was deemed to have failed in its attempts to meet Mark's needs. Mark, a young man with learning difficulties, wanted to live independently from his family. As part of the process of finding an appropriate long-term placement, an assessment of Mark's needs was carried out by Avon Social Services. However, the council's view of his needs conflicted with that of Mark and his family. Avon Social Services assessed that his needs could be met in an establishment that was considerably cheaper than the one preferred by Mark. It was this, rather than Mark's needs, that appeared to determine the decision. This conflict in opinion led Mark and his family to use the process of the law through judicial review to ensure that Mark's needs were met. The case of Mark Hazell (*R* v *Avon County Council, ex parte Hazell* [1992]) has ensured that local authorities 'cannot refuse on grounds of costs to provide accommodation chosen by an individual which they are already providing to others' (Braye and Preston-Shoot, 1997: 98). This ruling supports practitioners working from a needs-led perspective within a service-led, resource-driven practice arena.

For the anti-oppressive practitioner whose practice is informed by a social justice model, working with legislation which operates on an individual 'medical model of welfare' (Braye and Preston-Shoot, 1997) presents a number of ethical and moral challenges. Practice informed by anti-oppressive principles requires practitioners to ensure that the assessment of need and the consequent planning of services to meet that need is focused on extending and improving the range and quality of the existing service provision, rather than on overcoming the deficits of individuals and their families. As a practitioner your work should contribute to the process of change. It is not about *taking services off the shelf* but about taking account of the need that is identified and engaging in activities that will contribute to the development of needs-led provision. It is important to interpret the language of legislation in a way that will ensure that disabled people are not further disadvantaged by the concept of need. If, as Morris (2004) points out, assessment within the community care system continues to be based on 'dependency levels and eligibility criteria' (2004: 432) rather than needs, then disabled people will continue to have their human and civil rights denied. The purpose of needs-led assessment, therefore, must be understood by the practitioner (Sapey and Hewitt, 1991) and supported by legislative and administrative systems which are not underpinned by dependency models of need.

Assessments are not value free

Social workers and other professionals make decisions on a daily basis, which have important consequences for service users. The difficulties inherent in making professional judgements stem from the fact that the situations being assessed are fluid and uncertain. The narratives of the people we work with are complex, contradictory and changeable. 'For instance parents may want to misrepresent their interpersonal conflicts in an attempt to present an "ideal front" to a powerful outsider, who they might think is looking to find fault with them' (Benbenishty Rami et al., 2003: 138). Information being used may not be complete or understood by the individual making the assessment, the voices of less dominant players in the situation may not be heard or given due consideration. Our responses to complex and changing social situations will vary and consequently will shape and determine the decisions that we make.

The following case scenarios provide an opportunity to begin to think about the principles and dilemmas of assessing social situations. The first concerns the area of mental health work, which poses a number of challenges for health and social care practitioners working together, particularly where assessment of need may also lead to deprivation of liberty.

Case example: Bill Valentine

Councillor Davies has been contacted by a number of Bill Valentine's neighbours, who are concerned about him. They are aware that he has, on a number of occasions, left his flat door open while out shopping, and that he is using his gas cooker as a means of keeping warm. Bill is also known to have a few drinks. Bill regularly complains that someone is entering his flat and is stealing from him. Bill, who is 78 years old, lives alone following the death of his wife, Mary, a year ago. Mary died suddenly and Bill has found it hard coping with his feelings of loss. He has been prescribed anti-depressants but he does not always feel it is necessary to take them. His daughter, who lives locally, calls to see her father on a weekly basis and has noticed over a period of time that he has become distracted and disoriented and that he has taken to writing little notes to himself. She recently contacted Bill's GP, who was quite concerned about Bill's mental health. He subsequently called in a specialist. Bill was then admitted to hospital for an assessment. He was persuaded to go 'voluntarily', although the use of compulsory powers under the Mental Health Act 1983 or the National Assistance Act 1948 was considered. As a result of his admission he was diagnosed as having multi-infarct dementia.

The concerns of the people involved in Bill's life are encapsulated in some of the conversations that have taken place over the course of a couple of weeks.

Cllr Davies: From what I've heard Bill is a real danger to everyone in that block of flats. It's in everyone's interests, including Bill's, that he should be taken into hospital.

Social worker: The care plan which is in place at the moment is based on ensuring that Bill has the level of support that will enable him to remain safe and to continue to live in the community.

Daughter: My dad has always said that he wants to be able to stay at home and look after himself, ever since mum died. I respect that and want him to keep his dignity and his independence.

Cllr Davies: Well, from the reports I've heard Bill is not coping even with the level of support that is being offered. In fact he is a risk to himself and a danger to people living in the flats. He should be cared for properly. Is it dignified for a frail old man to be left at such risk to himself and others?

Social worker: It is very difficult to make judgements about depriving someone of their liberty. To remove someone against their will is a very drastic step and should only be considered once all the facts of the situation are fully understood and there is agreement with all involved about the action that needs to be taken.

GP: Well, my position is clear. He needs medical attention, and we have a duty to ensure that he receives it. If that means that his wish to remain at home has to be disregarded, then so be it.

Question: Can you identify some of the issues and dilemmas that are framed by each person in this scenario?

Two months after his discharge from hospital a request to complete an assessment of Bill under section 2 of the Mental Health Act 1983 is received by the duty approved social worker. If granted, this would lead to Bill's compulsory admission to hospital, where he could be detained for up to 28 days for assessment. To be 'sectioned' the law requires two medical recommendations – a psychiatrist and a GP. Both felt that Bill, as a consequence of his dementia and depression, would be a danger to himself and to others if he was to remain in the community. Bill has made it clear that he does not want to go into hospital. The social worker, in attempting to balance an assessment of Bill's social circumstances and the medical diagnosis that has been made, is finding it particularly difficult to agree with the medical recommendation.

The power to override the wishes of a vulnerable person or her or his family should not be abused. The needs and wishes of Bill should be listened to and the risk which he poses to himself and others should be balanced against his assessed strengths and abilities and the formal and informal support systems which can be put into place. Alternatives to hospital admission have to be actively considered. The approved social worker may only make an application for compulsory admission of Bill if it is 'in all circumstances. . . . the most appropriate way of providing . . . care and treatment' (Section 1(2), Mental Health Act 1983). The principles underpinning the Mental Capacity Act 2005 will further focus on the rights of the individual to make and be appropriately supported to make their *own* decisions.

In terms of anti-oppressive practice, all parties should be provided with information and made aware of the consequences of the infringement of people's civil liberties. Practitioners have responsibilities in relation to the 'liberty and custody, rights and risks' of individuals (Braye and Preston-Shoot, 1997: 7), therefore health and social care workers are expected to make assessments based on the best interests of the person concerned, as long as these do not conflict with the rights of others. An important principle here is that as far as possible the needs of the vulnerable person should drive the assessment process and they should be fully involved in the decision-making processes.

Case example: Zoe

During the course of her short life, Zoe has been accommodated on one occasion by the local authority due to concerns of neglect. Zoe, who is 8 years old and of dual heritage, is small for her age and at times can be withdrawn. During her early years, Zoe reached her developmental milestones at the appropriate time. Zoe attended a local playgroup for 6 months when she was 3 years old but May, her mother (white, aged 27), removed her when she was approached by staff about Zoe's aggressive behaviour towards other children.

When she was 5 years old, Zoe began primary school, where behavioural problems were noted. Zoe was often late for school and her attendance was poor. She was accommodated for the first time when she was 6 years old, after a neighbour rang social services to report that Zoe had been left alone. Zoe was placed with foster carers. At the case conference that was convened it was agreed that Zoe should return home and that attempts should be made to ensure that May was supported to continue to care for her daughter. Over the next few months the social services family support team social worker visited Zoe and May on a regular basis. Zoe was attending school regularly and Bea, her maternal grandmother (white, aged 54), cared for her granddaughter at weekends. After 8 months it was agreed that social services involvement was no longer necessary. It was agreed by all involved in the case that Zoe's basic needs were being met by her mother May and by Bea. However, it was felt that May's continued drug use could in the future undermine her ability to care for Zoe.

A year after the case was closed, Zoe's home situation began to deteriorate. May's partner of 6 months, Pete, is involved in selling drugs and it is thought that he may be using the family home to supply local people. May's increased drug use means that at times she is 'unavailable' to care for Zoe or to ensure that she attends school on a regular basis. Zoe's behaviour within school has deteriorated. Bea's recent diagnosis of a life-threatening illness has meant that she has not been able to offer the level of support that she previously was able to. There are reports of Zoe being seen out playing in the neighbourhood late at night during the week and wandering the streets at weekends. Neighbours are once again concerned about Zoe's safety.

You have been asked to undertake an assessment of this situation. The following questions may help you to begin to think about your role and some of the issues that may arise.

- What will you be bringing to the assessment relationship in terms of your experiences of working with some of the issues that this family faces?
- How far does your age, gender, class, ethnicity, and other social division membership assist your understanding of the lives of Zoe, May, Bea and Pete?
- How will you approach the assessment so that you fully engage with all the family members?
- What aspects of the legislation will you be working with?
- The assessment of a parent's ability to parent has a central legal position within child care legislation and policy – what knowledge, values and skills would you bring to this assessment task?
- If the needs of Zoe cannot be met by May, how would you work in partnership with both Zoe and May when looking for alternative carers?

Commentary

These are not easy questions, but it is helpful when approaching an assessment to think systematically about what information you may need to obtain and for what purpose. At the start of the assessment process you need to define and clarify the situation. Within the above scenario, for example, you will need to be clear as to who is saying that a problem exists. You may need to ask yourself why a problem exists and how serious is the problem. Your understanding of these questions will be based on how far you manage to facilitate each person being able to tell their story. Questions about the availability of resources, both formal and informal, within and external to the organization that you are located in, also need to be addressed. This will include the skills, experience and time that you have. You have to think about how you will work in partnership and the nature of the work that you or others may be engaged in. Finally, decision-making regarding possible courses of action needs to be thought through and explored with service users, carers and other professionals, including your line manager. Information that will assist your decision-making should be carefully and clearly recorded.

The following pointers provide a useful starting point for undertaking anti-oppressive assessments:

- *Assessment should involve those being assessed* and should be centred on the needs and strengths of the service user(s). Involvement of service users has to be really thought through and acted upon if it is to be a reality rather than rhetoric. Appropriate and sensitive communication is required. This may require practitioners to contact specialist agencies who can provide interpreters for people whose first language is not English or who have no hearing or require particular aids to assist communication. Practitioners need to be aware of the communication needs of the people they are working with. Asking well-thought-through, carefully phrased and concrete questions is important, as is being prepared to repeat or put certain questions to one side. Summaries of discussion, paraphrasing and sharing written copies of the information can also help in developing good communication (Parker and Bradley, 2003).

- *Openness and honesty should permeate the assessment process.* Service users have rights and practitioners have particular obligations which need to be made explicit. Therefore, service users should be made aware of the purposes of the assessment and agency policy in relation to, for example, confidentiality and its limits.
- *Assessment should involve the sharing of values and concerns.* The practitioner should be reflective and reflexive throughout the process.
- *There should be acknowledgement of the structural context of the process.* Individual situations need to be located within a social context.
- *The process should be about questioning the basis of the reasons for proposed action, and all those involved should consider alternative courses of action.*
- *Assessment should incorporate the different perspectives/narratives of all the people involved.*
- *Assessment should be holistic* so as to reflect the complexity of the service user's situation.
- *Practitioners need to be aware of the impact of legislative requirements on the assessment.* It is important to acknowledge that tension may exist between the requirements of the legislation, the practitioner's professional judgement of the situation and the views of service users and carers.

These pointers, when combined with a sound theoretical framework for assessment, contribute to the making of assessments that are not only robust and defendable but are informed by a meaningful dialogue between practitioner and service user(s). However, this task is made more difficult by the fact that there is 'a lack of any comprehensive assessment framework for assessment in social work' (Milner and O'Byrne, 1998: 2). Equally, Milner and O'Byrne suggest, there is limited discussion in the literature on assessment about the conceptual and theoretical underpinning of assessment frameworks. They point out that knowledge which assessment activity is based on is drawn exclusively from the disciplines of psychiatry and psychology and is, they claim, often used uncritically. An overarching framework for generic assessment, which can assist practitioners to make professional judgements about situations of need and risk and which can be used to critically evaluate the proliferation of official 'linear, prescriptive and stylised assessment formats' (Milner and O'Byrne, 1998: 2), has been developed by Derek Clifford. It is a framework that can be used by health and social care professionals engaged in multiprofessional and multidisciplinary assessments of 'complex individual and micro-social situations' (Clifford, 1998: 4).

Clifford's anti-oppressive social assessment framework[2] is informed by 'theoretical contributions from the social sciences' (Clifford, 1998: 4), debates within qualitative research, literature developed by black feminists and feminists from other social divisions, feminist moral philosophy and ethics, and perspectives drawn from the disability service user movement and other dominated social groups. The inclusion of the perspectives of those who have experienced multiple oppressions critiques and challenges conventional assumptions about the nature of need, and the quality and type of support that people may require. Central to Clifford's methodology is the concept of critical auto/biography. The slash represents the importance of the connection that exists between the individual(s) making the assessment and the person(s) being assessed. Assessment, Clifford argues, is a complex process. Consequently, practitioners need to be aware of how personal, structural and methodological factors influence and affect our understanding of people's situations. As practitioners working with vulnerable people, our interpretation of social situations requires that we hold a 'critical (and self critical) stance on issues to do with values and action' (Clifford, 1998: 7). Practitioners assessing and intervening in the lives of people need to take into account the fact that their involvement in the process, their values, perspectives, personal histories and identities, will ultimately shape and direct their actions. Making assessments, therefore, 'is an intellectually challenging, skilful and ethical process' (Clifford, 1998: 9).

The following interconnected anti-oppressive principles which Clifford has developed over a number of years provide a firm basis for practitioners wishing to engage in assessments that are theorized, holistic and informed by the perspectives of those who have experienced various forms of oppression. These principles can be used to critically analyse social situations as well as critically assessing to what extent assessment tools and documents are sensitive to anti-oppressive principles and values.

Social difference

When making assessments, it is important to systematically take into account the range of socially constructed differences that exist within contemporary society. These differences arise because of inequalities of power between dominant and dominated social groups. The major social divisions are often identified as 'race', class, gender, age, sexuality and disability. Other social differences such as physical and mental health, service user status, religion, geographic location, also exist, adding to the complexity of oppression faced by individuals. It is the interconnection between what could be called major social divisions and other dimensions of difference that contributes to the unique experiences of oppression people face as well as the complex nature of oppression. The principle of *social difference* is based on an understanding of how social divisions interconnect and shape the lives of people.

Reflexivity

When assessing situations, we have to remember that as practitioners we are both participants in and observers of social situations. Our values, social identity, perspectives and professional status affect and are in turn affected by our involvement with service users, carers, colleagues and other professionals. Our values and perspectives are central to the process of understanding social situations. The anti-oppressive principle of *reflexivity* reminds practitioners of the need to continually reflect on and actively consider the ways in which their membership of particular social divisions, their values and knowledge of social situations affect how far they can facilitate service users sharing their experiences with them. It is also important to remember that responses from service users and carers within the assessment process are also influenced by previous contact and interactions with different agencies, including the agency that you represent, and may not just be in relation to you as a person. Therefore, the nature and quality of the relationship is not just determined by social divisions and power issues but by the institutional position that is held by the practitioner.

The historical dimension

Individual, family, group or community experiences and events should be located within an historical and social context so that these experiences are not abstracted from reality but are given meaning by being placed within a specific time and place. Practitioners therefore need to understand how key events on a local, national or international level may influence behaviour and attitudes.

Interacting social systems

Personal life experiences and events should be placed within the wider context of social systems. Individual life situations should be viewed in relation to social systems such as the family, peer groups, organizations and communities. Understanding these systems and how they may have contributed to an individual's experiences is vital if practitioners are not to divorce individual behaviour from the social systems which may have contributed to shaping the attitudes and actions of the individual. The impact of health and social care agencies and organizations should also be taken into account, as they too are a 'crucial part of the user's social world' (Clifford, 1998: 685).

Power

Power, as we have discussed in Chapter 2, is a complex social concept. Power shapes and determines relationships on an individual, group, community, organizational and societal level. Therefore, power issues in social relationships need to be analysed at different levels, 'at the level of political, social and economic structures, and at the level of personal power arising from cultural, institutional and psychological factors' (Clifford, 1998: 685). When making social assessments, practitioners may wish to consider questions such as:

- What is the nature of the power that this person has?
- Does this relate to their membership of various social divisions?
- What physical, material and financial resources does this family have?
- What are the cultural and psychological strengths and vulnerabilities of this person, this family?

These questions and other similar questions can assist the practitioner attempting to make a systematic power analysis of situations and will assist decision-making regarding levels of vulnerability and potential strengths of individuals who are living in situations of risk. A critical understanding of the process of assessment and the concept of need will assist practitioners engaging in anti-oppressive practice. This critical perspective should inform your understanding of the relationship between assessments and the legislation.

Assessment and the legislation

The assessment of need is pivotal to effective intervention and the provision of good-quality preventive services. There are many situations which, legally, social care practitioners are expected to assess. These are multiple and complex, and can be controversial. Local authorities in England, under section 7 of the Local Authority Social Services Act 2000, implemented the *Framework for the Assessment of Children in Need and their Families* (Department of Health et al., 2000), in April 2001 (Garrett, 2003; Millar and Corby, 2005). The framework, it should be pointed out, lacks the full force of statute, but it is a tool used by practitioners to undertake systematic assessments under the Children Act 1989 (section 17) as well as build on responsibilities under section 47 of the Act. These assessments, informed by an ecological and strengths-based approach, address the context in which difficulties arise and confirm the value of multidisciplinary working with children and families. The framework, in conjunction with the revised *Working Together to Safeguard Children* (Department of Health, 1999c), emphasizes the importance of considering child protection concerns within the context of children and families in need. By refocusing the protective and paternalistic gaze of practitioners to one of addressing the needs of disadvantaged and vulnerable children and families, it is envisaged that 'optimal outcomes' (Department of Health, 1999c: ii) for children and their families will be achieved.

Assessments of need are of two types: initial and core. Initial assessments are carried out at the referral stage 'to ensure the systematic screening of needs early on in the process of engagement with families' (Millar and Corby, 2005: 2). The initial assessment should take place within seven days of a referral being received. A core assessment is an in-depth holistic assessment in which there may be safeguarding concerns. This assessment is likely to involve other professionals providing specialist information or advice regarding the situation. The core assessment has to be completed within 35 days and begins at the point the initial assessment ended or a decision is made to undertake enquiries under section 47 of the Children Act 1989 when a child 'is suffering or likely to suffer significant harm'. Analysis of the information obtained during this period should inform planning, the intervention strategy and the nature of the services that are required. Assessments using the framework should be 'planned, undertaken in partnership with children and families and recorded appropriately' (Parker and Bradley, 2003: 20). The framework focuses on three key areas:

- the developmental needs of children;
- the capacity of parents or caregivers to respond appropriately to those needs;
- the impact of wider family and environmental factors on parenting capacity and the child.

(Department of Health, 1999b: 17)

The above areas of assessment interconnect and interrelate. The task of the practitioner is to carefully explore how these three areas affect the child's welfare and safety. The Common Assessment Framework for Children and Young People (Department of Health, 2005a) is designed to be used alongside the *Framework for the Assessment of Children in Need and their Families*. All local authorities are expected to implement this assessment process between April 2006 and the end of 2008. This assessment tool is designed to alert practitioners to potential issues and difficulties in children's lives. It is envisaged that the Common Assessment Framework will promote more effective, earlier identification of children's additional needs and improve multi-agency working. The implementation of the Framework will help agencies meet the new obligations set by sections 10 and 11 of the Children Act 2004, regarding the duty to improve the welfare of children under 18, and can be used by all practitioners working with children, young people and their families within, for example, health, education or social care agencies. Guidance (Department of Health, 2005a) identifies that a common assessment could be undertaken:

- when a child is displaying difficult and challenging behaviour within school which may be a result of bullying;
- when a child is engaging in antisocial behaviour due to possible substance misuse;
- when a routine postnatal visit raises concerns for a health practitioner about the housing conditions and the possible impact these may have on a newborn baby;
- when a practitioner is considering making a referral to another agency, such as child and adolescent mental health services.

The commitment to interagency working and the provision of integrated needs-led services informs assessments in relation to adults. The single assessment process outlined in the National Service Framework for Older People (Department of Health, 2001c) is designed to ensure:

> that older people receive appropriate, effective and timely responses to their health and social care needs, and that professional resources are used effectively. In pursuit of these aims, the single assessment process should ensure that scale and depth of assessment is kept in proportion to older people's needs; agencies do not duplicate each others' assessments; and professionals contribute to assessments in the most effective way.
>
> (Department of Health, 2002a: 2)

It is an interdisciplinary, interprofessional, coordinated approach to assessment and care planning. It is also an attempt to address the concerns of service users and carers that service provision at times was experienced as disjointed and patchy (Johns, 2005). The single assessment process is based on four different levels of assessment:

- contact assessment (information collected on the presenting problem at first contact with formal services);
- overview assessment (carried out if the professional feels that the person needs a more rounded assessment);
- specialist assessments (to explore specific needs);
- comprehensive assessment (when prolonged/intensive support is

likely to be required or when the person requires specialist assessments across a range of areas).

(Glasby, 2004: 130)

The assessments should be based on the needs, strengths and abilities of the individual and should take into account the level of support that the older person receives from family members, relatives, and people in the community. The assessment should inform a care plan which is subject to regular review. Once the assessment is completed it should (normally with the consent of the service user) be shared between health and social care agencies. When gathering, sharing and storing information for an assessment, it is essential that practitioners are aware of the requirements of the human rights legislation in relation to issues of privacy and confidentiality (Baldwin and Walker, 2005). The Single Assessment Process, the *Framework for the Assessment of Children in Need and their Families*, and the Common Assessment Framework for Children and Young People have all been driven by the increasing recognition of the need for 'joined up solutions for joined up problems' (Glasby, 2004: 7; Glasby and Lister, 2004). This emphasis on interprofessional collaboration has its strengths, in terms of providing coordinated, effective and creative service provision.

However, the effectiveness of the collaborative process can be compromised by the very differences that exist between the various professionals involved. For example, interprofessional divisions can be caused by the different interpretation that each professional has of the others' role, function and status. The differential access which some professional groups have to resources will accentuate divisions between practitioners. Competing values and theoretical perspectives held by practitioners within the collaborative group can also impede clear communication and effective working relationships (Glasby, 2004; Glasby and Lister, 2004; Darlington et al., 2005).

These difficulties can be minimized and overcome if all involved in the process are committed and willing to actively work towards the principles of partnership, not just with each other but with service users and carers – this requires as a first step that practitioners are clear about their roles and responsibilities, that they are committed to the goals of joint working, and importantly that they are willing to critically analyse decisions made in the light of competing values, beliefs and theoretical perspectives and are confident that decision-making processes have been underpinned by anti-oppressive principles and a commitment to meeting the needs of service users and carers.

Chapter summary

The complex nature of assessments cannot be overemphasized. Holistic assessments underpinned by anti-oppressive principles are essential if assessments are to truly reflect the experiences of people we are attempting to work with. Assessments should take account of the power relations that exist between individuals, groups and communities. There must also be some understanding of the links between people's personal experiences of oppression and the reality of structural inequality. As critical, reflective practitioners we must be aware of ourselves in the assessment process and how both we and the people involved in the assessment will inevitably be changed by the relationship. In this chapter we have looked at assessment as a process and in relation to the legislation. An anti-oppressive theoretically informed assessment framework provides practitioners with a basis to engage in assessments that are robust and ethical. The framework along with the pointers for practice should assist practitioners in the difficult task of assessing situations of uncertainty.

Further reading

Baldwin, N. and Walker, L. (2005) Assessment, in R. Adams, L. Dominelli and M. Payne (eds) *Social Work Futures: Crossing Boundaries, Transforming Practice.* Basingstoke: Palgrave.
This chapter looks at assessment in relation to children and families, and adults and provides case studies to explore the process of assessment.

Parker, J. and Bradley, G. (2003) *Social Work Practice: Assessing Planning, Intervention and Review.* Exeter: Learning Matters.
This book is written to meet the requirements of the new social work degree. It is an accessible book, which enables the student to look at the relationship between assessment, planning intervention and review. Chapters 1 and 2 look at assessment and assessment tools.

Holland, S. (2004) *Child and Family Assessment in Social Work Practice.* London: Sage Publications.
This book provides a detailed, theorized discussion of child and family assessments. The book, rooted in original research evidence, promotes a critical and reflective approach to assessment. The inclusion of exercises encourages the links between theory and practice.

Clifford, D. (1998) *Social Assessment Theory and Practice.* Aldershot: Ashgate Arena.
This book introduces and systematically develops the idea of social assessments within the health and social care professions. The book provides an innovative

and comprehensive theoretical and practical basis for social assessments. It usefully examines both multidisciplinary and multiprofessional issues in the process of assessment with a range of service user groups.

Activities

Activity 1

- Pair up with a friend, colleague or fellow student. Take it in turns to tell a story about something that happened in your family (childhood or current family). This should be an important event but not a traumatic one.
- Tell the story again, this time using objects as props. Perhaps use some plastic figures, dolls or puppets to represent the characters or draw the scene.
- Review together the differences and similarities in the experiences of telling the stories using each style.
- Now discuss what this might mean for assessment practice using talking and other ways of communicating.

This exercise is taken from Holland (2004: 160).

Activity 2

There are a number of assessment schedules that are used by practitioners within the area of health and social care. It is important to familiarize yourself with the content of these. For this activity you need to look at an assessment schedule. You can obtain this from the agency in which you are working or undertaking a placement. Using the principles below (this is not a definitive list), critically assess this schedule. Alternatively, you could talk to someone involved in assessments of older people and carers and try to identify the principles that inform his or her practice before comparing them with the five core principles outlined below. If you have been the subject of an assessment, you might like to reflect on this experience and consider whether you feel that the core principles informed the process.

- Begin from the user's and the carer's definitions of the relevant problems or issues.
- Be comprehensive, that is, be flexible and adaptable to enable a wide range of factors and information to be collated, as appropriate to each individual person and her or his circumstances.
- Provide a coherent framework for understanding and prioritizing the complex information gathered from a range of different sources.

- Take account of issues of confidentiality.
- Offer a consistent standard of good practice to users and carers while also recognizing that the process of assessment involves the exercising of judgement, whether professional judgement or subjective judgement of users and carers (Hughes, 1993).

11 Planning

> It sounded like an excellent plan, no doubt, and very neatly and simply arranged; the only difficulty was, that she had not the smallest idea how to set about it...
>
> (Lewis Carroll, *Alice's Adventures in Wonderland*)

The language of health and social care practice is now more focused on planning. Legislation requires us to agree *care plans* with service users in both health and social care settings. Governments produce planning frameworks (Department of Health, 2004b: 65) and local authorities are expected to produce service and development plans. In practice this means that while planning was once seen as merely a link between assessment and intervention, it is now considered as a key skill for all practitioners (Holloway, 2005). Furthermore, Holloway notes, while the emphasis on the planning machinery contained within National Service Frameworks and the Care Standards Act 2000 may initially seem to be a technical process, within their daily tasks health and social care practitioners 'find themselves reaching for "planning" as the tool which may help them to reduce a complicated multi-faceted problem to a manageable situation' (Holloway, 2005: 55). Legislation, policy guidance and research recognize that if we are to meet the needs of both services and individuals, plans must be informed by the views of actual and potential users of the services. This in turn requires local authorities to engage more closely with their local communities in order to define needs and identify how they intend to respond to them. In this chapter we will therefore examine what planning means to service users and carers, practitioners and those who have responsibility to produce policy and practice strategies.

The legal framework

Since the early 1990s, through various pieces of legislation, agencies and practitioners have been required to involve and consult with service users in service management and planning (Beresford and Croft, 2004; Holloway, 2005; Hudson, 2005). For example, the Children Act 1989 and the accompanying guidance and regulations require local authorities to approach planning and decision-making in partnership with children and families (Morris, 2005). The Children Act 1989 (Amendment) (Children Services

Planning) Order 1996 requires local authorities to devise a variety of services in consultation with a wide range of agencies (Morris, 2005; Preston-Shoot and Wigley, 2005). The Children Act 2004 takes forward the government's commitment – evident in Part III of the Children Act 1989 – to actively involve children and their families in the design and delivery of needs-led and holistic services. Section 17 of the Children Act 2004 also requires local authorities to prepare and publish a Children and Young People's Plan (CYPP) which covers services for all children and young people aged from 0 to 19, young people aged 20 and over leaving care, and young people up to age 25 with learning difficulties (Department for Education and Skills, 2005). The Children and Young People's Plan, although prepared by the local authority, has to be completed in partnership with agencies within the voluntary and community sectors that have a role to play in safeguarding and promoting the welfare of children. The Local Safeguarding Children Board[1] will also have an important role to play in the planning of services. Joint planning is therefore seen as a major cornerstone of the development of effective, integrated service provision.

Under the National Health Service and Community Care Act 1990, local authorities are required to prepare, publish and regularly update local delivery plans for the provision of community care services. Health departments and social services departments have had to establish joint care planning teams to advise on the development of strategic plans. The plans are intended to meet the needs of the population they serve. Services and objectives should be provided, for example, in relation to older people who require support services, people who have physical or learning difficulties, and those who have mental health difficulties or who have drug and alcohol dependency and are in need of preventive and after-care services (Brayne and Carr, 2003). The intention of this section (section 46) is that authorities will respond to the identified needs of the communities they serve rather than plan the services that they think people should want: this links in with the social justice model approach to service provision. The plan should be regularly updated to ensure that services respond to expressed needs. Culturally sensitive community care provision will take into account the diverse needs of minority communities and ensure that services are planned in consultation with them. In addition, the Act provides for each individual to have her or his needs assessed (section 47) and the guidance states that 'all users in receipt of a continuous service should have a care plan' (Department of Health, 1991b: 61). There is an obligation to assess needs, even if the authority is unable to resource the needs identified. 'The extent to which needs must be met will depend on whether the authority has the power or a duty to meet that need' (Brayne and Carr, 2003: 485). Practitioners therefore have to be aware of where there is a statutory obligation to meet assessed needs.

Equally, in terms of anti-oppressive practice, where discretion is exercised by the authority to meet a particular need then practitioners should challenge the decision where 'human rights are breached, government direction is ignored, or the proposed provision does not in fact meet the assessed need' (Brayne and Carr, 2003). Failure to challenge professional and managerial control of the planning agenda can lead to practice that has 'profoundly conservative consequences' (Humphries, 2005: 280) for services users and the development of service provision. The incorporation of service users' direct experience of policy and practice into the discussion, analysis and development of services radicalizes and refocuses the managerialist debates that take place in relation to the provision of services. This focus on those on the receiving end of services critically shifts the emphasis of service planning away from developing services centred on the needs of the organization to one that is needs-led (McTernan, 2003). It also ensures that decisions that could be deemed illegal, practice that is inappropriate, and interventions that are driven by a lack of resources are not concealed.

Radical and transformatory practice is based on a true engagement of people who require services for themselves or those they care for. The involvement of service users, groups and communities in mapping needs can impact on the way in which resources are allocated to alleviate the social conditions which contribute to the social problems people face. The assessment of need, practitioner experiences, evaluation studies of services already in place, and information on best practice can be used not only to understand the nature of need within a community but to generate new understandings of the nature of social problems and how they can be resolved.

The importance of planning

Guidance suggests that good planning is essential 'if services are to be developed to meet the needs of children, young people, and families, if resources, assets and the workforce are to be deployed to best effect, and if all partners are to focus on achieving the best possible local outcomes' (Department for Education and Skills, 2005: 4). However, planning is only likely to be effective if it is underpinned by information based on wide-ranging consultation that ensures that rich and diverse data are acquired so that the voices of all stakeholders are heard. Obtaining information that can be used to develop services is not an easy task, and research findings regarding local authority planning processes and needs assessments 'suggest that plans vary in quality and are often not strategic documents. There are gaps in information, for example population surveys on unmet need, whilst user and community consultation are rare' (Preston-Shoot and Wigley, 2005: 258). This means that there is a need to make best use of resources so that those who need support have access to services that are relevant and effective. Planning has a number of purposes (Preston-Shoot and Wigley, 2005):

- **Securing better services.**
- **Obtaining better outcomes for services users**. For example, the white paper *Valuing People* (Department of Health, 2001d) requires that a plan is agreed for the future for all adults with a learning disability living with carers aged 70 and older. This is in recognition of the fact that early planning can prevent the need for more in-trusive crisis-orientated intervention when the carer is no longer able to cope or dies (Bowey and McGlaughlin, 2005: 1380).
- **Focusing on business planning.**
- **Effectively managing finite resources**. Joint planning is one way in which limited resources can be used to fully meet the needs of service users. The government has put into place a number of in-itiatives to ensure that there is good partnership working and joint planning across health and social care services that will ensure that all those involved are actively engaged in the process and feel that there is a continuum of health and social care. To this end, it has been recognized that discharge from hospital is a process rather than an isolated event, and one that should be properly planned so people are transferred from hospital to the right setting, with care options to ensure that their health and social care needs are identified and met. Problems that can occur if there is no planned process are that dis-charges from hospital:
  - occur too soon;
  - are delayed;
  - are poorly managed from the patient/carer perspective;
  - are to unsafe environments. (Health and Social Care Joint Unit and Change Agents Team, 2003: 2)
- **Providing information to the public.**

Communications between service users, other professionals and across disciplines, however, are textured by power, differences in values, beliefs and views of the world (White and Featherstone, 2005). To ensure that plans are truly developed in partnership with users, the challenges of participation also need to be acknowledged and the appropriate resources put into place to ensure that user involvement is not tokenistic. The planning of health and social care services is not a neutral, esoteric activity. Plans provide a con-ceptual and practical framework at the level of service planning and at the level of practice to take forward the ideological commitment to meet need in its many forms. Meeting the care needs of individuals across different settings to ensure a continuum of care requires careful planning. If we take the ex-ample of people who have been diagnosed with cancer, research indicates that the majority of cancer care occurs in outpatient settings (National Cancer Institute, 2002). This means that most of the responsibility of accessing services is borne by those requiring a service – the patient and their families. This is not an easy task as health care systems are complex. It is therefore important that a coordinated approach is taken by health care systems so that this particular service user group, their carers and families do not experience a fragmented service provision which fails to address their specific needs.

Planning is a skilled activity requiring practitioners to employ a range of communication, analytical and relational skills. For plans to be effective, they must not only provide a detailed picture of a situation, identify the people or agencies who will be involved, 'clearly state what action might be taken, and by whom these actions might be taken in order to meet assessed or identified needs' (Parker and Bradley, 2003: 64), but they must also be negotiated and agreed by all participants. Plans should be clear and include mechanisms for ongoing review and evaluation. Finally, resources and a commitment to see the plan succeed should underpin the planning process.

Planning has to take account of the fluid nature of situations. Plans cannot be viewed as tools that will impose rationality and order on situations since, despite our best efforts, there are times when plans do not work out, for a variety of reasons. They should therefore be seen as dynamic documents which are regularly reviewed so that new information and any changes within the situation can be used to further develop and modify the plan. For agencies to deliver negotiated interdisciplinary, needs-led, preventive services, the plans underpinning such activities have to be informed by a critical understanding of the concept of need, information about the local levels and nature of need, long-term preventive strategies, agreed priorities and mechanisms for monitoring, reviewing and evaluating the plans.

The provision of a needs-led service has to be based on accurate and reliable information. Practitioners therefore have an important role to play in identifying and shaping services. This role has increased and become much more explicit over the years as 'the modernizing services' agenda of the late 1990s, combined with the managerial drive for 'quality' and the efficient use of resources, has resulted in the proliferation of a series of policy directives. Planning within practice now has a dual purpose: that of ensuring that the needs of the service user are met and that of meeting the needs of managerialism. In short, the 'balancing act between professional considerations and management imperatives which the individual practitioner must achieve becomes crucially located within the planning task' (Holloway, 2005: 56).

Different types of plans

Practitioners have to complete a number of specific care plans as part of their work with service users in a range of situations. Through completing these plans the assessed needs of the individual and how they may be met become concretized. This process links individual care planning and service planning, as the identification of needs, and the nature of the services that are required to meet them, are inextricably linked. The following brief discussion of different types of plans evidences the relationship between planning and the legislation. However, it should be noted that planning in complex and unpredictable situations is neither an easy task nor a technical one in which plans can be produced just by following prescriptive guidance. It is about the reflective and reflexive engagement with service users. The creation of an effective and creative plan requires practitioners to have 'a diverse knowledge base spanning human behaviour, social structures, policy frameworks and local resources' (Holloway, 2005: 65), and the ability to use this knowledge to challenge traditional practice responses.

Care plans for adults

The domination of the 'social care entrepreneurship' model within the area of care management 'where the availability of services is tightly constrained by cost' (Lymbery, 2004a: 61) has led to practitioners working in the area to be concerned about the quality of the practice that they are able to engage in. Ten years ago when we interviewed a hospital-based social worker, she remarked that 'care planning is just about ticking boxes. There are no resources to meet the needs, so what is the point of doing it?' This experienced practitioner, working within a context of limited resources and time constraints, felt that rather than engaging in creative social work practice, she was assessing the needs of the individual in terms of physical resources rather than helping them to understand what their lives would be like once they were discharged from hospital. Social workers in such situations feel frustrated and disempowered as the complex task of practice is reduced to an administrative task, that is, organizing resources rather than using their skills as practitioners. They feel powerless because all they can see are finite resources, complex needs and no solutions (Postle, 2001).

The practitioners we interviewed for this edition had similar concerns regarding the vast amounts of assessment documentation they had to complete and the consequent impact that this task had on the time that they had available to directly engage with service users. However, the single assessment process (SAP) for older people, which was introduced in the National Service Framework for Older People (Department of Health, 2001c), and the revised guidelines on care planning, should promote user-centred approaches and the possibility of engaging in creative person-centred practice (Parker and Bradley, 2003; Lymbery, 2004a). Under the National Health Service and Community Care Act 1990 all individuals in receipt of community care services should have a care plan. The care manager, with the service user and/or carer, draws up a plan based on the assessment of need of the individual and the services that will be provided. 'The plan may be implemented in a variety of ways, drawing on providers from public, private and voluntary sectors and with the scope for direct provision and direct payments to enable the service user to arrange their own services' (Brammer, 2003: 313). Care planning – the putting together, developing and writing of care plans within care management – should be responsive to the diverse needs and social division membership of the individual, and account should be taken of the environmental factors that have contributed to the needs that the individual has. Details of the level of support that carers can provide and the level of risk which the user is willing to accept need to be included in the plan alongside information regarding any contribution to the care costs that users are asked to make (Parker and Bradley, 2003).

Person-centred planning

Person-centred planning provides a widely adopted framework for supporting people who have continuing life-long needs in the community (Holloway, 2005). Plans are made on the basis of what the individual feels is important to them given their particular social situation and their individual needs. Planning is informed by the principles of social inclusion, human rights and the social model of disability. Within person-centred planning the power to make decisions resides with the individual and not the professional. Unlike the process of assessment and care planning, person-centred planning is not linked to eligibility criteria. Planning is undertaken in relation to the needs of the individuals so that they can live the life that they choose within their own communities. There are five key features (Webb and Skills for People, 2002) that distinguish person-centred planning from other processes; they are as follows:

- *The person is at the centre.*
  This means that the individual is centrally involved in the process and is able to choose who is involved in meeting their needs and helping them to make plans for their future. The approach is informed by the concepts of rights, independence and choice.
- *Family members and friends are key partners in planning.*
  Person-centred planning is about enabling people to remain and to be active members within their communities. It is recognized that friends, family and other members of the community have a valuable contribution to make in relation to providing appropriate support for people with learning disabilities so that they can live as independently as is possible.
- *The plan shows what is important to the key person (now or in the future). It shows their strengths and the support that they need.*

Through involvement with and a deeper understanding of the individual's needs and desires, plans can evolve and develop so as to take into account what is important for the individual, their abilities and what is needed to ensure that identified goals are attained.

- *The plan helps the person to be part of their community and helps the community to welcome them. It is not just about services. It shows what is possible, not just what is on offer.*

Central to meeting this key feature is the principle of working together to make the necessary changes that are required for individuals to live their lives to their fullest potential.

- *Things do not just stop when the first plan is written. Everyone involved keeps on listening, learning and making things happen. Putting the plan into action helps the person to achieve what they want out of life.*

People change as they are exposed to a variety of experiences. Therefore, the plan should reflect the dynamic nature of people's lives and the fact that difficulties can be resolved. The experiences of working together can be used to inform the person's life, community developments and the delivery of appropriate needs-led services.

Children in need

Plans for working with children in need and their families are central to measuring the success of any subsequent work that is undertaken. The central role of planning and coordinating services is highlighted in the inquiry into the death of Victoria Climbié (see, for example, Recommendations 13 and 51).

The content of plans will vary in relation to practice situations. They will, however, contain some similar elements. Guidance contained in the *Framework for the Assessment of Children in Need and their Families* (Department of Health, 2000a) provides a useful checklist in relation to the elements that should be included in plans:

- The objectives of the plan – these should be clear.
- What services will be provided by the various professionals involved.
- The timing and the nature of the contact between professionals and the people who they are working with.
- The purpose of the services and professional contact.
- The commitment to be met by the user(s), for example obtaining alternative accommodation or attending a local family support group.
- The commitment to be met by the practitioners involved – provision of services which are responsive to social divisions and equal opportunities.

- Which elements of the plan are negotiable and which are not.
- What needs to change and what goals need to be achieved.
- What is unacceptable in terms of care.
- What sanctions will be used if the individual is placed in danger.
- What preparation and support children and adults will receive if they have to appear in court as witnesses in criminal proceedings.

The *Children in Need Plan* is completed at the end of a core assessment, which will involve the child, family members and appropriate agencies. A format for the plan can be found in the assessment records (Department of Health and Cleaver, 2000). Following enquiries and assessment under section 47 of the Children Act 1989, an interagency initial child protection conference is convened. The focus of this meeting should be the establishment of a *child protection plan* to safeguard and promote the welfare of the child (Department of Health, 1999c: para 5.81). This responsibility is also enshrined in Recommendation 13 of the Lord Laming Report of the Victoria Climbié inquiry (Brayne and Carr, 2003).

The child protection plan should:

- Identify risks of significant harm to the child and ways in which the child can be protected through an interagency plan based on assessment findings.
- Establish short-term and longer-term aims and objectives that are clearly linked to reducing the risk of harm to the child and promoting the child's welfare.
- Be clear about who will have responsibility for which actions – including actions by family members – within specified timescales.
- Outline ways of monitoring and evaluating progress against the plan.
  (Department of Health, 1999c: para 5.69)

Care plan for looked-after children

A child in need who is looked after by the local authority should have a care plan which identifies immediate and longer-term objectives. Care plans should, if used to inform practice, assist in 'permanency planning' and reduce the risk of children drifting within the care system and in and out of care. Care plans need to be prepared for 'a child who is the subject of a care or supervision order or for whom the plan is adoption' (Department of Health, 2000a: 61). The local authority circular, LAC (99)29 (12 August 1999) 'Care Plans and Care Proceedings under the Children Act 1989' sets out guidelines for the preparation of plans for court cases. The guidance provides practitioners with advice as to what the plan should contain (Brayne and Carr, 2003).

Personal education plans

The promotion of the education of children within the public care system is part of New Labour's agenda to tackle social exclusion and educational failure. Guidance in this area, by promoting better planning mechanisms and structures, attempts to address the lack of planned help and support for looked-after children within the school system (Hayden, 2005). Looked-after children (except those in respite care) are required to have a personal education plan or 'PEP' (Department of Education and Employment/Department of Health, 2000). Personal education plans should be completed by a social worker and the designated teacher in the school and the child. The plan should be completed within 20 school days of the child entering care or joining a new school. Personal education plans should be reviewed regularly and be part and parcel of the general planning process of children in the care system. Research evidence suggests that social services staff and teachers use personal education plans as a mechanism through which they can 'meet and co-operate in the planning of the education of looked after children' (Hayden, 2005: 351).

We can see from this brief overview of some of the planning structures that both practitioners and service providers are subject to the need to make plans. How far organizations have fulfilled the remit to involve service users in service organization planning and delivery is questionable. Research commissioned by the Social Care Institute for Excellence and completed by the University of Sunderland with the Sunderland Carers' Centre, suggests that there is evidence that carers had access to key decision-making forums and that 'a small number of respondents had referred to involving carers through modernization and reform group structures' (Hudson, 2005: 1) which are important strategic multiagency structures in which services could be developed. However, the effectiveness of user involvement has been questioned (Beresford and Croft, 2004). Hudson's research also highlights the barriers that organizations and users may face when attempting to overcome some of the difficulties of ensuring that involvement of users at a strategic level is effective. Structures need to be created in which carers feel they have genuine involvement with supporting agencies. Progress is patchy in this area and good practice is often constrained by limited funding, while the gap between legislative intent in relation to involvement of users and practical outcome still needs to be bridged (Hudson, 2005).

Planning in practice

Family group conferences

Family group conferences have been used as a method of working with children and families since the early 1990s (Holland et al., 2005). They provide a forum in which family and social networks and professional systems can collectively contribute their knowledge and expertise in the form of a plan. The aim of this plan is to safeguard and enhance the welfare of the child, by attempting to change and democratize the nature of decision-making and developing approaches that are driven by the needs of the service user. Family group conferencing is a valuable participatory approach which can be used to effectively work with children and their families and has become 'increasingly recognized as an effective planning process' (Morris, 2002: 131). By facilitating 'more democratic relations within families' (Holland et al., 2005: 59), family group conferences attempt to reduce the power differences which exist between professionals and families. The approach is used in a wide range of situations where decisions need to be made about children (Lawrence and Wiffen, 2002). However, as a way of working family group conferences have been open to criticism relating to how issues of power are managed within the familial network (Lupton and Nixon, 1999; Dalrymple, 2002; Holland et al., 2005). Criticisms pertinent to this discussion regarding planning can be couched in terms of the following questions: How far do the needs of the child inform the plan? How far are the existing power imbalances within the family further reinforced by a plan that effectively reflects the needs of those who are most dominant? How far is the voice of the child listened to, understood and acted upon? How far can the opinions of the child influence what is effectively an adult-dominated decision-making process? It has also been pointed out that 'not all families are able to come together and plan, and in exceptional circumstances to do so would be to place a child at further risk' (Morris, 2002: 133). Despite these concerns, evidence suggests that family group conferences are successful when compared to traditional practice approaches 'in terms of mobilising family involvement, [and] maintaining children's care within the family network ...' (Holland et al., 2005: 60). This means that family group conferences can, as part of a range of methods and approaches, contribute to the making of plans that are effective.

Concurrent planning

The importance of planning is nowhere more significant than in relation to ensuring that decisions regarding the placement of children are made within acceptable timescales. In section 1(2) of the Children Act 1989, one of the principles concerning the welfare of the child is the 'avoidance of delay' which creates uncertainty for children and can have a detrimental effect on the relationship between children and their parents (Department of Health, 1991b: para 1.8). It has been argued that the Act has not lived up to the initial promise of reducing court delay, and in fact evidence indicates that delay is becoming more common (McKeigue and Beckett, 2004). One remedy to this situation is that the court is required firstly to draw up a timetable to ensure that delay is minimal, and secondly 'give such direction as it considers appropriate for the purpose of ensuring, so far as is reasonably practicable, that that timetable is adhered to' (Brayne and Carr, 2003: 244). The National Adoption Standards for England (Department of Health, 2001b) also directly tackle the issues of drift and delay and requires local authorities to ensure that:

- the child's need for a permanent home will be addressed at the four-month review and a plan for permanence made;
- clear timescales will be set for achieving the plan, which will be appropriately monitored and considered at every subsequent review;
- where the plan is adoption, the adoption panel will make its recommendation within two months.

Additionally, 'section 109 of the 2002 Adoption and Children Act requires courts to draw up timetables for resolving adoption cases without delay together with directions that timetables are adhered to' (Wigfall et al., 2006: 43). Underpinning principles of concurrent planning are identified as 'the focus on the child, the promotion of permanence, the reduction in the number of moves, the tight timescales, and the concurrent exploration of two potential outcomes' (Wigfall et al., 2006: 47). As an approach to the permanent placement of children, concurrent planning can be seen as a possible solution to the problem of looked-after children languishing in the care system, failing to achieve their potential, and providing them with the opportunity to experience a permanent family. Concurrent planning, which has its origins in Seattle, USA (introduced to the UK in 1998), is a controversial approach to planning in the area of child care.

In brief,[2] concurrent planning aims to speed up the permanent placement of children. This is achieved by assessing the immediate birth family and the extended family – that is, looking at possibilities of rehabilitation and at the same time developing a care plan for placement outside the family. While work is being undertaken with the birth family, the child is placed with a family who are approved as both foster carers and adopters, who would, should rehabilitation plans fail or prove not to be possible, go on to adopt the child. Concurrent planning requires a clear, time-limited plan to be drawn up with the birth family which addresses the problems that precipitated the removal of the child and what is required for the child to be returned. The plan equally has to ensure that the need of the child for permanency is also met.

It should be acknowledged that concurrent planning poses a number of ethical and practice dilemmas for practitioners: for example, the investment of concurrent carers in the child that is placed with them is quite high, so how far are they able to actively engage and commit to the process of rehabilitation? Does the imposition of specific timescales facilitate or hinder birth parents making the necessary changes in their personal and social situations? In an evaluation study only 2 out of 24 children were returned to the birth family, indicating that rehabilitation was unlikely. It also has to be noted that research evidence from three pilot concurrency projects has suggested that concurrency planning in relation to babies under 12 months speeded up placement, and that fewer adoptions were contested (Wigfall et al., 2006). However, we are aware from research evidence that children who wait tend to be older, have complex needs, are black, Asian and of racially mixed parentage (Frazer and Selwyn, 2005). Will concurrent planning have an impact on the length of time that these children have to wait for permanent placements? As an approach, concurrent planning may in time become a more familiar tool in the range of options available to practitioners, but it is probably one that practitioners will not choose when there is a possibility of rehabilitation.

The issues raised by concurrent planning in relation to meeting the placement needs of children should be placed within the wider context of government policy, anti-oppressive practice and the interests of children and their families. Social workers undertaking assessments, while acknowledging the importance of making timely decisions, are aware that individual factors within cases may well make it difficult to maintain the principle of avoiding delay, and that at times to speed up decision-making processes may be counterproductive, undermining partnership arrangements, and may be detrimental to the long-term needs of the child (Clifford and Burke, 2004). Practitioners are committed to ensuring that the plans that they make take into account the best interests of service users. However, by failing to appreciate the complex ethical and practice issues involved when placing children, government policy adds to the already difficult task that practitioners face.

Chapter summary

Multiprofessional and interagency planning, commissioning and delivery of services requires that working relationships between different professional groups are constructive and that meaningful communication is engaged in. The achievement of a needs-led approach to the planning and delivery of services is dependent on practitioners undertaking comprehensive, multidisciplinary assessments of individuals who require a service and using information obtained to inform plans and intervention strategies. The emphasis on *working together* has led to the development of partnership arrangements within local authorities. This is a positive and essential move for effective planning. In this chapter we have looked at the role and purpose of planning within the legislative context, and looked at how the need for effective planning has had an impact on approaches to practice. The use of planning as a process to facilitate and promote user involvement is made possible within the framework of family group conferences. Using the example of concurrent planning within child care, the complex relationship between theory, practice and policy becomes evident – the needs of children and their families, professional considerations and values can collide with government and management imperatives to reduce the number of children who wait. Planning, if it is to be effective and of good quality, should incorporate the active involvement of users. The legislation provides the impetus for action in this direction.

Further reading

Parker, J. and Bradley, G. (2003) *Social Work Practice: Assessing, Planning, Intervention and Review*. Exeter: Learning Matters.
This is written for undergraduates and is an accessible book which enables the student to look at the relationships between assessment, planning, intervention and review. Chapter 3 looks at how plans are made in children and family work, as well as with adults. Guidance on and activities related to care planning are included.

Holloway, M. (2005) Planning, in R. Adams, L. Dominelli and M. Payne (eds) *Social Work Futures: Crossing Boundaries, Transforming Practice*. Basingstoke: Palgrave Macmillan, pp. 54–67.
This is a useful chapter which explores the task and processes planning. The chapter usefully includes a number of case studies.

Mandelstam, M. (2005) *Community Care Practice and the Law*, 3rd edn. London: Jessica Kingsley.
This book looks at the legal and policy changes affecting the field of community care and at the practical implications of the law.

Activity: Debra and Assim: case example revisited

Debra (age 22) is a white young woman with a long-standing drug habit. Her 3-year-old son Ricky, who is white, lives with his grandparents, Mary and Peter. She is expecting a baby and her partner, Assim (age 22), who is black, is the father. Assim is aggressive and hostile towards professionals and has been convicted of several violent offences. In the last three months of the pregnancy, Debra has managed to reduce her drug use and make a home for the forthcoming baby. However, she still sees Assim regularly and they are both saying that they are committed to each other.

The week before the baby is due there is a big domestic incident with Assim and the police are called. Debra is injured. As a result of the police enquiries it comes to light that Debra has been regularly assaulted throughout her pregnancy by Assim. Mary says that she feels the baby will not be safe with Debra and has offered to care for the baby after it is born. The social worker has tried to discuss with Debra and Assim the concerns raised by Mary and by the professionals involved with the family. Assim, during that interview, becomes hostile and threatening and has now refused to engage with the social worker in any further assessment. Debra is saying that she will do anything to keep the baby, including agreeing to seek further help with her drug dependency and separate from Assim.

There are a number of issues to think about here. First of all, the primary concern must be to safeguard the baby when it is born. This involves the assessment of Debra and Assim's parenting capacity, which the social worker has already started to do. Mary's offer to care for the baby would be an easy option and resolve many of the problems identified by the professionals. A potential problem here, though, for the baby growing up in a predominantly white household could be the development of a positive black identity. The social worker is aware that under section 47 of the Children Act 1989 and her statutory responsibilities in relation to *Working Together to Safeguard Children: A Guide to Inter-Agency Working to Safeguard and Promote the Welfare of Children* (Department of Health et al., 1999) and the *Framework for the Assessment of Children in Need and their Families* (Department of Health et al., 2000), there are a number of concerns to be addressed. However, Debra has the right to an opportunity to see if she can care for the baby, and Assim also has a right to be a parent. The social worker is working with Debra to identify her strengths. However, assessing the situation in the context of drug use and violence is complex. There needs to be re-engagement with Assim, but working in a climate where he is hostile to social services involvement is likely to be difficult. Debra's drug use structures her life in a particular way. She is a parent alongside trying to find money to feed her habit – this is difficult if she has to spend all day looking for a dealer while avoiding people she owes money to. Furthermore, for the social worker, if Debra is out and about, it is difficult to make a thorough assessment and/or to observe her interactions with her baby when it is born.

The process of assessment and planning are inextricably linked, however we would like you in this exercise to focus on planning how you would work with all the people involved in this case study. The Children Act 1989 identifies the importance of a negotiated and planned service provision. Using the case study draw up an appropriate plan of how you would work with Assim and Debra.

It is important when constructing a plan that you work openly, honestly and in partnership with all the participants. The plan has to be negotiated and owned by all the individuals it affects if it is to work. A number of challenges are presented in the above scenario. It is therefore important that the task of planning is not undertaken as a technical activity but one that is informed by care and concern and an understanding of the difficulties faced by the various participants.

12 Service user involvement

Last week I voiced my concerns about this plan. I spoke of the need to start with my son. To look at the way he chooses to communicate and encourage that. To find things that interest him and explore those with his classmates. I asked what would happen if my son was not interested in this communication system – would he be seen to have failed – again? It was noted that once again I was questioning professional opinion, obstructing any attempts to help my son. My words went unheard, my voice of knowledge and experience of my son was not listened to.

(Murray and Penman, 1996: 5)

For the last 20 years, the emergence and development of the idea of 'user involvement' has had a significant impact on the development of more liberatory social work (Beresford and Croft, 2004: 63). Involvement of service users and carers has been a priority for the UK government (Department of Health, 2001a) since consultation was first made a legislative duty in the early 1990s. Both the government and health and social care providers recognize that service users have a 'legitimate and distinct' (Miller, 2003) contribution to make to the planning and delivery of services. Since the Children Act 1989 and the National Health Service and Community Care Act 1990 made consultation a legislative duty, there have been increasing requirements for local authorities to actively involve service users and carers in service development. For example, directives on *Best Value* for local authorities have increased requirements for active service user (and carer) participation. Children and young people must be offered an independent advocate when they make a formal complaint.[1] An independent complaints advocacy service is linked to the Commission for Patient and Public Involvement in Health. National initiatives have been funded that recognize patient and public involvement,[2] and service users are required to be involved in all aspects of training for social workers.[3] These and many other initiatives indicate that the 'participatory rhetoric' associated with social care practice since the 1970s is now being mainstreamed into policy and practice (Beresford and Croft, 2004). However, developing effective user involvement is challenging for health and social care practitioners and organizations are developing so that:

The voices of patients, their carers, and the public generally are heard and listened to through every level of the service, acting as a lever for change and improvement.

(Department of Health, 2001a: para 2.1)

For example, the Mental Health Act Commission has a Service User Reference Panel with a remit to:

- provide the Commission with a service user perspective on all aspects of its current and planned activity;
- influence the Commission's work programme, including advising and commenting on visiting priorities, development work, and publications;
- advise on how the Commission can involve users meaningfully and effectively in its work.

http://www.mhac.org.uk/Pages/serviceuser.html

Patient Advice and Liaison Services (PALS) offer a one-stop advisory service within hospital and primary care trusts in England; and Patient and Public Involvement in Health forums are attached to National Health Service trusts and primary care trusts in England to make sure that the public is involved in decision-making about health and health services.

Despite progress in establishing principles of service user participation, however, the fact remains that 'user-participation initiatives require continual awareness of the context of power relations in which they are being conducted' (Carr, 2004: vii). Health and social care practitioners therefore need to consider ways of supporting the involvement of service users both in practice and in the process of theory-building (Beresford and Croft, 2000). Research indicates that user organizations are not satisfied with the process or outcomes of their involvement (Barnes and Shardlow, 1997; Carr, 2004). However, a major achievement of the National User Involvement project was that disabled people began to be perceived as experts to be consulted rather than 'service users' (Lindow, 2005). This immediately indicates a dilemma regarding terminology: both the term 'service user' and interpretations of user involvement are contested. In order to consider the problems of political interpretation and practical implementation that have frustrated both users of services and professionals (Robson et al., 2005), this chapter will begin by looking at terminology and consider different theoretical perspectives about user involvement. We will then go on to think about some practice models and issues and dilemmas in promoting participatory practice.

Service users – problems of definition

While we have chosen to use the term 'service user' throughout this book, the terminology used to describe the relationships between agencies providing services and people receiving them varies. For example, the word 'consumer' began to be favoured in the mid-1990s as a term that is reflected in a number of approaches aimed at gaining people's views about services. While this has never really been a term favoured by service user groups, consumerist initiatives – such as surveys, focus groups, panels and councils – which seek views on identified issues or particular services, reflect the view that services are provided for their consumers. However, people in receipt of health services are *patients*,[4] those living in supported housing or a care situation are *tenants* or *residents*, opticians and chemists refer to *customers* and other services work with *clients* or *service users*. Some academics use these last two terms interchangeably. For example, Dominelli considers that both are problematic in terms of the relationship between social workers and the people using social services, explaining that:

> I retain the word 'client' as it is understood more clearly worldwide, although I occasionally refer to 'users' to avoid constant repetition of the word 'client' when one use of it follows another in close proximity. I intend both terms to mean simply the person or persons that approach professional social workers for services or assistance.
>
> (2002a: 6)

Payne (2005a) also recognizes the international understanding of the word 'client', which he feels is the most inclusive and generally understandable term. However, he more specifically uses the word 'users' when referring to people who are receiving packages of services or referring to services for people with learning difficulties, where the term is most prevalent. In addition, language such as *public involvement, service user involvement* or *lay involvement* is variously applied when the perspectives of communities are sought on wider issues such as building a hospital, the development of initiatives such as Sure Start[5] or improving practice through National Service Frameworks.[6] In public health, the concept of 'lay involvement' is used to reflect the changing nature of the way people are involved in public services. The perception of the public not as passive recipients of expert health care but as active participants in the process of health improvement (Taylor, 2003) is the same as in other areas of health and welfare services, but 'lay involvement' appears to be a less contentious term.

Practitioners and academics initiate many of these debates, although they are based on a developing understanding of user perspectives through listening to their stories. The Shaping Our Lives National User Network uses the term 'service user' in an active and positive way, pointing out that the term should always be based on self-identification. The development of service user movements is a reaction to their negative experience of welfarist and professional responses and they are significantly different to other social movements who campaign *on behalf of* marginalized groups. Service user movements are:

- based on self-identification, such as movements of disabled people, mental health service users, psychiatric system survivors or older people;
- self-organized and self-run, that is, organized around local, national and international groups based on their own identities which they control, developing their own ways of working, philosophies and objectives;
- committed to parliamentary and direct action, for example the work of the disabled people's movement's Direct Action Network, the psychiatric system survivors Reclaim Bedlam and Mad Pride Campaigns, and NAYPIC,[7] a campaigning organization that was set up by young people in local authority care.

(Beresford and Croft, 2000)

However, use of the term 'service user' can still imply that a person is defined primarily as a passive recipient of a service. Service user organizations have challenged use of the term in this way on the basis that a service user is first a person, who cannot fit easily into categorizations around service divisions or client groups. The Shaping Our Lives National User Network identifies a number of meanings for the term 'service user':

- Being in an unequal and oppressive relationship with the state and society.
- Having an entitlement to receive welfare services. This includes the past when someone might have received a service and the present. Some people still need a service but for a number of reasons are not entitled to it.
- Sometimes having to use a service for a long time which separates service users from other people, and stigmatizes them as being inferior or having something wrong with them.
- Identifying and recognizing that service users share a lot of experiences with a wide range of people who use services. For example, care experienced young people, people with learning difficulties, mental health service users, older people, physically and/or sensorily impaired people, people using palliative care services and people with

drug and alcohol problems. The Network points out that recognition of the shared experiences of people who use services gives them a powerful voice.

(Levin, 2005: 20)

What is user involvement?

Defining exactly what is meant by the term 'user involvement' is equally problematic. The words 'partnership',[8] 'involvement', 'participation' and 'working together' have all been used in relation to thinking about user involvement, have become integrated into social policy and service provision (Powell, 2001) and are often used interchangeably. However, it has been suggested that the challenge for practitioners is actually putting the ideas underpinning these terms into practice (Levin, 2005). Nevertheless, there are some significant differences that indicate what happens and the associated levels of activity (or passivity). Firstly, people may be *involved* as individuals in decisions concerning their own lives (in agreeing their personal care plans; attending reviews, case conferences or other decision-making forums); as individuals in wider events (focus groups or consultation events); through membership of an organization – where service users have formed an identity (a self-help group or user-led organization such as Gingerbread[9] or Alcoholics Anonymous), or as a representative of a wider group (such as a network for carers or local community group). Involvement might be one-off or ongoing. For example, questionnaires and feedback forms, focus groups and group interviews, or consultation events provide an opportunity for a lot of people to contribute their views who might only be interested in a particular issue. On the other hand, people who live in residential care may have regular group meetings, young people may belong to a youth forum, service users may choose to join subcommittees and working groups, be part of a newsletter group or be regularly involved in specific activities such as recruiting and training staff. Involvement can also include activities that range from complaining (an open service is one that welcomes complaints and is prepared to act on what people say about the service), to fundraising and voluntary work.

Participation more precisely defines an activity where people are not just listened to or consulted, but are also able to influence and achieve change (Willow, 2002). Participatory approaches in development have been described as encouraging 'involvement in interventions that affect them and over which they previously had limited control or no influence' (Cooke and Kothari, 2001: 5). *Working together* is a term used in many contexts to describe ways of improving practice. For example, Monmouthshire Council[10] in Wales has a community strategy which focuses on working with communities to find out what people think, need and aspire to. It encourages local organizations to work together in order to create a shared vision in which the community knows where it wants to be and what it wants to look like. Salford City Council Community, Health and Social Care Services[11] in England routinely talk to and involve service users and carers in the planning, development, delivery and review of services. Their Joint Working Together Strategy stresses the importance of involving service users, carers and local citizens which is linked with the notion of building a sense of ownership and trust, as well as delivering services to better meet people's needs.

Case example: Communicating with Tony

Lisa is a social work student who had a placement in a residential home for people with learning difficulties which aimed to 'provide a home from home' and 24-hour support to encourage independent living. The residential home has a philosophy of care of participation, respect, information, choice, and individuality to help them provide an effective service and to involve each individual to develop their life skills. Tony, aged 36, is a white man who lives in the home. Lisa attended a meeting with Tony that was held to decide about his future. She found this meeting 'very fast and very verbal' and, unsurprisingly, Tony did not stay in the meeting for very long.

Lisa decided to try and find other ways of communicating with Tony so that he could be more involved in his meetings. She went to the library and found a book about picture exchange communication and used some of their ideas. Together, Tony and Lisa took photographs of things that he liked and disliked. Tony did not see why he should take pictures of things he did not like and so there was a larger list of likes. Lisa found that 'it was good seeing how such a simple technique could help communication'. She was realistic about the comments from some people that the enjoyment of the activity on a particular day could influence some of the pictures that he took. Nevertheless, it helped her to communicate with Tony and to provide work that he could take to the meeting to help the decision-making process. Lisa was disappointed that the professionals in the meeting did not take a great deal of notice of his work. However, she had started a process that had a number of potential outcomes for future work with Tony and other service users living in the same home:

- she developed ways of enabling Tony to communicate;
- she made people aware that Tony could be actively involved in decisions concerning his life;
- she ensured that a service user perspective became integral to work with all the people living in the home.

Lisa went back to the home after her placement finished and commented that Tony recognized her. For her this was evidence that the work that she had started with Tony had a positive impact.

One way of distinguishing the various experiences is through consideration of 'management-centred approaches to user involvement' where service users take part in existing organizational structures with an agenda that is defined by the organization; and 'user-centred user involvement' which means that the objectives and priorities of service users become those of the organization (Robson et al., 2005). Organizations engage with service users in different ways, and there is a risk in relation to management-centred approaches that initiatives to involve service users are 'conducted as externalised consultation exercises to approve of professional service planning and policy proposals rather than enabling service users to be integral partners for their fomulation' (Carr, 2004: 17). On the other hand, a study of three very different user-led mental health groups found that while their involvement did not have any significant impact on power relations within the mental health system, there was a change in some cases in the nature of the relationship between service users and providers. Significantly, it forced a level of accountability by providers. The service user groups were able to challenge the systems and make those in existing positions of power consider things in different ways (Barnes and Shardlow, 1997).

A second way of thinking about user involvement is through consideration of the ideological basis of involvement. Two approaches can be identified: consumerist and democratic. Consumerist/managerial approaches to user involvement have developed with the increasing use of market approaches within health and social care services. In the late 1970s emphasis on purchasing services meant that recipients of health and social care became active consumers. Their 'needs' were recognized and the responsiveness, accessibility and quality of services were emphasized. User involvement therefore meant 'improving the product' by getting feedback from customers in various ways. The principles of consumerism are:

- accessibility;
- information;
- choice;
- redress;
- representation.

Many of these are key elements of health and social care legislation. The consumerist model has been criticized, though, for being used 'both self consciously and implicitly as a means of "user intelligence gathering"' (Beresford, 2005: 79) through consultative methods of collecting information. While services may have become more responsive, flexible and relevant, they continue to be owned and controlled by the organizations or professionals delivering the service (Braye, 2000). This means that service user representation in the wider processes of health and social care planning and delivery is unlikely, and there are no opportunities for wider dialogue on health and social care issues (Taylor, 2003). A further problem with the consumerist approach is that it supports an increasing emphasis on the 'managerialist' element of service user involvement as legislation and policy initiatives now include service users in audit, inspection planning, individual assessment, complaints procedures and (consultatively) in service management (Beresford, 2005). How far choice is really possible in consumerism has also been questioned, as this will depend on who is really making the choice and the financial restrictions that inevitably limit availability of alternatives. It has been pointed out, though, that consumerism does at least create the chance for groups of service users to share their views within any consultative mechanisms that are in place. Taylor (2003) also notes the possibility for encouraging more participation, and therefore gaining more influence, if there are various opportunities available for service user involvement. An incremental development of participation may then lead to more democratic approaches, which we consider below.

The centrality of choice in consumerism

Choice in consumerism depends on who is making the choice and how it will be paid for. For example:

- There may be a lack of providers in certain areas, for example in rural communities where there can be less choice than in urban areas. One private social care provider may have a monopoly; in some areas local authorities have little or no provision of their own (in-house).
- Financial ceilings on the amount of support a person is awarded so that, for instance, a person might be seen as 'costing too much' for support at home and encouraged to use institutional care even if their choice is to continue living in their own home.
- Conflict or disagreement about the type or level of support needed. A person might not wish to be helped to get ready for bed at 5pm or might find that a 15-minute visit from a care worker to help with personal care is too rushed.

(Malin et al., 2002: 61)

Democratic approaches, on the other hand, are more concerned about ensuring that people have influence in relation to the services that they are using and the organizations that impact on them (including policy-making, resource allocation and management) so that they have more control over their lives (Beresford, 2005). The focus is not on welfare rights but participatory rights to:

- be heard;
- participate;
- exercise choice;
- define problems and action.

Since this approach is about changing service users' experience of service delivery collectively, rather than individually, it has been described as a political approach to involvement (Beresford, 2005) because its main concern is to ensure that service users are able to directly promote change.

> The goals will thus reside in the wider avenues of citizenship in which oppression and exclusion are experienced. They will be chosen by people themselves, rather than enacting professional agendas for meeting need.
>
> (Braye, 2000: 19)

While initiatives as a result of consumerist approaches have been limited in terms of impact on user/professional power relations, service user movements have been associated with changes in policy and the provision of health and social care services. Beresford and Croft (2004) point out that while these achievements should not be overstated, nor should they be underestimated, as they represent the development of transformative practice, disturbing dominant understandings and structures.

The impact of service user movements and organizations

- Developing a new discourse which has challenged traditional social work practice from a progressive and liberatory position (as opposed to the generally right-wing and negative media-related discourse).
- Placing a renewed emphasis on the human and civil rights of service users (rather than framing them in terms of 'needs' to be interpreted by outside 'experts').
- Developing social models and understandings of service users' situations and experience, in particular the 'social model of disability' (Oliver, 1990).
- Conceiving and pioneering new and different approaches to providing individual and collective support for service users, for example developments from 'direct payments', putting individual service users in control of personal 'packages of support', user-controlled services, development of independent advocacy and support roles.
- Providing a campaigning force to back up and provide pressure for the implementation of their progressive proposals. Local democratically constituted organizations controlled by service users have provided the basis for

local, national and international action to support service users' aims and objectives.

- Working for the inclusion of service users in health, social care and social work, employment and training.

(Beresford and Croft, 2004: 63)

We can see that the active involvement of service users as citizens rather than just recipients of services (Lister, 1998b) means that the relationships between practitioners, carers and service users are being reframed. This does not negate the value of professionalism because, as Powell notes, 'most citizens value professional support and advice, but they wish it to be accountable to the public it serves' (Powell, 2001: 141).

Models of involvement

Alongside the ideological approaches outlined above, a number of models of participation have developed to analyse the level and nature of user involvement. Each model incorporates a recognition that there are varying degrees of participation and, for any user involvement initiative to be successful, allies are needed within the organizations involved. The best-known model is the ladder of participation, first developed by Arnstein (1969) with reference to the involvement of citizens in housing and community development in the USA.[12] The ladder places degrees of participation on various rungs, with the bottom rung representing limited participation, where views may be expressed but not necessarily taken into account. Varying degrees on subsequent rungs move to the top of the ladder, representing total control and active citizenship. This model has been criticized for its simplicity and the suggestion that the lower rungs are not worthwhile. However, it has also been identified as a useful way of ensuring that we are vigilant about the true extent of user involvement and mechanisms that are apparently designed to empower service users (Willow, 2002).

An alternative model is that of a wheel (Treseder and Crowley, 2001), with varying degrees of participation depicted as spokes that may be applicable to a particular service user on a certain issue at a particular point in time. Research has shown that there needs to be a range of methods of involvement depending on how far service users want to commit themselves (Carr, 2004). This model recognizes that there is choice about the level of participation, recognition that at particular times people may want to be more or less involved for varying reasons, and that the involvement is real.

A third model is that of a bridge. This has been used to demonstrate effective user involvement in community care (Taylor and Upward, 1995) and to demonstrate the politics of participation for young people (John, 1996). John argues for this more dynamic model because it encompasses 'the construction of creative alliances with adults which forms the true basis of an emotional democracy on which, it could be argued, children's participation must be based' (John, 1996: 19). The strength of the bridge depends on the time, resources and personnel available to develop it, how far it allows flexibility on the agendas of both sides, and how far it reaches out to service users on one side and decision-making processes on the other. The bridge therefore needs firm foundations and ongoing maintenance at all times. The maintenance can be undertaken by individuals or collaboratively, with all parties negotiating together in a process whereby service users are not passive but active constructors and maintainers of the bridge.

Values – making user involvement a reality

A number of difficulties have been highlighted in the literature about implementing effective user-led change. One of the key points is to be aware that any user involvement requires us to be constantly conscious of the context of the power relations in which it is being conducted (Carr, 2004). The history of welfare involves a division between service users and professionals who are delivering services, with users seen as passive recipients of charity and care rather than active participants in any planning or delivery of services. Paternalism rather than partnership was the guiding principle. Decision-making power was with the providers of services, and professional expertise was seen as necessary for the effective implementation of their services. Research has shown that 'exclusionary practices and attitudes can still affect the extent to which service users can influence change. It appears that power sharing can be difficult within established mainstream structures, formal consultation mechanisms and traditional ideologies' (Carr, 2004: vii). This is demonstrated in findings from research about risk assessment and management and the involvement of mental health service users. Their involvement was variable and often depended on individual professional initiative. While some service users influenced the support they received, their role on the whole was to accept or reject what was offered. At the same time, there was not much use made of advocates and service users did not get a full picture about different available supports. The researchers suggested that the involvement of service users could improve the effectiveness of risk management, 'a willingness to take appropriate risks, talk about risk and look holistically at all aspects of a person's life may go some way to enable more effective risk management' (Lindow and Rooke-Matthews, 2005). The example in the box identifies some of these issues.

Case example continued: Tony's walks – risks and rights

Tony finds it difficult to communicate verbally. He enjoys walking and had been used to going out on long walks on his own. However for three months he had been unable to do this as the professionals involved considered that he was too vulnerable. A key pad on the front door effectively stopped him from leaving his home.

Lisa found that Tony's confinement affected him emotionally and physically. He was upset that he was not allowed out and this frustration caused situations of challenging behaviour such as ripping up his clothes and even going to hit out at individual support workers. He was also putting on weight because of the lack of exercise and would eat more because he was bored. All the people who shared a home with Tony were affected by this decision. Lisa recognized that the situation was also difficult for the support workers, who would worry when he went out for a walk (whether or not it was organized) and who also felt guilty about not allowing him to go out and having to explain to him why this decision had been made. Although Tony did have a one-to-one worker who was helping him to make a scrap book, as Lisa pointed out, 'he likes doing the scrap book but that isn't fresh air – he is a fresh air person. Being indoors all day must be a nightmare for him.' But sitting in the small garden was not enough either – because what he liked to do was to walk.

Lisa was concerned that Tony's human rights were being violated under Article 5 of the Human Rights Act. She asked if it was legal to restrict Tony's liberty in this way and was told that he could be considered as *de facto* detained. She didn't understand what this meant and so went to her law books to find out. She could not find anything about it. However, she was so sure that it was against the Human Rights Act for this to be happening to Tony that she continued to ask questions and look for more information. She found out about *de facto* detention in Mental Health Law and read about the decision in the European Court of Human Rights in the case of *H.L. v The United Kingdom* (Application no. 45508/99).

The decision concerned H.L., a 49-year-old man with autism. He was deemed to lack capacity. He had been an 'informal' patient at Bournewood Hospital for over 30 years. That is, he was not subject to detention under the Mental Health Act 1983 and although use of legislation was considered, it was not deemed necessary by the responsible consultant because H.L. was compliant and had not resisted admission and had not tried to 'run away'. In 1994 he was discharged to reside (successfully) with paid carers. On 22 July 1997 the day centre he attended reported concerns for H.L. and alerted the hospital. H.L. was returned to hospital in his own 'best interests' under the common law doctrine of necessity. This happened without the knowledge of the paid carers and when they requested his discharge it was refused. Challenges went all the way to the

House of Lords and then to the European Court of Human Rights as to what constituted legal detention, and eventually a decision from the European Court found that H.L.'s human rights had been breached under Articles 5.1 and 5.4 of the Human Rights Act 1998 – these being the right to liberty and security and the right to have legality of detention reviewed. (For a full summary of the case and decision, see the European Court of Human Rights internet site: *http:// www.echr.coe.int.*)

This decision led to what is known as the 'Bournewood Gap' and at the time of writing it has been the subject of various case law as to what constitutes 'detention'. The contradictory rulings do not make it clear as to what can be considered detention or deprivation of liberty, not even in locked wards. It was thought that the new Mental Capacity Act 2005 would clarify the issue, but guidance for the Act already states that the 'Bournewood Gap' still exists. There has been concern that the UK may have thousands of 'informal' patients who lack capacity. It was at first thought that all of these patients may have to be assessed under the Mental Health Act 1983, although this does seem to be the case now.

Decisions are made on a case by case basis, which highlights ethical dilemmas. Somebody would need to alert an assessing body to review the restrictions imposed on an informal patient. If the patient had no family members/ carers or advocates, then review may not be requested. Safeguards that are in place to protect detained patients under Mental Health Act 1983, namely the Mental Health Act Commission, cannot intervene in the case of informal patients. Therefore Lisa's involvement in ascertaining the legal rights of her service user was good anti-oppressive practice.

As a result of Lisa's work and her highlighting her findings to the home, it was agreed that Tony should not be restricted from leaving his home. Lisa found ways of helping Tony to keep safe when he went for a walk on his own. He knew that if he got lost he should go to a police station and he always had his name and address written on a card in his pocket.

Involving service users

Advocacy

The last two decades have seen the growth of independent advocacy services. Advocacy is one of the oldest forms of support (Brandon, 1995). It has developed in a *formal* way in relation to legal services where the role of advocates in court (lawyers) is to represent the interests of their clients, speak up on their behalf and protect their rights (Wertheimer, 1996). Principles of service user involvement can be identified in the emergence of self-advocacy. At its most basic, self-advocacy can be described as the earliest form of advocacy which many people use every day (Brandon, 1995a) and simply means speaking out or standing up for one's rights as a person (Goodley, 2000). Much of the literature about self-advocacy relates to adults with learning difficulties, and self-advocacy has been described as challenging the identity they have been assigned (Brandon, 1995a). More broadly, the term has been used to delineate the self-determination of minority groups, particularly those with learning difficulties, and members of the group are therefore known as self-advocates (Goodley, 2000). For *individuals* this is about having the confidence and ability to express one's own feelings, to make choices and to influence decisions either as part of an individual programme plan, or in relation to education, work and living situations (Simons, 1998). Participating in self-advocacy *groups* means that rather than be passive recipients of welfare, people demonstrate their ability to control their own lives – and so reclaim their identity (Barnes and Shardlow, 1996).

Health and social care practitioners often act as advocates for service users and carers will act for the people they are caring for. But sometimes support is needed from an independent person who does not have to worry about agency or professional interests. Within health and social care practice various forms of advocacy have become established as an accepted method of working with people who are marginalized and oppressed. *Independent advocacy* is defined by the Scottish Executive as:

> . . . a crucial element in achieving social justice. It is a way to ensure that everyone matters and everyone is heard – including people who are at risk of exclusion and people who have particular difficulties in making their views known.
>
> (Scottish Executive, 2001)

In their guide to commissioners of advocacy services, the Executive also begins to explore the power relations that exist in the provision of services, recognizing that professionals are in a powerful position because they are often expected to make judgements that impact on the lives of service users and control resources. This does not make the advocate a better person but, as the Executive puts it: 'They just stand in a different place and see things from a different perspective' (2001).

Most literature about advocacy focuses on two areas of advocacy: case advocacy, referring to work with individuals or small groups (such as families); and cause or systemic advocacy, referring to work with larger groups, usually aimed at structural changes in relation to legislation, policy or practice. However, advocacy at both levels are interrelated (Mickelson, 1995) and the two forms can be linked together in a framework for understanding advocacy (Preston, 1995). The relationship between case and systemic advocacy is important as individual situations provide the information needed to promote change in legislation, systems and policies. In the UK, there are a range of independent organizations that offer varying forms of advocacy,[13] but essentially all have the following principles:

- empowerment;
- autonomy;
- citizenship;
- inclusion.

(Atkinson, 1999)

Case example: Annie

Annie was worried about who would be at her child protection conference – she wanted to be there herself but did not want to see her stepfather. So she met with the chairperson before the conference and as a result her stepfather was excluded from the meeting until the decisions were made. Annie also talked to the chairperson about where she wanted to sit and was in the room before the professionals were invited in. Ground rules were agreed about what the meeting was talking about – that is, the risk. The advocate and Annie each had paper and a pen to make notes. Sometimes the discussion was quite adult, but the chairperson stopped and summarized it in easier language. Annie really felt that she was the focus of the meeting – not in an embarrassing way – but that the decision was about her. Things that she said were included in the plan. She also had views about registration and at the review when Annie was de-registered she felt that people should have been more worried about her and that she should have been kept on the register.

(Dalrymple, 2005)

The advocate is:

> an 'unambigous ally, standing alongside and shoulder to shoulder with their partner; speaking out against injustice, discrimination and 'system abuse'.

(Atkinson, 1999: 12)

The independent advocate does not of course have to be self-sufficient and have all the answers. It is appropriate for the advocate to seek support, advice, information and assistance from others, providing that the position of the service user is not compromised. The role of an advocate demands a complex mixture of skills, and challenges the traditional assumptions about the nature of the relationships between workers, carers and users. In practice it can evoke a wide range of responses, from open hostility to enthusiastic support. For that reason an advocate needs to be independent in order to function effectively.

Case example: Mr Williams

Mr Williams is 78 years old, has mobility problems, is in chronic pain and is incontinent. He approached his local advocacy service for help because:

- his income support credits had stopped;
- he needed help preparing for social services to reassess his care needs;
- he needed help to pursue compensation for disrepair through the local ombudsman.

The advocate negotiated on his behalf with social services, the occupational therapist, the ombudsman and the local authority complaints manager. In supporting Mr Williams the advocate recorded sending 18 letters or faxes, making 28 telephone calls and 3 visits.

The care manager's decision following the assessment was to take away home care. This ran contrary to all the evidence presented, but was attributed to new national guidelines. The advocate pursued this with social services, the local councillor and via a solicitor.

(adapted from Jones, 2004a)

There are many who feel that social workers, carers, health visitors, general practitioners, teachers or any person close to the user involved can be an advocate. While all practitioners should use advocacy skills and advocate on behalf of people they are working with, there are occasions when an independent advocate would be a preferred option. An independent advocate only promotes the view of the user, irrespective of other considerations. For example, it can be disempowering for both the user and the person acting as an advocate if the advocate feels constrained by their employer. Carers, equally, can feel constrained by their own obligations and duties and therefore find it difficult to advocate if their own needs conflict with the needs of the person they are caring for. The advocacy role envisaged for carers in mental health and mental incapacity law reforms does not appear to recognize this potential difficulty (Keywood, 2003). Perhaps even more disempowering for the user is when someone appears to be acting as an advocate, and yet continues to act in her or his own role, such as social worker, nurse or probation officer. There are clearly dilemmas for both practitioners and carers, and to take on the advocacy role for service users who already feel powerless may be as distressing for practitioners as it is for users (Barford and Wattam, 1991). The skill then is to assess when we can act as an advocate ourselves and when it would be better to obtain independent advocacy support.[14]

Case example: Jasmine

John and Louise are foster carers with a private fostering agency. They are supported by Emma, a social worker from the agency. 14-year-old Jasmine has been living with them for a year and has recently given birth to a baby boy. She has her own local authority social worker, Lee, and the social services department pays for the placement. As Jasmine was about to be discharged from hospital, John and Louise were told that the fostering agency was raising the fee as it would now become a mother and baby placement. Lee told Jasmine that his team manager had made the decision to find an alternative placement.

Jasmine became very upset and refused to talk to Lee, asking Emma to support her and her carers at a meeting organized by Lee to discuss the situation. Although Emma knew that it was Lee's role to support Jasmine, she agreed with John and Louise that they had a joint responsibility to support Jasmine. However, at the meeting she was challenged by Lee about the agency raising the cost of the placement to such a degree and was told that the local authority did not have unlimited resources. Emma found herself in a dilemma as an employee of a profit-making organization but believed that Jasmine's wishes and needs were being ignored because of financial considerations. Unable to advocate for Jasmine, she realized that an independent advocate was needed if her voice was to be heard in the decision-making process.

Research

The importance of involving the perspectives of service users has been highlighted by both the UK government and funders of services in order to inform policy and practice. This consumerist approach has been challenged by service user groups who have questioned the purpose and merits of user involvement in research. Among these concerns are questions about:

- the ideological basis of involvement;
- whose discourse?;
- the purpose of research; and
- the nature of research values.

(Beresford, 2005)

For example, arguments for child-centred approaches to research (Mahon et al., 1996; Mauthner, 1997) start with the recognition that adult-centric research and the unequal power relations that exist between adults and children make it easy for children to become objects of the research process. Debates about informed consent, vulnerability and competence show the dominance of protectionist perspectives. Adult gatekeepers insist that consent has to be obtained from parents, school teachers, social workers or other key adults, depending on the research, which means that children often do not have the opportunity to either agree or refuse to participate. Of course, once access had been gained there is nothing to stop researchers giving young people the opportunity to opt in or out, since 'children are, in a variety of ways, capable of deciding whether or not they wish to be interviewed' (Mahon et al., 1996: 150), particularly if they are given full information and prepared for the research. The right of children to give consent has been vigorously debated through *Gillick*,[15] but subsequent rulings have restricted 'their ability to contribute to research and so to influence old beliefs about childhood and restrictive policies and practices that affect children' (Alderson, 1995: 75).

Discussions about children's rights in relation to decision-making are ongoing and, in the case of research, unresolved (France et al., 2000). Masson (2000) points out that there is a need to ensure that children and young people do not feel that they have to participate:

> Where the person seeking children's participation is in a powerful position over them, as in the case of a teacher or carer, children may feel that they have to agree, or, worse still, that they will be penalised if they do not.
>
> (Masson, 2000: 40)

While most commentators agree that consent should be gained from relevant adults (Cohen and Mannion, 1994; Alderson, 1995), we can see from children's rights perspectives the complementary yet conflictual nature of participation, provision and protection (Alderson, 2000). The notion of informed consent at first glance seems unproblematic, that is, that children and young people are given full information about the research (appropriate to their level of understanding) and can then volunteer to participate if they wish. Despite arguments that the child's consent should be the primary consideration, it would be difficult for a child to participate against the wishes of their parents – or, for example, a keyworker in a residential unit, a foster carer or social worker: the 'corporate parent' (France et al., 2000) and some people feel that the will of the parents should be respected in the case of parents or corporate parents (Butler and Williamson, 1994). However, this means, in effect, that children and young people are seldom able to make their own decision about whether or not to participate in the research (Masson, 2000). The role of the gatekeepers is a powerful one and, while rightly protecting children and young people from harm, it has been noted that:

> It is indeed a marker of the control exercised over children's lives, knowledge and rights in the UK that children's own consent to research is not considered adequate.
>
> (Mayall, 2000: 133)

It is important, then, for us as critical practitioners to be aware of the oppressive elements of ongoing debates and of our role not only in contributing to those debates but also to actively ensure that service users are able to decide for themselves whether or not to participate when they are asked to be involved in research projects. Equally, as professional education increasingly encourages us to instigate our own research projects, we have to be mindful of how we conduct such projects.

However, there is also an increasing body of user-led research that is having an impact on policy and practice. *Strategies for Living* (Faulkner and Layzell, 2000) was a programme of work in adult mental health based on a belief in the value of 'expertise by experience' which supports, promotes and encourages user-led research so that we can learn from the expertise of service users. Projects included:

- A healthy benefits research project – initiated by mental health service users trying to access essential welfare benefits.
- Mental Health Advocacy in Wales – carried out by members of Cymar, the Welsh Association of Patients Councils and Advocacy Schemes.
- The ups and downs of being a carer for someone with bi-polar disorder – initiated by the author because of her personal experience of coping with bi-polar disorder and maintaining a positive relationship with her carer.
- Self-help groups for people who self-harm – came out of the researchers' personal experience of attending a self-help group for people who self-harm, their own experiences of the benefits gained and also the difficulties of sustaining a group with no funding and little, if any, external support.

Social work education

The requirement to include user and carer involvement in the social work degree represents a significant achievement for the service user movement which has worked at a national and strategic level to get this as a central requirement within the new degree. Newly established institutions such as the Social Care Institute for Excellence (SCIE) recognize the importance of including user perspectives and support the *Shaping Our Lives National User Network* project. However, despite the successes of the user movement influencing the national development of the social work degree service, users and carers have expressed concerns about the tokenistic nature of their experiences, arguing the need for positive principles that need to underlie best practice user involvement in social work education and training (Turner, 2004). Principles[16] outlined by the Shaping Our Lives National User Network address these concerns:

- Involvement should be planned and structured.
- Involvement should be based on work with organizations that are controlled and run by service users, with the interests of service users and carers being addressed as distinct issues.
- There should be recognition of service users' contributions through the payment of fees and expenses.
- Good practice should include access to education and training courses for service users.

(cited in Levin, 2004)

The challenge for universities is to develop ways of working in partnership with service users and carers. Any user and carer representatives working within the bureaucratic structures of a university will need support both to understand the context in which they may be asked to be involved and further support to preserve their own perspectives.

Access to files

Involving service users in both collating and storing information is experienced as empowering for service users. This involves sharing what is written in case records and kept in agency files and making files easily accessible to service users. Sharing records equalizes the relationship between service users and providers and enhances participation. The Access to Personal Files Act 1987 gave the right to service users to see their personal files. It also provided the impetus for work within social welfare agencies to be a 'more open activity' (Payne, 1989).

The practice of sharing decisions with users and opening up records presents a number of ethical issues, however, and demonstrates the difficulties that workers face when they attempt to work within a participatory framework. The access to records debate highlights the importance of working in partnership with users. Record keeping should involve users' views if records are to be used to guide and inform practice decisions. However, workers can find it difficult to share information honestly with users when the relationship is an unequal one, particularly where information is gathered for the purpose of evidence (such as in cases of child abuse, abuse of older people).

Despite these problems, we would argue that if involvement with users is to be successful then the power relations that exist between users and service providers have to be acknowledged. One way of attempting to do this is by sharing recorded information. Knowledge of recorded information is the means by which users can verify what is written about them and their situation and correct inaccurate information. It enables users to control information about them. Finally, but importantly, sharing information in an open and honest way demonstrates respect. This is clearly shown by the following comments from people who have received copies of letters concerning them (Department of Health, 2004a):

> A relative whom I have been helping with a mental health problem recently received a copy of a psychiatrist's letter (at our specific request) following the consultation, and it made such a difference to our confidence. It showed that the doc had understood what we were saying and wasn't just fobbing us off. It also helped us understand and remember their advice. Such a boost for trust in the relationship. As an ex-NHS manager and citizen, I got such a thrill in seeing how well our Service can work.
>
> (A carer)

> Sometimes for whatever reason you don't fully take on board what the doctor has told you. I found the letter useful to read over and digest properly what was written.
>
> (Dr Diana Jelley and Caron Walker)[17]

Issues of accountability to the user and to the agency are also addressed by access to files policies. Assessments and plans are subject to critical evaluation, which is an important aspect of the development of an ethical practice. 'Greater openness and sharing in decision making reflects a greater preparedness to be flexible about the acceptable norms in social work interactions' (Payne, 1989: 132). The legislation governing access to records exists and it needs to be actively used to ensure that work with users is based on true partnership and accountability.

Principles for user involvement

A number of guiding principles have been identified to make user involvement a reality in services and organizations (Croft and Beresford, 1993), which can help practitioners, while working within the framework of the law, to engage positively with service users.

1. *Resources.* Involving people requires resources (both material and human) and this has to be recognized by those seeking to promote genuine participation.

2. *Information.* Information is power and needs to be shared. To be effective information should:
   - be of immediate relevance, clear, attractive and brief;
   - be appropriate to people's abilities, experience, knowledge, language and culture;
   - take into account particular needs of members of minority ethnic communities, people with limited ability, people with sensory disabilities, people with limited literacy skills;
   - link verbal and written information;
   - be available from clear contact points;
   - offer the chance to get to know the information given, to develop trust and confidence.

3. *Training.* Participation will be tokenistic if there is no acknowledgement that people have skills but these need to be developed through training. Professionals have had access to specialized training in order to carry out their tasks. In order to empower people to be able to participate on an equal footing they must also have access to training. This does not mean that participation should be conditional on training, but there needs to be a recognition that we all have training needs. The best training is where everyone is involved together and users contribute to the training process.

4. *Research and evaluation.* Obviously it would be contrary to the whole notion of participation not to involve users in any research undertaken or evaluation of services and projects.

5. *Equal access and opportunities.* People cannot say something about services unless they have access to them.

6. *Forums and structures for involvement.* It is important to have participatory structures and forums where people can feel comfortable about airing their views.

7. *Language.* Language is not neutral and we should check out that we all have a common understanding of what is being said.

8. *Advocacy.* There are many forms of advocacy, which ensure that people who are in receipt of services have a voice that is respected and valued. This ensures that the views of users are listened to and acknowledged.

These guiding principles can be used to help us, through the framework of the law, to work positively with users. We discussed in Chapter 3 the importance of knowing our own value base and understanding that of the law. Such principles are informed by an empowerment perspective and user involvement can only be effective if we accept and acknowledge those principles. The example in the box shows how one organization, with principles like these underpinning their work, has made involvement a reality.

Wiltshire and Swindon User Network (WSUN)

WSUN has been used as an example of good practice in a number of documents (see, for example, Carr, 2004). It was formed in 1991 in response to the 1990 NHS and Community Care Act which said that service users should be key stakeholders in social care. It was financially supported by Wiltshire Social Services Department with a service agreement drawn up by the users in the Network. It is managed by a planning group of 12 service users and up to 4 social services allies elected annually. 'Users' are defined as anyone who chooses to define themselves as such, but usually long-term users of service, ex or potential users. The distinctive features of their model of involvement are:

- an independent user-controlled organization resourced to 'do user involvement';
- a network of individual users and groups (with any perspectives/professional care group label) supported by organizational infrastructure to participate in many different ways;
- a pro-active approach to negotiate user participation in as many different ways as possible – riddling the system;
- service users have a democratic right as citizens to participate in the services they receive;
- within their own democratic organization users can empower each other and gain the confidence to participate effectively with professionals;
- users have valuable expertise from their experience of using services and are paid a small fee for their regular participation in addition to all costs incurred by attending meetings;
- informed by the social model of disability;
- service users set their own agenda and priorities for change;
- outreach is provided to marginalized users.

The Network aims to promote user involvement in all aspects of community care by supporting the empowerment of users; direct involvement of users to bring about change; promoting good practice in user involvement and developing and managing user-controlled projects (in the areas of information, independent living and advocacy).

Chapter summary

The legislative mandate for involving service users has had an impact on policy and practice. Despite the debates about the meaning of involvement, the fact is that the involvement of people in the planning and development of services is challenging 'traditional modes of thinking and operation' (Carr, 2004: 28). However, there are a number of approaches and models of user involvement which we need to understand as critical practitioners in order to challenge the barriers to user involvement. Effective service user and carer involvement involves all of us thinking about how we work and being prepared to work in new ways (Levin, 2005). However, we need to be aware of the danger that new ways of working may become mechanized techniques for practice. One way of doing this is to use any guidelines available to us as value-based principles for involving service users (Beresford, 2003). This means being constantly aware of the power relations that impact on individuals and systems and being prepared to challenge the structures, practices and attitudes that exclude service users and deny them the opportunity to influence either decisions relating to their own lives or the services they need.

Further reading

There is an increasing body of knowledge and practice expertise developing in this area and you are encouraged to look at health and social care journals for up to date accounts of ongoing work and research. Many user organizations have their own websites with examples of the work that they are doing. SCIE (Social Care Institute for Excellence) *www.scie.org.uk* includes developments in service user involvement in continuous updates of its website. Government initiatives can be found on the Department of Health website *www.dh.gov.uk*.

Carr, S. (2004) *Has Service User Participation Made a Difference to Social Care Services?* Bristol: SCIE/The Policy Press.
A position paper from the Social Care Institute for Excellence reviewing and analysing the impact of service user participation in social care services.

Kemshall, H. and Littlechild, R. (eds) (2000) *User Involvement and Participation in Social Care: Research Informing Practice*. London: Jessica Kingsley.
A useful reader exploring ways of involving service users in the planning, delivery and evaluation of services.

Means, R. and Smith, R. (1998) *Community Care: Policy and Practice*. Basingstoke: Macmillan.

Chapter 4 of this book provides a comprehensive account of strategies for user empowerment and ways to manage this.

Roberts, K. and Chapman, T. (2001) *Realising Participation*. Aldershot: Ashgate. Based on research this book explores how opportunities are being provided to enable users to be actively involved in their care.

Willow, C. (2002) *Participation in Practice: Children and Young People as Partners in Change*. London: The Children's Society.
Six case studies are used in this book to demonstrate ways that children and young people can be involved in decision-making in a range of settings.

Activity

Angelica is 12 years old. Her mother is Irish and her father is Jamaican. Her parents are divorced and she has no contact with her father. She has been looked after in local authority care for several years since her mother went to Ireland temporarily. On her return to England her mother visited Angelica sporadically but was not sufficiently settled to provide a home for her. The plan is that Angelica will eventually be reunited with her mother.

The staff in the children's unit where she was placed are mainly white. Angelica is well liked by the staff because, they say, she does not present any 'behavioural problems'. At the last review it was decided that Angelica should be accommodated with foster carers, and discussions about the kind of placement are taking place. First, the residential social worker and Angelica discuss the kind of family she would like. Secondly, the field social worker and Angelica have a discussion, and then all three talk together. The field social worker raises the subject of a black family, but Angelica and the residential social worker do not feel that this is a good idea.

The task is for you as the person involved in working with Angelica to prepare her for the next review. Whether you are the residential social worker or the field social worker you have a role to play in the process. It is important to consider what preparation needs to occur prior to the review, and what needs to be done during and after the review to support Angelica (adapted from Coombe and Little, 1986: 151).

How do you work with Angelica so that she can participate fully in this crucial decision concerning her life?

Compare your ideas with those listed below. They were developed out of a training exercise designed by the authors. The participants were residential social workers who were asked to think about the issues concerning the involvement of young people in meetings.

Before the meeting:

The young person needs to:

- know the purpose of the meeting;
- have information about who will attend and why;
- have the option to request that certain people do not attend;
- be introduced to participants before the meeting;
- have had access to and understood previous minutes (such as child care conference notes, review notes);
- be able to go through the report to be presented at the meeting in advance (with an appropriate person);
- be aware of delicate issues that might be brought up at the meeting;
- be able to discuss how she or he might feel and react to information presented at the meeting;
- have the opportunity to participate in a 'mock' meeting if they wish;
- meet the chair of the meeting;
- feel comfortable about the timing of the meeting (not to have to miss school or work).

During the meeting:

- The young person should be properly introduced to the participants of the meeting and made aware of its purpose.
- The young person should be allowed to communicate in a way that is comfortable to her or him.
- The young person should have a right to leave at any point. This is to be agreed prior to the start of the meeting and if necessary a short break in the proceedings is to be allowed.
- Participants need to be aware of the possible reactions of the young person.
- A support strategy must be developed and agreed so that it is clear who is to support the young person and how this should be managed.
- Thought should be given to the length of the meeting. This means that there should be clear aims and objectives so that only pertinent information is discussed.

After the meeting:

- The young person should have the opportunity to discuss the process and the decisions taken and
  - (a) be able to express any feelings that she or he may have;
  - (b) be able to explore the implications of the decisions made.
- The young person should have access to support.
- The young person should receive her or his own copy of the minutes.

The following points can help the process:

- A code of conduct needs to be sent out to all participants prior to the meeting.
- Chairs should have access to training.
- The young person should not be referred to as the 'subject' in written documentation.

This is not a complete list and you may well wish to add to it. Although they are specifically related to young people, the principles can be transferred and used with other groups. These are general guidelines. In some situations it will be necessary to adapt them to meet the needs of an individual. For example, it may be that a person with learning difficulties will become distressed by having to sit too long in one position, or may become frustrated with all the written work presented at the meeting. Guidelines about how the needs of a particular person may be met should therefore be circulated to all participants.

Note for Practice

In an account of the use of advocacy by children and young people in advancing their participation rights within the child protection system, the project helped the child protection coordinator and the person chairing the conference to be pro-active and to modify previous ways of working. So, for example, the agenda for the Child Protection Conference was rearranged for one young man:

> . . . so that when the young person was discussed the conference also made their decision re registration and recommendations at that point instead of moving to his sister. This ensured the young person didn't have to keep leaving the conference, thus making his participation more meaningful.
>
> (Wyllie, 1999)

13 Evaluation

> Evaluation of one's mental and physical state is unlikely if the space so essential to the unhurried frame of mind is absent, so we need to ponder the value of creating space and contemplate the disposition generated by being in a hurry.
>
> (Rees, 1991: 121)

The essence of evaluating is to make the 'space' that Rees talks about here, so that we can 'ponder', not only the value of creating that space but also to remind ourselves about what we are doing and why we are doing it. Our interaction with people should make a difference to their lives and to our lives – but we will only know if it does make a difference if we make the time to find out.

The agenda for the delivery of public services has moved from its direct provision by public bodies to those same bodies being responsible for performance management of service providers. Local authorities are responsible for the performance management of voluntary and private providers and primary care trusts are responsible for provision by hospital trusts as well as voluntary and private sector provision. This means that 'we live in an age where efficacy is a key issue, particularly in respect of the use of public funds' (Williams and Fisher in the preface to Carpenter, 2005). Evaluation can be undertaken by people outside organizations, for example through inspection, or with the involvement of all stakeholders: participatory evaluation. It can take place within the organization and at an individual level where evaluation may include reflection and self-evaluation of personal practitioner activity. In this chapter we will consider evaluation at both practice and policy levels and what legislation tells us about it. We will go on to look at definitions of evaluation, the role of reflection within practice and the revolutionary potential of evaluation and research.

Legislation and evaluation

We live in a performance culture where 'the languages of cost-effectiveness, service-user satisfaction, empowerment, management by effectiveness, quality, service contracts, partnership, staff supervision, financial decentralisation and targeted measurement have permeated the planning, management and delivery' (Shaw, 1996: 19) of health and social care services. The use of performance indicators are now a feature of public management, and with new government initiatives there are numerous evaluation requirements and targets. For example, policy initiatives such as Sure Start, which provides support for children in socially disadvantaged areas who are under the age of 4; New Deal for Communities, which is a regeneration programme for local communities; and the Children's Fund, set up as part of the UK government's commitment to tackle disadvantage among children and young people, have all required both national and local evaluation.

Unfortunately, the positive elements of evaluation are often negated as the political pressure for results makes it difficult for agencies on the receiving end of such initiatives to manage the process. This means that workers struggling to set up innovatory projects can find evaluation a burden. This is not helped by the fact that people who commission evaluations of projects, including governments, are not always sure about their purpose or if the proposed research is realistic in terms of timescales and resources (Lewis and Utting, 2001). The demands of monitoring and reporting for statutory and voluntary agencies and community groups – especially when the experience is of 'duplication, repetition and overload' (Alcock, 2004: 220) – can damage the processes of partnership and participation that are essential elements of anti-oppressive practice. However:

> This should not surprise us. By and large, routinely generated in-dicators are not designed to answer questions about the outcomes of specific policy initiatives. Nor are they focussed on the impact of collaborative working across agencies involved in partnerships to address cross-cutting policy problems. There is a long way to go be-fore the commitment to partnership working is reflected in systems of performance monitoring which assess performance in collabora-tion and in working with service users and communities, rather than in meeting regulatory requirements defined for individual agencies.
> (Barnes, 2004: 56)

On the other hand, evaluation is not just about regulatory requirements or the effectiveness of outcomes. While it is important and necessary to take account of the legal, political, social and economic context of practice and to acknowledge the requirements of audit and quality assurance (at the same time maintaining a critical stance as to its effectiveness) evaluation is also a key element of practice (Adams, 1998a; Lishman, 1999). Evaluation literature has both critiqued and developed the theory and methods of evaluation to ensure its centrality as a dimension of practice (Shaw, 1996; Shaw and Lishman, 1999; Shaw and Gould, 2001) with evaluation described as 'a study which has a distinctive purpose; it is not a new or distinctive research strategy' (Robson, 1993: 170). The need to evaluate our work is necessary both to understand and develop practice and because 'accountability to both funders and service users cannot now be taken off the agenda' (Gould, 1999: 77). Furthermore, in examining what comprises legitimate knowledge in the light of many stakeholder views, we can find, through evaluation, that talking to service users, as well as to those involved in the commissioning and provision of services – sharing stories, skills and knowledge – can be a valuable means of understanding how practice is constructed.

What is evaluation?

While there are many definitions of evaluation, Parsons suggests that evaluation involves judging by applying rules and/or standards to a given activity or set of activities, or to put it simply, 'evaluation lets one know how one is doing' (1998: 205). Newburn (2001) suggests that a definition by Patton incorporates many of the characteristics of evaluation activity:

> The practice of evaluation involves the systematic collection of information about the activities, characteristics and outcomes of programmes, personnel and products for use by specific people to reduce uncertainties, improve effectiveness, and make decision with regard to what those programs, personnel, or products are doing and affecting.
>
> (Patton, 1981: 15)

The key elements identified here are:

- the need for systematic collection of information;
- the wide range of topics to which evaluation had been applied;
- that to be effective the evaluation has to be used by someone;
- the variety of purposes of evaluation.

(Newburn, 2001)

It could be said that evaluation is a tool for measuring quality. Essentially evaluation is a series of procedures which are carried out in order to collect information. This will then *improve the quality* of a service by underpinning the decision-making as well as allowing us to *judge the quality* of the services we offer (Edwards, 1991). Such a process involves first examining aims and objectives, in order to question and examine what we are doing. Having done that we are then able to contribute to decision-making (that is, by providing new information which can lead to changes) and improve the quality of service provision. Evaluation may address issues of either practice or service.

Service evaluation concentrates on understanding and/or changing ways that services are delivered while *practice evaluation* looks at daily work that may be considered separately from its agency context. However, in reality, no evaluation fits one category and most will involve both service and practice evaluation (Shaw, 1996). However, evaluation should not just be a private enterprise – it is about opening up our work to public scrutiny. This is significant if we are to be accountable for how public resources are used to meet the needs of people who require a service. Parsons (1998) points out that, in terms of assessing the outcome of a piece of work or 'intervention', evaluation can be as helpful to the service user as it is to practitioners and agencies. Evaluation is a continuous process and should be an integral part of the way we work. It should also incorporate the views of everyone involved in the process of providing health and social care services.

Evaluation is often referred to as *formative* or *summative*. Formative evaluation is carried out at regular intervals and the information can be used to provide continuous feedback to inform and reshape the process. Discussing the evaluation of empowerment practice, Parsons (1998) suggests that formative, or what she terms *process* evaluation, assesses the processes used to achieve the desired outcome. Summative evaluation is concerned with outcomes and effectiveness. Its purpose is to provide a final report about a project or programme but it will not be used for continuous reshaping. Parsons (1998) uses the term *outcome* evaluation to described summative evaluations. Both qualitative and quantative approaches can be used to determine outcomes. Newburn (2001) points out that the distinctions between these two approaches can be confused and also identified too closely with differences between 'process' and 'outcome' evaluation. The first is about what is happening in a programme or intervention and the latter is concerned with the impact. Table 13.1 looks at how the formative and summative evaluations might be compared and contrasted.

Evaluation can be likened to monitoring a journey. Formative evaluation is about continually checking where we are going to make sure we are on the right track. When we have reached the end of the journey, we provide a summative evaluation which should attempt to answer these questions: Have we arrived at our destination?

- If 'no', where are we?
- If 'yes', or 'no', how did we arrive there?
- If 'yes', or 'no', is it worth going on?

(Phillips et al., 1994: 4)

Those of us who work in public services are accountable to the people we work for and with. Governments recognize the need to evaluate and monitor the laws they produce and oversee as public servants. While the evaluation

Table 13.1 Formative and summative evaluations

	Formative	Summative
Target audience	Programme managers, practitioners	Policy-makers, funders
Focus of data collection	Clarification of goals	Implementation issues
Role of evaluator	Interactive	Independent
Methodology	Quantitative and qualitative (but with emphasis on qualitative)	Emphasis on quantitative
Frequency of data collection	Continuous monitoring	Limited
Reporting	Informal via discussion	Formal
Frequency of reporting	Throughout study	On completion of evaluation

Source: Herman et al., 1987

and dissemination of information about how legislation is functioning is inevitably a political activity (Taylor and Balloch, 2005a), we nevertheless can use their reports and statistics to inform our practice and actively to involve ourselves and service users in debate. Through this process people can be made aware of their rights and campaign to ensure that those rights are respected.

Reflection

Reflection has been described as 'the worker's ability to pattern or make sense of information, in whatever form, including the impact of her own behaviour and that of her organisation on others' (Smale et al., 2000: 220). Making sense of information through reflection means that we are creating knowledge, which is necessary for ongoing evaluation. Taylor (2000) links understanding of reflection to a more generally understood meaning which is about throwing back rays like heat, sound or light, for example. So for her:

> . . . reflection means the throwing back of thoughts and memories, in cognitive acts such as thinking, contemplation, meditation and any other form of attentive consideration, in order to make sense of them, and to make contextually appropriate changes if they are required.
>
> (Taylor, 2000: 3)

Development of reflective approaches are primarily attributed to Donald Schön (1983, 1987; Agryis and Schön, 1976), who argued that knowledge and theory are developed by practitioners who, in the context of a given situation, can develop an understanding of how they practice. Reflection-in-action occurs in our minds as we are acting in a particular situation, and reflection-on-action happens after the event when we consider and try to understand our experience.

Reflection, then, is an element of reviewing our practice and has been described as the final stage of the fourfold processes of:

- assessment,
- planning,
- intervention, and
- review.

(Bell, 2005)

Before beginning a piece of work the practitioner gathers evidence about potential interventions in order to decide with a service user what will be the most effective intervention – this is described as evidence-based practice. Combining this with critical reflection during and after the work enables its evaluation, including its effect on the service user, which in turn informs practice theory and knowledge. Bell (2005) notes the complexity of reviewing, however. First, there are three main areas to explore:

1. Inputs, such as the resources that have been put into an intervention.
2. Process, what happens during the work, what is the throughput?
3. Outcome, which includes output and the value of output.

Any review is determined by the objectives of the intervention so that any inputs, outputs and outcomes can be assessed. However, the objectives of those involved may conflict. Tensions between the objectives of service users and agencies, and between those of different professionals will then make it difficult to assess the outcomes of any intervention. Thompson (2000b) therefore suggests that 'systematic practice' is helpful to enable a clear focus on our work. He uses a framework that involves focusing on three questions in any situation:

- What are we trying to achieve?
- How are we going to achieve it?
- How will we know we have achieved it?

He outlines a process to address these questions, which he describes in terms of five stages, similar to those of Bell: assessment, intervention, review, termination and evaluation. He points out though that this is not a rigid inflexible process but a framework that has to be used sensitively and 'is geared towards facilitating reflective practice, rather than replacing it' (Thompson, 2000b: 139).

Reflective practice involves an openness to new ideas, new perspectives and new approaches which should enable us to avoid uncritical, routinized practice (Thompson, 2000b). This then leads us to consider the concept of critical reflection. Drawing on early formulations of reflective practice, feminism and postmodernist thinking about knowledge, Fook (2002) shows how critical reflection places importance on understanding how reflective practice uncovers power relations and questions dominant power relations. She summarizes the process of critical reflection in three stages:

1. Description of your practice and the situation (or context). This means telling your story so that it can be analysed. She suggests that diary records start as an exercise in writing your story of what has happened which can later be analysed and understood in different ways. Stories can also be written creatively through poetry.
2. Reflective questioning, reflection-on-action (or deconstruction), focusing on issues of power and how notions of power are constructed. By looking at a diary entry or practice record we can start to look for gaps, biases, themes and missing themes.
3. Redeveloping practice and theory (reconstruction), particularly in relation to how power relations and structures can be changed to be more emancipatory.

While we are thinking about personal critical reflection here, the principles apply to all evaluation of practice, since it can be seen as 'a value-driven activity that depends on an understanding of the power relationship between commissioners, policy makers, service providers, service users and evaluators' (Taylor and Balloch, 2005a: 5).

Throughout the book we talk about reflection as an essential element of anti-oppressive practice. Combining reflection and anti-oppressive practice is no easy task, though, as Issit (2000)[1] points out in her discussion about feminist anti-oppressive reflective practice: 'an anti-oppressive feminist/ womanist approach would seek to connect the personal, professional and the political dimensions with reflection as a systematic activity' (Issit, 2000: 129). Critical reflection enables examination of all these dimensions and enables practitioners to develop their own theories of practice through their work.

Poetry as evaluation

Introducing the media of story writing, poetry and collage to first year nursing students to reflect on their practice enabled them to 'capture notable perceptive experiences and provide them with an opportunity to experience a set of words that describe something that previously the person had been unable to articulate' (Newton, 2004: 159). She quotes Holmes and Gregory (1998), who suggest that 'poetry is a way in which nurses can reveal their perception in their work and how these new perceptions can add depth and meaning to their experience' (Holmes and Gregory, 1998: 1194).

Extract of poem by student B

I sat with a patient of mine, there was a look in her eye
She wanted to be beneath the blue sky
I'm old and grey but young at heart . . .
My legs aren't that good, I've replaced both hips
Both of them broken from having trips
My eyes are shortsighted and longsighted too
Show me around and I'll follow your cue
I had teeth and I lost them too
Bloody annoying, now I can't chew
Vitamised diet they said would be good
They should try it, I think they should . . .

Extract from poem by student C

Sitting tilted, molded to the chair
Blankets covering thin, little legs,
Food crumbs around the mouth and dusted down her skivvy.
Awkward head movements, but knowing sad eyes
I greet her warmly,
No verbal responses, but acknowledgement in those eyes.
My thoughts brim with uncertainty – what am I supposed to Do Here???
Wash, change nappy and put cream on her genitalia!
What? Is this my task?
How can I do this and not embarrass her,
Or do I mean myself?!
Dignity, dignity, dignity
A mantra I repeat continually in my mind
No strength in her body – bloody stroke!
How long has she been like this?
Everyday, cared for in the most personal way by different people, Me – a stranger, using gloved hands to put cream in her most vulnerable parts . . .

These poems capture the insight of these students into their experiences of working in nursing homes and the levels of reflection show elements of theoretical reflectivity. Both students are questioning the everyday care/practice given to older people. Student B tries to share the fact that a taken for granted assumption, the patients's diet, which seems to be an acceptable practice by staff, did not fit with either the patient's or the student's perspective:

> I had teeth and I lost them too
> Bloody annoying, now I can't chew
> Vitamised diet they said would be good
> They should try it, I think they should...

Student C similarly questions everyday practice and reflects on her commitment to nursing and the nursing care that she was expected to provide, questioning both the care and the contradictions within herself:

> Wash, change nappy and put cream on her genitalia
> What?! Is this my task?
> How can I do this and not embarrass her, Or do I mean myself?!

Evaluation and research

Fook (2002) suggests that the process of critical reflection can function at the same time both as a way of evaluating practice (through systematic and constant scrutiny of what we are doing) and as research of practice (because it involves ongoing documentation of practice which in turn provides data about how practice maybe changed). She argues that without engagement in the critical reflective process, development of practice theory and knowledge through evaluation and research is unlikely.

Practitioner researchers such as Howes (2005) identify the need to evaluate practice so that good practice can be highlighted and disseminated. A similar point is made by Ferguson (2003a) who argues for the need to move beyond a 'deficit approach' where the focus is on what does not get done (well), to create a perspective where learning occurs in terms of best practice which is set out as a model for developing systems and practice competencies. He suggests that this requires a broadening of the concept of evidence-based practice to include qualitative research methods and the experience of professionals, service users and the production of 'practice-based evidence'. Howes demonstrates how this may be done by describing how, as a social work practitioner in a busy social work office, she was able to consult with professionals and service users, following concerns expressed about the fact that young people did not know about the purpose of a child protection conference and how it might affect them. Social services managers in the county where the research took place responded positively to her fndings. Through focus groups, role plays, workshops and individual interviews, Howes was therefore able to identify how young people can contribute to the development of good practice as well as demonstrating that 'innovative social work practice has the potential to lead to service improvement' (Howes, 2005: 591).

Any evaluation and research takes place within a political context and within power structures where different stakeholder views and interests are expressed from positions of more or less power. Most services and evaluations of them are constructed within legislative and funding processes and are shaped by contexts of practice that reflect unequal power relations. Clifford's principles for anti-oppressive assessment provide a useful framework for understanding the issues of power that impact on the evaluation process.

Anti-oppressive principles for evaluation

The principles developed by Clifford and others (Clifford, 1995; Burke and Harrison, 1998; Clifford and Burke, 2001) drawing on black feminist and other non-dominant perspectives can enable us to reflect on how evaluation and research relates to wider power issues through:

- Analysis of social difference with attention to the varying power relations between different stakeholders and other differences that interact in the lives of all those involved in evaluation and research.
- Evaluation of the differing kinds of power dimensions that arise in situations where people are using a service.
- Evaluation of the different effects and levels of interacting systems in the situations where people are using a service.
- Consideration of how personal and organizational histories lead to and mould the understanding and behaviour of individuals involved in the receipt and provision of services.
- Analysis of the mutual interaction between the evaluator/researcher and those involved in the evaluation/research (reflexivity).

Service user involvement in evaluation

There are two key issues that have arisen in relation to service user involvement in evaluation. The first is service users' definitions of outcomes (Shaping Our Lives National User Network, 2003). The second relates to the questions being raised by service users and service user researchers about 'whose agendas, issues, concerns and interests user involvement in research and evaluation is seeking to advance' (Beresford, 2005: 80). In many ways the two issues raise the same concerns.

The Shaping Our Lives project was set up in 1996 to bring together lessons from service users and to develop their views about user-led outcomes (Shaping Our Lives National User Network, 2003). The project drew together ideas of user-defined outcomes, worked with and supported user groups in four development projects[2] and shared common themes and learning across the projects. However, issues raised when thinking about services in terms of outcomes demonstrated that service users wanted to look at their lives and their needs as a whole. For example, the process of getting a service and how it is delivered will impact on how they experience it. Problems included:

- poor access to services;
- delays in service provision;
- poor treatment from service providers;
- lack of consultation or consultation which was ignored or not acted upon.

Experiences like this affect the outcome of the service and so users did not see the process as separate to the outcome. Discussing mental health advocacy services, Platzer suggests that evaluation 'needs to concentrate as much on process as outcomes, and question the underlying mechanisms if it is to make a useful contribution to developing good practice' (2005: 94). Service users also viewed outcomes from a holistic perspective which would cover areas like housing, transport, employment, income and benefits and broader issues around discrimination and equality. In their consideration of user-defined outcomes, service users felt that while it was important to evaluate services in terms of their outcomes, the subjective perspectives of individual users should be included, recognizing that this can be supported by an objective measurement. The example used was a suggestion by a mental health service user that effective services could be measured in relation to spending on drugs and that effective support would lead to less spending on drugs. The work of this project clearly identified how service users wanted to think about outcomes and the difficulties of doing this in the way that many services are organized.

A key message for practitioners and academics involved in evaluation is that the ideas of user-defined outcomes cannot be separated from action to define and achieve them. Service users did not just want to monitor and evaluate service delivery. They needed to be involved in defining the outcomes and then working towards achieving them – which in turn requires time and resources. Furthermore, the project found that users felt that services continued to show a lack of respect. The value of their own outcomes was neither acknowledged or valued. This brings us back to the service users questioning of the purpose of research and evaluation.

Considering whether the increasing requirements for user involvement in evaluation is consistent with their interests or empowerment, Beresford (2005: 81) asks some pertinent questions:

- Will their involvement just be an 'add-on' which will serve to advance the service system and/or dominant government discourse and knowledge base?
- How helpful is such involvement likely to be to the development and advancement of service users' own body of knowledge and cannon of work, analysis and discourse – or might it actually conflict with them?
- Is it enough to be involved merely to advance the dominant discourse and debate in the process providing more knowledge for the state and service system, which may have oppressive potential?

These questions suggest that the empowering potential of legislation depends on whether evaluation is primarily concerned with changing and improving the lives of people who are using services or whether it is about extending the body of knowledge.

One way of ensuring that evaluation has an impact on the lives of service users is through participatory evaluation. In fact, it has been suggested that policies requiring a high degree of public participation should consider such approaches to evaluation as this is one way of involving all stakeholders in a meaningful way, especially service user groups. There are a number of approaches to participatory evaluation and a great deal of ongoing debate about its empowering potential.[3] Characteristics of participatory evaluation have been identified as:

- drawing on local resources and capacities;
- recognizing (or even prioritizing) the wisdom and knowledge of local people;
- ensuring that stakeholders are a key part of the decision-making process;
- enabling participants to *own* the evaluation process rather than being 'subjected' to it;
- working together on the evaluation, usually as a group with the role of a facilitator being to support their work (yet only acting as a catalyst for others' ideas);
- ensuring that all parts of the evaluation process are relevant to the participants rather than being imposed upon them.

(Graham and Harris, 2005: 100)

Evaluation as revolution

Evaluation can be seen as a political (Taylor and Balloch, 2005b) and revolutionary activity (Phillips et al., 1994). From a political perspective, Taylor and Balloch identify it as an activity that is affected by power relations between commissioners, policy-makers, service providers, service users and evaluators. The revolutionary element is the movement to more active involvement of service users which questions the power relations within the politics of evaluation:

> The concept of user empowerment, in the name of which many new schemes are being set up and evaluated, is breathtakingly radical in its implications for shifts of power and influence in service planning and modes of service provision.
>
> (Phillips et al., 1994: 24)

Phillips' observations are still relevant as service users raise concerns about their involvement in evaluation and research (Beresford, 2005).

Many of us within the health and social services do not allow ourselves the time to 'ponder'. The pressures of work are such that finding the space to really consider the experiences of service users, to read, reflect, and evaluate our practice can be difficult. In a society where policies are shaped by dominant values and norms, little account is taken of the needs of oppressed groups. We therefore need to monitor and evaluate the effectiveness of legislation by making ourselves aware of relevant research and law reports.

Legislation expects users to participate in decisions made about their own lives at a personal level, as well as being involved at the structural level of policy and planning. Without proper evaluation of personal practice, of the impact of the legislation and policies and procedures deriving from them, it can be easy to delude ourselves into believing that a commitment to user involvement means that it is actually happening. Then there is no revolution.

Chapter summary

In this chapter we have explored the current culture of practice that increasingly demands performance assessment and evaluation of routine targets and indicators. This can negate the positive elements of evaluation, which goes beyond regulatory requirements to consideration of the empowerment potential of participatory evaluation. We have seen that critical reflection is a key element of evaluation and anti-oppressive practice. However, since evaluation takes place within a political context it involves many stakeholder views within structures that reflect unequal power relations. We have therefore looked at some of the difficulties of anti-oppressive evaluation and identified principles for understanding the power issues involved. Evaluation is therefore seen as part of a continual learning process which health and social care practitioners in the public domain need to recognize as part of their accountability to service users.

Further reading

Shaw, I. (1996) *Evaluating in Practice*. Aldershot: Arena.
A well-known text aimed at social workers which is a useful practical guide to evaluation.

Shaw, I. and Lishman, J. (eds) (1999) *Evaluation and Social Work Practice*. London: Sage Publications.
This book looks at the issues for evaluation in social work practice.

Taylor, D. and Balloch, S. (eds) *The Politics of Evaluation: Participation and Policy Implementation*. Bristol: The Policy Press.
This book focuses on evaluation as a political activity and is a key resource for all stakeholders who are interested in promoting change through evaluation.

Parsons, R.J. (1998) Evaluation of empowerment practice, in L. Gutiérrez, R.J. Parsons and E.O. Cox (eds) *Empowerment in Social Work Practice*. Pacific Grove: Brooks/Cole.
An accessible text that looks at the issues in evaluating empowerment programmes.

Useful websites

www.mande.co.uk A news service focusing on monitoring and evaluation methods.
www.ukes.co.uk The website of the UK Evaluation Society.

Activity 1: Evaluation in practice

The service manager at a resource centre for older people decided that it was important to evaluate the range of activities that the centre was offering to the users. She brought it to one of the monthly user forums. Before the meeting she spoke to Arthur, who was the chair of the group, and told him that as the centre was due to be inspected she wanted to find out what service users thought about the activities, as she knew that she would be asked about service user feedback. She was particularly proud of the Old Time Musical Evening that she personally arranged every three months. Arthur agreed to invite her to the meeting, although he pointed out that there was already a full agenda. He told her that she would only have minutes and she assured him that this would be fine.

The service users had organized the forum so that meetings lasted no longer than an hour. Usually the service manager did not attend. However, on this occasion Arthur informed the meeting that she had especially asked to go along to get feedback about what people thought about the activities at the centre. This upset a few people and Arthur had to stop further discussion about the invitation. When she arrived the service manager gave out a questionnaire which took some time to complete. Points of clarification were brought up and some people indicated that they would have preferred more time to consider their responses. One person did not have her reading glasses to hand. The service manager then spoke for 20 minutes about the inspection. Some of those present were nodding off at this stage.

The meeting went on for nearly two hours. Only one item was discussed, despite the fact that there was a prearranged agenda. At the end of the meeting the service manager, pleased with getting the information she needed to help her evaluate the service, told the group that she would pass their comments on to the rest of the staff group at the next team meeting. This would help her evaluate the services offered. Some of the users felt the need for a stiff drink! Arthur considered that he had not managed the meeting well. He had initially thought that inviting her to the meeting would be helpful but it turned out to be a nightmare.

In terms of the above scenario, how far do you feel that the users were consulted or involved in the process of evaluation? Consider the following questions:

- What was the purpose of this evaluation?
- Do you think that the service manager actually gathered the information she needed?
- Do you think that the service manager would have the correct information in order to meet the needs of the users?
- How far do you think that the actions of the service manager empowered the people who attended the forum?
- Do you feel that following the staff meeting a useful summative evaluation could be obtained?

Activity 2: Self-evaluation

We all need a system of self-evaluation to help us to develop an anti-oppressive perspective. These questions can help your personal critical evaluation of practice:

1. What theories and values inform my caring practice?
2. What is the likely impact of my perspective on users or the person I care for? In our interactions with others we respond differently depending on their social divisions membership. Service users will also respond to the differences they perceive in us. Taking account of the complexity and tensions in the dynamics of the situation, you therefore also need to ask:
3. How do I respond to all these differences?
4. Do I have a system of constantly analysing difference? This could be a series of questions that you ask yourself and might include, for example:

   - Am I making any assumptions about the social divisions membership of the people I am working with?
   - What differences are there *within* each social divisions category, for example what is the nature of the disability, ethnicity, age group that are relevant to this particular situation?

5. What is my understanding of oppression?
6. How does this understanding inform my practice?
7. What assumptions do I make about power, who has it, where it comes from, what it allows you to do?
8. How do I use my personal and professional power? These questions are individual challenges. To work in isolation saps our energy and can be demoralizing. Therefore a final question is:
9. What is my support network internally (within the team, with specialist forums and so on) and externally – locally, nationally and internationally (with national and international groups such as non-governmental agencies and campaigning organizations, service user groups, professional groups, trade unions and political parties)?

Our responses to these questions will change as we are exposed to a range of experiences.

Activity 3: Personal evaluation

We all have the capacity to evaluate a particular situation. It might be at an individual level, a team level or an organizational level. You may be nursing on a large medical ward, caring for a dependent relative, working in a small voluntary organization or part of a social work team. This exercise is intended to help you to evaluate your own practice and identify whether you are providing a quality service.

To begin, use the following questions in relation to your own situation:

1. Clearly define your aims and objectives.
    (a) What is it that you really want to achieve?
    (b) What obstacles stand in the way of your task?
    (c) What do you need to do to overcome the obstacles?
    (d) What will the reward be?
    (e) Is the task worth the reward?
2. Think about your answers and evaluate them.
    (a) Are your aims and objectives realistic?
    (b) Can they be achieved in the time available?
    (c) Are they appropriate (to the family, your agency, yourself)?
    (d) Are they compatible with policies, guidelines, procedures, legislation?
    (e) Are they in the best interests of the service user?
    (f) Are they measurable?

14 The REALITY OF ANTI-OPPRESSIVE PRACTICE

Working from an anti-oppressive position brings with it a fundamental transformation not only on an individual level but also on an organisational level. Implications for practice are expressed by Micheline Mason, one of the founder members of the Liberation Network of People with Disabilities, who says of professional intervention:

It will involve looking at your fears about disability, and exploring your own feelings of being oppressed. It will involve giving over information which you, as professionals, have been given and which we need. It will involve practical support for initiatives which we take, and will involve redesigning your role as 'helper' into one of enabler. Most of all it will involve making friends with us on our own terms. This may feel painful, frightening, difficult or even humiliating to you, as it does to us, but we are certain that it is necessary for all of us to get through this period of fundamental change in order to live together and enjoy each other as equals.

(Campling, 1984:25)

Anti-oppressive theory, the law and practice

Academics, practitioners, service users and carers have, over the last 10 years, contributed to the development of anti-oppressive theory and practice. There is now a body of literature available that provides a wealth of material to inform debate and develop practice (See for example Adams, 1998b, Clifford, 1998, Dominelli, 2002a, Healy, 2005, Pinkney, 2000, Wilson and Beresford, 2000, Tomlinson and Trew, 2002). The context of health and social care practice has become more complex and for professionals the challenges of everyday practice are exacerbated by the fact that they operate within a context where the values of caring are potentially pushed aside by managerial discourse and emphasis on outcome based practice. Ever changing legislation, policies and directives proceduralise professional responses to complex human situations. The tyranny of targets leave little room for professional autonomy in relation to creative and innovative practice. Professional knowledge and skills are devalued as professionals become increasingly marginalized from decision making processes. For example the need for re-lational skills to facilitate assessment and decision making becomes less im-portant in an environment where assessment and care management are separated from direct service provision (Jordan and Jordan, 2000).

Given the context of contemporary practice how can we use principles of anti-oppressive practice to engage effectively with people who use services? A commitment to change requires a 'sense of outrage' (Simey 1993) which we talked about in the introduction. The sense of outrage felt by Margaret Simey was shaped by the many contexts of her life: material, social, political, eco-nomic and cultural. Margaret Simey was a white middle-class woman who was born in 1906. As a young woman she was influenced by Eleanor Rathbone who was an outstanding social reformer and pivotal in the development of social work training at Liverpool University. At that time her sense of outrage about the position of women was her driving force. In the following quote she reflects on the impact of the declaration by the Liverpool Women Citizen's Association, which in the 1920's campaigned to win for women the right to vote so that they could be full citizens. They demanded the right to educa-tion, to opportunity and to independence. They were brought together by the 'passion of their conviction' (Simey, 1996) that they all had a right and a duty to actively participate in their own communities.

> It is impossible to convey to the 1990's the long lasting-impact of that declaration on me and my generation after the First World War. We were that unfortunate band who faced life dubbed 'Superfluous Women'. The label was deadly accurate. We were literally super-fluous; superfluous to the needs of the marriage market sharply di-minished by the consequences of war, superfluous on the economic market where the long shadow of the Great Slump already cast a gloom over all our lives. Unwanted even on the home front since to keep unmarried daughters in idleness was a luxury many middle-class families could no longer afford. And politically of no account. (I still remember, sixty years on, the precise moment when, for the first time ever, I cast my vote in a polling booth). Miraculously, these Women Citizens turned our resentment against the injustice of our condemnation to futility and frustration into a moral conviction which totally redeemed our situation. Our salvation lay in their undeviating loyalty to the principle of the universal right of every member of the community to play their part as responsible citizens.
>
> (Simey, 1996:3)

Margaret Simey spent most of her adult life living in an area of Liverpool which she graphically describes as having 'only one industry and that a singularly flourishing one, the manufacture of social problems' (1996:123). She commented that what her academic colleagues called the cycle of deprivation was a daily inescapable reality to the people who lived there. Practicing in often hostile and difficult circumstances and overwhelming structural inequalities Margaret Simey, as a community activist and later as a local politician, was motivated into taking action by the passion of her respect for the capacity of the ability of the people in the area to survive in circumstances that she acknowledged she herself could never cope with. She never became immune to the circumstances of people's lives. Her core principles included giving 'a profoundly respectful hearing' (1996:124) to those who called on her for help. In addition she recognized that the personal problems of service users might only be understood if they are contextualised. For her 'to attribute the troubles of such determined survivors to the inadequacies or misfortunes of individuals' was 'an injustice of the highest order' (1996:124). Her belief in making the systems work on behalf of users of services meant that firstly she believed that as a worker she was accountable primarily to the people she worked with and for. Margaret Simey put her professionalism and experience at the service of the people in the community from whom her authority was derived. Secondly she advocated a co-ordinated approach in order to meet the needs of people who used services. The value of anti-oppressive practice today has been questioned – has it lost its potency and become commodified into a professionalized response to inequalities? We believe that the critical challenges for current practitioners are resonated in the work of Margaret Simey and that it is possible to hold on to its core elements and its radicalism.

Practice that is informed by a political commitment to social equality and justice which is ethical and transformative needs to be based on a critical understanding of our own values and the context of practice. Throughout the book we have identified a number of underpinning principles which are set out in Figure 14.1.

Engaging in practice informed by these principles can help us to maintain the 'sense of outrage' necessary to galvanise us into action. The principles are not fixed. They are general principles which may be adapted by critical reflective practitioners working within varying practice contexts. Commitment to change is about being prepared to reflect, challenge and rethink taken-for-granted views of the structures within which we operate. The principles of the Commission of Social Care Inspection reflects a critical understanding of the context of practice of its work and a commitment to anti-oppressive practice.

Ten years ago the Disability Discrimination Act 1995 was passed in the UK and welcomed as an important piece of legislation to protect and promote the rights of disabled people. It was a hard won fight after years of campaigning by the disability movement. Assessing the impact of the Act O'Hara,

Principles for Anti-oppressive Practice

As anti-oppressive practitioners we should be able to:

- Continually consider how our values, social difference and power affects our interaction with others both emotionally and intellectually – reflexivity (Burke and Harrison, 1998, Clifford, 1998)
- Acknowledge and work with differences and commonalities with service users, carers, colleagues and other workers
- Understand and be committed to justice and equality principles within a human rights framework
- Incorporate a critical understanding of the concept of power
- Locate individual problems within a social context
- Recognise other people, including service users, as knowing subjects and knowledge creators (Dominelli, 2004)
- Work in true partnership with service users and other professionals where each in the partnership are respected and valued and given some autonomy within that relationship
- Minimise the intrusiveness of intervention
- Democratise service provision by working with service users and learning from their experience and expertise to shape and inform services
- Recognise and use the possibilities of personal and structural change
- Use national, international and global perspectives to inform our practice
- Challenge ways in which the policies or activities of government, organisations or society create or contribute to structural disadvantage, hardship and suffering, or militate against their relief (BASW Code of Ethics)
- Continually reflect on and evaluate our practice

Figure 14.1

writing in *The Guardian* (8 June 2005), identifies how the legislation has put disability rights on the human rights agenda, emancipating disabled people. Applauded as a landmark victory it is a complex piece of legislation with room for improvement. Nevertheless it can been used as a powerful tool for challenging oppression. Quoting research by Wright and Easthorne (2003), Sayce (2005) identifies how disabled students trying to enter nursing could have challenged the discrimination they faced on the grounds of health and safety. For example deaf people are assumed to be a health and safety risk to service users as they may not be able to hear alarms. Sayce points out that good practice under the Disability Discrimination Act 1995, which requires employers and service providers to make reasonable adjustments so that disabled people are not treated 'less favourably', could change this. Flashing lights as alarms as well as sirens or co-working with colleagues so that deaf people are alerted to an emergency could enable them to practice without

Principles of the Commission for Social Care Inspection
Put the people who use social care first

- People who use social care can trust us to act in their interests at all times
- We'll be guided by what they tell us, and support them to live independent lives with dignity
- We'll speak and act in a way that makes sense, and respects rights and choices

Improve services and stamp out bad practice

- We'll be a visible force for good, rewarding and promoting good practice
- We'll be firm but fair in raising standards and stamping out bad practice
- Our work will be driven by what matters to the people who use social care, not by regulation for its own sake

Be an expert voice on social care

- We'll be experts in our field, making our case based on high-quality evidence
- We'll give leadership to social care
- We'll stand up for the rights of people who use social care
- We'll help the people who work in social care to make it better
- We'll be an independent body with clout, respected and listened to by government and the media

Practice what we preach in our own organisation

- We'll live up to the standards of management and behaviour we expect from others
- We'll create a single, well-managed organisation for which people are proud to work
- We'll learn from our own staff and respect their professionalism and passion

Figure 14.2

danger. Another example of successful use of the legislation is demonstrated by Anthony Ford-Shubrook, who has cerebral palsy. He wanted to study IT at the only 6th form college in his area that offered the course he wanted. The IT department was on the 1st floor but there was no lift, which created a problem. Anthony's parents would have bought a 'climbing' wheelchair but this was seen as a health and safety risk. He won his case under the Disability Discrimination Act and the local Learning and Skills Council did then work with the college to enable him to take up his place and go to IT courses.

There are disagreements about definitions of disability and impairment often resulting in failed cases at tribunal because 'experts' or doctors argue that the person involved does not meet the criteria of 'disabled'. It is not enough therefore to rely on the taken-for-granted assumption that the rights enshrined in the law are sufficient to promote equality. The legislation can and has been used positively by disabled people to facilitate change and promote their rights. However critical practitioners need to be aware that 10 years after the legislation was passed the Disability Rights Commission is still documenting stories of persistent discrimination. Furthermore there are paradoxes in the progress of disabled people's rights. For example, it is planned that the Disability Rights Commission in the UK will be absorbed into the Commission for Equality and Human Rights. On the one hand this can be viewed as positive in ensuring that there will be an overall strategy for all excluded groups. However rights campaigners are concerned about how effective it will be in championing the needs of individual groups, in this case, disabled people. The new body will have an advisory rather than an advocacy role, reducing the necessary expertise available to support legal challenges. Another paradox is the development of policies that seem to contradict and undermine the progress of disabled people's rights. For example anticipated changes in regulations for incapacity benefit are likely to push more disabled people into seeking work. If they are unable to work then they will be forced into poverty with insufficient income to live on, which further excludes them from active participation in society. The legislation has contributed to a cultural shift from welfare to rights, but as critical practitioners we must be aware that the structural barriers within society remain.

This example, as with other examples within the book, demonstrates that it is possible to promote change and that legislation can be used as a tool for anti-oppressive practice. We see the law as a powerful force. That power can be problematic in that it can be oppressive, but it can be used to empower people who are marginalized within society. We identify and take the positive aspects of the law to support anti-oppressive practice.

In considering the principles in Part II and the practice in Part III we have made the links between the personal and the structural. By understanding both the structure and people's personal biographies we have a 'rich explanation of the interactive process of change' (Juckes and Barresi, 1993:214). The purpose of this book is to enable practitioners, service users and carers to make the links between issues of power and oppression that lie at the heart of health and social care practice. We have attempted to develop a practice that addresses power relations by using the powerful structure of the law to achieve change. We therefore need to conclude by thinking about that process of change.

We have argued that change is only possible through understanding the link between individual and structural inequalities. This means recognising the complexity and interconnections of the social divisions that impact on the lives of service users, carers and practitioners (Clifford, 1998, Dominelli, 2002a, Langan, 1992). Equality, equity and accessibility have been identified as vital social and political goals in the delivery of health and social care services (Phillips et al., 1994). There are many ways of attempting to achieve these goals. However, there are divergent opinions as to how to do so, affected by different theoretical approaches and understandings of oppression within society.

Many health and social care practitioners are committed to promoting change. But it is not easy and can have both financial and personal costs (Healy, 2005). Lack of resources characterizes the delivery of health and social care services in Europe. For example, over 10 years ago Twigg and Atkin found in their research focusing on carers that in relation to the work of occupational therapists 'the realities of their day-to-day work, in the context of waiting lists and backlogs, means that practice is much more narrowly focused' (1994:64). This theme is reflected in current debates about policy and practice in public services (Jones, 2001, Jordan and Jordan, 2000). For example Parton (1999) has noted that reduced resources make it impossible to develop the wide ranging preventative family support strategies required by the Children Act 1989. Stepney states that 'in the restructured and marketised welfare state, social work is now required to have a narrower and more instrumental focus' (2000:9). To widen the focus in all areas of practice requires a commitment to challenging inequalities. Rooney (1987) identified strong resistance to change from central and local government in relation to avoidance of the financial costs of that change. This means that the personal costs to practitioners and carers in fighting for change are directly related to fighting for increased resources as well as having to fight the ideological battles. However, as Rooney points out, 'Where change did come about it was through the ability to find and use power, no great measure of it but little bits here and there' (1987, p.97). We have said the law is a powerful resource. If we can use that power as an opportunity system (Solomon, 1976), even 'little bits here and there', then we can promote change.

In a busy week, with few resources, you may feel that it is unrealistic even to consider strategies for promoting change – it is all you can do to keep things going! However, we are not talking about changing the world overnight, we are talking about using our practice to challenge oppression and develop an agenda for change. This may include the development of a plan of action which goes beyond a passive commitment to anti-oppressive principles. It is a process that involves looking at the terrain. It is not a pleasant walk across a park but a hard scramble on rocky ground. Other people have travelled these paths before. The work of Margaret Simey, discussed earlier, and other social activists such as Josephine Butler or more recently, Nelson Mandela, illustrate this. Others are on their journey – many advocacy organizations are testament to this. This involves networking and using the expertise that exist in local groups and organizations who witness the impact of social and economic policies – they know the terrain. You may find the following points helpful when you are thinking about an agenda for change. Although not directly related to social work the following example shows the need for social problems to be addressed by professionals working together.

Identify the issue, problem or goal

Consider the following statistics. Of the 9,880 pupils excluded from school in 2003-4, Black children and young people were nearly three times more likely to be punished in this way than white pupils (*The Guardian*, Wednesday October 5th 2005). The Birmingham LEA & schools formal investigation found that Black pupils were four times more likely to be suspended than white pupils; Black pupils were suspended on average at a younger age and after shorter periods and fewer incidents of disruption. They were also less likely to be readmitted to the school. The activity below asks some critical questions which can be used to consider why this is a problem.

Break down the issue, problem or goal so that it is manageable

The goal here would be to develop ways of working with Black young people and their families so that they can return to mainstream education. Alongside this is the need to ensure that the education system can meet the diverse needs of its pupils. Assessments should take account of the factors that impinge on the lives of Black young people regarding their ability to cope with their home and school environments.

Set a time limit or target (this is dependent on the task)

While the government has set its own targets in relation to reducing school exclusions (Social Exclusion Unit, 1998) the imposition of mechanisms like quality assurance systems, league tables or OFSTED[1] inspections can both exacerbate social disadvantage and fail to make a difference to rates of school exclusion. At the same time the professional autonomy of teachers is being reduced as their activities are prescribed through having to deliver the set state curriculum (Cooper, 2002). Targets for practitioners working with children and their families could therefore include:

- Understanding the range of factors that affect school exclusion;
- Accessing training and support to enable creative practice;
- Negotiating for resources for the development of specialized schemes (e.g. mentoring, counselling, parenting groups);
- Developing inter-professional working relations (between social workers, teaching staff, support staff, psychological services, general practitioners, health visitors, police and other relevant workers);
- Reviewing practice;
- Developing policies and procedures.

Review and evaluate
Some examples of questions to consider are:

- Is there a record of factors affecting school exclusion and is that information regularly analysed and used (e.g. to support families; give genuine attention to poverty issues or set up specific projects to meet local need)?
- Have any additional training needs been identified and met?
- Have adequate support systems been put in place?
- Have adequate resources been obtained (innovative projects need to be part of a long-term strategy)?
- Do all staff have opportunities to meet regularly in order to share knowledge and expertise as well as negotiate any differences?
- Are systems in place to encourage sharing of good practice and examining the impact of policies and procedures? For example teachers who are trying to maintain teaching practice and values that respect the learning needs of a diverse range of pupils could share with other professionals their struggles within the context of new Labour education policy with it's narrow emphasis on academic success. Other professionals, working with families and the community, would be able to discuss issues affecting the lives of the young people concerned such as being young carers, child protection issues, mental health concerns or physical health problems.

Make links with others
There is always resistance to change. Staff will therefore need support within their own professional teams, with colleagues from other agencies and within the community they are located in.

In 2003 the charity *Coram Family* in London recognized that the statistics mentioned above were unacceptable. It saw that schools unable to tolerate difference and diverse needs appear to pathologise pupils who have different ways of behaving and are then labeled as 'deviant', 'disruptive', or, as one mother stated 'just another troublesome Black boy' (*The Guardian*, Wednesday October 5th 2005). These pupils, once labeled, are penalized and excluded because they do not fit in. It therefore set up a mentoring scheme in 2003 to work with excluded Black pupils up to the age of 13 in order to get them back into mainstream school. An initial 12 week programme was provided which included a discussion group, basic skills training and activities ranging from sports to computer based music and film projects. A weekly parents support group was also available. Ongoing support is provided by mentors for up to a year. One of the features of the project is that the mentors are mainly male and part of the thinking of the project is to provide a positive Black male role model. The success of this project should be measured by its ability to challenge both dominant discourses about Black young men and the ideologies of schools, which, through their exclusion of these pupils perpetuate the notion of education as regulatory rather than a humanizing and liberating experience (Cooper, 2002, Haydon, 1997). Foucault's idea about the role of education as producing 'docile bodies', that is children and young people who are compliant and do not challenge the dominant values of the school or society, has been described as 'a fruitful one for explaining school exclusions' (Cooper, 2002:34).

In order to develop practice which incorporates such strategies we must simplify the issue while remembering that oppression is complex. It has to be tackled at both *personal* and *structural* levels and solutions might not always be straightforward. We can often manage the practical concrete elements of a problem but it is more difficult to challenge the ideologies which maintain oppressive practices. Ideological change incorporates an understanding of the linkages and interconnections between various oppressions. However, it is a lot more difficult to promote such change. It is necessary for ideological and concrete change to go hand in hand if any effective permanent change is to occur. It is easy to be 'overwhelmed by the sheer scale and range of issues' (Lynn 1991, p. 13) in relation to anti-oppressive practice. In discussing empowerment we put forward a model for practice which enables us to appreciate that oppression operates at a number of levels. The benefit of working from such a model is that it enables you to think about how, and at which level, work needs to be undertaken.

If we are committed to anti-oppressive practice then we have a duty to ensure that the rights of users are not violated. Legislation can be used to deny rights but we need to be aware of our role in minimizing the oppressive aspects of practice and the law and we must endeavour to maximize the rights to which all people are entitled. It is for this reason that we see the law as an instrument to protect people's rights. It is a powerful instrument but it is one that we can control and we should not therefore become subservient to it. The following statement clearly states how the law can be used to inform our practice and the role we have in contributing to change:

> It is up to practitioners to utilize the law in the improvement of practice. It is there. It is a gift. Use it. By setting precedents, case law will improve our practice. Leave it to the policy makers to curtail our action. Don't limit ourselves. Use the arena or platform of the law for change.
>
> (Paul Wilcox, project manager 1994)

Notes

Chapter 1

1 Other influential publications are Dominelli (1997), Thompson (1997) now in its third edition and, more recently, Dominelli (2002).
2 A similar Bureau of Organized Charities developed in the USA.
3 These are outlined below, but see Pease and Fook (1999), Healy (2000), Martin (2003) and Healy (2005) for further historical analyses.
4 Best practice for the contributers meant describing practical ways of meeting needs rather than dwelling on past failures.
5 See Chapter 13 for further discussion on critical reflection.

Chapter 2

1 The Macpherson Report into the death of a young black man, Stephen Lawrence, found institutional racism prevalent in British society.
2 Already noted in Chapter 1, radical social work. In Adams et al. (2005) the first chapter looks at contemporary understandings of transformational practice.
3 The process of critical reflection is examined in more detail in Chapter 13.

Chapter 3

1 The Third Way is the name given to the political philosophy and strategy of the New Labour government in the UK. It is also the title of a publication by Tony Blair *The Third Way: New Labour Politics for the New Century*. London: The Fabian Society. Anthony Giddens has also written a book called *The Third Way: Renewal of Social Democracy*. Cambridge: Polity Press.
2 This case study is based on a case taken from the DRC website: *www.drc-gb.org/thelaw/success.asp*
3 In *Gillick v West Norfolk and Wisbech Area Health Authority* [1986] AC 112 (the *Gillick* case) the relationship between parent and child and the responsibilities of the parent in that relationship was debated. The House of Lords indicated that there is a tapering relationship between parents and their children which means that the older and more mature a child becomes the less the parent has

the right to know about their affairs. It was established that a child, under 16 years old, who does have capacity is 'Gillick competent' and can give consent for medical treatment if they had sufficient understanding of the proposed medical treatment and had expressed their wishes.

* It should be noted that it is a judge who makes a declaration of incompatibility pursuant to section 4 of the Human Rights Act 1998 if a primary legislation or a secondary legislation is incompatible with Convention rights. In the case of primary legislation being incompatible with Convention rights the Secretary of State responsible for the legislation must make amends, and in the case of secondary legislation Her Majesty in Council must make amends (section 10 of the Human Rights Act 1998).

Chapter 4

1   See Chapter 13 for further discussion of these terms.

Chapter 5

1   Adapted from Brenda DuBois and Karla Krogsrund Miley, *Social Work: An Empowering Profession.* Copyright © 1992 by Allyn and Bacon. Reprinted by permission.
2   See Chapter 3 for more about the Third Way.

Chapter 6

1   A range of guidelines for partnership working are now available – for example, Taylor, 1995; Audit Commission, 1998; Stewart et al. 1999; LGA 1999, 2001, 2002; Department of Health, 2001.

Chapter 7

1   Some of these terms are discussed further on in this chapter and in Chapter 12.
2   The principle that every adult has a right to make their own decisions is the basis of the law and the role of practitioners in some situations is to support people to understand what decisions they are being asked to make. The leaflet *Helping People Who Have Difficulty Making Decisions for Themselves – A Guide for Social Care Professionals, www.dca.gov.uk/family/mi/mibooklets/guides5.htm* is a useful guide to the law in this respect.

3   For example, in the case of *R (on application of M) v Secretary of State for Health 2003* a women did not want her adoptive father, who was the nearest relative according to the list outlined in Section 26 of the Mental Health Act 1983, to have access to her records or be involved in the decision-making. She argued that there was no trust or relationship between them and under Article 8 (respect to private life) Section 26 was declared incompatible with the Convention.

Chapter 8

1   Ageism is defined as prejudice and discrimination towards older people on the grounds of age: Bytheway, B. (1995) *Ageism.* Buckingham: Open University Press. See also Crawford, K. and Walker, J. (2004) *Social Work with Older People.* Exeter: Learning Matters Ltd. for discussion about the concept.
2   See Chapter 10 for more discussion about assessment.
3   Chapter 6 of the document.
4   For example, section 3(1) and section 7(1) of the Carers and Disabled Children Act 2000 provide power to the secretary of state to make provision in regulations for local authorities to issue vouchers for short-term breaks.
5   Here the speaker is talking about the eligibility bands of Fair Access to Care (see box).

Chapter 9

1   The Children's Fund was a prevention programme rolled out across England in 2000. It was established to provide support for children and their families before they reached crisis, with the aim of reducing the future probability of poor outcomes and maximizing their life chances.
2   This was the government's response to the report into the death of Victoria Climbié. Laming, H. (2003) *The Victoria Climbié Inquiry.*
3   National Society for the Prevention of Cruelty to Children.
4   The examples of Parentline and NEWPIN were informed by the work of Smith (1999).
5   **fsu** is a charity established in the UK in 1948 to work with hard to reach, vulnerable and excluded children and their families. It aims to create new ways of engaging with the most marginalized and excluded families.
6   See Chapter 6 on partnership.
7   This Unit was set up by the government in 1997. The work of the Social Exclusion Unit includes specific projects to tackle specific issues and programmes to assess past policy and identify future trends.
8   Centrepoint is a national charity working to improve the lives of socially

excluded, homeless young people. It provides a range of accommodation-based services.

9 Connexions is a service that provides integrated information, advice and guidance for 13–19-year-olds in England.

10 National Association for the Care and Resettlement of Offenders.

Chapter 10

1 The former County of Avon subsequently became the unitary authorities of Bristol, Bath and North East Somerset, North Somerset and South Gloucestershire.

2 Clifford uses the term 'social assessment' in relation to assessing the needs of individuals and small groups to refer to 'social as distinct from psychological or medical assessment – that is, assessment which is centred on *social* explanation – and will draw on social science concepts' (Clifford, 1998: xix).

Chapter 11

1 Local safeguarding children boards replace non-statutory area child protection committees (ACPC). The Children Act 2004 required all local authorities to establish a local safeguarding children board by April 2006. The intention to establish local safeguarding children boards was first proposed in *Every Child Matters*, and *Keeping Children Safe* and was influenced by a Joint Chief Inspectors' report which found that ACPC arrangements were not working well in some areas for a nbumber of reasons. Local safeguarding children boards are required to co-ordinate and ensure the effectiveness of local arrangements and services to safeguard and promote the welfare of children. A broader list of core agencies must, by law, be represented on the Board than is the case on an ACPC.

2 A fuller account can be found in Wigfall, V., Monck, E. and Reynolds, J. (2006) Putting programme into practice: the introduction of concurrent planning into mainstream adoption and fostering services, *British Journal of Social Work*, 36: 41–55.

Chapter 12

1 Adoption and Children Act 2004.

2 See the National Health Service Framework and the Expert Patient (Department of Health, 2000).

3   Department of Health (2002) *Requirements for Social Work Training*. London: Department of Health.

4   However, the term 'service user' is also used in the health services, and the Nurses Agency Regulations indicate that a service user can be an individual or an institution or organization.

5   Sure Start is a UK government programme to deliver the best start in life for every child. It brings together early education, child care, health and family support.

6   National Service Frameworks are long-term strategies for improving specific areas of care in the UK and a rolling programme of National Service Frameworks started in April 1998. They:

- set national standards and identify key interventions for a defined service or care group;
- put in place strategies to support implementation;
- establish ways to ensure progress within an agreed timescale;
- form one of a range of measures to raise quality and reduce variations in service.

Each National Service Framework is developed with the assistance of an external reference group which brings together health professionals, service users and carers, health service managers, partner agencies, and other advocates.

7   National Association of Young People In Care.

8   The concept of partnership is discussed in more detail in Chapter 6.

9   An organization for lone parents run by lone parents.

10 See *www.monmouthshire.gov.uk/.../YourCouncil/PolicyStrategy/Monmouthshire_ Partnership/Community_Strategy.htm* for more information.

11 See *www.salford.gov.uk/living/health.htm* for more information.

12 The model has been adapted for other forms of participation, for example in relation to children and young people. See Hart, R. (1992) *Innocenti Essays No. 4. Children's Participation: From Tokenism to Citizenship*. Florence: UNICEF International Child Development Centre.

13 See further reading at the end of this chapter for detailed accounts of the various forms of advocacy such as self-advocacy, citizen advocacy, peer advocacy, professional advocacy.

14 For social workers there is an expectation that they will be able to demonstrate an ability to do this in order to reach the level required to qualify (Key Role 3 National Occupational Standards for Social Work).

15 This ruling is described in a footnote in Chapter 3.

16 See below for a fuller account of guiding principles for user involvement.

17 'Shouldn't everyone know what is being written about them?' A pilot study in the northeast of England 2002 (*www.doh.gov.uk/patientletters/issues.htm*).

Chapter 13

1   Issit spoke to 34 women in a research project during 1997/1998, reporting on
    their perspectives and experiences of reflective practice in order to develop a
    critical understanding of such practice.
2   The groups were diverse – disabled people, mental health users and older
    people – and had a strong representation of the lives of people from black and
    minority ethnic groups.
3   The following authors examine the pitfalls and limitations of participatory
    approaches to evaluation and research and lead the debates about its libera-
    tory potential.

    Cooke, B. and Kothari, U. (2001) The case for participation as tyranny, in B.
    Cooke and U. Kothari (eds) *Participation: The New Tyranny*. New York: Zed
    Books Ltd.

    Hickey, S. and Mohan, G. (eds) (2004) *Participation: From Tyranny to Trans-
    formation?* London: Zed Books.

    Taylor, D. and Balloch, S. (eds) (2005b) *The Politics of Evaluation: Participation
    and Policy Implementation*. Bristol: The Policy Press.

Chapter 14

1   Ofsted is a non-Ministerial government department, led by Her Majesty's
    Chief Inspector of Schools in England (HMCI), that arranges and pays for
    inspections. Similar bodies exist in the other countries of the UK – HMI
    Inspectors for Schools (Scotland), Estyn, Wales and the Department of Edu-
    cation Northern Ireland.

Bibliography

Adams, R. (1998a) *Quality Social Work*. London: Macmillan.

Adams, R. (1998b) Social work processes, in R. Adams, L. Dominelli and M. Payne (eds) *Social Work: Themes, Issues and Critical Debates*. Basingstoke: Macmillan.

Adams, R. (2002) *Social Policy for Social Work*. Basingstoke: Palgrave.

Adams, R., Dominelli, L. and Payne, M. (eds) (1998) *Social Work: Themes, Issues and Critical Debates*. Basingstoke: Macmillan.

Adams, R., Dominelli, L. and Payne, M. (eds) (2002) *Critical Practice in Social Work*. Basingstoke: Palgrave.

Adams, R., Dominelli, L. and Payne, M. (2005a) *Social Work Futures: Crossing Boundaries, Transforming Practice*. Basingstoke: Palgrave Macmillan.

Adams, R., Dominelli, L. and Payne, M. (2005b) Transformational social work, in R. Adams, L. Dominelli and M. Payne (eds) *Social Work Futures: Crossing Boundaries, Transforming Practice*. Basingstoke: Palgrave Macmillan.

Agryis, C. and Schön, D. (1976) *Theory in Practice: Increasing Professional Effectiveness*. San Francisco: Jossey-Bass.

Ahmad, B. (1990) *Black Perspectives in Social Work*. Birmingham: Venture Press.

Ahmed, S., Cheetham, J. and Small, J. (1986) *Social Work with Black Children and Their Families*. London: B.T. Batsford.

Alcock, P. (2004) Targets, indicators and milestones: what is driving area-based policy action in England?, *Public Management Review*, 6: 211–27.

Alderson, P. (1995) *Listening to Children: Children, Ethics and Social Research*. London: Barnardos.

Alderson, P. (2000) Children as researchers: the effects of participation rights on research methodology, in P. Christensen and A. James (eds) *Research with Children, Perspectives and Practices*. London: Falmer Press.

Allan, J. (2003) Theorising critical social work, in J. Allan, B. Pease and L. Briskman (eds) *Critical Social Work: An Introduction to Theories and Practices*. Crows Nest, NSW: Allen & Unwin.

Allison, A. (2005) Embracing diversity and working in partnership, in R. Carnwell and J. Buchanan (eds) *Effective Practice in Health and Social Care: A Partnership Approach*. Maidenhead: Open University Press.

Angelou, M. (1994) *Wouldn't take nothing for my journey now*. London: Virago Press.

Arnstein, S. (1969) A ladder of citizen participation in the USA, *Journal of the American Institute of Planners*, 35: 216–24.

ASPEN (1983) For my apolitical sisters, in the Raving Beauties (ed.) *In the Pink*. London: The Women's Press.

Atkinson, D. (1999) *Advocacy: A Review*. Brighton: Pavilion Publishing Ltd/Joseph Rowntree Foundation.

Badham, B. (2002) Preface, in C. Willow (ed.) *Participation in Practice: Children and Young People as Partners in Change*. London: The Childrens Society.

Bailey, D. (2002) Mental health, in R. Adams, L. Dominelli and M. Payne (eds) *Critical Practice in Social Work*. Basingstoke: Palgrave.

Bailey, R. and Brake, M. (1975) *Radical Social Work*. London: Edward Arnold.

Bailey, R. and Brake, M. (1980) *Radical Social Work and Practice*. London: Edward Arnold.

Baldwin, M. (2004) Critical reflection: opportunities and threats to professional learning and service development in social work organisations, in N. Gould and M. Baldwin (eds) *Social Work, Critical Reflection and the Learning Organisation*. Aldershot: Ashgate Publishing Ltd.

Baldwin, N. and Walker, L. (2005) Assessment, in R. Adams, L. Dominelli and M. Payne (eds) *Social Work Futures: Crossing Boundaries, Transforming Practice*. Basingstoke: Palgrave Macmillan.

Bamford, F. N. and Wolkind, S. N. (1988) *The Physical and Mental Health of Children in Care*. London: ESRC.

Banks, S. (1995) *Ethics and Values in Social Work*. Basingstoke: Macmillan.

Banks, S. (2001) *Ethics and Values in Social Work*. Basingstoke: Palgrave.

Banks, S. (2004) *Ethics, Accountability and the Social Professions*. Basingstoke: Palgrave Macmillan.

Banks, S. and Williams, R. (2005) Accounting for ethical difficulties in social welfare work: issues, problems and dilemmas, *British Journal of Social Work*, 35: 1005–22.

Barclay Report (1982) *Social Workers: Their Role and Tasks*. London: Bedford Square Press.

Barford, R. and Wattam, C. (1991) Children's participation in decision making, *Practice*, 5: 93–101.

Barker, R. and Roberts, H. (1992) The uses of the concept of power, in D. Morgan and L. Stanley (eds) *Debates in Sociology*. Manchester: Manchester University Press.

Barnes, D., Carpenter, J. and Bailey, D. (2000) Partnerships with service users in interprofessional education for community mental health: a case study, *Journal of Interprofessional Care*, 14: 189–200.

Barnes, M. (ed.) (2004) *Assessing the Impact of the Children's Fund: The Role of Indicators*. Birmingham: NECF.

Barnes, M. and Shardlow, P. (1997) From passive recipient to active citizen: participation in mental health user groups, *Journal of Mental Health*, 6: 289–300.

Barnett, S. A. (1898) Review of the possibilities of settlement life, in W. Reason (ed.) *University and Social Settlements*. London: Methuen.

Bartlett, P. and McHale, J. (2003) Mental incapacity and mental health: the development of legal reform and the need for joined-up thinking, *Journal of Social Welfare and Family Law*, 25: 313–24.

BASW (2002) *The Code of Ethics for Social Work*. Birmingham: BASW.

Bates, J. (2005) Embracing diversity and working in partnership, in R. Carnwell and J. Buchanan (eds) *Effective Practice in Health and Social Care: A Partnership Approach*. Maidenhead: Open University Press.

Batsleer, J. and Humphries, B. (2000) Welfare, exclusion and political agency, in J. Batsleer and B. Humphries (eds) *Welfare, Exclusion and Political Agency*. London: Routledge.

Batty, D. (2005a) Asylum seeker families' benefits cut. *The Guardian*.

Batty, D. (2005b) Family face benefit cut despite court victory. *The Guardian*.

Beauchamp, T. and Childress, J. (2001) *Principles of Biomedical Ethics*. Oxford: Oxford University Press.

Beckett, C. (2005) *Values and Ethics in Social Work*. London: Sage Publications.

Begley, A. M. (2005) Practising virtue: a challenge to the view that a virtue centred approach to ethics lacks practical content, *Nursing Ethics*, 12: 622–37.

Behan, D. (2003) ADSS Position Statement in Response to the Victoria Climbie Inquiry Report.

Bell, L. (2005) Review, in R. Adams, L. Dominelli and M. Payne (eds) *Social Work Futures: Crossing Boundaries, Transforming Practice*. Basingstoke: Palgrave Macmillan.

Benbenishty, R., Osmo, R. and Nora, G. (2003) Rationales provided for risk assessments and for recommended interventions in child protection: a comparision between Canadian and Israeli professionals, *British Journal of Social Work*, 33: 137–55.

Beresford, P. (2003) *It's Our Lives: A Short Theory of Knowledge, Distance and Experience*. London: OSP for Citizen Press.

Beresford, P. (2005) Service-user involvement in evaluation and research: issues, dilemmas and destinations, in D. Taylor and S. Balloch (eds) *The Politics of Evaluation: Participation and Policy Implementation*. Bristol: The Policy Press.

Beresford, P. and Croft, S. (2000) Service users' knowledges and social work theory: conflict or collaboration?, *British Journal of Social Work*, 30: 489–503.

Beresford, P. and Croft, S. (2004) Service users and practitioners reunited: the key component for social work reform, *British Journal of Social Work*, 60: 53–68.

Beresford, P., Croft, S. and Harding, T. (2000) Quality in personal social services: the developing role of user involvement in the UK, in C. Davies, L. Finlay and A. Bullman (eds) *Changing Practice in Health and Social Care*. London: Sage Publications.

Berridge, D. (1985) *Children's Homes*. Oxford: Blackwell.

Bisman, C. (2004) Social work values: the moral core of the profession, *British Journal of Social Work*, 34: 109–23.

Blakemore, K. (1998) *Social Policy, an Introduction*. Buckingham: Open University Press.

Bowey, L. and McGlaughlin, A. (2005) Adults with a learning disability living with elderly carers talk about planning for the future: aspirations and concerns, *British Journal of Social Work*, 35: 1377–92.

Brammer, A. (2003) *Social Work Law*. Harlow: Pearson Education Ltd.

Brandon, D. (1995) *Advocacy: Power to People with Disabilities*. Birmingham: Venture Press.

Braye, S. (2000) Participation and involvement in social care: an overview, in H. Kemshall and R. Littlechild (eds) *User Involvement and Participation in Social Care*. London: Jessica Kingsley.

Braye, S. and Preston-Shoot, M. (1992) *Practising Social Work*. London: Macmillan.

Braye, S. and Preston-Shoot, M. (1995) *Empowering Practice in Social Care*. Buckingham: Open University Press.

Braye, S. and Preston-Shoot, M. (1997) *Practising Social Work Law*. Basingstoke: Macmillan.

Braye, S. and Preston-Shoot, M. (2005) On systematic reviews in social work: observations from teaching, learning and assessment of law in social work education, *British Journal of Social Work Advanced Access*, 17 October, 22.

Brayne, H. and Broadbent, G. (2002) *Legal Materials for Social Workers*. Oxford: Oxford University Press.

Brayne, H. and Carr, H. (2003) *Law for Social Workers*, 2nd edn. Oxford: Oxford University Press.

Brayne, H. and Carr, H. (2005) *Law for Social Workers*, 3rd edn. Oxford: Oxford University Press.

Brayne, H. and Martin, G. (1990) *Law for Social Workers*. London: Blackstone Press.

Brechin, A. (2000) Introducing critical practice, in A. Brechin, H. Brown and M.A. Eby (eds) *Critical Practice in Health and Social Care*. London: Sage Publications Ltd.

Brenton, M. (1985) *The Voluntary Sector in British Social Services*. London: Longman.

Brink, A. (2003) *The Other Side of Silence*. London: Vintage Publications.

Brodie, D. (2004) Partnership working: a service user perspective, in J. Glasby and E. Peck (eds) *Care Trusts: Partnership Working in Action*. Abingdon: Radcliffe Medical Press Ltd.

Burke, B. and Harrison, P. (1998) Anti-oppressive practice, in R. Adams, L. Dominelli and M. Payne (eds) *Social Work: Themes, Issues and Critical Debates*. Basingstoke: Macmillan Press Ltd.

Butler, I. and Williamson, H. (1994) *Children Speak: Children, Trauma and Social Work*. Harlow: Longman.

Butt, M. (1996) *Social Care and Black Communities: A Review of Recent Research Studies*. London: HMSO.

Bytheway, B. (1995) *Ageism*. Buckingham: Open University Press.

Camilleri, P. (1999) Social work and its search for meaning: theories, narratives and practices, in B. Pease and J. Fook (eds) *Transforming Social Work Practice: Postmodern Critical Perspectives*. London: Routledge.

Campling, J. (1984) On our own terms, *Community Care*, 5 April: 25–6.

Carnwell, R. and Carson, A. (2005) Understanding partnerships and collaboration, in R. Carnwell and J. Buchanan (eds) *Effective Practice in Health and Social Care: A Partnership Approach*. Maidenhead: Open University Press.

Carpenter, J. (2005) *Evaluating Outcomes in Social Work Education*. Dundee/London: Scottish Institute for Excellence in Social Work Education/Social Care Institute for Excellence.

Carr, S. (2004) *Has Service User Participation Made a Difference to Social Care Services?* Bristol: SCIE/The Policy Press.

Cemlyn, S., and Briskman, L. (2003) Asylum, children's rights and social work, *Child and Family Social Work*, 8: 163–78.

Centrepoint (2001) Centrepoint response to SEU consultation on young runaways.

Chahal, K. and Ullah, A.I. (2004) *Experiencing Ethnicity: Discrimination and Service Provision*. York: Joseph Rowntree Foundation.

Charles, M. and Butler, S. (2004) Social workers' management of organisational change, in Lymbery, M. and Butler, S. (eds) *Social Work Ideals and Practice Realities*. Basingstoke: Palgrave Macmillan.

Chestang, L. (1972) *Character Development in a Hostile Environment*. Chicago: University of Chicago Press.

Children's Rights Alliance for England (2004) State of Children's Rights in England: Annual Review of UK Government Action on 2002 Concluding Observations of the United Nations Committee on the Rights of the Child.

Chima, G. (2003) The juggling act, in V. Cree (ed.) *Becoming a Social Worker*. Abingdon: Routledge.

Clark, C.L. (2000) *Social Work Ethics: Politics, Principles and Practice*. Basingstoke: Macmillan.

Clegg, S.R. (1989) *Frameworks of Power*. London: Sage Publications.

Clifford, D. (1998) *Social Assessment Theory and Practice*. Aldershot: Ashgate Publishing.

Clifford, D. and Burke, B. (2004) Moral and professional dilemmas in long-term assessment of children and families, *Journal of Social Work*, 4: 305–21.

Cohen, L. and Mannion, L. (1994) *Research Methods in Education*. London: Routledge.

Colton, M., Sanders, R. and Williams, M. (2001) *Working with Children: A Guide for Social Workers*. Basingstoke: Palgrave.

Commission for Racial Equality (2002) *Statutory Code of Practice on the Duty to Promote Race Equality*. London: Commission for Racial Equality.

Conway, M. (1979) *Rise Gonna Rise*. New York: Anchor.

Cooke, B. and Kothari, U. (2001) The case for participation as tyranny, in B. Cooke and U. Kothari (eds) *Participation: The New Tyranny*. New York: Zed Books.

Cooke, P. and Ellis, R. (2004) Exploitation, protection and empowerment of people with learning disabilities, in M. Lymbery and I. Butler (eds) *Social Work Ideals and Practice Realities*. Basingstoke: Palgrave.

Coombe, V. and Little, A. (1986) *Race and Social Work*. London: Tavistock.

Cooper, A. (2005) Surface and depth in the Victoria Climbié inquiry report, *Child and Family Social Work*, 10: 1–9.

Cooper, C. (2002) Researching secondary school exclusion and projects of docility, *Research Policy and Planning*, 20: 31–40.

Corby, B. (2002) Child abuse and child protection, in B. Goldson, M. Lavalette and J. McKechnie (eds) *Children, Welfare and the State*. London: Sage Publications.

Corrigan, P. and Leonard, P. (1978) *Social Work under Capitalism: A Marxist Approach*. London: Macmillan.

Crawford, K. and Walker, J. (2004) *Social Work with Older People*. Exeter: Learning Matters.

Cree, V. and Wallace, S. (2005) Risk and protection, in R. Adams, L. Dominelli and M. Payne (eds) *Social Work Futures: Crossing Boundaries, Transforming Practice*. Basingstoke: Palgrave Macmillan.

Cree, V.E. (2003) Becoming and being a social worker, in V.E. Cree (ed.) *Becoming a Social Worker*. Abingdon: Routledge.

Crimmens, D. and Milligan, I. (2005) Residential care: becoming a positive choice, in D. Cimmens and I. Milligan (eds) *Facing Forward: Residential Child Care in the 21st Century*. Lyme Regis: Russell House Publishing.

Crisp, B.R., Anderson, M.R., Orme J. and Lister, P. (2005) *Learning and Teaching in Social Work Education: Textbooks and Frameworks on Assessment*. London: Social Care Institute for Excellence.

Croft, S. and Beresford, P. (1989) User involvement, citizenship and social policy, *Critical Social Policy*, 26: 5–18.

Croft, S. and Beresford, P. (1993) *Citizen Involvement: A Practical Guide for Change*. London: Macmillan.

Croft, S. and Beresford, P. (2000) Empowerment, in M. Davies (ed.) *The Blackwell Encyclopaedia of Social Work*. Oxford: Blackwell Publishers.

Cull, L.-A. and Roche, J. (2001) *The Law and Social Work: Contemporary Issues for Practice*. Basingstoke: Palgrave.

Dalrymple, J. (2002) Family group conferences and youth advocacy: the participation of children and young people in family decision making, *European Journal of Social Work*, 5: 287–99.

Dalrymple, J. and Burke, B. (2000) Anti-oppressive practice, in M. Davies (ed.) *The Blackwell Encyclopaedia of Social Work*. Oxford: Blackwell Publishers.

Darlington, Y., Feeney, J.A. and Rixon, K. (2005) Practice challenges at the intersection of child protection and mental health, *Child and Family Social Work*, 10: 239–47.

Dartington Social Research Unit (2004) *Refocusing Children's Services Towards Prevention: Lessons from the Literature*. London: DfES.

Davis, A. and Garrett, P.M. (2004) Progressive practice for tough times: social work, poverty and division in the twenty-first century, in M. Lymbery and S. Butler (eds) *Social Work: Ideals and Practice Realities*. Basingstoke: Palgrave Macmillan.

Dawson, C. (2000) *Independent Successes: Implementing Direct Payments*. York: York Publishing Services/Joseph Rowntree Foundation.

Denney, D. (1998) *Social Policy and Social Work*. Oxford: Oxford University Press.

Department for Education and Skills (2004) *Every Child Matters*. Norwich: The Stationery Office.

Department for Education and Skills (2005) Guidance on the Children and Young People's Plan, Nottingham DfES Publications.

Department of Education and Employment/Department of Health (2000) *Education of Young People in Public Care: Guidance*. London: Department for Education and Employment/Department of Health.

Department of Health (1991a) *Care Management and Assessment Practitioners' Guide*. London: Department of Health.

Department of Health (1991b) *The Children Act 1989 Guidance and Regulations, Volume 1: Court Orders*. London: HMSO.

Department of Health (1991c) *Working Together under the Children Act 1989: A Guide to Inter-Agency Cooperation for the Protection of Children from Abuse*. London: HMSO.

Department of Health (1995) *Building Bridges: A Guide to Arrangements for Inter-Agency Working for the Care and Protection of Severely Mentally Ill People*. London: Department of Health.

Department of Health (1998) *Modernising Social Services: Promoting Independence, Improving Protection, Raising Standards*. Cm. 4169, London: The Stationery Office.

Department of Health (1999a) *Caring about Carers: A National Strategy for Carers*. London: The Stationery Office.

Department of Health (1999b) *Framework for the Assessment of Children in Need and their Families*. London: The Stationery Office.

Department of Health, Home Office, Department of Education and Employment (1999c) *Working Together to Safeguard Children*. London: The Stationery Office.

Department of Health (2000a) *Framework for the Assessment of Children in Need and their Families*. London: The Stationery Office.

Department of Health (2000b) *No Secrets: Guidance on Developing and Implementing Multi-Agency Policies and Procedures to Protect Vulnerable Adults from Abuse*. London: The Stationery Office.

Department of Health (2001a) *Involving Patients and the Public in Health Care*. London: The Stationery Office.

Department of Health (2001b) *The National Adoption Standards for England*. London: Department of Health.

Department of Health (2001c) *National Service Framework for Older People*. London: Department of Health.

Department of Health (2001d) *Valuing People: A New Strategy for Learning Disability for the 21st Century – A White Paper*. London: HMSO.

Department of Health (2002a) *Guidance on the Single Assessment Process*, HSC 2002/ 00:LAC(2002)1.

Department of Health (2002b) *Safeguarding Children: A Joint Chief Inspectors Report on Arrangements to Safeguard Children*. London: Department of Health Publications.

Department of Health (2003) *Direct Payments Guidance. Community Care Standards for Carers and Children's Services (Direct Payments) Guidance, England*. London: Department of Health Publications.

Department of Health (2004a) *Copying Letters to Patients: Good Practice Guidelines*. London: Department of Health.

Department of Health (2004b) *National Standards, Local Action: Health and Social Care Standards and Planning Framework 2005/06–2007/08*. London: Department of Health.

Department of Health (2005a) *Common Assessment Framework for Children and Young People: Guide for Service Managers and Practitioners*. London: Department of Health.

Department of Health (2005b) *Independence, Well-Being and Choice: Our Vision for the Future of Social Care for Adults in England*. Norwich: The Stationery Office.

Department of Health (2006) *Mental Capacity Act 2005 – Summary*. London: Department of Health.

Department of Health, Department of Education and Employment and Home Office (2000) *Framework for the Assessment of Children in Need and their Families*. London: The Stationery Office.

Department of Health, Home Office, Department of Education and Employment (1999) *Working Together to Safeguard Children: A Guide to Inter-Agency Working to Safeguard and Promote the Welfare of Children*. London: The Stationery Office.

Department of Health and Cleaver (2000) *Assessment Recording Forms*. London: The Stationery Office.

Department of Health and Home Office (2003) *The Victoria Climbie Inquiry: Report of an Inquiry by Lord Laming*. London: The Stationery Office.

Department of Health Social Services Inspectorate (1995) *The Challenge of Partnerships in Child Protection: Practice Guide*. London: HMSO.

Descombes, C. (2004) The smoke and mirrors of empowerment: a critique of user-professional partnership, in M. Robb, S. Barrett, C. Komaromy and A. Rogers (eds) *Communication, Relationships and Care: A Reader*. London: Routledge.

Despain, J.E., Leinicke, L.M., Ostrosky, J.A. and Rexroad, W.M. (2003) Work values at Caterpillar: a process, *Organizational Dynamics*, 32: 405–14.

Dominelli, L. (1998) Anti-oppressive practice in context, in R. Adams, L. Dominelli and M. Payne (eds) *Social Work: Themes, Issues and Critical Debates*. Basingstoke: Macmillan Press.

Dominelli, L. (2002a) *Anti-Oppressive Social Work Theory and Practice*. Basingstoke: Palgrave Macmillan.

Dominelli, L. (2002b) Changing agendas: moving beyond fixed identities in anti-oppressive practice, in D.R. Tomlinson and W. Trew (eds) *Equalising Opportunities, Minimising Oppression: A Critical Review of Anti-Discriminatory Policies in Health and Social Welfare*. London: Routledge.

Dominelli, L. (2002c) Values in social work: contested entities with enduring qualities, in R. Adams, L. Dominelli and M. Payne (eds) *Critical Practice in Social Work*. Basingstoke: Palgrave.

Dominelli, L. (2004) *Social Work: Theory and Practice for a Changing Profession*. Cambridge: Polity Press.

Downie, R.S. and Telfer, E. (1980) *Caring and Curing: A Philosophy of Medicine and Social Work*. London: Methuen.

Doyal, L. and Gough, I. (1991) *A Theory of Human Need*. Basingstoke: Macmillan.

Dubois, B. and Krogsrund Miley, K. (1992) *Social Work: An Empowering Profession*. Boston: Allyn and Bacon.

Eby, M. (2000) The challenge of values and ethics in practice, in A. Brechin, H. Brown and M.A. Eby (eds) *Critical Practice in Health and Social Care*. London: Sage Publications.

Ely, P. and Denney, D. (1987) *Social Work in a Multi-Racial Society*. Aldershot: Gower Publishing Company.

Faulkner, A. and Layzell, S. (2000) *Strategies for Living: A Report of User-led Research into People's Strategies for Living with Mental Distress*. London: Mental Health Foundation.

Fawcett, B. and Featherstone, B. (1996) 'Carers' and 'caring', in B. Humphries (ed.) *Critical Perspectives on Empowerment*. Birmingham: Venture Press.

Fawcett, B. and Featherstone, B. (2000) Setting the scene: an appraisal of notions of postmodernism, postmodernity and postmodern feminism, in B. Fawcett, B. Featherstone, J. Fook and A. Rossiter (eds) *Practice and Research in Social Work: Postmodern Feminist Perspectives*. London: Routledge.

Ferguson, H. (2003a) Outline of a critical best practice perspective on social work and social care, *British Journal of Social Work*, 33: 1005–24.

Ferguson, H. (2003b) The Sixth Sense, *The Guardian*.

Ferguson, H. (2004) *Protecting Children in Time: Child Abuse, Child Protection and the Consequences of Modernity*. Basingstoke: Palgrave Macmillan.

Ferguson, H. (2005) Working with violence, the emotions and psychosocial dynamics of child protection: reflections on the Victoria Climbie case, *Social Work Education*, 24: 781–95.

Finch, J. and Mason, J. (1993) *Negotiating Family Responsibilities*. London: Routledge.

Flekkoy, M.G. and Kaufman, N.H. (1997) *The Participation Rights of the Child: Rights and Responsibilities in Family and Society.* London: Jessica Kingsley Publishers.

Fook, J. (2000) Constructing and reconstructing professional expertise, in B. Fawcett, B. Featherstone, J. Fook and A. Rossiter (eds) *Practice and Research in Social Work: Postmodern Feminist Perspectives.* London: Routledge.

Fook, J. (2002) *Social Work Critical Theory and Practice.* London: Sage Publications.

Fook, J. (2003) Critical social work: the current issues, *Qualitative Social Work,* 2: 123–30.

Fook, J. (2004) Critical reflection and organisational learning and change: a case study, in N. Gould and M. Baldwin (eds) *Social Work, Critical Reflection and the Learning Organization.* Aldershot: Ashgate.

Foucault, M. (1980) *Power/Knowledge: Selected Interviews and Other Writings 1972–77.* New York: Semiotext.

Foucault, M. (ed.) (1989) *Foucault Live. Interviews 1996–1984.* New York: Semiotext.

France, A., Bendlow, G. and Williams, S. (2000) Researching the health beliefs of children and young people, in A. Lewis and G. Lindsay (eds) *Researching Children's Perspectives.* Buckingham: Open University Press.

Franklin, B. (1995) The case for children's rights: a progress report, in B. Franklin (ed.) *Children's Rights: Comparative Policy and Practice.* London: Routledge.

Frazer, L. and Selwyn, J. (2005) Why are we waiting? The demography of adoption for children of black, Asian and black mixed parentage in England, *Child and Family Social Work,* 10: 135–47.

Freeman, M. (1983) *The Rights and Wrongs of Children.* London: Francis Pinter.

Freeman, M. (1992) *Children, their Families and the Law: Working with the Children Act.* London: Macmillan.

Freire, P. (1972) *Pedagogy of the Oppressed.* Harmondsworth: Penguin.

Galper, J. (1980) *Social Work Practice: A Radical Perspective.* Englewood Cliffs: Prentice-Hall.

Garrett, P.M. (2003) Swimming with dolphins: the assessment framework, New Labour and new tools for social work with children and families, *British Journal of Social Work,* 33: 441–63.

George, V. and Wilding, P. (2002) *Globalisation and Human Welfare.* Basingstoke: Palgrave.

Gilchrest, A. (2003) Community development and networking for health, in J. Orme, J. Powell, P. Taylor, T. Harrison and M. Grey (eds) *Public Health in the 21st Century: New Perspectives on Policy, Participation and Practice.* Maidenhead: Open University Press.

Gilchrest, A. (2004) *The Well-Connected Community: A Networking Approach to Community Development.* Bristol: The Policy Press.

Glasby, J. (2004) Social service and the single assessment process: early warning signs?, *Journal of Interprofessional Care,* 18: 129–39.

Glasby, J. and Lister, H. (2004) Cases for change in mental health: partnership working in mental health services, *Journal of Interprofessional Care,* 18: 7–16.

Glasby, J. and Peck, E. (2004) Introduction, in J. Glasby and E. Peck (eds) *Care Trusts: Partnership Working in Action*. Abingdon: Radcliffe Medical Press.

Goldson, B. (2002) Children, crime and the state, in G. Barry, L. Michael and M. Jim (eds) *Children, and the Welfare State*. London: Sage Publications.

Goldson, B. (2003) Anti-social assault on the poor, *Socialist Worker Online*.

Golightley, M. (2004) *Social Work and Mental Health*. Exeter: Learning Matters Ltd.

Gorman, H. (2005) Frailty and dignity in old age, in R. Adams, L. Dominelli and M. Payne (eds) *Social Work Futures: Crossing Boundaries, Transforming Services*. Basingstoke: Palgrave Macmillan.

Gould, N. (1999) Qualitative practice evaluation, in I. Shaw and J. Lishman, (eds) *Evaluation and Social Work Practice*. London: Sage Publications.

Graham, K. and Harris, A. (2005) New Deal for Communities as a participatory public policy: the challenges for evaluation, in D. Taylor and S. Balloch (eds) *The Politics of Evaluation: Participation and Policy Implementation*. Bristol: The Policy Press.

Graham, M. (2002) *Social Work and African-Centred Worldviews*. Birmingham: Venture Press.

Grier, A. and Thomas, T. (2005) Troubled and in trouble: young people, truancy and offending, in R. Adams, L. Dominelli and M. Payne (eds) *Social Work Futures: Crossing Boundaries, Transforming Practice*. Basingstoke: Palgrave Macmillan.

GSCC (2002) *Codes of Practice for Social Care Workers and Employers*. London: General Social Care Council.

Gutierrez, L. M. (1990) Working with women of color: an empowerment perspective, *Social Work*, 30: 149–53.

Gypsy Survey (1993) *From Myth to Reality: Building Perceptions and Meeting the Need of the Gypsy Community in the 1990's*. Tyne and Wear: Northern Gypsy Council.

Hardiker, P., Exton, K. and Barker, M. (1991) *Policies and Practices in Preventive Child Care*. Aldershot: Ashgate.

Harlow, E. (2003) New managerialism, social service departments and social work practice today, *Practice*, 15: 29–41.

Hart, R. (1992) *Innocenti Essays No. 4: Children's Participation: From Tokenism to Citizenship*. Florence: UNICEF International Child Development Centre.

Hasenfield, Y. (1987) Power in social work practice, *Social Services Review*, 61: 470–83.

Haugaard, M. (2002) *Power: A Reader*. Manchester: Manchester University Press.

Hayden, C. (2005) More than a piece of paper? Personal education plans and 'looked after' children in England, *Child and Family Social Work*, 10: 343–52.

Haydon, D. (1997) 'Crisis' in the classroom, in P. Scraton (ed.) *Childhood in 'Crisis'*. London: UCL Press Ltd.

Hayes, D. (2005) Social work with asylum seekers and others subject to immigration control, in R. Adams, L. Dominelli and M. Payne (eds) *Social Work*

Futures: Crossing Boundaries, Transforming Practice. Basingstoke: Palgrave Macmillan.

Health and Social Care Joint Unit and Change Agents Team (2003) *Discharge from Hospital: Pathway, Process and Practice.* London: Department of Health.

Healy, B. (1996) In doing you learn: some reflections on practice research on an advocacy project, in J. Fook (ed.) *The Reflective Researcher.* St. Leonards: Allen & Unwin.

Healy, K. (2000) *Social Work Practices: Contemporary Perspectives on Change.* London: Sage Publications.

Healy, K. (2005) *Social Work Theories in Context: Creating Frameworks for Practice.* Basingstoke: Palgrave Macmillan.

Henfrey, J. (1988) Race, in D. Hicks (ed.) *Education for Peace.* London: Routledge.

Heron, G. (2004) Evidencing anti-racism in student assignments: where has all the racism gone? *Qualitative Social Work,* 3: 277–95.

Hick, S. (2002) Introduction. Anti-Oppressive Practice: Challenges for Social Work, *Critical Social Work.*

Hick, S. (2005) Reconceptualising critical social work, in S. Hick, J. Fook and R. Pozzuto (eds) *Social Work: A Critical Turn.* Toronto: Thompson Educational Publishing.

Hickey, S. and Mohan, G. (eds) (2004) *Participation: From Tyranny to Transformation?* London: Zed Books.

Hill-Collins, P. (1990) *Black Feminist Thought: Knowledge, Consciousness, and the Politics of Empowerment.* London: Unwin Hyman.

Hitchings, E. (2005) R(On the Application of Spink) v Wandsworth Borough Council [2004] EWHC 2314; EWCA Civ 302, *Journal of Social Welfare and Family Law,* 27: 333–81.

Holden, C. (2000) Globalisation and social work, in M. Davies (ed.) *The Blackwell Encyclopaedia of Social Work.* Oxford: Blackwell Publishers.

Holdsworth, L. (1991) *Social Work with Physically Disabled People.* Norwich: University of East Anglia.

Holland, S. (2004) *Child and Family Assessment in Social Work Practice.* London: Sage.

Holland, S. and Scourfield, J. (2004) Liberty and respect in child protection, *British Journal of Social Work,* 34: 21–36.

Holland, S., Scourfield, J., O'Neill, S. and Pithouse, A. (2005) Democratising the family and the state? The case of family group conferences in child welfare, *Journal of Social Policy,* 34: 59–77.

Holloway, M. (2005) Planning, in R. Adams, L. Dominelli and M. Payne (eds) *Social Work Futures: Crossing Boundaries, Transforming Practice.* Basingstoke: Palgrave Macmillan.

Holton, M. (2001) The partnership imperative: joint working between social services and health, *Journal of Management in Medicine,* 15: 430–45.

hooks, b. (1981) *Ain't I a Woman: Black Women and Feminism.* London: Pluto Press.

hooks, b. (1989) *Talking Back: Thinking Feminist, Thinking Black*. Boston: South End Press.

Howe, D. (1995) *Attachment Theory for Social Work Practice*. Basingstoke: Macmillan.

Howell, A. M. (2003) A minority experience, in V. Cree (ed.) *Becoming a Social Worker*. Abingdon: Routledge.

Howes, M. (2005) Introducing a research project into social work practice – a model for the future? *Social Work Education*, 24: 585–92.

Hudson, B. (2002) Interprofessionality in health and social care: the Achilles heel of partnership? *Journal of Interprofessional Care*, 16: 7–17.

Hudson, V. (2005) Plan with care, *http://communitycare.co.uk*.

Hughes, B. (1993) A model for the comprehensive assessment of older people and their carers, *British Journal of Social Work*, 23: 345–64.

Humphries, B. (1996) Contradictions in the culture of empowerment, in B. Humphries (ed.) *Critical Perspectives on Empowerment*. Birmingham: Venture Press.

Humphries, B. (2004) An unacceptable role for social work: implementing immigration policy, *British Journal of Social Work*, 34: 93–107.

Humphries, B. (2005) From margin to centre: shifting the emphasis of social work research, in R. Adams, L. Dominelli and M. Payne (eds) *Social Work Futures: Crossing Boundaries, Transforming Practice*. Basingstoke: Palgrave Macmillan.

Hutchinson, J. and Campbell, M. (1998) *Working in Partnership: Lessons from the Literature*. London: Department for Education and Employment.

Ife, J. (2001) *Human Rights and Social Work: Towards Rights-Based Practice*. Cambridge: Cambridge University Press.

Ife, J., Healy, K., Spratt, T. and Solomon, B. (2005) Current understandings of critical social work, in S. Hick, J. Fook and R. Pozzuto (eds) *Social Work: A Critical Turn*. Toronto: Thompson Educational Publishing.

International Association of Schools of Social Work (IASSW) and International Federation of Social Workers (2001) International definition of social work, *http://www.iassw.soton.ac.uk*.

Issit, M. (2000) Critical professionals and reflective practice: the experience of women practitioners in health, welfare and education, in J. Batsleer and B. Humphries (eds) *Welfare, Exclusion and Political Agency*. London: Routledge.

Iversen, R. R., Gergen, K. J. and Fairbanks II, R. P. (2005) Assessment and social construction: conflict or co-creation? *British Journal of Social Work*, 36: 689–708.

Jenkins, P. (1995) Advocacy and the UN Convention on the Rights of the Child, in J. Dalrymple and J. Hough (eds) *Having a Voice: An Exploration of Children's Rights and Advocacy*. Birmingham: Venture Press.

Jervis, M. (1989) The dilemma of intervention, *Social Work Today*, 7 December.

John, M. (1996) Voicing: research and practice with the 'silenced', in M. John (ed.)

Children in Charge: The Child's Right to a Fair Hearing. London: Jessica Kingsley Publishers.

Johns, R. (2003) *Understanding the Law in Social Work.* Exeter: Learning Matters Ltd.

Johns, R. (2005) *Using the Law in Social Work,* 2nd edn. Exeter: Learning Matters Ltd.

Johnson, T. (1989) *Professions and Power.* London: Macmillan.

Jones, C. (2001) Voices from the frontline: state social workers and New Labour, *British Journal of Social Work,* 31: 547–62.

Jordan, B. (1990) *Social Work in an Unjust Society.* Hemel Hempstead: Harvester Press.

Jordan, B. (2001) Tough love: social work, social exclusion and the Third Way, *British Journal of Social Work,* 31: 527–46.

Jordan, B. with Jordan, C. (2000) *Social Work and the Third Way: Tough Love as Social Policy.* London: Sage Publications.

Jordan, J. (1989) *Moving towards Home: Political Essays.* London: Virago.

Juckes, T. J. and Barresi, J. (1993) The subjective-objective dimension in the individual-society connection: a quality perspective, *Journal for the Theory of Social Behaviour,* 23: 197–216.

Katz, I. (1995) Approaches to empowerment and participation in child protection, in C. Cloke and M. Davies (eds) *Participation and Empowerment in Child Protection.* Chichester: John Wiley & Sons Ltd.

Kaur, R. (2005) *Partnerships for Older People Projects: A Policy Perspective.* London: Department of Health.

Keating, F. (1997) *Developing an Integrated Approach to Oppression.* London: CCETSW.

Kelly, L. and Lovett, J. (2005) *What a Waste: The Case for an Integrated Violence Against Women Strategy.* London: DTI.

Kennedy, H. (1993) *Eve was Framed: Women and British Justice.* London: Vintage Books.

Kennedy, H. (2004) *Just Law: The Changing Face of Justice – and Why it Matters to Us All.* London: Chatto and Windus.

Keywood, K. (2003) Gatekeepers, proxies, advocates? The evolving role of carers under mental health incapacity law reforms, *Journal of Social Welfare and Family Law,* 25: 355–68.

Kieffer, C. (1984) Citizen empowerment: a developmental perspective, in J. Rappaport, C. Swift and R. Hess (eds) *Studies in Empowerment: Steps Toward Understanding and Action.* New York: Haworth Press.

Klug, F. (2000) *Values for a Godless Age: The Story of the United Kingdom's New Bill of Rights.* London: Penguin.

Kolb-Morris, J. (1993) Interacting oppressions: teaching social work content on women of colour, *Journal of Social Work Education,* 19: 99–110.

Laing, J. (2003) Reforming mental health law and the ECHR: will the rights of mentally vulnerable adults be protected? *Journal of Social Welfare and Family Law*, 25: 325–42.

Laming, H. (2003) *The Victoria Climbié Inquiry*. London: The Stationery Office.

Lamont, S. S. (1999) Participating in theory, *British Medical Journal*, 219.

Langan, M. (1992) Introduction: women and social work in the 1990's, in M. Langan and L. Day (eds) *Women, Oppression and Social Work: Issues in Anti-Discriminatory Practice*. London: Routledge.

Langan, M. and Lee, P. (1989) Whatever happened to radical social work? in M. Langan and P. Lee (eds) *Radical Social Work Today*. London: Unwin Hyman.

Lawrence, P. and Wiffen, J. (2002) *Family Group Conferences: Principles and Practice Guidance*. London: Barnardos/Family Rights Group/NCH.

Leat, D. and Perkins, E. (2000) Juggling and dealing: the creative work of care package purchasing, in C. Davies, L. Finlay and A. Bullman (eds) *Changing Practice in Health and Social Care*. London: Sage Publications.

Leece, J. (2004) Money talks, but what does it say? Direct payments and the commodification of care, *Practice*, 16: 211–21.

Legrand, J. (1990) *Quasi-Markets and Social Policy*. Bristol: University of Bristol, School for Advanced Urban Studies.

Leigh, S. and Miller, C. (2005) Is the Third Way the best way? Social work intervention with children and families, *Journal of Social Work*, 4: 245–67.

Levin, E. (2005) *Involving Service Users and Carers in Social Work Education*. London: SCIE.

Lewis, J. and Utting, D. (2001) Made to measure? Evaluating community initiatives for children: introduction, *Children and Society*, 15: 1–4.

Lindow, V. (2005) *Evaluation of the National User Involvement Project*. London: Joseph Rowntree Foundation.

Lindow, V. and Rooke-Matthews, S. (2005) *A Survivor's Guide to Working in Mental Health Services*. London: Mind Publications.

Lishman, J. (1999) Introduction, in I. Shaw and J. Lishman (eds) *Evaluation and Social Work Practice*. London: Sage Publications.

Lister, R. (1998a) Citizenship on the margins: citizenship, social work and social action, *European Journal of Social Work*, 1: 5–18.

Lister, R. (1998b) In from the margins: citizenship, inclusion and exclusion, in M. Barry and C. Hallett (eds) *Social Exclusion and Social Work: Issues of Theory, Policy and Practice*. Lyme Regis: Russell House Publishing.

Littlechild, R. and Blakeney, J. (1996) Risk and older people, in H. Kemshall and J. Pritchard (eds) *Good Practice in Risk Assessment and Risk Management*. London: Jessica Kingsley Publishers.

Lloyd, G., Stead, J. and Kendrick, A. (2005) *'Hanging on in There': A Study of Inter-Agency Work to Prevent School Exclusion in Three Local Authorities*. London: National Children's Bureau/Joseph Rowntree Foundation.

Lorde, A. (1984) *Sister Outsider: Essays and Speeches*, CA 95019. London: The Crossing Press/Freedom.

Lowenstein, S. F. (1976) Integrating content on feminism and racism into the social work curriculum, *Journal of Social Work Education*, 12: 91–6.

Lukes, S. (1974) *Power: A Radical View*. London: The Macmillan Press.

Lukes, S. (1986) *Power: Readings in Social and Political Theory*. Oxford: Blackwell.

Lupton, C. and Nixon, P. (1999) *Empowering Practice? A Critical Appraisal of the Family Group Conference Approach*. Bristol: The Policy Press.

Lymbery, M. (2004a) Managerialism and care management practice with older people, in M. Lymbery and S. Butler (eds) *Social Work Ideals and Practice Realities*. Basingstoke: Palgrave Macmillan.

Lymbery, M. (2004b) Responding to crisis: the changing nature of welfare organisations, in M. Lymbery and I. Butler (eds) *Social Work Ideals and Practice Realities*. Basingstoke: Palgrave Macmillan.

Lynn, E. (1999) Value bases in social work education, *British Journal of Social Work*, 29: 939–53.

MacKinnon, C. (2005) *Women's Lives, Men's Laws*. Cambridge, Mass.: Harvard University Press.

Macpherson, W. (1999) *The Stephen Lawrence Inquiry*. London: The Stationery Office.

Mahon, A., Glendinning, C., Clarke, K. and Craig, G. (1996) Researching children: methods and ethics, *Children and Society*, 10: 145–54.

Marchant, C. (1993) Within four walls, *Community Care*, 10: 11–20.

Marshall, K., Tisdall, K., Cleland, A. and Plumtree, A. (2002) *'Voice of the Child' under The Children (Scotland) Act 1995: Giving Due Regard to Children's Views in All Matters that Affect Them Volume 1 – Mapping Paper*. Edinburgh: The Stationery Office.

Martin, J. (2003) Historical develoment of critical social work practice, in J. Allan, B. Pease and L. Briskman (eds) *Critical Social Work: An Introduction to Theories and Practices*. Crows Nest NSW: Allen and Unwin.

Maslow, A. H. (1970) *Motivation and Personality*. London: Harper and Row.

Maslow, A. H. (1973) *The Farther Reaches of Human Nature*. Harmondsworth: Penguin Books.

Mason, P., Morris, K. and Smith, P. (2005) A complex solution to a complicated problem? Early messages from the National Evaluation of the Children's Fund Prevention Programme, *Children and Society*, 19: 131–43.

Masson, J. (2000) Researching children's perspectives: legal issues, in A. Lewis and G. Lindsay (eds) *Researching Children's Perspectives*. Buckingham: Open University Press.

Mauthner, M. (1997) Methodological aspects of collecting data from children: lessons from three research projects, *Children and Society*, 11: 16–18.

Mayall, B. (2000) Conversations with children: working with generational issues, in P. Christensen and A. James (eds) *Research with Children, Perspectives and Practices*. London: Falmer Press.

Mayhew, J. (1997) *Psychological Change: A Practical Introduction*. Basingstoke: Macmillan.

McAteer, E. (2002) The subtle lessons of a tragic case, *Community Care*.

McKeigue, B. and Beckett, C. (2004) Care proceeding under the 1989 Children Act: rhetoric and reality, *British Journal of Social Work*, 34: 831–49.

McNay, M. (1992) Social work and power relations: towards a framework for an integrated practice, in M. Langan and L. Day (eds) *Women, Oppression and Social Work: Issues in Anti-Discriminatory Practice*. London: Routledge.

McTernan, E. (2003) Maps and charts in planning family support: the development of children's services planning in Northern Ireland, *Child Care in Practice*, 9: 199–212.

Means, R., Richards, S. and Smith, R. (2003) *Community Care Policy and Practice*. Basingstoke: Palgrave Macmillan.

Means, R. and Smith, R. (1998) *Community Care: Policy and Practice*. Basingstoke: Macmillan.

Mental Health Foundation (2005) Executive briefing: the Mental Capacity Act, *Need 2 Know*.

Mickelson, J. S. (1995) *Advocacy*. New York: NASW Press.

Millar, M. and Corby, B. (2005) *The Framework for the Assessment of Children in Need and their Families* – A basis for a 'therapeutic' encounter? *British Journal of Social Work Advance Access*, 1–13.

Miller, C. (2003) Public health meets modernisation, in J. Orme, J. Powell, P. Taylor, T. Harrison and M. Grey (eds) *Public Health for the 21st Century: New Perspectives on Policy, Participation and Practice*. Maidenhead: Open University Press.

Miller, C. (2004) *Producing Welfare: A Modern Agenda*. Basingstoke: Palgrave Macmillan.

Milner, J. and O'Byrne, P. (1998) *Assessment in Social Work*. Basingstoke: Macmillan.

Mind (2005) Mind concerned as Government still promotes Bill of compulsion not compassion, *http://www.mind.org.uk/News+policy+and+campaigns/Press/govtresponsetopls.htm*

Minhas, A. (2005) Dependent upon outside help: reflections from a service user, in R. Carnwell and J. Buchanan (eds) *Effective Practice in Health and Social Care: A Partnership Approach*. Maidenhead: Open University Press.

Mistry, D. and Chauhan, S. (2003) Don't leave race on the side, *Community Care*.

Mitchell, G. (1989) Empowerment and opportunity, *Social Work Today*.

Moberly Bell, E. (1962) *Josephine Butler: Flame of Fire*. London: Constable.

Moreau, M. (1979) A structural approach to social work practice, *Canadian Journal of Social Work Education*, 5: 78–94.

Moreau, M. (1990) Empowerment through advocacy and consciousness-raising: implication of a structural approach to social work, *Journal of Sociology and Social Welfare*, 17: 53–67.

Morgan, D. (1989) Able to intervene, *Community Care*, 30 December.

Morris, A. E. and Nott, S. N. (1991) *Working Women and the Law: Equality and Discrimination in Theory and Practice*. London: Routledge.

Morris, J. (ed.) (1989) *Able Lives: Women's Experience of Paralysis*. London: The Women's Press.

Morris, J. (1993a) Feminism and disability, *Feminist Review*, 43: 57–70.

Morris, J. (1993b) *Independent Lives? Community Care and Disabled People*. London: Macmillan.

Morris, J. (2004) Independent living and community care: a disempowering framework, *Disability and Society*, 19: 427–42.

Morris, K. (2002) Family-based social work, in R. Adams, L. Dominelli and M. Payne (eds) *Critical Practice in Social Work*. Basingstoke: Palgrave.

Morris, K. (2005) From 'Children in Need' to 'Children at Risk' – the changing policy context for prevention and participation, *Practice*, 17: 67–77.

Mullaly, B. (1993) *Structural Social Work*. Toronto: Oxford University Press.

Mullaly, B. (1997) *Structural Social Work: Ideology, Theory and Practice*. Ontario: Oxford University Press.

Mullaly, R. P. and Keating, E. F. (1991) Similarities, differences and dialectics of radical social work, *Journal of Progressive Human Services*, 2: 49–78.

Mullender, A. and Ward, D. (1991) *Self-Directed Group Work: Users Take Action for Empowerment*. London: Whiting and Birch.

Mullender, A. and Ward, D. (1993) Empowerment and oppression: an indissoluble pairing for contemporary social work, in J. Warmsley, J. Reynolds, P. Shakespeare and R. Woolfe (eds) *Health, Welfare and Practice: Reflecting Roles and Relationships*. London: Sage.

Munro, E. (2005) A systems approach to investigating child abuse deaths, *British Journal of Social Work*, 35: 531–46.

Murray, C. and Hallett, C. (2000) Young people's participation in decisions affecting their welfare, *Childhood*, 7.

Murray, P. (2000) Disabled children, parents and professionals: partnerships on whose terms? *Disability and Society*, 15: 638–98.

Murray, P. and Penman, J. (eds) (1996) *Let Our Children Be. A Collection of Stories*. Sheffield: Parents with Attitude.

National Cancer Institute (2002) Transitional Care Planning 208/05471.

National Evaluation of the Children's Fund (2004) *Prevention and Early Intervention in the Social Inclusion of Children and Young People: Emerging Lessons from the First Round of Case Studies Undertaken by NECF*. London: DfES.

Newburn, T. (2001) What do we mean by evaluation? *Children and Society*, 15: 5–13.

Newman, C. (1989) *Young Runaways: Findings from Britain's First Safe House*. London: The Children's Society.

Ng, S. M. and Chan, C. L. (2005) Intervention, in R. Adams, L. Dominelli and M.

Payne (eds) *Social Work Futures: Crossing Boundaries, Transforming Practice.* Basingstoke: Palgrave Macmillan.

Nicholas, E. (2003) An outcomes focus in care assessment and review: value and challenge, *British Journal of Social Work*, 33: 31–47.

Norton, D. C. (1978) *The Dual Perspective: Inclusion of Ethnic Minority Content in the Social Work Curriculum*. Washington, DC: Council on Social Work Education.

Oliver, M. (1990) *The Politics of Disablement*. Basingstoke: Macmillan.

Orme, J. (2002) Social work: gender, care and justice, *British Journal of Social Work*, 32: 799–814.

Parker, J. and Bradley, G. (2003) *Social Work Practice: Assessing Planning, Intervention and Review*. Exeter: Learning Matters Ltd.

Parmar, P. (1990) Black feminism: the politics of articulation, in J. Rutherford (ed.) *Identity: Community, Culture, Difference*. London: Lawrence and Wishart.

Parrott, L. (2005) The political drivers of working in partnership, in R. Carnwell and J. Buchanan (eds) *Effective Practice in Health and Social Care: A Partnership Approach*. Maidenhead: Open University Press.

Parsons, R. J. (1998) Evaluation of empowerment practice, in L. Gutiérrez, R. J. Parsons and E. O. Cox (eds) *Empowerment in Social Work Practice*. Pacific Grove: Brooks/Cole.

Parton, N. (1996) *Social Theory, Social Change and Social Work: An Introduction*. London: Routledge.

Parton, N. (1999) Reconfiguring child welfare practices: risk, advanced liberalism, and the government of freedom, in A. S. Chambon, A. Irving and L. Epstein (eds) *Reading Foucault for Social Work*. New York: Colombia University Press.

Parton, N. (2000) Some thoughts on the relationship between theory and practice in and for social work, *British Journal of Social Work*, 30: 449–63.

Parton, N. (2001) Risk and professional judgement, in L.-A. Cull and J. Roche (eds) *The Law and Social Work: Contemporary Issues for Practice*. Basingstoke: Palgrave.

Parton, N. (2006) *Safeguarding Childhood: Early Intervention and Surveillance in a Late Modern Society*. Basingstoke: Palgrave Macmillan.

Parton, N. and O'Byrne, P. (2000) *Constructive Social Work: Towards a New Practice*. Houndsmill Basingstoke: Macmillan.

Pattinson, S. (2001) Are nursing codes of practice ethical? *Nursing Ethics*, 8: 5–17.

Patton, M. Q. (1981) *Creative Evaluation*. Newbury Park, CA: Sage.

Payne, M. (1989) Open records and shared decisions with clients, in S. Shardlow, (ed.) *The Values of Change in Social Work*. London: Tavistock/Routledge.

Payne, M. (1991) *Modern Social Work Theory*. London: Macmillan.

Payne, M. (1993) *Linkages: Effective Networking in Social Care*. London: Whiting and Birch.

Payne, M. (1994) Routes to and through clienthood and their implications for practice, *Practice*, 6: 169–80.

Payne, M. (1997) *Modern Social Work Theory*, 2nd edn. Basingstoke: Macmillan.

Payne, M. (1999) The moral bases of social work, *European Journal of Social Work*, 2: 247–58.

Payne, M. (2000) *Anti-Bureaucratic Social Work*. Birmingham: Venture Press.

Payne, M. (2005a) *Modern Social Work Theory*, 3rd edn. Basingstoke: Palgrave Macmillan.

Payne, M. (2005b) *The Origins of Social Work: Continuity and Change*. Basingstoke: Palgrave Macmillan.

Pease, B. and Fook, J. (1999a) Postmodern critical theory and emancipatory social work practice, in B. Pease and J. Fook (eds) *Transforming Social Work Practice*. London: Routledge.

Pease, B. and Fook, J. (eds) (1999b) *Transforming Social Work Practice: Postmodern Critical Perspectives*. London: Routledge.

Peckham, S. (2003) Who are the partners in public health?, in J. Orme, J. Powell, P. Taylor, T. Harrison and M. Grey (eds) *Public Health in the 21st Century: New Perspectives on Policy, Participation and Practice*. Maidenhead: Open University Press.

Penketh, L. (2000) *Tackling Institutional Racism: Anti-Racist Policies and Social Work Education and Training*. Bristol: The Policy Press.

Penketh, L. and Ali, Y. (1997) Racism and social welfare, in M. Lavalette and A. Pratt (eds) *Social Policy*. London: Sage Publications.

Phillips, C., Palfrey, C. and Thomas, P. (1994) *Evaluating Health and Social Care*. Basingstoke: Macmillan.

Phillipson, J. (1992) *Practising Equality: Women, Men and Social Work*. London: CCETSW.

Philpot, T. (2004) A life of service, *Community Care*.

Pinderhughes, E. B. (1983) Empowerment for our clients and for ourselves, *Social Casework*, 64: 331–8.

Pinkerton, J. (2002) Child protection, in R. Adams, L. Dominelli and M. Payne (eds) *Critical Practice in Social Work*. Basingstoke: Palgrave Macmillan.

Pinkney, S. (2000) Anti-oppressive theory and practice in social work, in C. Davies, L. Finlay and A. Bullman (eds) *Changing Practice in Health and Social Care*. London: Sage Publications.

Pitts, J. (1990) *Working with Young Offenders*. London: Macmillan.

Platzer, H. (2005) Best value but not best interests: can service users instruct mental health advocates?, in D. Taylor and S. Balloch (eds) *The Politics of Evaluation: Participation and Policy Implementation*. Bristol: The Policy Press.

Postle, K. (2001) The social work side is disappearing. I guess it started with us being called care managers, *Practice*, 13: 13–26.

Powell, F. (2001) *The Politics of Social Work*. London: Sage Publications.

Powell, J. (2005) 'Value talk' in social work research: reflection, rhetoric and reality, *European Journal of Social Work*, 8: 21–37.

Poxton, R. (2004) What makes effective partnerships between health and social care? in J. Glasby and E. Peck (eds) *Care Trusts: Partnership Working in Action.* Abingdon: Radcliffe Medical Press.

Preston, J. (1995) *1995 Annual Report,* Vancouver, Office of the Child, Youth and Family Advocate.

Preston-Shoot, M. (2003) Teaching and assessing social work law: reflections from a post qualifying programme, *Social Work Education,* 22: 461–78.

Preston-Shoot, M., Roberts, G. and Vernon, S. (2001) Values in social work law: strained relations or sustained relationships? *Journal of Social Welfare and Family Law,* 23: 1–22.

Preston-Shoot, M. and Wigley, V. (2005) Mapping the needs of children in need, *British Journal of Social Work,* 35: 255–75.

Quinn, M. (2003) Immigrants and refugees: towards anti-racist culturally affirming practices, in J. Allan, B. Pease and L. Briskman (eds) *Critical Social Work: An Introduction to Theories and Practices.* Crows Nest NSW: Allen and Unwin.

Ramazanoglu, C. (1989) *Feminism and the Contradictions of Oppression.* London: Routledge.

Ramussen, D. M. (1996) Critical theory and philosophy, in D. M. Ramussen (ed.) *The Handbook of Critical Theory.* Oxford: Blackwell Publishers.

Rappaport, J. (1981) In praise of paradox: a social policy of empowerment over prevention, *American Journal of Community Psychology,* 9: 1–25.

Rappaport, J. (1984) Studies in empowerment: introduction to the issue, *Prevention in Human Services,* 3: 1–7.

Rappaport, J. (1985) The power of empowerment language, *Social Policy,* 17: 15–21.

Rappaport, J. (1987) Terms of empowerment/exemplars of prevention: toward a theory for community psychology, *American Journal of Community Psychology,* 15: 121–44.

Rees, S. (1991) *Achieving Power: Practice and Policy in Social Welfare.* North Sydney: Allen and Unwin.

Reid, W. J. and Epstein, L. (1972) *Task-Centred Casework.* New York: Colombia University Press.

Reigate, N. (1997) Networking, in M. Davies (ed.) *The Blackwell Companion to Social Work.* Oxford: Blackwell.

Rimmer, A. (2005) What is professional social work? Social work and social justice, in S. Shardlow and P. Nelson (eds) *Introducing Social Work.* Lyme Regis: Russell House Publishing.

Robson, C. (1993) *Real World Research.* Oxford: Blackwell Publishers.

Robson, P., Begum, N. and Lock, M. (2005) *Developing User Involvement: Working Towards User-Centred Practice in Voluntary Organisations.* Bristol: Joseph Rowntree Foundation/The Policy Press.

Roche, J. (2001) Social work values and the law, in C. Lesley-Anne and J. Roche (eds) *The Law and Social Work: Contemporary Issues for Practice.* Basingstoke: Palgrave.

Rojek, C., Peacock, G. and Collins, S. (1988) *Social Work and Received Ideas*. London: Routledge.

Rooney, B. (1987) *Racism and Resistance to Change: A Study of the Black Social Worker's Project in Liverpool Social Services Department*. Liverpool: Merseyside Area Profile Group.

Rose, S. M. and Black, B. L. (1985) *Advocacy and Empowerment: Mental Health Care in the Community*. Boston: Routledge and Kegan Paul.

Rosenfield, J. M. (1989) *Emergence from Extreme Poverty*. Paris: Science and Service, Fourth World Publications.

Rowe, J., Hundleby, M. and Garnett, L. (1989) *Child Care Now*. London: British Association of Adoption and Fostering (BAAF) Research Series 6.

Royal College of Nursing (2000) Developing a national plan for the new NHS, June.

Sapey, B. and Hewitt, N. (1991) The changing context of social work practice, in M. Oliver (ed.) *Social Work: Disabled People and Disabling Environments*. London: Jessica Kingsley Publishers.

Sawicki, J. (1991) *Disciplining Foucault: Feminism, Power, and the Body*. London: Routledge.

Sayce, L. (2005) Risk, rights and anti-discrimination work in mental health: avoiding the risks in considering risk, in R. Adams, L. Dominelli and M. Payne (eds) *Social Work Futures: Crossing Boundaries, Transforming Practice*. Basingstoke: Palgrave Macmillan.

Scarman, L. (1981) *The Brixton Disorders*, 10–12 April 1981. Cmnd 8427. London: HMSO.

Schofield, J. and Thoburn, J. (1996) *Child Protection: The Voice of the Child in Decision Making*. London: IPPR.

Schön, D. (1983) *The Reflective Practitioner*. London: Temple-Smith.

Schön, D. (1987) *Educating the Reflective Practitioner*. San Francisco: Jossey-Bass.

Scottish Executive (2001) *Independent Advocacy: A Guide for Commissioners*. Norwich: The Stationery Office.

Seebohm, F. (1968) Report of the Committee on Local Authority and Allied Personal Social Services (Seebohm Report).

Sennett, R. (2003) *Respect: The Formation of Character in an Age of Inequality*. London: Penguin.

Sennett, R. and Cobb, J. (1972) *The Hidden Injuries of Class*. New York: Vintage.

Shaping Our Lives National User Network (2003) *Shaping Our Lives: What People Think of the Social Care Services They Use*. York: Joseph Rowntree Foundation.

Shaw, I. (1996) *Evaluating in Practice*. Aldershot: Arena.

Shaw, I. and Lishman, J. (1999) *Evaluation and Social Work Practice*. London: Sage Publications.

Shemmings, D. (2000) Professional attitudes to children's participation in decision making: dichotomous accounts and doctrinal contests, *Child and Family Social Work*, 5: 235–43.

Sibeon, R. (1990) Comments on the structure and forms of social work knowledge, *Social Work and Social Sciences Review*, 1: 29–44.

Simey, M. (1993) Unpublished lecture, Liverpool John Moores University.

Simey, M. (1996) *The Disinherited Society: A Personal View of Social Responsibility in Liverpool in the Twentieth Century*. Liverpool: Liverpool University Press.

Singh, G. (2000) *Exploring and Promoting the Needs of Black Practice Teachers*. Coventry: Coventry University.

Singh, G. (2002) The political challenge of anti-racism in social care, in D. R. Tomlinson and W. Trew (eds) *Equalising Opportunities, Minimising Oppression*. London: Routledge.

Sivanandan, A. (2005) *Why Muslims Reject British Values*. London: Guardian Unlimited.

Skelcher, C. (1993) Involvement and empowerment in local public services, *Public Money and Management*, 13: 13–20.

Skidmore, R. A., Thackery, M. G. and Farley, O. W. (1991) *Introduction to Social Work*. Englewood Cliffs, N.J.: Prentice-Hall.

Skinner, A. (1992) *Another Kind of Home: A Review of Residential Care*. Edinburgh: SWSI.

Smale, G., Tuson, G. and Statham, D. (2000) *Social Work and Social Problems: Working Towards Social Inclusion and Social Change*. Basingstoke: Palgrave.

Small, J. (1986) Transracial placements: conflicts and contradictions, in S. Ahmed, J. Cheetham and J. Small (eds) *Social Work with Black Children and Their Families*. London: Batsford.

Smith, M., Nursten, J. and McMahon, L. (2004) Social workers' responses to experiences of fear, *British Journal of Social Work*, 541–59.

Smith, T. (1999) Neighbourhood and preventive strategies with children and families: what works? *Children and Society*, 13: 265–77.

Social Exclusion Unit (1998) *Truancy and School Exclusion*. London: SEU.

Social Services Inspectorate (1991) *Care Management and Assessment: Practitioner's Guide*. London: HMSO.

Sohng, S. S. L. (1998) Research as an empowerment strategy, in L. Gutiérrez, R. J. Parsons and E. O. Cox (eds) *Empowerment in Social Work Practice*. Pacific Grove: Brooks/Cole.

Solomon, B. (1976) *Black Empowerment: Social Work in Oppressed Communities*. New York: Colombia University Press.

Solomon, B. (1987) Empowerment: social work in oppressed communities, *Journal of Social Work Practice*, May: 79–91.

Soydan, H. and Williams, C. (1998) Exploring concepts, in C. Williams, H. Soydan and M. R. D. Johnson (eds) *Social Work and Minorities: European Perspectives*. London: Routledge.

Spelman, E. (2006) Room for the lambs, *London Review of Books*, 28: 22–3.

Spender, D. (1980) *Man Made Language*. London: Routledge and Kegan Paul.

Stainton, T. and Boyce, S. (2004) 'I have got my life back': Users' experience of direct payments, *Disability and Society*, 19: 443–54.

Stepney, P. (2000) Implications for social work in the new millennium, in P. Stepney and D. Ford (eds) *Social Work, Models, Methods and Theories*. New York: Russell House.

Stepney, P. and Ford, D. (2000) *Social Work Models, Methods and Theories: A Framework for Practice*. Lyme Regis: Russell House.

Stevenson, O. and Parsloe, P. (1993) *Community Care and Empowerment*. London: Joseph Rowntree Foundation.

Stevenson, S. (1989) Taken from home, in S. Shardlow (ed.) *The Values of Change in Social Work*. London: Tavistock/Routledge.

Swift, C. (1984) Empowerment: an antidote for folly, *Prevention in Human Services*, 3: xi–xv.

Swift, C. and Levin, G. (1987) Empowerment: an emerging mental health technology, *Journal of Primary Intervention*, 8: 71–94.

Taylor, B. J. (2000) *Reflective Practice: A Guide for Nurses and Midwives*. Buckingham: Open University Press.

Taylor, D. and Balloch, S. (2005a) Introduction, in D. Taylor and S. Balloch (eds) *The Politics of Evaluation: Participation and Policy Implementation*. Bristol: The Policy Press.

Taylor, D. and Balloch, S. (eds) (2005b) *The Politics of Evaluation: Participation and Policy Implementation*. Bristol: The Policy Press.

Taylor, M. (1997) *The Best of Both Worlds: The Voluntary Sector and Local Government*. York: YPS for the Joseph Rowntree Foundation.

Taylor, P. (2003) The lay contribution to public health, in J. Orme, J. Powell, P. Taylor, T. Harrison and M. Grey (eds) *Public Health for the 21st Century: New Perspectives on Policy, Participation and Practice*. Maidenhead: Open University Press.

Taylor, P. and Upward, J. (1995) *Bridge Building for Effective User Involvement in Primary Care*. Birmingham: Birmingham Family Health Services Authority.

The Howard League for Penal Reform (2005) Major national campaign to end the deaths of children in custody launched by the Howard League for Penal Reform, press release.

The Nursing and Midwifery Council (2002) *Code of Professional Conduct*. London: The Nursing and Midwifery Council.

The Sainsbury Centre for Mental Health (2000) *Taking Your Partners: Using Opportunities for Inter-Agency Partnership in Mental Health*. London: The Sainsbury Centre.

The Social Exclusion Unit (2002) *Young Runaways*. London: SEU.

Thomas, N. and O'Kane, C. (1999) Experiences of decision-making in middle childhood: the example of children 'looked after' by local authorities, *Childhood*, 6: 369–87.

Thompson, N. (1993) *Anti-Discriminatory Practice*. London: Macmillan.

Thompson, N. (1995) *Age and Dignity: Working with Older People*. Aldershot: Arena.

Thompson, N. (1998) The ontology of ageing, *British Journal of Social Work*, 695–707.

Thompson, N. (2000a) *Theory and Practice in the Human Services*. Buckingham: Open University Press.

Thompson, N. (2000b) *Understanding Social Work: Preparing for Practice*. Basingstoke: Macmillan.

Thompson, N. (2001) *Anti-Discriminatory Practice*. Basingstoke: Palgrave Macmillan.

Thompson, N. (2002) *Building the Future: Social Work with Children, Young People and their Families*. Lyme Regis: Russell House Publishing.

Thompson, N. (2003) *Promoting Equality: Challenging Discrimination and Oppression in the Human Services*. Basingstoke: Palgrave Macmillan.

Throssell, H. (ed.) (1975) *Social Work: Radical Essays*. St. Lucia: University of Queensland Press.

Timms, N. (1983) *Social Work Values: An Enquiry*. London: Routledge and Kegan Paul.

Tisdall, K., Bray, R., Marshall, K. and Cleland, A. (2004) Children's participation in family law proceedings: a step too far or a step too small? *Journal of Social Welfare and Family Law*, 26: 17–33.

Tisdall, K., Marshall, K., Cleland, A. and Plumtree, A. (2002) Listening to the views of children? Principles and mechanisms within the Children (Scotland) Act 1995, *Journal of Social Welfare and Family Law*, 24: 385–99.

Tomlinson, D. R. and Trew, W. (2002) *Equalising Opportunities, Minimising Oppression: A Critical Review of Anti-Discriminatory Policies in Health and Social Welfare*. London: Routledge.

Tong, R. (1989) *Feminist Thought: A Comprehensive Introduction*. Sydney: Allen and Unwin.

Treseder, P. and Crowley, A. (2001) *Taking the Initiative: Promoting Young People's Participation in Decision Making: Wales Report*. London: Carnegie Young People's Initiative.

Trevithick, P. (2000) *Social Work Skills: A Practice Handbook*. Buckingham: Open University Press.

Troyna, B. and Hatcher, R. (1992) *Racism in Children's Lives: A Study of Mainly White Primary Schools*. London: Routledge/National Children's Bureau.

Tsui, M.-S. and Cheung, F. C. H. (2004) Gone with the wind: the impacts of managerialism on human services, *British Journal of Social Work*, 34: 437–42.

Twigg, J. and Atkin, K. (1994) *Carers Perceived*. Buckingham: Open University Press.

Ungerson, C. (1993) Caring and citizenship: a complex relationship, in J. Bornat, C. Pereira, D. Pilgrim and F. Williams (eds) *Anthology: Charter in Community Care. A Reader*. London: Macmillan/Open University Press.

Ungerson, C. (2004) Whose empowerment and independence? A cross-national perspective on 'cash for care' schemes, *Ageing and Society*, 24: 189–212.

Utting, W. (1991) *Children in Public Care*. London: The Stationery Office.

Victor, C. (1991) *Health and Healthcare in Later Life*. Buckingham: Open University Press.

Ward, D. (2000) Totem not token: groupwork as a vehicle for user participation, in H. Kemshall and R. Littlechild (eds) *User Involvement and Participation in Social Care: Research Informing Practice*. London: Jessica Kingsley Publishers.

Ward, D. (2005) Asylum measures inhuman and disastrous, London: *The Guardian*.

Ward, D. and Mullender, A. (1991) Empowerment and oppression: an indissoluble pairing for contemporary social work, in J. Walmsley, J. Reynolds, P. Shakespeare and R. Woolfe (eds) *Health and Welfare Practice: Reflecting Roles and Relationships*. London: Sage.

Wasserstrom, R. A. (1964) Rights, human rights and racial discrimination, *Journal of Philosophy*, 61: 628–9.

Watson, N., McKie, L., Hughes, B., Hopkins, D. and Gregory, S. (2004) (Inter)-dependence, needs and care: the potential for disability and feminist theorists to develop an emancipatory model, *Sociology*, 38: 331–50.

Webb, R. and Tossell, D. (1999) *Social Issues for Carers: Towards Positive Practice*. London: Edward Arnold.

Webb, T. and Skills for People (2002) *Planning With People – Accessible Guide*. London: Department of Health.

Weeks, J. (1990) The value of difference, in J. Rutherford (ed.) *Identity: Community, Culture and Difference*. London: Lawrence & Wishart.

Weick, A., Rapp, C., Sullivan, W. P. and Kisthardt, W. (1989) A strengths perspective for social work practice, *Social Work*, 34: 350–4.

Weick, A. and Vandiver, S. (1982) *Women, Power and Change*. Washington DC: The National Association of Social Workers.

Welsh Office (2003) *Guidance on Accommodating Children in Need and their Families*. Cardiff: National Assembly for Wales.

Wertheimer, A. (1996) *Advocacy: The Rantzen Report*. London: BBS Educational Developments.

Westwood, S. (2002) *Power and the Social*. London: Routledge.

Whelehan, I. (1995) *Modern Feminist Thought: From the Second Wave to 'Post-Feminism'*. Edinburgh: Edinburgh University Press.

White, S. and Featherstone, B. (2005) Communicating misunderstandings: multi-agency work as social practice, *Child and Family Social Work*, 10: 207–16.

Wigfall, V., Monck, E. and Reynolds, J. (2006) Putting programme into practice: the introduction of concurrent planning into mainstream adoption and fostering services, *British Journal of Social Work*, 36: 41–55.

Williams, F. (1989) *Social Policy: A Critical Introduction*. Cambridge: Polity Press.

Williams, F. (1996) Postmodernism, feminism and the question of difference, in N. Parton (ed.) *Social Work, Social Theory and Social Change*. London: Routledge.

Williams, J. (2001) 1998 Human Rights Act: social work's new benchmark, *British Journal of Social Work*, 31: 831–44.

Williams, J. (2004) Social work, liberty and law, *British Journal of Social Work*, 34: 37–52.

Willow, C. (2002) *Participation in Practice: Children and Young People as Partners in Change*. London: The Children's Society.

Wilson, A. and Beresford, P. (2000) 'Anti-oppressive practice': emancipation or appropriation? *British Journal of Social Work*, 30: 553–73.

Wise, S. (1995) Feminist ethics in practice, in R. Hugman and D. Smith (eds) *Ethical Issues in Social Work*. London: Routledge.

Womens National Commission (2003) *Unlocking the Secret: Women Open the Door on Domestic Violence. Findings from a Consultation with Survivors*. London: DTI.

Wright, D. J. and Easthorne, V. (2003) Supporting adults with disabilities, *Nursing Standard*, 18: 37–42.

Wyllie, J. (1999) *The Last Rung of the Ladder: An Examination of the Use of Advocacy by Children and Young People in Advancing Participation Practice within the Child Protection System*. London: The Children's Society.

Index